Lord Salisbury

Cambridge Studies in the History and Theory of Politics

EDITORS
MAURICE COWLING
G. R. ELTON
E. KEDOURIE
J. G. A. POCOCK
J. R. POLE
WALTER ULLMANN

*For complete list of books in this series
see page* 387

Lord Salisbury on Politics

*A selection from his articles in the
Quarterly Review, 1860–1883*

*Edited with an introduction and notes
by*

PAUL SMITH
Lecturer in History, King's College London

CAMBRIDGE
at the University Press 1972

CAMBRIDGE UNIVERSITY PRESS
Cambridge, New York, Melbourne, Madrid, Cape Town, Singapore, São Paulo

Cambridge University Press
The Edinburgh Building, Cambridge CB2 8RU, UK

Published in the United States of America by Cambridge University Press, New York

www.cambridge.org
Information on this title: www.cambridge.org/9780521083867

© Cambridge University Press 1972

This publication is in copyright. Subject to statutory exception
and to the provisions of relevant collective licensing agreements,
no reproduction of any part may take place without the written
permission of Cambridge University Press.

First published 1972
This digitally printed version 2007

A catalogue record for this publication is available from the British Library

Library of Congress Catalogue Card Number: 74-174256

ISBN 978-0-521-08386-7 hardback
ISBN 978-0-521-04457-8 paperback

Contents

Preface	*page* vii
List of abbreviations	viii
Editor's introduction	1
Bibliographical note	110
'The Budget and the Reform Bill' (April 1860)	111
'The House of Commons' (July 1864)	159
'The Reform Bill' (April 1866)	193
'The Change of Ministry' (July 1866)	226
'The Conservative Surrender' (October 1867)	253
'The Programme of the Radicals' (October 1873)	292
'Disintegration' (October 1883)	335
Index	377

Preface

My thanks are due to Mr Maurice Cowling, who suggested this edition, and has cast a helpful editorial eye over it (without, of course, incurring any responsibility for its blemishes); to the Marquis of Salisbury, who has very kindly allowed me to quote from the Salisbury Papers at Christ Church, Oxford; to the librarian of Christ Church, Dr J. F. A. Mason, who most courteously aided my work there; to Messrs Hodder and Stoughton, for permission to quote from Lady Gwendolen Cecil's life of her father; and not least to my wife, who has patiently borne with my unreasonable working habits.

A few words are necessary about the editing of the articles. Each is prefaced by an introductory note, designed to supply the essential background. Otherwise, annotation has been kept to a minimum, in the belief that a heavy apparatus of footnotes would be more of an impediment than an aid to the articles' use. An outline historical knowledge has been assumed in the reader, and therefore of the very large number of events, persons, and pronouncements, historical and contemporary, to which Salisbury alludes, only those not figuring prominently in general history receive notes. In the introductory note and footnotes to each article, Lord Salisbury is given the title by which he was known when the article was written (i.e. Lord Robert Cecil to 1865, Viscount Cranborne from 1865 to 1868, and Lord Salisbury thereafter).

PAUL SMITH

King's College London
November 1971

List of Abbreviations

B.Q.R.	*Bentley's Quarterly Review*
Cecil, *Biographical Studies*	Lady Gwendolen Cecil, *Biographical Studies of the Life and Political Character of Robert Third Marquis of Salisbury*
Cecil, *Salisbury*	Lady Gwendolen Cecil, *Life of Robert Marquis of Salisbury*
Q.R.	*Quarterly Review*
S.R.	*Saturday Review*

Editor's Introduction

SALISBURY'S JOURNALISM

THE third Marquis of Salisbury led the Conservative party for twenty-one years (the first four in tandem with Sir Stafford Northcote), and was prime minister for nearly fourteen of them. He was arguably 'the most formidable intellectual figure that the Conservative party has ever produced'.[1] He was also one of the dominant European, indeed world, statesmen of the last quarter of the nineteenth century, hardly inferior in stature even to Bismarck. Yet, compared to men like Peel or Disraeli, he has not occupied the place in the Conservative hall of fame or received the attention from historians that might seem to be his due.

The failure to bulk more largely in party hagiography is perhaps not difficult to understand. Though the Conservative party enjoyed what was in many ways its heyday under Salisbury's leadership, it is hard to say that his role was crucial to its success, or that he gave to it any distinctive impulse or policy that can be accounted fundamental in its development. Both Peel and Disraeli can be seen, with varying degrees of accuracy, as having played a vital part in the making of the modern party by fostering its adaptation to the political consequences of economic and social change, as crystallised in the Reform Acts of 1832 and 1867. Salisbury's Conservatism, though not diehard, was more of the resistant than of the adaptive variety: the core of his early political career was his virulent opposition to 'democracy' as expressed in the Reform movement of the sixties, and in power he seemed to men like Lord Randolph Churchill to be unsympathetic to the cultivation of mass support made necessary by the extension of the franchise. His mature achievement, and interest, lay rather in the field of foreign and imperial affairs than in home policy. In an age of democratic politics centred largely on social issues, Salisbury seems to belong to a distant and antipathetic tradition, the last grand aristocratic figure of a political system that died with Victoria, or even before, a great whale irretrievably beached on the receding shore of the nineteenth century. Into the 'progressive' strain of modern Conservatism he simply will not fit.

[1] R. Blake, *Disraeli* (1966), p. 499.

EDITOR'S INTRODUCTION

There are other things which make him a slightly uncomfortable subject for Conservative piety. Despite the conventionality of his background and the orthodoxy of his fundamental beliefs, he was an odd kind of Conservative, as odd in his way as Disraeli and possessing little more in common with the majority of his followers. Partly this was a matter of temperament and personality; largely it was a matter of intellect. Conservatives, Derby told Disraeli in 1875, 'are weakest among the intellectual classes: as is natural'.[1] Salisbury went some way to make up the deficiency. He was an intellectual of a highly critical and sceptical temper, and, if he adhered to the same principles as the mass of his party, he professed to sustain them on the basis of a rigorously empirical and even utilitarian approach, which showed little apparent regard for some of the claims of sentiment, tradition, and interest that operated as nutriments of Conservative feeling in less clear or less cutting minds. He was one of those untypical and sometimes uncongenial figures, like Peel, or Disraeli, or Churchill, by whom the Conservative party allows itself from time to time to be led, because it needs the qualities of intellect, or imagination, or character which they can supply. His leadership never sat quite easily on the party: they trusted and admired him, but they did not fully understand him, and they found him aloof. He had no deep attachment to the party as such: he saw it simply as a mechanism for specific purposes, and declared that, were it to abandon the principles for which he supported it, he would walk down the steps of the Carlton for the last time without a backward glance or a feeling of regret.[2]

From historians, Salisbury's career still awaits comprehensive examination and assessment. Since the fourth volume of Lady Gwendolen Cecil's remarkable, but unhappily unfinished, life of her father appeared in 1932, he has received no major biography. But his foreign policy has been the object of detailed modern study, and recently Mr Michael Pinto-Duschinsky's *The Political Thought of Lord Salisbury 1854–68* (1967) has surveyed what is undoubtedly one of the most interesting sides of his personality, his corpus of ideas, seeing in him a paradigm of the empirical strand in English Conservative thinking. Salisbury's ideas on society and politics are hardly less worthy of attention than his practical statesmanship. No doubt he regarded the former as very much secondary to the latter: he had small taste for theorising, and did not set out to be

[1] Derby to Disraeli, 18 Aug. 1875: Hughenden Papers, B/XX/S/968.
[2] Cecil, *Salisbury*, iii, 301. Cf. *Biographical Studies*, p. 40.

a political thinker in any large or systematic sense. Yet his fundamental feelings and beliefs, if they were never consciously organised into a political philosophy, were necessarily prime determinants of his political action. Moreover, they represent very well an important strain of Conservative thought. It is not, despite large elements in common and a virtual identity of practical outcome, typical Toryism: Salisbury was too utilitarian, too lacking in reverence for authority, prescription, and tradition, too cynical and pessimistic perhaps, for that. It is an intellectual and sophisticated Toryism, which employs an apparatus of close empirical reasoning to support the conclusions at which it is programmed by instinctive predilection to arrive. It is, or desires to be, a clear, hard, logical creed, realistic and sceptical, seeking an argumentative basis for resistance to radical change not in the sentimental or mystical idealisation but in the rational justification of the existing order. It is, in short, Toryism for the clever man. From Salisbury it received more extensive and more explicit expression than from most practising politicians, and not only in his speeches. Though he never wrote a political treatise, he produced between 1856 and 1894, but mainly in the 1860s, when he was in his thirties, a considerable body of journalism, in which the character of his political thinking is abundantly displayed.

Salisbury[1] left Oxford in 1850, at the age of twenty, ill-health having curtailed his university career to two years and an honorary fourth class. After nervous illness had forced him to abandon studies for the bar, he was sent on a long sea voyage to South Africa, Australia, and New Zealand, which did a good deal to make him more robust. Returning to England in 1853, he was successful in gaining a fellowship at All Souls, and, in August, was returned unopposed at a by-election for Stamford, the pocket borough of his cousin, the Marquis of Exeter. The opening of his journalistic career followed shortly upon his entry into Parliament. It is possible that he contributed to the *Morning Chronicle* and the *Standard* in the mid and late fifties, but the first piece of journalism that can certainly be attributed to him appeared in the weekly *Saturday Review* in December 1856.[2] The *Saturday* was owned by his brother-in-law,

---

[1] Robert Arthur Talbot Gascoyne-Cecil was known as Lord Robert Cecil until the death of his elder brother in June 1865, and then as Viscount Cranborne until he succeeded to the marquisate in April 1868. For the sake of simplicity, he is called 'Salisbury' throughout this introduction.

[2] On Salisbury's writings, see M. Pinto-Duschinsky, *The Political Thought of Lord Salisbury 1854–68* (1967), ch. ii and annotated list of published writings, pp. 157–88; Cecil, *Salisbury*, i, ch. iii; J. F. A. Mason, 'The Third Marquess of Salisbury and the *Saturday Review*', *Bulletin of the Institute of Historical Research*, xxxiv (1961),

EDITOR'S INTRODUCTION

Alexander Beresford Hope, and between 1856 and 1868 he contributed to it 608 unsigned pieces, leaders, 'middles', and book reviews, his output reaching its peak with 422 pieces in 1861-4. In the early years at least, a prime motive of this productivity was cash. Salisbury, his daughter tells us,[1] did not like writing, and did it only reluctantly. But he was a younger son, and the financial disabilities of that position were greatly reinforced when, in July 1857, he contracted a marriage of which his father, precisely on financial grounds, disapproved. Journalism was a ready means of supplementing his inadequate income in the first years of married life.[2]

The *Saturday Review* articles were mostly quite short – about two columns – and covered a very wide field. Some were serious pieces on politics, history, literature, and current affairs; others were comparatively light-hearted sketches of the social and political scene, or sardonic reviews of the latest novels. Salisbury had not been writing them long before he began to produce much more substantial contributions to rather weightier periodicals. In 1858 he contributed 'The Theories of Parliamentary Reform' to the series entitled *Oxford Essays*, and in 1859-60 he was closely connected with the short-lived *Bentley's Quarterly Review*, for which he wrote certainly two, and possibly four, long political articles.[3] These latter pieces, with their characteristically scathing wit, attracted some attention and admiration, and this may have helped, when *Bentley's* failed, to bring about the opening of their author's long association with John Murray's *Quarterly Review*.

The *Quarterly* was, and remained, the leading Tory journal of the day, with a remarkably distinguished list of contributors, which included men like Acton, Matthew Arnold, Gladstone, Froude, and Henry Maine.

36-54. For the *Saturday Review*, see M. M. Bevington, *The Saturday Review 1855–1868* (1941).

[1] Cecil, *Salisbury*, i, 70-1.
[2] He seems to have made only about £300 from his *Saturday* contributions in 1856-60, but in the next four years the figure probably went up to well over £300 *per annum*, a substantial addition to a household income which Lady Gwendolen Cecil estimates at perhaps £700 *p.a.* in the early years of marriage. As time went on, he gained a certain amount from business directorships, but in 1866 he was badly hit by the failure of Overend, Gurney & Co., and had to ask his father for help in finding the £5,000-£6,000 needed to meet immediate engagements (see his letters to the 2nd Marquis, 14 May, [?17 May], 12 June, 22, 26, 28 July, 8 Sept. 1866 (typescript copies): Salisbury Papers).
[3] 'English Politics and Parties' and 'The Faction-Fights' (*B.Q.R.*, i [March-July 1859], 1-32 and 343-74) are certainly his; 'France and Europe' and 'The Coming Political Campaign' (*ibid.* ii [Oct. 1859-Jan. 1860], 1-32 and 303-34) may well be. They are, of course, unsigned: for the attributions, see Pinto-Duschinsky, pp. 33-5.

SALISBURY'S JOURNALISM

Its politics, in the era of Derby and Disraeli, tended to be somewhat right of the Conservative leadership, and to incline to the more 'stern and unbending' school of Toryism which Salisbury so powerfully reinforced. His first contribution to it appeared in April 1860, and between then and October 1883 he produced altogether thirty-three articles, averaging just over thirty-four pages, or roughly 15,500 words, each. Seventeen of these were mainly devoted to current domestic politics, with the Reform issue bulking very large up to 1867. Four were on foreign affairs and three on ecclesiastical questions; three were biographical studies of Pitt and Castlereagh; three, in 1861–5, dwelt on the lessons of the American Civil War; and three discussed the miscellaneous subjects of 'Competitive Examinations', 'The Income Tax and its Rivals', and 'Photography'. The great majority of the articles appeared in the first six years – twenty-four in the twenty-six issues of the *Quarterly* between April 1860 and July 1866 (when Salisbury became a cabinet minister). After that they dwindled to a trickle – one in each of the years 1867, 1869, and 1870, two in 1871, one in 1872 and 1873, and then a long gap while Salisbury was again in office, until the last two articles in 1881 and 1883. The falling-off was presumably due not only to Salisbury's ministerial commitments in 1866–7 and 1874–80, and to his assumption of the leadership of the Conservative party in conjunction with Sir Stafford Northcote in 1881, but also to the fact that his succession to the marquisate in April 1868 removed any remaining financial motive for writing. From 1874, though the editor, William Smith, continued to ask him for articles, his main contribution to the *Quarterly* consisted in giving advice on its political content,[1] and in 1883 his irritation at the failure to respect his anonymity in the discussion provoked by his celebrated article on 'Disintegration' led him to decide that he would write for it no more. That, however, was not quite the end of his journalistic career, for between 1883 and 1894 he published four fairly short signed articles in the new Conservative periodical, the *National Review*, dealing with artisans' dwellings, electoral reform, and the position of the House of Lords.

The *Quarterly* articles form much the most substantial part of Salisbury's writings, and they are a vital source for his political thinking. The three devoted to the lives of Pitt and Castlereagh, and the three of 1863–4 on 'Poland', 'The Danish Duchies', and 'The Foreign Policy of England', were reprinted in 1905 by John Murray, as, respectively, *Essays by the late Marquess of Salisbury K.G.: Biographical* and *Essays by the late*

[1] See Smith's letters, in the Salisbury Papers.

5

EDITOR'S INTRODUCTION

Marquess of Salisbury K.G.: Foreign Politics. But a number of the others have equal claims to resurrection. The present selection merits reprinting not only as illustrating the essentials of Salisbury's outlook and ideas, but also as furnishing an important document on the politics of his day, seen from a particular type of Conservative standpoint, and as constituting some of the most vigorous and distinguished political journalism of the late nineteenth century.

As a source for Salisbury's thought, the articles must, of course, be used with a degree of caution. They were not intended to embody a systematic exposition of his beliefs, and fall a long way short of doing so. Their purpose was not the elaboration of social or political theory, but the concrete discussion of current issues; and only once, in the disquisition on the ground of the right to vote, in July 1864,[1] did their author feel obliged to attempt anything like an extended statement of general theoretical principles. Salisbury was producing journalism for the market, not a set of slowly evolved and delicately constructed intellectual treatises. Much of the time he was working under pressure: between 1860 and 1865 he was turning out several thousand words a week for the *Saturday* and the *Quarterly* combined, besides having to attend to the business of Parliament when it was in session. Moreover, the fact that he was writing for a partisan review, to stimulate and encourage a largely converted audience, did not conduce to the pursuit of detached objectivity or to cautious and carefully qualified expression. His daughter notes that, compared with his contemporary parliamentary speeches, his writings are 'distinctly more highly coloured'.

The criticisms are stronger, the confidence expressed is more absolute, the indifference shown to his opponents' opinions is less mitigated. In the one case the phrasing was restricted to that shade of emphasis for which the speaker was himself willing to be responsible, – in the other the limiting criterion was that required by the party character of the periodical in which the articles appeared anonymously.[2]

Salisbury would not have wanted to stand by every word he said in his articles, or to endorse for all time every nuance and inflection. He seems to have considered his writings too incidental and imperfect to be worthy to represent him, for he never spoke voluntarily of them, and resented any allusion to them by others in his presence.[3]

Nonetheless, it is reasonable to use the articles as a guide to the nature of his mind and opinions. Allowance made for exaggerations of

[1] *Q.R.*, cxvi (1864), 263–71.
[2] Cecil, *Salisbury*, i, 81.
[3] *Ibid.* i, 71.

tone and excesses of combative zeal, there is no cause to doubt that what he wrote represented what he felt and believed. Indeed, the exaggerations and excesses were often representative too, of deeper emotions and more instinctive attitudes than his calmer moods were willing to acknowledge. Perhaps he knew this: it is conceivable that his dislike of allusion to his writings arose partly from a sense that they rendered him vulnerable by revealing more than he wished. Writing is a dangerous act for very private souls like his: each paragraph is an involuntary confession. Salisbury's articles may not set out to define his feelings and beliefs, but they inevitably go some way towards doing so. It is true that much has to be gleaned from inference and implication, rather than from direct statement. But a good deal is more or less explicit. Even Salisbury's distrust of theorising and refusal to enter into formal discussion of first principles create less difficulty than might be anticipated in establishing the structure of his thought, for behind them lies a mind that combines with its empiricism a strong generalising tendency. In the middle of the most matter-of-fact discussions of current questions, Salisbury is continually either referring to or seeking to sketch out general propositions established by experience. His intense interest in the particular is partly a reflex of his interest in the general: the facts are ultimately sacred because of their utility for the verification or the formulation of general ideas. So that despite his distaste for 'theory', his writings contain a good deal of it, though usually in rather undeveloped form. If he hardly ever attempts to elaborate general principles, they are everywhere immanent, and are constantly breaking through the surface. What emerges for the observer is something less than a political 'philosophy' in the fullest sense, but something more than a mere congeries of disorganised attitudes and opinions.

For the politics of the period, the articles provide both a lively and penetrating commentary and a notable illustration of some of the operative elements. Salisbury is almost never dull; and even when he is dealing in the small change of the current political scene, the interest of what he has to say is seldom merely ephemeral, for he is invariably concerned to relate the phenomena of the moment to the large and continuing themes which form the constant focus of his attention. Within the ample limits of the *Quarterly*, he seeks to produce not a hasty review of events as they slip past but a considered estimate of their significance in the general movement of politics and society. The growth of class conflict and the trend towards 'democracy' are the overriding preoccupations which form a unifying thread in his treatment of them. The attitudes he expresses,

EDITOR'S INTRODUCTION

while they cannot, especially in their intensity, be called typical of Conservative feeling, are nevertheless representative in essentials of an important part of it – a part whose failure to prevail outright has led to the underestimation of its size and influence.

The force of Salisbury's views gains much from the skill with which he presents them. As political journalism, the articles are of a high order. True, their style is not impeccable: in particular, there is a certain amount of prolixity and repetition, which seems to result from a stretching-out of matter to fill up the required quota of pages. But the argument is factual and closely reasoned, the writing lucid and vigorous. Salisbury's fondness for reducing the abstract to the concrete and for rendering the remote in terms of the familiar finds issue in a succession of vivid images and metaphors, and his talent for the verbal sketch – or sometimes caricature – produces many sharp vignettes. Humour, of the distinctly non-indulgent variety, is always present. A continual irony – frequently plain sarcasm – pervades Salisbury's work: sardonic banter is perhaps his most characteristic tone, and his most frequent method of attack. His capacity to flay the doctrines and personalities he dislikes is formidable, and it is mercilessly employed. As Lady Gwendolen Cecil points out,[1] his purpose is to smash the opposition, not to convert it; his polemics are designed not to bring the enemy to a better frame of mind but to hammer him into the ground. There is no question of sympathetic understanding of the alien point of view; there is little admission of the possibility of virtue on the other side. This, of course, while it heightened the immediate impact, was bound to limit the wider influence of the articles. Though several of them – notably those of April 1860, October 1867, and October 1883 – created a considerable stir on their appearance (the screen of anonymity collapsing in the process), it is hard to think that they did much to affect the political situation. Probably their tone repelled as many as it attracted. Salisbury constantly invites the charge which he himself levels against Disraeli: 'He is very apt to fall into the error from which few great masters of sarcasm are exempt, of preferring the glitter of a brilliant display to the gold of solid victory.'[2]

Undoubtedly, Salisbury's combative instincts sometimes exceed reasonable bounds. When he is roused, there is virtually no exaggeration of his opponents' wickedness too crude to employ. His attitude to the Union side in the American Civil War provides an example: he compares the North in point of atrocity to, among others, Ghenghis Khan and Tamerlane, for purposing, as he alleges, the 'wholesale extermination'

[1] *Ibid.* i, 76–7. [2] *Q.R.*, cviii (1860), 277.

of the Confederates.[1] His powers of personal abuse are extensive. Disraeli, who suffered most from them, was, if anything, guilty of understatement in describing him, perhaps in a belated flash of resentment, as 'a great master of gibes, and flouts, and jeers'.[2] No doubt the harshness of some of Salisbury's language can be partially ascribed, at least in the early days, to his need to command notice. Taken to task by his father for the vitriolic attack on Disraeli in the July 1859 number of *Bentley's*, he replied:

> The style in which such views may be conveyed is naturally more pointed than the style in which I should convey them to you. But it must be remembered that I write for money. Various concurring circumstances have left me no other means of gaining money on which I have any ground for relying except writing. I must therefore write so as best to gain money. I am bound of course to write no opinion that I do not hold, but what I do write I must write in the style that is most likely to attract, and therefore to sell.[3]

Under fire for repeating the offence in his first contribution to the *Quarterly*, he wrote: 'Readers in this rapid age are too hasty and too thoughtless to give much heed to strictures which are not flavoured with the relish of a personal application.'[4] But it is difficult to believe that only crowd-pulling was responsible for the bitterness of his invective. The virulent language was the sign of a dryly passionate emotion. Salisbury's writing often seems to lack warmth: 'his characteristic hard, cold, melancholy clarity of style, like the blue of a northern sky as the light begins to fade'.[5] Yet it carries marks of inner turbulence, clearly visible. Beneath the taut membrane of rational discourse lies a tense and agitated mind.

THE CAST OF MIND

In order to understand the character of the mind which Salisbury brought to bear upon society and politics, it is necessary to make some reference to the circumstances of his early life and the formation of his personality. He was one of those human beings who have serious difficulty in coming to terms with the world around them and in achieving a tolerable mode of living. As a child, losing his mother before he was ten, he was solitary and starved of the affection which his nature demanded. He was frail, delicate, highly-strung, and intensely cerebral,

---

[1] *Ibid.* cxvii (1865), 269.
[2] *Hansard's Parliamentary Debates*, 3rd series, ccxxi, 1358–9 (5 Aug. 1874).
[3] To 2nd Marquis, 25 July 1859, in Cecil, *Salisbury*, i, 86. He also argued that the responsibility for what appeared in a review lay solely with the chief editor.
[4] *Q.R.*, cviii (1860), 290. [5] Blake, *Disraeli*, p. 474.

EDITOR'S INTRODUCTION

lacking both the physical force and the nervous stability to cope easily with the rough-and-tumble of boyhood and the pains of adolescence. At Eton his shy and rather aloof sensitivity and his precocious talent for theology set him apart from his schoolfellows, who showed their sense of his separateness by bullying him severely: he lived in real fear of a childish brutality to which he could offer no reply beyond a violent but impotent rage, and the experience may well, as his daughter suggests,[1] have done permanent harm both to his nerves and to his capacity for personal relations. Oxford proved less bruising and less lonely, and it was there that he began to make some mark among his contemporaries, becoming secretary and treasurer of the Union. But he was still a somewhat isolated figure, reserved, painfully fastidious, and so absolute in his moral and intellectual attitudes and opinions as to make friendship with those who disagreed with them virtually impossible. He emerged from Oxford almost pathetically under-equipped to cope with adult life. The combination of physical frailty, which the sea voyage of 1851-3 only partially cured, low animal spirits, extreme nervous sensibility, and exceptional intelligence was nicely calculated to render his adjustment to society as difficult as possible. Even routine social intercourse was a trial to this lanky, stooping, shortsighted young man, with his unrelenting seriousness and his shyness towards women. Upon his mind and outlook, the nature of his physical and nervous endowment and the acute problems of his childhood and early manhood had lasting effects.

Such is the impression of mass and solidity, both physical and moral, presented by Salisbury in his later years that it is hard to realise how far, as a young man, he was a neurotic of the first water. In a weak and often ailing body, fretted by a powerful and remorselessly active intellect, his nervous system proved inordinately susceptible to strain. All his life, he would be liable to the crises which he called 'nerve storms', bringing depression, lassitude, and a hypersensitiveness of touch and hearing. Even minor jolts readily produced a state of tension which issued in physical symptoms: when his father made the highly uncongenial proposal that he should become colonel of the Middlesex militia it gave him stomach ache for a whole morning.[2] Political or intellectual combat brought him to a high pitch of nervous exaltation. The exhilaration of battle overrode his habitual intellectual pessimism to produce a confidence

[1] Cecil, *Salisbury*, i, 15-16.
[2] *Ibid*. i, 50. A vital consideration for Salisbury in replying was whether the regiment had volunteered for foreign service. 'If so', he wrote, 'all hesitation is at an end. I have no vocation for fighting' (to 2nd Marquis, 11 April 1855: Salisbury Papers).

THE CAST OF MIND

in victory which was succeeded by the most bitter disappointment when the result was defeat. The intensity of his emotional involvement in political issues is strikingly illustrated by the impact upon him of the American Civil War. At times, his passionate identification with the Confederate cause placed him under such nervous stress as to give his wife reason to fear for his mental stability. She found him one night, after he had taken to sleep-walking, 'standing at the wide open window of a second-floor bedroom, fast asleep, but in a state of strong excitement and preparing to resist forcibly some dreamt-of intrusion of enemies – presumably Federal soldiers or revolutionary mob leaders'.[1]

The depth and turbulence of Salisbury's nervous engagement in political conflict go far to explain some of the characteristics which he displayed in controversy. The 'deadly earnestness' already noticeable in his Oxford Union days,[2] the violence of tone against his opponents, the nature of his humour, aimed less at amusing the audience than at ridiculing and humiliating its object, were a reflection of strong and febrile emotion, the root of which seems sometimes to have lain in a deep nervous apprehension. When he confronted those forces which were charged for him with a quality of personal menace because they seemed to threaten the security of his world – atheism, democracy, socialism, the trade unions, the armies of the Northern states – he experienced at moments the fear that stems from the consciousness of physical and emotional vulnerability, and fear triggered the impulse to strike out and to wound which can be glimpsed in flashes through the polished surface of his speech and writing. The high-pitched invective, tinged occasionally with something close to hysteria, and the brutal sarcasms were at once the defensive carapace and the means of compensation for the felt weaknesses and vividly conceived dreads of their author. Frequently in their expression, and sometimes in their inner substance, the politics of the young Salisbury were the politics of nervous hypertension.

They were, too, the politics of pessimism and disillusion. It would be surprising if the hurts to which the over-sensitive nature was exposed had not bred a certain reserve about the prospects of human happiness and the possibilities of human improvement. With his idealism, his fastidiousness, and his passionate moral earnestness, the young man suffered in contact with the rawness and corruption of the world, and what his daughter calls 'the pitiless sincerity of his mental outlook'[3]

[1] Cecil, *Salisbury*, i, 170.
[2] H. A. Morrah, *The Oxford Union 1823–1923* (1923), p. 129.
[3] Cecil, *Salisbury*, i, 121.

EDITOR'S INTRODUCTION

prevented his trying to find comfort in self-delusive hopes. Instead, he sought both to cover his wounds and to protect himself against their repetition by cultivating an outer skin of cynical realism. It was not a very tough skin, however, for a residual hope and trust would continually pierce it, inviting and incurring renewed disappointments; and the cynicism, which was so pronounced in the earlier years, seems gradually to have been softened down by time.[1] More durable was the feeling of pessimism, in which the lessons of experience came to reinforce the natural result of low vitality and weak nerves. This, though momentarily overcome in the excitement of battle, was throughout life a fundamental feature of Salisbury's outlook. It consisted not merely in scepticism about the likelihood of things getting better but in a conviction that they were steadily getting worse. Even at the normally hopeful age of twenty, Salisbury was telling the Oxford Union: 'We are not the same people that we have been, either in our social characteristics, in our patriotic sentiments, or in the tone of our moral and religious feelings.'[2] Seventeen years later, on the eve of the struggle over the second Reform Bill, he wrote to a friend: 'I have for so many years entertained a firm conviction that we were going to the dogs that I have got to be quite accustomed to the expectation.'[3] For him, the evidence pointed so clearly to dismal conclusions that to adopt any others could result only from a failure of moral nerve. He would talk of 'the essential cowardliness of optimism (in his use of that word an irrational or unproved foundation was always presumed)'.[4] Disillusioned and pessimistic himself, he savaged the illusions and vain hopes of others as though he were seeking a kind of emotional compensation in exposing their minds and hearts to the cold winds which had cut into his own.

One important result of Salisbury's temperament and early experience was to induce in him an almost morbid diffidence. This was intensified by his intellectual attachment to an ideal of moral perfection which he knew human nature to be inherently incapable of realising, but which nonetheless imposed on him a constant sense of unworthiness for his falling short of it. All his life he had a deep consciousness of personal inadequacy and an exaggerated capacity for self-deprecation, most strongly revealed, perhaps, in his inability to believe himself capable of pleasing or influencing others. It was this side of his personality, coupled with his distaste for the more sordid aspects of the world's business, that led him in moments of fatigue or depression to want to

[1] *Ibid.* i, 78–9. [2] Speech of February 1850, quoted in Morrah, p. 139.
[3] To H. W. Acland, 4 Feb. 1867, in Cecil, *Salisbury*, i, 211.
[4] *Ibid.* iii, 19.

THE CAST OF MIND

extricate himself from public, or even from ordinary social, life. His ill-adjustment to the world and its demands, with all the nervous strain that it entailed, produced an impulse of rejection and withdrawal, never strong enough to dominate him completely, but continuously manifest in a variety of ways, such as his profound aversion from casual contact with strangers, and having as its effect to increase the distance across which his mind received the impress of the reality outside.

That distance was sometimes marked, and the nature of Salisbury's apprehension of external reality requires comment. He had in many respects a very limited direct experience and perception of it. His sensory receiving apparatus, finely tuned in some directions, was conspicuously defective in others. For instance, he was remarkably lacking in visual sense and in powers of direct observation:[1] much of the outward appearance, and therefore some of the inward content, of things left no impression on him. Nor could imagination supply what he failed to sense, for that faculty was not, except in moments of nervous excitement, strong in him. Nothing better illustrates his difficulty in grasping hold of the external world than his lack of capacity for making contact with other people. In part, this derived from a self-centred indifference to them. 'Outside the circle of those connected with him by business or by close and established intimacy', notes his daughter, 'he had no interest in individual human nature.'[2] In part, too, the trouble was the diffidence which prevented his reaching out for response. But to a large extent it was simply that he did not possess the power of animal apprehension of another personality. It was symptomatic that he could not make an instinctive judgement of character. Mere physical confrontation told him little: he needed concrete evidence of a man's work and abilities in order to be able to assess him.[3] His intuitive understanding of others was so weak that their motives and feelings were frequently incomprehensible to him – something that appears very clearly in his articles.[4]

It was with his intellect, rather than with his senses, that Salisbury caught hold of the external world, and with his intellect that he comprehended and ordered it. Reality presented itself to him in large part not through direct experience or perception but through report, through the refractive medium of language, and was assimilated and assessed in the quiet recess of the mind. Salisbury preferred this mode of receiving

---

[1] *Ibid.* i. 174; ii, 7–8. [2] Cecil, *Biographical Studies*, p. 49.
[3] Cecil, *Salisbury*, i, 56.
[4] In 1886, to take a good example, Salisbury, devoid of sentimental attachment to his own party, was quite at a loss to understand the pain experienced by the Liberal Unionists at breaking with theirs. *Ibid.* iii, 300–2.

EDITOR'S INTRODUCTION

it, perhaps because it was less taxing and confusing, but also because the more direct approach had little value for him in terms of increased understanding. Politics were much of his life, and the great political arena was the House of Commons, but after he had left that chamber in 1868, on his accession to the peerage, he apparently never revisited it as a spectator, so that in later years 'there were several men of distinction in the political world whose faces he had never even seen'.[1] He was not interested in seeing them, and his grasp of their outlooks and actions would scarcely have been enhanced had he done so. It was not necessary, or useful, for him to take the measure of things at first hand; it was enough to ponder their evidences in the seclusion of his mind. He liked to assess them undisturbed by what he seems to have found the distracting and confusing influence of others' opinions, and his need to work out his own conclusions in his own fashion brought him to the point of intellectual isolation. He found it intensely difficult to collaborate with others. When he was at the Foreign Office, he would formulate policy on major questions entirely by himself, disliking even to discuss matters until careful scrutiny of the facts had led him to a firm decision.[2] This remarkable intellectual self-sufficiency, with its accompanying moral certitude, was undoubtedly one of his great strengths; but it was probably also one of his great weaknesses, contributing as it did to a tendency towards narrow views and contracted sympathies that might have been less evident had he formed his opinions more in friction with the minds of others.

There was, then, a degree both of abstraction and of isolation in Salisbury's apprehension of reality. He saw it, or much of it, at one remove, and came to terms with it in lonely cerebration. The knowledge so achieved was sometimes more of form than of substance: while the facts were firmly grasped, the spirit slipped out through their interstices. Thus what is brought under review in Salisbury's articles is frequently not a world directly felt, seen, and understood, but rather one that has been mentally reconstructed – often, especially as regards human personality, on somewhat mechanistic lines – from the verbal evidence to hand. Intelligence has been made the substitute for empathy, and acuteness of analysis is not matched by keenness of sensibility. Such was the extent of Salisbury's intellectual detachment that when it was pierced by immediate contact with something that had hitherto been only mentally realised, the jolt could be severe. He was familiar enough intellectually with the sordid aspects of human nature and politics, and

[1] *Ibid.* i, 295.   [2] *Ibid.* ii, 234–5; iii, 205–7; iv, 282.

THE CAST OF MIND

indeed made them the object of much cynically knowing castigation, but when the formation of his first ministry, in 1885, forced him to confront directly men's appetites, including his friends', for places and honours, he was shocked, and found the experience 'a revelation'.[1]

Yet, as we have seen, intellectual detachment in this sense did not necessarily mean any lack of emotional engagement. Salisbury might be partly insulated from the immediate impact of reality, but it did not always follow that the vigour of his response was thereby attenuated. Indeed, the way in which he established his hold on external phenomena may sometimes have tended to produce a more intense reaction than direct experience and absorption would have done. The images he built up in his mind by piecing together and brooding over the evidence might on occasion be larger and more highly coloured than a nearer acquaintance with the reality would have shown to be justified, especially when it was a question of those things which threatened his sense of security and therefore disturbed the equability of his judgement – democracy, say, or trade unionism. The feelings evoked in him were heightened accordingly, and the process may provide a further key to the exaggeration of tone and the brutality of invective which occur in his articles, and are hardly to be explained away entirely as a necessary journalistic spice or a mere partisan fillip to the zeal of Tory readers.

The young Salisbury's neuroticism, his pessimism, his diffidence, the difficulties he experienced in establishing communication with the external world, posed an obvious threat to his mental and emotional stability, and it is a question why he did not break down under their pressure. Two factors seem to have been paramount in enabling him to make the transition to the massive calm of his later years: one was his marriage, and the other, and probably the more important, was his religion. Marriage in 1857 to Georgina Alderson gave him a partner who could supply the qualities of gaiety, optimism, and extroversion which he lacked, and could perform the vital function of mediating between him and common humanity. It rescued him from continual depression, and provided the secure domestic happiness on the basis of which a great public career could be endured. But if we seek the fundamental binding force which prevented the disintegration of a personality so flawed and strained, it is primarily to religious faith that we have to look.

Salisbury's religion was an act of unconditional intellectual surrender. It is customary to lay stress on the critical and sceptical temper of his mind, and in general terms there is every justification for such an

[1] *Ibid.* iii, 142.

EDITOR'S INTRODUCTION

emphasis; but the unrestricted subjection of every thought and feeling, every facet and problem of human existence to the corrosive and disintegrating power of his intellect would have rendered life intolerable to him. There had to be an area in which the rational and critical faculties fell silent, an area of unreserved and ingenuous belief which could provide the sense of the meaning and the coherence of things that was necessary to make of life more than the brief and insignificant passage of a particle through a void. In the religion of Christianity Salisbury found the framework of existence which he needed, and he accepted it with an absolute faith which seems to have owed virtually nothing to conviction of the intellectual kind. Through 'that personal surrender in love and trust to the living Christ, which lay at the heart of his religion',[1] he achieved emotional security and was able to release his fundamental idealism in a sphere where it was, by definition, protected against damage from the lessons of experience or the questionings of reason. Vigorously though he might employ his rational and critical powers on the intellectual subtleties of theology, a subject in which he was strongly interested and where he was no more inclined than in other realms to follow authority, he insisted that the essential core of religion was a mystery, impenetrable to human intellect and intractable to precise definition and analysis. In the end, one believed or one did not, guided by moral feelings and perceptions beyond the reach of reason either to dissect or to subvert.[2] Religious faith was for Salisbury the necessary sheet-anchor of his mind, and against it no current of sceptical examination could be suffered to run.

Religion satisfied the hankering after final truth which was always so pronounced in Salisbury, but it was not enough for him to worship the truth in amorphous and unspecific form. He needed a determinate creed and an earthly church, and he found them in the Church of England. He regarded dogma as a precondition of firm belief and active zeal, and abominated 'that shapeless, formless, fibreless mass of platitudes which in official cant is called "unsectarian religion"'.[3] His strong churchmanship did not carry him so far as to maintain that other Christian communions were outside the operation of divine grace, but it did lead him to scout attempts to achieve an accommodation with them which involved the dilution of the distinctive beliefs that he saw as the Church's essence.

---

[1] *Ibid.* i, 122; and see in general ch. iv for the character of Salisbury's religion.
[2] For an illustration of Salisbury's inclination deliberately to subordinate the intellect to the demands of 'the moral feelings', see his letter to Lady Blanche Balfour, 30 Sept. 1851 (Salisbury Papers).
[3] *Q.R.*, cxiii (1863), 266. Cf. *ibid.* cxviii (1865), 206–8.

THE CAST OF MIND

Whatever reserve he might feel towards other varieties of Christian, however, was trifling beside his fierce hostility towards those who denied Christianity itself. It was his belief that Christianity could not co-exist with, but must destroy, civilisations which rejected it.[1] His hatred of systems of belief which dispensed with religion in the accepted sense altogether, and sought to explain and to order the world in purely secular terms, was extreme. Not only did they elevate false gods, and negate the truth of the Christian world view which alone held salvation, but in doing so they attacked the very foundation of Salisbury's mental and emotional stability. They faced him with a possibility which he could not contemplate, and perhaps, too, their critique of religious belief threatened the fatal arousal of his own faculty of scepticism, in this sphere so well anaesthetised. In his bitter opposition to them the *odium theologicum* was reinforced by the fear of a personal dissolution.

Because it was so essential to the security of Salisbury's mind, religion furnishes the most important example of the subordination of his intellectual powers to needs and feelings arising at the deepest level of his being. But it is not the only one. In other areas it can be seen that despite the bent for rational and sceptical enquiry with which he is rightly credited, his beliefs could sometimes be rooted less in rigorous observation and analysis than in instinct, emotion, and prejudice. True, these latter factors seldom revealed themselves in very gross or unsophisticated form, and from many of their most common manifestations he was freer than the average of men – witness for instance his resistance to racial prejudice and his distaste for the cruder kinds of nationalism. But he was far from immune to them, and their influence can be traced in some of his most fundamental attitudes. Certain cases in point will appear later, but one which it is convenient to cite here is his view of the capacities of women. This was very little in advance of the ordinary male prejudice of his time. Though he had just married a highly intelligent woman, he could still write, in September 1857, that women were 'fatally deficient in the power of close consecutive thought', and that men had 'too much experience of the sex's charming ways ever to trust them with government or political economy, or moral philosophy, or oratory, or science'.[2] Twenty-six years later, a letter to his friend Lady John Manners was more revealing of the limitations of his own outlook than of the new developments in higher education for women which he discussed.

[1] Cecil, *Salisbury*, i, 108.
[2] *S.R.*, iv (1857), 238. The piece was entitled 'Bloomeriana'.

EDITOR'S INTRODUCTION

I have heard [he wrote] a good deal about the Ladies' Colleges at Oxford & Cambridge...From all I hear the young ladies do not become very amiable or attractive members of society. Speaking of them generally these Colleges are decidedly freethinking. Do you know Jack Wallop by chance – a son of Lord Portsmouth. I have heard him describe Meetings at Cambridge of these young ladies. Instead of going to Church they used to assemble on Sunday morning at the rooms of a free-thinking Don, & as they called it 'search after truth' – that is discuss all conceivable forms of unbelief.

I dare say these Colleges are useful as furnishing a diploma to ladies who wish to be Governesses: but for any other purpose I should do my utmost to dissuade any female relation over whom I had influence from going there. I must add that I have heard many instances of young ladies suffering permanently in health in consequence of attempting to study like men at an age when men can do it safely but they cannot.[1]

In the end, Salisbury's primary responses, like other people's, were determined more by visceral than by cerebral processes. Around them, like others, he built an elaborate masking structure of rational justification, deploying the skills of the intellect to give a formal logical sanction to the compelling promptings of the instinctive mind. His sceptical and combative intelligence, his capacity for critical examination, could not be turned inwards on those promptings: that would have been a kind of suicide, and one, in any case, impossible to perform. They had to be turned outwards, and brought to bear with passionate force upon those feelings and beliefs which, denying the validity of his own, sapped the base on which the security of his personality rested. Their first task was self-defence, not the pursuit of objective truth, and they operated from premises in the formation of which they had at best a secondary role.

Much of Salisbury's thought was thus rational more in its formal elaboration than in its fundamental origin. But the overt style, as displayed in his writing, was always logical, sceptical, and empirical, bringing to the discussion of society and politics a semblance of the methods with which he was familiar through his interests in science.

---

[1] Salisbury to Lady John Manners, 7 Oct. 1883 (typescript copy): Salisbury Papers, vol. 'Manners', pp. 216–17. He did, however, tell the same correspondent on 6 May 1884 that he was 'all for ladies studying men's subjects who have a taste for them' (*ibid.* p. 231); and in face of the enfranchisement of the agricultural labourer he also came to feel more kindly towards female suffrage. He did not, he wrote, regard it as a question of high importance, 'but when I am told that my ploughmen are capable citizens, it seems to me ridiculous to say that educated women are not just as capable. A good deal of the political battle of the future will be a conflict between religion and unbelief: & the women will in that controversy be on the right side' (to Lady John Manners, 14 June 1884: *ibid.* p. 235). Cf. his words at Edinburgh, 29 Nov. 1886, quoted in C. Rover, *Women's Suffrage and Party Politics in Britain 1866–1914* (1967), p. 106.

THE CAST OF MIND

Empiricism was the salient characteristic of his intellectual approach, where it was not hamstrung by predispositions and predilections that the intellect did not control.[1] His mind hankered always after the actual, the concrete, the facts, and he was deeply averse from metaphysical abstraction and mere theoretical speculation. General ideas unverified by experience and beliefs not supported by the evidence evoked his impatient ridicule. Most especially was this so when they came in the guise of authority and received opinion. There was a strong instinct of contrariness in Salisbury's mentality: a proposition had only to wear the halo of orthodoxy for him to want to find grounds for contesting it.[2] He had a deep distrust of the experts: 'people', he once wrote, 'are fully alive to the danger of superstition in priests – in course of time they will find out that the weakness is universal & that professors may be just as bad'.[3] His intelligence was essentially a critical and pugnacious, rather than a creative, one, finding its inspiration and fulfilment in the destruction of false doctrines and unthinking acceptances.

The sharpest weapon in his critical armoury was his insistence on close analysis of the meaning of phrases and concepts. '"Would you mind defining?" was', says his daughter, 'the familiar and stimulating request with which he punctuated conversational discussion with the junior members of his family';[4] and precise definition formed for him a prerequisite of connected argument. His mind strove incessantly after clarity, sharpness of outline, the exactly realised; it abhorred vagueness, ambiguity, the blurring of edges. Once definition had been achieved, and one literally knew what one was talking about, it was possible to examine the propositions under review both in terms of their internal logic and in their relation to the empirical evidence. The evidence of experience furnished the ultimate test of truth, the basis of sure knowledge and right judgement, and Salisbury's concentration on it was almost passionate. In the assessment of any opinion, any phenomenon, any situation, everything in the end depended, or seemed to depend, on the evidence. Salisbury placed the highest value on meticulous observation of the facts and on the obtaining of as much accurate, detailed information as possible. It is significant that one of the sources of his keen interest in photography was his realisation of the advantages brought to scientific

---

[1] For a discussion of Salisbury's empiricism, see Pinto-Duschinsky, pp. 54–67, who is concerned to contrast it with the intuitive, religion-based, semi-mystical strain of Conservative thought.
[2] Cecil, *Salisbury*, i, 101.
[3] Salisbury to Sir L. Mallet, 26 Dec. 1876 (typescript copy): Salisbury Papers, vol. 'Lytton III to Mallet', p. 252.
[4] Cecil, *Salisbury*, i, 78.

EDITOR'S INTRODUCTION

enquiry by the accuracy of observation which it permitted.[1] It is wholly characteristic that when official duty brought the Mohammedan world within his purview he should have begun a serious study of the Koran, and that his fourth son's commissioning in the Guards should have led him to a reading of Lord Wolseley's *Soldier's Pocket Book*.[2] On whatever subjects or questions his mind was required to deal with, he wished to be as thoroughly informed as he could. Only so could he subject theories and beliefs to the test of empirical verification; only so could he build up from the ground (or, where they were already predetermined, confirm by selective reference) his own opinions, and establish the general propositions that his mind, for all its emphasis on particular cases and limited verities, still sought to discern in the complexity of things. It was this innate hunger for precise definition, exact and complete data, and rigorous empirical testing of ideas that both engendered and was developed by his interest in scientific pursuits, beginning with youthful botanising and progressing to experiments in chemistry and electricity. Science offered possibilities of exact observation and measurement, orderly classification, and mathematically precise conclusion that he would have liked to find in the study of social and political phenomena, into which he could not resist trying to import scientific method and scientific metaphor. But society and politics could not be reduced to formulae, nor could they be experimented with in the laboratory. The best that Salisbury could do was to extract the utmost from the haphazard experimentation of which they had been the subjects in the laboratory of history. It was history, necessarily, which supplied him with much of the data for their empirical analysis. Characteristically, he preferred the detailed and statistical to the anecdotal and impressionistic kind, and the attention he devoted to its study and the constant reference he made to it reflected its importance to his mode of thought.

The empirical approach formed the conscious habit of Salisbury's mind, and, even when vitiated by pressures of a sub- or super-rational nature, set the pattern of his treatment of problems and events. Applying it to the pursuit of truth meant far more to him than the mere satisfaction of an intellectual impulse: it was the fulfilment of an imperative moral duty. 'The right functioning of a man's judgment', he once declared, 'is his most fundamental responsibility.'[3] It was almost as though he believed that one could enable oneself by sheer moral endeavour to know the good and to embrace it.

[1] See *Q.R.*, cxvi (1864), 498–9.
[2] Cecil, *Salisbury*, i, 107; iii. 26.
[3] *Ibid*. iii, 20.

SOCIETY AND POLITICS

The basic characteristics of Salisbury's mind show up very strongly in his thinking on problems of society and politics. His views were moulded after the peculiar configuration of his own personality, and deeply influenced by the milieu into which he had been born; rooted as much in instinct and feeling as in dispassionate analysis, they were expressed and justified in carefully rational form.

The tendency of his brand of neuroticism was to cause him to be easily alarmed by the prospect of sudden or drastic change, and to place supreme value upon stability, security, balance, and order. He had a low opinion of human nature,[1] seeing man as essentially selfish, and this, with his habitual pessimism, made him deeply sceptical of the possibilities of the 'progress' in whose name change was often demanded. His natural bent, therefore, was towards the maintenance of the status quo, where that could be undertaken with some conviction of reasonableness. Moreover, the status quo of mid-nineteenth-century England was one in which he occupied a particularly privileged position, and, while he accepted that the advantages to which he had been born carried with them an obligation of service, he was not inclined to regard them as an object for doubts and questionings, or to look with favour upon attempts to remodel the socio-political system which sustained them. He was a member of one of the most historic families of the ruling class, an aristocrat, and, after 1868, a great landowner; and in most essential respects, though with greater intellectual subtlety and personal idiosyncrasy than many of his peers, he thought and behaved like one.

As he looked out on to the world through the windows of Hatfield, it was difficult for him not to feel that the order of things which placed him there was a natural and a proper one, and impossible for him to escape the conditioning influence of his social role. Because he was in some prominent aspects untypical of his class and party, it is easy to forget how little he diverged from them in his basic instincts and assumptions. It did not require a very deep scratch to reveal beneath the sceptical intellectual the patrician member of the landed interest. Despite his aversion from many of the common pursuits of the landed class, his daughter goes so far as to assert that 'by temper and character he was essentially a squire', with the squire's 'abnormal sensitiveness to any interference, legislative or individual, with his rights as a landlord'.[2]

---

[1] On which, see Pinto-Duschinsky, pp. 86–94.
[2] Cecil, *Biographical Studies*, p. 25.

EDITOR'S INTRODUCTION

He possessed an instinctive knowledge of, and except when 'the indolent plea of privilege' was involved, an instinctive sympathy for, the 'squire's' viewpoint.[1] He saw the landed interest as in some sense the foundation of the country's stability and prosperity, writing of 'the specially national character of its wealth',[2] and its defence, as his articles illustrate, was one of his most fundamental political preoccupations.

Yet the attachment to the established order produced by temperament and social position could not, for Salisbury, be an uncritical, undiscriminating, and unreasoned one. His intellect demanded that it be capable of rational justification; and for this purpose the arguments of custom and prescription, the feelings of awe and veneration, which might suffice less cerebral conservatives, were clearly inadequate. The need for rationalisation, however, did not lead him either into the construction of a systematic political theory or into argumentation on an absolute moral base, for both those activities were foreign to his intellectual nature. He approached politics not as a theoretical study but as a living process in which he was deeply engaged. He had no bent for abstract, *a priori* reasoning, and he worked not from first principles but from the desire to achieve specific ends. He was not concerned to evolve general theories – though his mind had a generalising impulse – but rather practical maxims and recommendations. In short, he was not a political philosopher but a politician with a keen analytical and historical sense. As a politician, and an empiricist, responding to particular problems and cases, he did not want to be too constricted by preconceived schemes or immutable principles. Constancy to 'principle', indeed, if vital where fundamentals were at stake, was not a major theme in his conduct of day-to-day matters.

The greater number of the principles by which his political action was guided were essentially utilitarian in character and founded on what may be called the higher expediency. There were but a few of them for which he would have admitted any independent or permanent existence apart from the circumstances in which they operated.[3]

He was not inclined to treat politics as a department of ethics, and to claim for his opinions derivation from an absolute and eternal morality. He had a strong sense that ethical codes were more relative than absolute, and that, rather than shape their action in conformity to them, human beings tended to formulate them so as to justify their action. 'Opinions

[1] Cecil, *Salisbury*, ii, 3.
[2] *Q.R.*, cvii (1860), 532.
[3] Cecil, *Biographical Studies*, p. 14.

upon moral questions', he wrote, 'are more often the expression of strongly felt expediency than of careful ethical reasoning; and the opinions so formed by one generation become the conscientious convictions or the sacred instincts of the next'; and he recognised that as conditions changed so too would the morality which society found conducive to its interests.[1] Arguments of abstract, 'natural' right came into the same category of webs sophistically spun to cover selfish claims. If morality and right were relative to specific circumstances, then their invocation in abstract and universal form was an unsatisfactory method of establishing a political position, and since not they but pragmatic self-interest formed the basis of politics, it could not be expected to have much influence on men's conduct:

In the real business of life no one troubles himself much about 'moral titles' No one would dream of surrendering any practical security, for the advantages of which he is actually in possession, in deference to the *a priori* jurisprudence of a whole Academy of philosophers.[2]

Of this dictum, Salisbury himself, as a representative of the governing and propertied classes, was no mean example.

Politics was an activity directed not towards the realisation of truth or virtue but towards the attainment of more limited and prosaic objectives, stability, balance, and security. The test of right or wrong was not some abstract principle or ideal but utility in relation to those objectives. Salisbury was interested not in the theoretical merits of courses of action but in their practical effect. It was as early as 1858, in his contribution on 'The Theories of Parliamentary Reform' to *Oxford Essays*, that he made explicit his attachment to the utilitarian mode of political thinking. Reviewing the current debate on Reform, he wrote:

The rights of caste and the rights of man have been alike consigned to a blessed oblivion. Indeed, the tacit unanimity with which this generation has laid aside the ingenious network of political first principles which the industry of three centuries of theorists had woven, is one of the most remarkable phenomena in the progress of thought.

Expediency was now the governing consideration, and though men still appealed to 'principles', 'no one acts on them or reasons from them'. 'The only principle upon which, in the present day, any thinking politician really acts, is "the greatest happiness of the greatest number".'[3]

[1] *S.R.*, xix (1865), 532; quoted in Pinto-Duschinsky, p. 76. Cf. *Q.R.*, cxxiii (1867), 534, where Salisbury speaks of 'the proneness of mankind to shape their conduct by their desires, and to devise afterwards the code of morality necessary to defend it'.
[2] *Q.R.*, cxvi (1864), 263.
[3] 'The Theories of Parliamentary Reform', *Oxford Essays* (1858), pp. 52-3.

EDITOR'S INTRODUCTION

Salisbury's utilitarianism informed his approach to almost all political questions, and did much to set the distinctive tone of his political discourse. The voice was that neither of the philosopher nor of the moralist, still less of the traditionalist or the obscurantist, but of the political artificer, concerned with the appropriation of rational means to at least overtly rational ends. It was in terms of social usefulness, not of theoretical correctness or abstract moral rectitude, that the essentials of the established order were to be justified; it was by close empirical reasoning that their defence was to be sustained. Yet despite Salisbury's compulsion to buttress his political attitudes with an apparatus of carefully rational argument, he recognised that rational argument was not the only test of political wisdom, and that it was in the last resort something deeper which determined a man's political conduct. His own dislike of far-reaching change was almost beyond the power of argument to dispel. 'Under any circumstances, change is abstractedly an evil', he wrote in 1858,[1] and seven years later he declared:

The perils of change are so great, the promise of the most hopeful theories is so often deceptive, that it is frequently the wiser part to uphold the existing state of things, if it can be done, even though, in point of argument, it should be utterly indefensible.[2]

Just as Salisbury did not see the institutions and arrangements he was impelled to defend as possessing transcendental philosophical or moral validity, so he did not regard them as definitive and immutable forms representing the terminus of historical evolution. On the contrary, he knew very well that in the longest perspective they were the product merely of a transitory stage in that evolution. For a man with a deep distaste for change, he had an almost paradoxically strong sense of its permanence and inevitability in history. He saw history as flux, and never entertained the illusion that it might be possible to produce stasis. Essentially, history was the working out of God's design, but man had no means of knowing what that design was and what historical developments forwarded it.[3] Nevertheless, Salisbury did not think it impossible to discern some broad patterns in the maelstrom. He never set down his thoughts on history in systematic fashion, but there are several indications in his writings of how he saw its movement. In general he seems to have viewed it as dominated by 'the law of action and reaction which governs every movement in the moral world',[4] and therefore subject to fluctuations comparable to the swing of a pendulum or to the ebb and flow of tides.

[1] *Ibid.* p. 53.
[2] *Q.R.*, cxvii (1865), 550.
[3] Cecil, *Salisbury*, i, 111.
[4] *Q.R.*, cxviii (1865), 208.

SOCIETY AND POLITICS

He also regarded societies and nations as quasi-organisms, exhibiting a cycle of birth, growth, and decay. 'It is patent on the face of history', he wrote, 'that the aggregates of men who form communities, like the aggregates of atoms that form living bodies, are subject to laws of progressive change – be it towards growth or towards decay';[1] and he talked of a finite 'span of national life'.[2] In linear 'progress' he believed only in a very restricted sense. His statement in 1865 that it was 'quite true' that the history of the human race had been 'the record of a continual progress' requires the qualification that he provided a few years later, when, tilting at the orthodox belief in progress, he accepted the scientific and material varieties, but argued that political progress, which required moral evolution, was a different matter.[3]

Such a conception of history might seem to reduce the mass of human beings to the status of helpless puppets, animated by an inscrutable divine will, and jerked hither and thither by movements and processes outside their control. Salisbury, indeed, with his penchant for self-abasement, would cite with 'quasi-exultation' historical examples of the failure of individual effort to 'deflect the larger currents of human action'.[4] But his sense of the individual's ultimate impotence in the face of history was far from inducing in him passivity or fatalism. The fighting instinct in his nature was too strong: the course of events was not something to be nobly borne, but demanded a vigorous engagement and effort.

Even if the overall purpose and direction of the historical process defied man's comprehension, he could still try to understand and affect its detailed operation in the world around him. Salisbury, while temperamentally uninterested in producing anything like a theoretical model of contemporary politics, was nonetheless led by the organising bent of his mind to form a fairly schematic picture of them, which he would have liked to think possessed some of the precision of scientific analysis. He actually spoke of himself as engaged in 'the investigation of political science', studying the 'pathology of states', and regarded history and current events as furnishing in some sense a set of laboratory data, referring to the Franco-Prussian War, for example, as 'a very remarkable experiment in illustration of political science', which had demonstrated the 'comparative dynamic value' of the two governments involved.[5] His view of what powered the actions of men and provided the dynamic of

---

[1] *Ibid.* clvi (1883), 570. Cf. *ibid.* cxxx (1871), 280, for a reference to 'political organisms'.
[2] *Ibid.* cxxxiii (1872), 586 (and cf. 583).
[3] *Ibid.* cxvii (1865), 267; cxxxi (1871), 570.
[4] Cecil, *Salisbury*, iii, 20.
[5] *Q.R.*, cx (1861), 249; cxxx (1871), 269. Cf. *ibid.* cxxxv (1873), 574.

politics was predominantly materialistic. Except when gripped by religious enthusiasm, human beings were not moved primarily by ideas and doctrines, but by considerations of material interest. The theories which politicians propagated were a secondary growth, 'prized for the purpose of throwing a veil of decency over the naked passions by which political convulsions are brought about'.[1] The pursuit or retention of economic and social advantage lay, for Salisbury, at the root of most politics. He had a strong sense of the need to look at the economic and social base if history was to be properly understood, and stressed the importance of economic and social factors in creating political conflict, especially where the working classes were concerned.[2] In his *Quarterly* article of July 1864, he went so far as to represent nearly all political issues as being at bottom matters of property. Church controversies were 'in essence only a struggle between different sets of persons for the possession of certain rates, or tithes, or lands'. Finance was a contest between classes over the distribution of taxation. Foreign policy was mainly a question of property, in that most people's feelings about it were dictated by 'material interests alone'. Property furnished

> almost the only motive power of agitation. A violent political movement (setting aside those where religious controversy is at work) is generally only an indication that a class of those who have little see their way to getting more by means of a political convulsion.[3]

The battle for economic and social advantage was fought by classes. Salisbury laid continual stress upon class struggle as the motive force in modern politics, to such an extent that his writings acquired at times an almost Marxian tone.[4] He saw the conflict as increasingly one not between different sections of the propertied classes but between the propertied classes taken as a whole and the rest: 'The struggle for power in our day lies not between Crown and people, or between a caste of nobles and a bourgeoisie, but between the classes who have property and the classes who have none.'[5] This contest between 'possession and non-possession' had been 'the fatal disease of free communities in ancient times';[6] transcended since the Reformation by religious issues,

---

[1] *Ibid.* cxvi (1864), 263.
[2] See, for example, *ibid.* cviii (1860), 287–8; cxvii (1865), 545; clvi (1883), 576–7.
[3] *Ibid.* cxvi (1864), 265–6.
[4] Though not apparently well acquainted with his ideas, Salisbury had certainly heard of Marx. In 1861 he reviewed the latter's pamphlet *Herr Vogt*, with the remark: 'It will add something to the secret history of 1848, and much to the vocabulary of any Englishman desiring to learn the art of German imprecation' (*S.R.*, xi (1861), 80).
[5] *Q.R.*, cxii (1862), 542.   [6] *Ibid.* clvi (1883), 576–7.

and obscured by dissensions within the possessing classes, it was now starkly re-emergent.

Salisbury never attempted to work this interpretation out in detail, and its lack of refinement is obvious. He defined neither 'class' nor the precise composition of the classes whose antagonisms he portrayed. Nor did he put forward any very exact view about the relation of the fundamental pattern of class conflict which he postulated to political conflict as experienced in practice. The latter was clearly something more complex than a simple collision between groupings representing the opposed material interests of classes. Salisbury, of course, knew that. He recognised at least one other principle of political division than that of class, a psychological dichotomy between types of individual temperament, about whose relationship to lines of class – which was patently not one of perfect correspondence – he was unclear. He wrote in 1872:

> The two parties represent two opposite moods of the English mind, which may be trusted, unless past experience is wholly useless, to succeed each other from time to time. Neither of them, neither the love of organic changes nor the dislike of it [sic], can be described as normal to a nation. In every nation, they have succeeded each other at varying intervals during the whole of the period which separates its birth from its decay. Each finds in the circumstances and constitution of individuals a regular support which never deserts it. Among men, the old, the phlegmatic, the sober-minded, among classes, those who have more to lose than to gain by change, furnish the natural Conservatives. The young, the envious, the restless, the dreaming, those whose condition cannot easily be made worse, will be *rerum novarum cupidi*. But the two camps together will not nearly include the nation: for the vast mass of every nation is unpolitical.[1]

Nonetheless, class struggle was for Salisbury the great underlying reality in politics, and there was no doubt as to where he stood in relation to it. He was passionately anxious that the classes endowed with property and education should prevail, or at least succeed in holding the forces of indigence and ignorance in check. Only thus could political stability and good government be maintained. His preference for the rule of the well-to-do and the educated over that of mere numbers was fundamentally, of course, instinctive: he belonged to the well-to-do and the educated himself. He did not, however, contend that the upper social strata, or any section of them, had any indefeasible natural or hereditary right to govern. Their supremacy and privileges must be justified by their performance: power was validated only by the right exercise of it. He did not suppose that members of the upper and middle classes were

[1] *Ibid*. cxxxiii (1872), 583–4.

inherently and necessarily better in a moral sense than members of the lower. Indeed, he was sharply conscious of how many of the former fell below the standards of responsibility and effort which ought to attach to their social position: for example, '"Clubland" (his usual synonym for the "idle rich") was always referred to with contemptuous condemnation'.[1] All the same, he found it difficult, if not impossible, to exclude the notion that there were qualitative distinctions between classes, taken as a whole.[2] Of those distinctions, material possessions, which might be to some extent both their cause and their effect, served as a rough-and-ready sign: hence he spoke of 'the intellectual advantages and moral securities which property as a rule implies'.[3]

It was his feeling that the rule of property and education was 'natural', in the sense of being the outcome of the natural processes of social evolution. He thought that probably all civilised countries had passed through the same stages. Men started off with 'institutions of absolute equality' and held their lands in 'perfect community', but over the centuries 'the inevitable operation of natural laws centres the common power in a few persons, and divides the common lands among a few owners'.[4] Some men, in other words, came to predominate over others: though he did not use the term, Salisbury seems to have believed in something like a process of natural selection. It followed that political equality had no natural existence in developed societies, and that the attempt artificially to institute it must lead to disaster, since it involved setting aside the 'natural leaders' whom it was the peculiar function of the propertied and educated classes to provide, and whose attributes of disinterestedness and responsibility, together with their attachment to the maintenance of stability, were the best obtainable guarantees of good government.

Political equality is not merely a folly – it is a chimera. It is idle to discuss whether it ought to exist; for, as a matter of fact, it never does. Whatever may be the written text of a Constitution, the multitude always will have leaders among them, and those leaders not selected by themselves. They may set up the pretence of political equality, if they will, and delude themselves with a belief of its existence. But the only consequence will be, that they will have bad leaders instead of good. Every community has natural leaders, to whom, if they are not misled by the insane passion for equality, they will instinctively

[1] Cecil, *Salisbury*, iii, 27.
[2] Cf. Pinto-Duschinsky, pp. 84–5.
[3] *Q.R.*, cxii (1862), 542.
[4] *S.R.*, xi (1861), 405. Inequality of power appears as a necessary consequence of the emergence of private property and its differential accumulation: 'the equality of property once gone, the equality of power will not long survive it'.

SOCIETY AND POLITICS

defer. Always wealth, in some countries birth, in all intellectual power and culture, mark out the men to whom, in a healthy state of feeling, a community looks to undertake its government. They have the leisure for the task, and can give to it the close attention and the preparatory study which it needs. Fortune enables them to do it for the most part gratuitously, so that the struggles of ambition are not defiled by the taint of sordid greed. They occupy a position of sufficient prominence among their neighbours to feel that their course is closely watched, and they belong to a class among whom a failure in honour is mercilessly dealt with. They have been brought up apart from temptations to the meaner kinds of crime, and therefore it is no praise to them if, in such matters, their moral code stands high. But even if they be at bottom no better than others who have passed through greater vicissitudes of fortune, they have at least this inestimable advantage – that, when higher motives fail, their virtue has all the support which human respect can give. They are the aristocracy of a country in the original and best sense of the word. Whether a few of them are decorated by honorary titles or enjoy hereditary privileges, is a matter of secondary moment. The important point is, that the rulers of the country should be taken from among them, and that with them should be the political preponderance to which they have every right that superior fitness can confer. Unlimited power would be as ill-bestowed upon them as upon any other set of men. They must be checked by constitutional forms and watched by an active public opinion, lest their rightful pre-eminence should degenerate into the domination of a class. But woe to the community that deposes them altogether![1]

The formal argument for the supremacy of property and education was thus basically a utilitarian one: the classes which possessed them were in general better equipped and more likely to govern well (in Salisbury's sense of 'well') than those which did not. The positive side of the argument was, however, rather less stressed by Salisbury than the negative. The virtues of rule by the possessing classes were pale by the side of his characterisation of the evils of the alternative – 'democracy'.

The dominant theme of Salisbury's political writing was his hostility to democracy, by which he meant not necessarily 'one man, one vote', but any system which gave practical supremacy to the lower classes. His polemics against democracy were marked by such strong feeling that it is clear that it represented for him not simply a defective and dangerous form of government but a type of both social and political organisation repugnant to his deepest instincts. The root of his attitude probably lay in his diffidence and shyness, and in the tensions and difficulties involved for him in all forms of social intercourse. The relatively moderate amount of public exposure and currying of public

[1] *Q.R.*, cxii (1862), 547–8.

EDITOR'S INTRODUCTION

favour demanded by politics as they were when he first entered them was ordeal enough; the prospect of having to cultivate a mass electorate composed largely of the lower orders, and of experiencing the gradual erosion of the barriers of social distinction and deference which protected men of his class from the familiarity of the classes beneath, filled him with nervous revulsion. He resisted the admission of overpowering numbers of working men to the franchise as though he were resisting their imminent irruption into his own drawing-room. But if his opposition to democratic ideas had a powerful emotional content, it was strongly supported by argument. He drew a little on the views of others, like de Tocqueville and J. S. Mill, but in the main his criticism of democracy rested on his own observation of historical examples, and in particular of the United States, which, furnishing the first modern instance of the application of democratic theory to the government of a large country, served him as a case-study.[1]

'First-rate men will not canvass mobs; and if they did, the mobs would not elect the first-rate men.'[2] Salisbury thought that democracy was bound to be vitiated from the start by lack of adequate leadership and a sound political personnel. The propertied and educated classes who provided a nation's 'natural leaders' would not go begging for the popular vote, when 'those from whom they have to beg are their inferiors in the ordinary concerns of life, are rough and coarse in their manners, and delight in humiliating a "gentleman", and require him to swallow the most claptrap pledges as the condition of their support'.[3] They would rather opt out of politics. Salisbury detected the process already in operation in some of the larger English borough constituencies, even under the restricted franchise of 1832. He wrote in 1859:

There is something so filthy in the humiliations that a Marylebone candidate has to undergo that none but mere political adventurers will stand...Out of the 21,000 who form the register only 10,000 recorded their votes in the animated contest which resulted in sending Mr. Edwin James to the House of Commons. The refined and educated population, who give to Marylebone the wealth of which its demagogues boast, who are the fountain of all its outward show of luxury and prosperity, hold themselves as much aloof from the filthy turmoil of borough politics as if they lived in New Orleans or New York. The publicans and their customers have fairly driven out the inhabitants of the stately streets and squares, extending from Portland-place to Westbournia, who are as destitute

---

[1] See especially the article 'Democracy on its Trial', *Q.R.*, cx (1861), 247–88. De Tocqueville is quoted several times in this piece, and Mill's *Representative Government* is one of the works ostensibly under review.
[2] *Q.R.*, cx (1861), 281.
[3] *Ibid.* cxvi (1864), 273. Cf. *ibid.* cxii (1862), 549–51.

SOCIETY AND POLITICS

of political rights as Jews in modern Rome or plebeians under the early Consuls. Wealth, intellect, distinction, are all lost and buried in the mass of 10 *l.* householders. The pewter-pot alone remains supreme. This is the species of constituency which Mr. Bright wishes to extend.[1]

Men of substance and culture could have no place in democratic politics, since the masses were 'wholly incapable of appreciating men whose understanding, refinement, and morality are so totally at variance with their own'.[2] The result of their exclusion was a 'poverty of greatness'[3] very dangerous to the state in moments of crisis, and a general mediocrity among politicians not likely to produce good government in ordinary times. Without the influence of 'the higher class', politics lost 'its position as a vocation' and became merely another way of making a living, 'the refuge of educated men who have lost their character, and of ready-tongued adventurers', the pursuit of self-interested professionals, out to make a killing, and promoted from the background by the 'wire-pullers and caucus-mongers', the party managers, with whom real control rested.[4]

Politicians of this type, far from providing the wise counsel and firm leadership which might guide and tame democracy's passions, were reckless and weak, ready to do anything to satisfy the whims of the voters. Government in their hands was a corrupt, inefficient, and vacillating thing, subservient to every passing mood of popular feeling. The prospect of an executive completely and instantly obedient to a democratically elected assembly's interpretation of the popular will was a nightmare to Salisbury. In America, the control of the electorate and its representatives over governmental policy was at least checked between elections by the entrenched power of the executive, embodied in the president. But there was no such safeguard in the British constitution. The experience of America and France seemed to Salisbury to teach that

if you will have democracy, you must have something like Caesarism to control it. The feeble and pliable Executive of England is wholly unsuited to such an electoral body. A Government that yields and must yield to the slightest wish of the House of Commons, is only possible so long as that House of Commons is the organ of an educated minority.[5]

Under constitutional arrangements evolved to suit the supremacy of a propertied minority, democracy seemed likely to produce a more

[1] *S.R.*, vii (1859), 777. [2] *Q.R.*, cx (1861), 281.
[3] *Ibid.* cxii (1862), 545, referring to the weakness of the American federal government.
[4] *Ibid.* cxvi (1864), 273-4; cxii (1862), 547-9.
[5] *Ibid.* cxix (1866), 279.

absolute supremacy of the unpropertied majority in England than elsewhere. The people would rule in a very real and immediate sense. Salisbury had no doubt that the unrestrained domination of the numerical majority meant tyranny, when that majority was drawn from the people at large, rather than from an educated and propertied élite. Democracy, claimed as the embodiment of freedom, in the sense of the faculty for every man to have a voice in the conduct of government, might prove in fact the negation of freedom, in the perhaps more fundamental sense of the liberty of the individual, under the law, from undue coercion and interference, whether by the state or by other citizens, in the conduct of his affairs, the enjoyment of his property, and the expression of his beliefs. How could freedom in this latter sense stand up against an assault by a majority purporting to represent that ultimate authority of a democratic state, 'the will of the people'? The Radical advocates of an extended franchise seemed to Salisbury to be working from a concept of freedom entirely different from, and inimical to, his own. 'They look', he wrote, 'to the origins of the supreme power in the State, and if that satisfies them they care little about the limitations by which it is restricted. Freedom, in their definition, is the supreme, unchecked power of the majority.' The majority embodied the people's will, 'and against the people individuals have no rights'.

It is the multiplication table which furnishes in the last resort the essential test that distinguishes right from wrong in the government of a nation. If one man imprisons you, that is tyranny; if two men, or a number of men imprison you, that is freedom.[1]

Not the least frightening feature of the tyranny of the majority was that it extended to more than just government and legislation: 'it exercises', wrote Salisbury with reference to America, 'a despotic control over the life and actions of private individuals more minute and more penetrating than it would be physically in the power of an absolute monarch to carry out'.[2] Like Mill in the *Essay on Liberty*, Salisbury saw that a man might be coerced in far more fundamental matters and with far greater efficiency by his fellows than by the state, and that it was as much from social pressures, backed by social sanctions, as from political decrees that the threat to freedom of behaviour and opinion came. Democracy had to be regarded as a social as well as a political system, and once the structures of status and deference which supported the upper classes above the lower had been undermined by its egalitarian

[1] *Ibid.* cxvii (1865), 284–5. [2] *Ibid.* cx (1861), 264.

presuppositions, an enforced outward conformity to the tastes and prejudices of the mass was to be apprehended as its logical result.

An inevitable concomitant of popular majority rule was, in Salisbury's view, an attack on the property of the well-to-do classes. Once the latter had lost electoral supremacy, no methods would suffice to maintain their independent power. 'By unwearied canvassing or lavish expenditure they may beg or bribe back a semblance of it for a time; but even that shadow, so dearly purchased, of their former influence, they will retain on sufferance.'[1] Nothing, in the long run, could protect them from the spoliation implicit in the materialistic politics of class conflict. 'Wherever democracy has prevailed', Salisbury wrote, 'the power of the State has been used in some form or other to plunder the well-to-do classes for the benefit of the poor.'[2] This was not because the poor were in general more rapacious and wicked than the average of men, but simply because they were no less so. Salisbury conceded that the despotism of universal suffrage

would be liable to all the influences which do modify human selfishness, and prevent the world from being nothing else than a battle-field of rival self-interests. It is not to be supposed that the working classes, more than any other classes, would commit an act of glaring robbery unless they had some very strong motive to do so, and something in the nature of a pretext to cover from the eye of their own consciences the nudity of the operation.

But motives and pretexts were not likely to be lacking: 'the pressure of want or the intoxication of passion will overpower the conscience of a democracy', and where an appetite existed, the sophisms would be forthcoming to justify its satisfaction. 'The good intentions or the good feeling of the multitude...may serve for ordinary times, and in the absence of special temptation; but they will not stand a strain.'[3] In the end, the people would apply their political supremacy to the redistribution of wealth.

It did not, however, follow that because the propertied minority would be unable effectively to resist this process through the political system, they would passively acquiesce in it. For Salisbury, one of the most dangerous features of democracy was its tendency so grossly to outrage the rights and susceptibilities of minorities as to cause them to appeal to force against it. The moderation with which minorities were treated in well-governed states was impossible in democracies, because they were guided by passion – a word Salisbury used frequently when talking of the democratic temper.

[1] *Ibid.* cxix (1866), 280. [2] *Ibid.* cvii (1860), 524.
[3] *Ibid.* cxvi (1864), 269–70.

EDITOR'S INTRODUCTION

In the collective deliberations of any body of men, reason gains the mastery over passion exactly in proportion as they are educated and as they are few. Passion is fostered equally by the two main characteristics of the democratic sovereign – ignorance and numbers.[1]

The result was that, having no hope of fair treatment, a minority in a democracy might well feel compelled, in desperation and fear, to fight to defend itself. It was precisely in these terms that Salisbury interpreted the origins of the American Civil War.[2] Democracy was thus inherently unstable and prone to internal violence. But it was also prone to external violence: like many of its opponents, Salisbury thought it peculiarly susceptible to the temptations of foreign adventure. 'Wherever it has had free play', he wrote, 'in the ancient world or the modern, in the old hemisphere or the new, a thirst for empire, and a readiness for aggressive war, has always marked it.'[3] The feverishness and intolerance of democratic multitudes, their liability to be swept by sudden and intense emotions, and their incapacity for self-control, seemed to Salisbury to guarantee that ultimately democratic experiments must collapse in a more or less bloody disillusionment and chaos, whether caused by the impossibility of finding a stable internal consensus, or by external war, or by both. What happened when the people got out of control he knew, or thought he knew, as many of his generation did, from the example of the French Revolution, which held a strong fascination for him, and on which, at Hatfield, he assembled a remarkable library.[4] To a man whose mind enclosed the images of September 1792 and the Terror, it is not surprising that democracy was not freedom, was not progress, was not the new dawn, but tyranny, barbarism, and night.

In order to avoid these highly coloured horrors, the classes endowed with property and education must reconcile themselves to the necessity of constant political exertion to keep democracy from coming fully into being. Perhaps the greatest danger to them lay in their own apathy and false sense of security, and Salisbury was insistent in warning them against it, especially when it was aggravated by an apparent lull in the political battle. 'More fortresses', he reminded them, 'have been lost by heedlessness than by panic.'[5] Of course, much of politics was a grubby business, which they would find distasteful: there was 'no greater sacrifice made by the highly educated classes in England to their country's welfare than the part which they take in politics'.[6] But the sacrifice had to be

[1] *Ibid*. cx (1861), 269.
[2] *Ibid*. cx (1861), 268–70.
[3] *Ibid*. cxv (1864), 239.
[4] Cecil, *Salisbury*, ii, 13.
[5] *Q.R.*, cvii (1860), 534.
[6] *Ibid*. cxviii (1865), 194.

SOCIETY AND POLITICS

made, and their political duty accepted, if their values and interests were to be preserved. Nor did Salisbury think that politics was only a matter of regrettable and vulgar necessity. It could express high and honourable aspirations:

> Real power to control the destinies and be in some degree the architect of the welfare of our fellow-men must always be the ambition of the loftiest class of minds: and it is an ambition which is noble, and above all shade of cavil.[1]

The 'comfortable classes' must labour in the political arena without expectation of respite, still less of final victory, for the battle in which they were engaged was by its nature incapable of being brought to a conclusion. The contest between the forces of conservation and those of innovation was eternal, whatever its changing forms, and the strenuous maintenance of a precarious balance all that could realistically be hoped for. 'Conflict in free states', Salisbury believed, 'is the law of life',[2] and therefore both natural and, in some sense, a sign of health. During the Reform crisis of 1866, he contemptuously dismissed the notion that it might be possible through some settlement to reach an era of repose, in which struggles for political power between classes would disappear.

> We might as well hope for the termination of the struggle for existence by which, some philosophers tell us, the existence or the modification of the various species of organized beings upon our planet are determined. The battle for political power is merely an effort, well or ill-judged, on the part of the classes who wage it to better or to secure their own position. Unless our social activity shall have become paralyzed, and the nation shall have lost its vitality, this battle must continue to rage. In this sense the question of Reform, that is to say, the question of relative class power, can never be settled.[3]

For all his yearning after harmony and stability, Salisbury had the keenest possible sense of the permanence of conflict and flux. Whatever state of affairs might momentarily be achieved, the demand for change would remain. 'There can be no finality in politics.'[4]

What there could be, if the conservative forces fought hard enough, was a degree of defensive success, fluctuating with the movement of the pendulum which Salisbury seems to have regarded as the natural pattern of politics. He saw the struggle between the forces of conservation and those of innovation as subject to a process of alternating predominance.[5] The impulse of each force would differ widely in successive generations, 'according to the teaching of events'. 'The pressure of abuses which have been bred by stagnation, or the memory of the disorders which

---

[1] *Ibid.* cxxvii (1869), 553.   [2] *Ibid.* cxviii (1865), 198.
[3] *Ibid.* cxx (1866), 273.   [4] *Ibid.* cxxiii (1867), 557.
See *ibid.* cxxxiii (1872), 583-4, quoted above, p. 27.

EDITOR'S INTRODUCTION

have been caused by change, will alternately depress one or the other extremity of the balance.'[1] But whichever side momentarily preponderated, a kind of automatic corrective mechanism operated to strengthen the other. Between the opposite poles of politics lay a great mass of moderate men of varying shades, 'who, according to the exigencies of the time and as they see that the extremists on the one side or the other are likely to become predominant, lean to the deficient side with irresistible force and redress the balance that is wanting to save the equilibrium of the Constitution'.[2] If the conservative forces could not hope, then, to eradicate the spirit of innovation and achieve a static peace, they had at least the assurance that their opponents could no more eliminate them, and that even in the high periods of political unrest the ultimate return of stability was virtually guaranteed, if they defended themselves vigorously.

Social stability is ensured, not by a cessation of the demand for change – for the needy and the restless will never cease to cry for it – but by the fact that change in its progress must at last hurt some class of men who are strong enough to arrest it. The army of so-called reform, in every stage of its advance, necessarily converts a detachment of its force into opponents. The more rapid the advance the more formidable will the desertion become, till at last a point will be reached where the balance between the forces of conservation and destruction will be redressed, and the political equilibrium be restored.[3]

That equilibrium was necessarily an unstable one, to be maintained only by the unremitting effort that had been required to establish it, and then for a limited space of time. But it was to Salisbury the highest achievement that practical politics could offer, and if each successive regaining of it marked in fact a regression from the position which the conservative forces had previously occupied, at least they could ensure by their exertions that the retreat was orderly and slow.

In the conduct of the unending struggle against the tides of radical 'reform', conservative tactics must combine resolution with a prudent flexibility. Salisbury's prime emphasis, of course, always lay on the former. Where essentials were in question, not even the threat of the direst consequences should deter the defenders of established order from doing their duty. Their fathers, Salisbury wrote, were blamed for their desperate resistance to the first Reform Act:

It is said, – and men seem to think that condemnation can go no further than such a censure – that they brought us within twenty-four hours of revolution...

[1] *Ibid.* cxxiii (1867), 557.
[2] Speech of 27 June 1883, quoted in Cecil, *Salisbury*, iii, 68.
[3] *Q.R.*, cxxvii (1869), 551–2.

SOCIETY AND POLITICS

But is it in truth so great an evil, when the dearest interests and the most sincere convictions are at stake, to go within twenty-four hours of revolution?[1]

And yet, while it might be necessary to be prepared to fight on the barricades, there was much to be said for avoiding actually getting killed on them. Salisbury was not a die-hard in the strict sense, and saw no practical use in hanging on to an untenable position until it was overrun. 'Resistance', he thought, 'is folly or heroism – a virtue or a vice – in most cases, according to the probabilities there are of its being successful.'[2] Where further resistance was clearly hopeless, sensible men gave ground. The art of conservative politics was to calculate what, in any given juncture, could be preserved, and what must eventually be abandoned.

Consistent firmness would reduce the need for retreats to a minimum. Salisbury believed that if only the conservative forces exercised with a strong hand the predominance they normally possessed in government, they would be able to avert a great deal of trouble. In the performance of the central tasks of government, the maintenance of order and the securing of life and property, statesmen should not shrink from employing almost any means that might be necessary, especially in moments of crisis threatening the stability of the state. Justifying Castlereagh's use of bribery in effecting the Irish union, Salisbury wrote: 'In the supreme struggle of social order against anarchy, we cannot deny to the champions of civilised society the moral latitude which is by common consent accorded to armed men fighting for their country against a foreign foe.'[3]

Given the vital importance of overt strength in politics, it was necessary to be very cautious in considering any concession to the forces of change. Too often, concession was the beginning of a slippery slope, each well-intentioned instalment serving only to create the impression of weakness and to stimulate the appetites it was designed to appease. Salisbury saw a good example in the French Revolution. Writing in approbation of the repressive policy adopted in the 1790s by the younger Pitt, he said that if any fact was clear amid the 'bewildering confusion' of the revolution, it was that 'the gentleness, the concessions, the morbid tenderness of Louis XVI had only tended to precipitate his own and his people's doom, and aggravate the ferocity of those he tried by kindness to disarm'.[4] Conciliation of malcontents, he was ready to agree, was far better than coercion where it could be successfully brought off, but any kind of

[1] *Ibid.* cxxiii (1867), 543.   [2] *Ibid.* cxvii (1865), 550.
[3] *Ibid.* cxi (1862), 204.   [4] *Ibid.* cxi (1862), 538–9.

EDITOR'S INTRODUCTION

attempted conciliation that looked like a timorous yielding to pressure for the sake of avoiding trouble was futile. 'Conciliatory legislation only conciliates', he declared in 1882, in reference to the Irish problem, 'when there is a full belief on the part of those with whom you are dealing that you are acting on a principle of justice and not on motives of fear.'[1]

Salisbury's preoccupation with the need for firm and determined government, however, did not make him blind to the dangers of upheaval if it should be too rigid, too repressive, too divorced from public feeling, and too reluctant to concede necessary reforms. He was fully alive to the threat of ossification, and he saw, too, the possibility that long and secure tenure of power would result in the ruling class's governing exclusively in its own interest, remarking:

A little Radicalism is a very useful thing for the purpose of keeping in check the natural selfishness of the classes who are the tenants of power. A feeling that their own overthrow is possible, if not probable, keeps jobbing within bounds, and provokes occasional attempts at practical reform.[2]

The power and influence of the conservative forces could, he knew, be maintained and justified only so long as they were exercised in a responsible and adaptive manner. If the conservative cause degenerated into the mere defence of sectional and vested interests, if it took the shape of automatic and unreasoning hostility to all alteration of a status quo invested with semi-mystical sanctity, then it ceased to be either morally and rationally defensible or practically viable. It was essential for its adherents to avoid the delusion that existing arrangements were necessarily ideal, and to accept the degree of change that was made inevitable by the movement of the times. Salisbury's anxiety to moderate and slow down change never led him into the foolishness of supposing that it could be brought to a stop; nor did his distaste for the thing in general prevent his recognising that some applications of it were desirable and beneficial. Change was constant, and institutions, customs, and policies must constantly be adapted to take account of new realities. 'The commonest error in politics', Salisbury thought, 'is sticking to the carcasses of dead policies.'[3] Adaptation was both the means and the price of effective conservation. The substance of the established order could be secured only by a standing readiness to modify its forms and

[1] Speech of 5 June 1882, quoted in Cecil, *Salisbury*, iii, 48.
[2] *S.R.*, xiii (1862), 637.
[3] Letter to Lytton, 25 May 1877, quoted in Cecil, *Salisbury*, ii, 145.

practices in such a way as to accommodate the consequences of social development and to deflect the criticisms of its radical opponents. In his attitudes both to political institutions and to economic and social arrangements, Salisbury showed himself by no means uncritical of what existed or obdurate against all change.

In judging the nation's political institutions, Salisbury insisted, it was necessary to appreciate that they did not purport to be based on any theory or intellectual process, but were rather the unplanned and irregular outcome of a long period of natural growth. The representative system, for example, was incapable of defence before 'a jury of philosophers': it was

a collection of the trophies of centuries of conflict – an accumulation of the deposits which have been left behind by the varying tides of political sentiment that from age to age have flowed over our island – the resultant of all the political forces, which, working in harmony or antagonism, have combined to propel England along the track in which it has been her destiny to travel.[1]

Institutions so evolved could be regarded as analogous to living organisms. This meant, of course, that their existence was finite: 'institutions like the House of Lords', Salisbury once told Alfred Austin, 'must die, like all other organic beings, when their time comes'.[2] But it meant too that until their time came it was a matter of high delicacy and danger to submit them to major surgery. Salisbury was particularly contemptuous of the foolish arrogance of those who thought to improve institutions which, however untidily constructed, were serving their purposes well by remodelling them according to the dictates of abstract reason and logic. He categorised them as 'symmetrical Reformers', 'the children of Abbé Sieyes and the *doctrinaires*', whose 'mania' was 'to introduce the accuracy of a machine and the proportions of a geometrical figure into the institutions which are to secure the happiness and carry out the wishes of capricious, inconsistent, illogical mankind'.[3] Even when an institution was defective, the perils of drastic alteration had to be carefully weighed, and Salisbury was a stout adherent of what he called 'the central doctrine of Conservatism, that it is better to endure almost any political evil than to risk a breach of the historic continuity of government'.[4] It was not through tinkering with institutions on the

[1] *Q.R.*, cxvi (1864), 271. Cf. 'The Theories of Parliamentary Reform', *Oxford Essays*, pp. 67–71.
[2] Salisbury to Austin, 29 April 1888 (typescript copy): Salisbury Papers, vol. 'Acland to Beach', p. 54.
[3] 'The Theories of Parliamentary Reform', *Oxford Essays*, p. 67.
[4] *Q.R.*, cxxxv (1873), 544.

EDITOR'S INTRODUCTION

basis of rational analysis and prescription that real political progress could, in any case, be obtained:

> Political progress is little, if at all, dependent on intellectual discovery... in essence it is a moral change. Its problems are not solved by thinking. Its achievements are not the work of studious or ingenious brains. Peace and goodwill – the objects to which it ought to tend – will not be the result of some clever contrivance which men by much debating and many experiments may hope to hit upon. If they attain it at all, it will be by rooting out the selfishness which good fortune nurtures, and the recklessness which springs from misery.[1]

Nonetheless, gradual adjustments to existing institutions, respecting their character and spirit, might well be both feasible and desirable, especially when they removed plausible grounds of attack. During the Reform debate of the mid-sixties, Salisbury became anxious to do away with the worst anomalies of the representative system, not because he thought they did any harm, but because the desire for a theoretically tidy arrangement made them sources of weakness.[2] He was in favour of a substantial reform of the House of Lords, in a bid to strengthen its influence by making it more representative of national opinion.[3] What he could not admit was that the necessity of adaptation to the needs of the age could ever require a whole political system to undergo such a sudden and sweeping transformation as he believed to be involved for the political system of England in the Reform Act of 1867. When that transformation was brought about, his response was to begin to wonder whether the institutions thus, as he saw it, denatured and perverted in their purpose were any longer viable.

While Salisbury in general accepted the system of government under which he found himself in England, he never thought it ideal. It is clear from his writings that representative government as such, the rule of an elected assembly, did not greatly appeal to him. As an undergraduate he had been the highest of Tories, 'an absolutist, contemning all forms of popular government, accepting Strafford as his ideal of an historical hero'.[4] He used to lament as a young man 'that he had not been born under a more actively monarchial constitution; he should have far preferred service to a king than to a parliament'.[5] Government, he

---

[1] *Ibid.* cxxxi (1871), 570.
[2] *Ibid.* cxvii (1865), 572–3. Under the influence of the prevailing demand for symmetry and logic, he grumbled, 'hard-headed Englishmen seem for the time as if they were metamorphosed into German Professors'.
[3] Below, p. 59.   [4] Cecil, *Salisbury*, i, 22.
[5] *Ibid.* iii, 180.

SOCIETY AND POLITICS

seems to have felt, came best from on high: he did not want to derive its authority from the will of 'the people', or to see its actions regulated by their fluctuating moods. In Australia in 1852, at the height of the gold rush, he ascribed the relative orderliness of the goldfields, which much impressed him, to the fact that

> the government was of the Queen, not of the mob; from above, not from below, holding from a supposed right (whether real or not, no matter) and not from 'the people the source of all legitimate power'...A hundred years ago the Americans had this spirit among them, – fifty years hence we shall not have it among us. But there it stands, a last protest against the principles of modern squeezability.[1]

Salisbury saw the purpose of government largely in negative and defensive terms. Of 'the two great opposite functions which are the final cause, the *raison d'être*, of all political institutions', the repression of rebellion and the upholding of liberty,[2] he placed at least as much emphasis on the former as on the latter. Forms of government were 'in their nature, precautions against disturbance';[3] their major objects were the maintenance of order and the protection of lives and, above all, property. What statesmen needed for these tasks was first and foremost strength and determination: if they possessed them, it was unnecessary and undesirable that they should worry overmuch about pleasing popular feeling. 'A Government which is strong enough to hold its own will generally command an acquiescence which with all but very speculative minds, is the equivalent of contentment.'[4]

Of course, Salisbury did not think that government could be stable and lasting without taking some pains to cultivate the goodwill of its subjects, or that it was nothing more than a contrivance for the preservation of order and property. But he did not see it as an emanation from or instrument of the people, whose primary duty was a constant effort to elicit and satisfy what at any given moment they thought to be their wishes.[5] Thus he felt that it ought not to be unduly sensitive to the movements of public opinion. It was not that he ignored the importance of public opinion as a political factor, or failed to listen to it: as a party leader, he took a certain amount of trouble to ascertain what it was.[6] But he did not think it right for responsible statesmen to pander to it, and, in any case, he believed that a good deal of what

---
[1] Lord Robert Cecil to Rev. C. Conybeare, 11 July 1852: quoted *ibid*. i, 31–2.
[2] *Q.R.*, cxii (1862), 543.   [3] *Ibid*.
[4] *Ibid*. cxvii (1865), 550.
[5] See 'The Theories of Parliamentary Reform', *Oxford Essays*, pp. 58–60.
[6] Cecil, *Biographical Studies*, p. 27; *Salisbury*, iii, 196.

EDITOR'S INTRODUCTION

passed for public opinion was an artificial product, assiduously manufactured by 'the journalists, the literary men, the professors, the advanced thinkers of the day'.[1]

No doubt his coolness towards representative government in general, as towards the democratic form of it in particular, had much to do with his shrinking from the direct contact with the multitude which it entailed, especially at election time. Sitting for the small pocket borough of Stamford without a single contest, he was spared the real horrors of electioneering, but the description of the humiliations of canvassing which he wrote in 1859 shows vividly the effect on a weak stomach of 'the nauseous mire of a general election'. He speaks of

The days and weeks of screwed-up smiles and laboured courtesy, the mock geniality, the hearty shake of the filthy hand, the chuckling reply that must be made to the coarse joke, the loathsome, choking compliment that must be paid to the grimy wife and sluttish daughter, the indispensable flattery of the vilest religious prejudices, the wholesale deglutition of hypocritical pledges...[2]

At least, in the constituency which politicians faced in 1859, education and property still had some secure predominance. After 1867, that predominance seemed to Salisbury to have gone, and he could not avoid the question whether the type of representative government of which it had been a more or less unspoken premise could endure or be tolerable without it.

Just as he had reservations about the representative system in principle, so Salisbury had criticisms of its detailed operation, even in what he would come to see in retrospect as its mid-century heyday. He was not much troubled by the charge that its machinery was ramshackle and in parts archaic. Indeed, he freely and amusingly admitted it. The House of Commons, he acknowledged in 1864, did its work 'in a fitful, slovenly, accidental sort of fashion'.

The system under which it is chosen is anomalous to the last degree. The various constituencies who return its members have nothing to show that entitles them to the proud privilege which they enjoy, except the fact that they are in possession. The limit of suffrage upon which the representation reposes, owes its existence to no other fact than that it happens to be represented by a round number, and that it presented some unexplained fascination to Lord Russell's mind at a critical period of English history. The elections are

[1] Q.R., cxxiii (1867), 563. Cf. ibid. cvii (1860), 532; cxi (1862), 229; Salisbury's letters to Lord Lytton (Salisbury Papers).
[2] B.Q.R., i (1859), 355. Cf. Q.R., cxviii (1865), 199. If the electors of Stamford were indeed treated to the spectacle of their rather priggish young member essaying a chuckling reply to a coarse joke, it must have been a sight to savour.

SOCIETY AND POLITICS

deformed by every kind of theoretical defect... The proceedings of the House itself, and the regulations under which they are placed, would not be more satisfactory to a theoretical politician. They are uncouth, complicated, often unmeaning, founded upon circumstances which have ceased to exist, often defensible by no reasons applicable to the present state of things, and liable at any time to misuse, which would bring the whole business of the country to a standstill.[1]

All this mattered little, because the success of the system depended less on its forms than on the common-sense spirit of the men who worked it. Yet there were structural features which were more disturbing, because offering threats to good government which common sense might not always be enough to dispel. One of these was the subordination of the executive to the legislature. Salisbury argued in 1864 that the Commons could, if they pleased, exert complete control over the executive, and that that 'brings the nation and the Government into so close a connection, that any policy which is approved by the mass of the nation is certain to be promptly adopted by its rulers'.[2] It is doubtful whether Salisbury thought this an unmixed blessing even in relation to the very limited political 'nation' of 1864; after 1867, it was precisely what most frightened him.

Another major source of unease was the party system. Salisbury never really came to terms with party. He regarded it as no more than a faintly sordid mechanism for securing common ends, and invested no sentiment in it. He was acutely conscious of the danger of its degenerating into faction, and of the tendency of party strife to imperil sound and stable government, though he himself was a most furious partisan, pursuing the victory of his cause by every means consistent with honour.[3] He expressed the fundamental defect of the party system pithily: 'it invites to the struggle for places; it professes to honour the battle for principles; but it will not allow any set of men to be successful in both these fields of political achievement'. In the pursuit of office and power, principle was inevitably sacrificed. Moreover, those who were indifferent to office could impose their sectional demands on their party as the price of their continued support, while the mass of faithful back benchers whose support could be taken for granted got 'neither the triumph of principle nor the gratification of place'.[4] There was another serious fault:

So long as we have government by party, the very notion of repose must be foreign to English politics. Agitation is, so to speak, endowed in this country.

[1] *Q.R.*, cxvi (1864), 247-8.
[2] *Ibid.* cxvi (1864), 257.
[3] Cecil, *Salisbury*, iii, 300-2.
[4] *Q.R.*, cxxxv (1873), 569-70.

EDITOR'S INTRODUCTION

There is a standing machinery for producing it. There are rewards which can only be obtained by men who excite the public mind, and devise means of persuading one set of persons that they are deeply injured by another. The production of cries is encouraged by a heavy bounty. The invention and exasperation of controversies lead those who are successful in such arts to place, and honour, and power. Therefore, politicians will always select the most irritating cries, and will raise the most exasperating controversies that circumstances will permit.[1]

Salisbury, of course, thought that this was particularly applicable to the Radicals: 'a party whose mission it is to live entirely upon the discovery of grievances are apt to manufacture the element upon which they subsist'.[2]

The most critical detail of the representative system was obviously the franchise, which defined the political nation, and must ultimately determine the character and working of the system as a whole. Salisbury did not think that there was any special magic about the franchise ruling when he entered politics. He recognised that it was arbitrary and contained anomalies, and that its terms were merely a reflection of a particular state of society, a particular balance of forces, which was subject to change. But it kept the great bulk of political power in the hands of the upper and middle classes, the condition on which alone he found representative government palatable, and he was deeply reluctant to contemplate its substantial remodelling. To revise it in such a way as greatly to increase the electoral power of the poorer classes and give them the means of exerting serious pressure on the House of Commons was unthinkable. In order to justify restricting the poorer classes to a very limited role, Salisbury was driven to try to provide an appropriate definition of the basis on which the franchise ought to rest. It was an exercise foreign to his temperament, with its aversion to theorising, and the idea that there was a fundamental principle whose application should decide the right to vote consorted uneasily with his view of political arrangements as matters of convenience shaped by historical evolution rather than by logical design. The argument he adopted was a classic piece of backwards reasoning, the premises following from the conclusion, in the sense that they were carefully formulated to produce the conclusion to which he was already committed.

Sketched out in his writings of 1858–9, his position was most fully developed in the *Quarterly* article of July 1864, following Gladstone's famous pronouncement that 'every man who is not presumably in-

[1] *Ibid.* cxxxi (1871), 578.
[2] Speech at Edinburgh, 24 Nov. 1882, quoted in Cecil, *Salisbury*, iii, 65.

capacitated by some consideration of personal unfitness or political danger is morally entitled to come within the pale of the Constitution'. Salisbury felt bound to allow that

If everybody came into the common concern with an equal contribution, it would be just that he should possess an equal share of power over the whole. So far as Government has to do with the disposal of life and limb, each man stands before it with a tolerably equal claim, and may demand an equal voice.[1]

His way of escape from the conclusion of equal manhood suffrage was via the very shaky contention that life and limb had been superseded as the primary concern of government. 'The chief object of Government, in England at least, is the protection of property...the main business of Parliament is to make laws to define and to secure in some form or other the distribution of property.'[2] The amounts of property which men had 'invested' in the 'concern' were not equal, and consequently it was inequitable that they should have an equal say in its management:

To give 'the suffrage' to a poor man is to give him as large a part in determining that legislation which is mainly concerned with property as the banker whose name is known on every Exchange in Europe, as the merchant whose ships are in every sea, as the landowner who owns the soil of a whole manufacturing town...two day-labourers shall outvote Baron Rothschild.[3]

Just as no commercial joint-stock company would operate on such an absurd basis, neither should states. 'The bestowal upon any class of a voting power disproportionate to their stake in the country, must infallibly give to that class a power *pro tanto* of using taxation as an instrument of plunder, and expenditure and legislation as a fountain of gain.' 'Natural right' could not be made to justify an equal suffrage without equal property to protect. 'The common consent of mankind, expressed in the management of their own concerns, has agreed that in the government and administration of common property, men should vote in proportion to their shares.'[4]

Salisbury thus had a principle. 'Not the number of noses, but the magnitude of interests, should furnish the elements by which the proportions of representation should be computed.'[5] It was far, however,

[1] *Q.R.*, cxvi (1864), 265.
[2] *Ibid.* Salisbury had taken this line in 1858: 'Setting aside the measures which originate in our religious disputes, Parliament exists almost exclusively for the purpose of regulating taxation and guarding property' ('The Theories of Parliamentary Reform', *Oxford Essays*, p. 62; and cf. p. 63). In 1864 he pressed it further, trying to show that virtually all political issues, including church questions, were at bottom matters of property (above, p. 26).
[3] *Q.R.*, cxvi (1864), 266.   [4] *Ibid.* cxvi (1864), 269–70.
[5] *B.Q.R.*, i (1859), 28.

from being an entirely satisfactory one. The analogy on which it rested was highly dubious: Salisbury himself was well aware that the state might be regarded as something grander than a mere joint-stock company for the preservation of life and property.[1] Moreover, it posed the difficulty for a conservative that it could be used to attack the existing franchise from almost opposite directions. The 1832 franchise did not, of course, proportion votes to property or 'interests'. Salisbury contended, indeed, that its 'uniform suffrage', giving one vote to the small taxpayer as to the large, reduced property to 'political defencelessness', from which its holders could extricate themselves only through such 'indirect and circuitous' means as electoral corruption and intimidation, not in themselves very desirable, but better than leaving wealth without any securities at all.[2] He saw, too, that one might argue, from a rather different viewpoint, that if votes ought to be proportioned to 'shares', then it was wrong that many working men who certainly had a 'share', however small, should have no vote. This second corollary of his principle was more troublesome than the first, and he evaded it by jettisoning the principle itself and resuming his normal empirical attitude towards political institutions. 'Such an objection to the existing state of things', he agreed, 'would be unanswerable, if our representative arrangements professed to be based on any kind of theory. That is very far from being their character.'[3] In the end, the nature and level of the franchise were bound to be for Salisbury matters of expediency, not logic.

What expediency demanded was that the practical supremacy of property and education should be preserved. 'The classes that represent civilisation, the holders of accumulated capital and accumulated thought, have a right to require securities to protect them from being overwhelmed by hordes who have neither knowledge to guide them nor stake in the Commonwealth to control them.'[4] It was the provision of those securities that was the essential point. If they were provided, in impregnable form, there was no particular reason why enfranchisement of the working classes should be ruled out. Salisbury never committed himself to the position that working men as such should not have votes: his contention was simply that they should not have them on such terms as to give them an absolute preponderance of political power over all other sections of the community. 'Supposing, of course', he allowed, 'that property is sufficiently represented to insure due consideration to its rights, then,

[1] *Q.R.*, cxvi (1864), 267.
[2] 'The Theories of Parliamentary Reform', *Oxford Essays*, pp. 73–6; *B.Q.R.*, i (1859), 28. Cf. *Q.R.*, cxvi (1864), 271–2.
[3] *Ibid.* cxvi (1864), 270.   [4] *B.Q.R.*, i (1859), 29.

SOCIETY AND POLITICS

as long as the standard of representation does not degenerate, the legislator cannot extend the suffrage too liberally or too far.' There might even be some advantage in a widened suffrage, as likely to increase popular loyalty and contentment, provided that effective control remained in safe hands: 'it may be said that the best form of Government (setting aside the question of morality) is one where the masses have little power, and seem to have a great deal'.[1] Salisbury showed interest in the various schemes devised to combine a wide suffrage with the safeguarding of the power of property. In 1858, for instance, he spoke well of the idea adopted by the state of Victoria – plurality of votes with universal suffrage. 'The result of the experiment of course depends entirely on the proportion in which wealth is allowed to confer votes. But it is the only combination which is at once logically unassailable, and yet likely to work fairly in practice.'[2] Something of this kind was the natural product of his principle of representation according to 'shares'. It is not surprising, however, that he never really took it up. Extra votes for property were readily acceptable, but even with that counterpoise manhood suffrage was too much to stomach, however logical it might be. The dangers of so radical an alteration of the representative system were too great. Once concede that every man had a right to vote, and the gates were opened to the flood-tide of democracy, against whose pressure no checks and safeguards could be guaranteed to hold.

When he turned from political institutions to the economic and social system which underlay them, Salisbury's consciousness of imperfection was again matched by a keen sense both of the danger and of the probable futility of drastic or hasty reformation. Whatever their demerits, structures, relations, and habits that had grown out of the life of a people could not be altered for the better overnight. It was often a question how far they could be altered for the better at all, especially by external agency. Salisbury's low view of human nature and scepticism of 'progress' rendered him pessimistic about the possibilities of sweeping social improvement. The conviction of original sin precluded faith in secular formulae for moral or material advance: 'his certainty that in the Gospel alone could be found a remedy for the world's evil made him impatient of any claim in competition with it'.[3] Much of what was unfortunate in the world he saw as more or less ineradicable. 'The flood of evils', he declared, writing about philanthropy in 1863, 'wells up ceaselessly; and it requires no small philosophy to labour on, baling it out little by little,

[1] 'The Theories of Parliamentary Reform', *Oxford Essays*, pp. 65-6.
[2] *Ibid.* p. 64, n.   [3] Cecil, *Salisbury*, i, 120.

EDITOR'S INTRODUCTION

with the certainty that no exertions that we can make will ever materially abate its flow.'[1] Attempts even at the alleviation of social ills were to be assessed sceptically: nothing more aroused his scorn than the sort of unrealistic and ill-conceived philanthropic effort that was just as likely to harm as to help those who were its objects.[2]

Salisbury shared the common view of his age that such moral and material improvement as was possible must depend primarily on the individual's free and rational exercise of his faculties in self-help. His respect for the liberty and responsibility of the individual was so profound that he was averse from giving moral counsel even to his own children, and would make no attempt to oversee the morality of the tenants on his estates.[3] Still less, therefore, did he believe in the wholesale reformation of society through the operations of government. The business of government was to provide security and to administer the common concerns, rather than to try to make men better or happier. In 1874, as a cabinet minister, he explicitly warned the Lords against entering 'the regions of paternal Government', especially in view of the danger, made so much more real by the second Reform Act, of 'laying down new principles of legislation which, upon other subjects and under a political system where power resided with the greatest numbers, would some day be used most disadvantageously against them'.[4] He was speaking on liquor licensing, an issue peculiarly adapted to bring out his deep dislike of attempts to perform a task 'which it is impossible for any Legislature to perform – namely, by the action of Government to insure morality among the people'.[5]

Yet Salisbury was far from seeing the role of government in relation to society as one merely of police and administration. There were areas and contingencies in which the positive intervention of government for social ends was not only permissible but might be essential, circumstances

[1] *S.R.*, xv (1863), 232; quoted in Pinto-Duschinsky, p. 89.
[2] His letter to Lady Blanche Balfour from Cape Town, 30 Sept. 1851 (Salisbury Papers), furnishes an amusing example: 'As perhaps you know Sidney Herbert's distressed Needlewomen was a total failure. He packed about fifty of these creatures into a ship & sent them off as emigrants. Before they got to the Cape, the surgeon, Captain, mates, & a couple of passengers had seduced – if such a term is applicable – nearly all of them. When they came here they took to the streets & as Herbert had consigned them to the Bishops care, & as he at first interfered in their behalf, until the truth was proved – they were called the Bishop's women. So much for philanthropic efforts.' For other complaints at this time about the influence of 'philanthropic nonsense', see his letters of 25 Sept. and 7 Nov. 1851 to his father (*ibid.*).
[3] Cecil, *Salisbury*, ii, 4–5; iii, 15–16. [4] *Hansard*, 3rd series, ccxx, 1190.
[5] *Ibid.* ccxi, 90 (May 1872). For Salisbury's opposition to 'Puritanical' regulation of the drink trade, see P. Smith, *Disraelian Conservatism and Social Reform* (1967), pp. 168, 210–12.

in which government could and should act as an agent of change and reform. The maintenance of freedom itself required an apparatus of legislation and state action designed to prevent some men from denying it to others or from suppressing it among themselves, or to counteract the force of economic and social circumstance which could render it no more than a mocking legal abstraction.[1] There was, too, a range of reforms of wide acceptability whose nature, scope, and cost put them patently beyond the compass of private and voluntary effort: to this category belonged most of the measures which fell within Salisbury's conception of what it was proper to do for the poorer classes.

He was always ready to endorse a degree of cautious and practical intervention by government in the name of social betterment. His first election address at Stamford in 1853 pledged support for 'measures tending to social and sanitary improvements and the amelioration of the conditions of the labouring classes'.[2] Six years later, he was complaining about the obsession of Parliament with partisan strife, when there was important work to be done, such as legal reform and the renovation of 'many a municipal and parochial institution that has outlived its age'.[3] Lady Gwendolen Cecil asserts that 'within the limits which his dread of national extravagance imposed legislation for social reform, provided that it was of a severely practical character, was that which appealed most effectively to his sympathies'.[4] The greater part of his concern for social reform centred on questions relating to the welfare of the poor. While the subject never excited his deepest interest and emotion, he showed sympathy for the poor from undergraduate days, when he was shocked by the low level of wages, and supported in the Oxford Union the motion 'that the amelioration of the social and moral condition of the working classes is the only means of preserving the present constitution of this country'.[5] 'It is right,' he declared in a speech of November 1882, 'to be forward in the defence of the poor; no system that is not just as between rich and poor can hope to survive.'[6] Here more than anywhere else a tinge of old-fashioned Tory paternalism appeared in his outlook. He had some of the sense of responsibility for the poor which Tories liked to assert was characteristic of the landed class, and felt no overriding

---

[1] For Salisbury's realisation that economic circumstances, 'stronger than law', could result in a 'practical serfdom' for the poorer classes, see his remarks on unemployed Lancashire factory girls in *S.R.*, xiv (1862), 567.
[2] Quoted in Pinto-Duschinsky, p. 141. [3] *B.Q.R.*, i (1859), 343.
[4] Cecil, *Biographical Studies*, p. 95.
[5] Cecil, *Salisbury*, i, 22; Pinto-Duschinsky, p. 191.
[6] Quoted in Cecil, *Salisbury*, iii, 65.

EDITOR'S INTRODUCTION

difficulty of principle about state aid to them. According to his daughter, he was not greatly impressed by the argument of 'the moral injury inflicted by State assistance upon the self dependence or energy of its recipients'. 'As an incentive to action the dread of destitution was certainly not valued by him to anything like the same degree as the hope of benefit.'[1] Nonetheless, his basic individualistic precepts were not submerged. The state might help, and in such a way as to stimulate rather than to demoralise, but in the long run it was not state action that could ensure the raising of the condition of the poor. Discussing measures to assist the rural working class, shortly before the general election of 1892, Salisbury said:

> We must learn this rule, that no men and no class of men ever rise to any permanent improvement in their condition of body or mind except by relying upon their own personal efforts... The only true lasting benefit which the statesman can give to the poor man is so to shape matters that the greatest possible liberty for the exercise of his own moral and intellectual qualities should be offered to him by law.[2]

To help men to help themselves must be the aim of social reform.

Exactly what the state should do for the poor was a matter of empirical determination. Perhaps the most fundamental factor governing their condition was the structure and working of the economy, and here state interference was of doubtful utility. In economic matters, once he had outgrown a youthful Tory attachment to protection as 'an essential element of the constitution of the country',[3] Salisbury accepted the conventional wisdom of free trade. Of course, it was against his nature to do so uncritically. He would have none of the Liberals' attempt to ascribe the tide of mid-Victorian prosperity to the creed which they claimed almost as a private possession,[4] and in the eighties and nineties, when the tide had gone out, and the cry had arisen for the shielding of the home economy from foreign competition and tariffs, he was ready so far to modify free trade as to consent to retaliatory duties, while steadily demurring to protection as both inexpedient and, because of the unpopularity of food taxes, politically impossible.[5] But he did not doubt that freedom of trade, enterprise, and contract was a fundamental of economic health, and, as such, a precondition of social well-being. The

---

[1] Cecil, *Biographical Studies*, p. 94.
[2] Speech at Exeter, 2 Feb. 1892, quoted in Cecil, *Salisbury*, iv, 401.
[3] Speech in the Oxford Union, 14 Feb. 1850, quoted in Morrah, p. 139.
[4] *Q.R.*, cxvii (1865), 546–8. The real causes, he alleged, had been the coming of railways and the gold discoveries in California and Australia.
[5] Cecil, *Salisbury*, iv, 177–82; *Biographical Studies*, pp. 86–9.

way to help the poor was not to embark on the sort of state intervention which would damage the economy to whose vigour their prospects of betterment were directly related. Basic problems like the rate of wages, governed by economic processes and laws whose disruption would be disastrous, could hardly be dealt with by legislative action.[1] Especially fatal would be the introduction of measures aiming at the redistribution of wealth through fiscal or other means. Anything that tended to 'confiscation' and threatened the security of property was not merely grossly unjust but calculated, by destroying capitalists' confidence, to dry up the flow of investment upon which the employment and wages of the poor depended. The best method of aiding the poor was to foster economic expansion and the creation of new wealth, not to encourage them, as Radicals did, to battle with the well-to-do over the partition of existing wealth.[2] Here the dictates of economic reason conveniently reinforced the defensive instincts of the possessing classes.

Other limitations on social legislation of which Salisbury was keenly conscious were those imposed by financial prudence and by the interests of the landed and agricultural classes to which he belonged. The influence of the latter is perhaps seen at its strongest in his approach to popular education. He had no zeal for the educational advancement of the poor: he was 'not naturally sensitive to the appeal of intellectual privation, – curiously less so than he was to that of material destitution or physical suffering'.[3] But it was his concern over the charge on landed property and over interference with the supply of juvenile agricultural labour, as well as over the educational position of the Church, that more than anything else made it hard for him to support enthusiastically an expansion of popular education based on rating and compulsory attendance.[4] His support of the bill making elementary education free which his ministry passed in 1891 seems to have derived more from a feeling that if the state compelled poor people to send their children to school it must help with the cost, and from the conviction that if the issue were left to the Liberals they would tackle it in such a way as to injure the Church schools, than from any deep regard for education as such.[5]

Elsewhere, however, Salisbury's support for social reform was less

[1] Thus, for example, while agreeing that agricultural labourers' wages were too low, Salisbury thought that the only remedy was emigration. Letter to Lady John Manners, 3 June 1886 (typescript copy): Salisbury Papers, vol. 'Manners', p. 280. He often corresponded with Lady John on social questions.
[2] Speeches at Edinburgh, 24 Nov. 1882, Dumfries, 21 Oct. 1884, Lambeth, 4 Nov. 1885, quoted in Cecil, *Salisbury*, iii, 65–6, 262–4.
[3] *Ibid.* i, 120.   [4] See Smith, pp. 133, n. 2, 177.
[5] Cecil, *Salisbury*, iv, 156–8.

EDITOR'S INTRODUCTION

constricted, and he did useful practical work. As a young member of Parliament, he backed factory legislation and was active in the largely successful agitation of the mid-sixties for the better treatment of paupers, especially the pauper sick.[1] In 1871 he was concerned with other prominent Conservatives in the New Social Movement, an abortive attempt to secure co-operation between a group of leading trade unionists and a group of peers and M.P.s on measures for the benefit of the working classes.[2] Of the important social measures over which he presided when prime minister, at least one, the Housing Act of 1885, owed a good deal to his personal interest and impulsion. He had advocated the provision of cheap money for building working-class dwellings in the *National Review* in November 1883[3] – his only major article on a social question – and had moved for a Royal Commission on working-class housing the following year. It was the main recommendations of that Commission, on which he sat, that he carried into law, extending the availability and lowering the interest of Treasury loans and taking new measures against slums.[4] He did not allow himself to be deterred by the allegation that he was infringing the tenets of political economy. In the end, these questions were empirical ones for him, to be determined according to circumstance rather than principle. Towards the end of his career, under the need to satisfy both an exigent 'democracy' touched by the ideas of socialism and a Radical ally, Chamberlain, he was prepared to accept even so far-reaching a proposal as old-age pensions. His words to the Lords in August 1895, while they do not precisely contradict, certainly contrast curiously with his younger pronouncements. He was taking the commonplace Conservative line that what the country wanted was not the organic change pursued by the Liberals but the practical improvements which the Conservatives would provide, and he said it was 'proclaimed to both Parties' that

> it is not the rearrangement of political machinery, but it is the improvement of the daily life of struggling millions and the diminution of the sorrows that so many are condemned to bear, which is the task – the blessed task – that Parliaments are called into existence to perform; and which, I trust... henceforth all Governments will feel to be the highest, the exclusive duty that any statesman,

[1] For the latter question, see *ibid*. i, 129–30; Smith, pp. 58–63.
[2] Smith, pp. 149–53.
[3] 'Labourers' and Artisans' Dwellings', *National Review*, ii (1883–4), 301–16. He had taken up the housing question at Birmingham in March, and it had been further brought into prominence by the pamphlet *The Bitter Cry of Outcast London* and by an article in the October issue of the *Fortnightly Review*.
[4] Cecil, *Salisbury*, iii, 77–83. He and Dilke collaborated on the measure.

SOCIETY AND POLITICS

or advisers of the Queen, or Leaders of Parliamentary Parties can be called upon or privileged to perform.[1]

It is unlikely that Salisbury was much less sceptical about social reform or much more fervently attached to it than he had been thirty years earlier. His change of emphasis recognised a change in the times. When large social reforms were clearly inevitable, it was not the part of a wise Conservatism to play Canute to the advancing tide.

Salisbury's ideas on international society and politics were just as much influenced as his views on internal questions by his pessimism about human nature and his overriding desire for stability and security. He started from the observation that international relations were something like a Hobbesian state of nature, the nations existing in a condition of virtual anarchy, without a common law. It was this that made it ridiculous and dangerous to follow what he lampooned as 'the preaching school of politicians' in wishing to direct the country's foreign policy according to the mild and precise morality that was properly applicable to the conduct of individuals:

as individuals and as nations we live in states of society utterly different from each other. As a collection of individuals, we live under the highest and latest development of civilization, in which the individual is rigidly forbidden to defend himself, because society is always ready and able to defend him. As a collection of nations we live in an age of the merest *Faustrecht*, in which each one obtains his rights precisely in proportion to his ability, or that of his allies, to fight for them.

So-called international law helped to mitigate disputes, but it could not stop aggression. 'In practice it is found that International Law is always on the side of the strong battalions.'[2] A nation had to look after itself: its policy had to be egoistical, and the statesmen who conducted that policy held a trust to act accordingly, even if this meant pursuing in the interest of the state a course of selfishness which their principles would preclude in private life.[3] Salisbury saw that the central factor in inter-

---
[1] *Hansard*, 4th series, xxxvi, 54.
[2] *Q.R.*, cli (1881), 542–4. Writing to the foreign secretary, Lord Stanley, on 23 Nov. 1866 (typescript copy: Salisbury Papers, vol. 'Stanley', p. 25) Salisbury had spoken of 'the prerogative of every sovereign state to determine for itself what are the doctrines of international law by which it will be bound'.
[3] See Cecil, *Biographical Studies*, p. 72, for Salisbury's attitude on this point. The courses which he was in principle prepared to sanction ran even as far as preventive occupation of a neighbour state whose inability to defend itself against outside aggression posed a threat to one's own security. 'It is puerile...to apply to the dealings of a nation with its neighbour's territory the morality which would be

EDITOR'S INTRODUCTION

national politics was power, and expressed his vivid contempt for the type of thinking about external relations common among his political opponents, which, lulled by years of apparent insular security, had become so abstract and moralistic that it was doubtful whether it could grapple with the hard problems involved in maintaining England's position in an era when her relative physical force in the world was declining.[1] He had no patience with the kind of pacific optimism that he detected, for example, in Gladstone's budget speech of 1860, evoking

> the vista of an age of security and peace – disbanded armaments, forgotten jealousies, immunity not only from the scourge but from the panic of war; pleasant dreams, constantly belied by experience, constantly renewed by theorists, but too closely linked to the hopes of all who believe either in material progress or in the promises of religion ever to be abandoned as chimeras.[2]

Aggression and conflict were not so easily banished, and the nation must have the will and the means for its self-defence.

A necessary egoism backed by strength was one thing, however; truculence and vainglory were quite another. Salisbury's attachment to his country was hardly touched by patriotism of the emotional and bellicose sort, and he had no desire to seek prestige by picking quarrels. The first aim of external policy might be the protection and furtherance of the national interest, but in the long run the best means to this was the promotion of international peace and security. This involved on the one hand abstaining from needless interference with the concerns of other countries and from the support of movements likely to disturb the international scene, and, on the other, being ready to help maintain by positive action a measure of equilibrium and respect for public law in Europe.

A disinclination to meddle was fundamental to Salisbury's approach to other states, as to other individuals. In 1859 he wrote:

> though it is England's right to enforce the law of Europe [i.e. treaties] as between contending states, she has no claim, so long as her own interests are untouched, to interfere in the national affairs of any country, whatever the extent of its misgovernment or its anarchy.[3]

---

applicable to two individuals possessing adjoining property, and protected from mutual wrong by a law superior to both' (*Q.R.*, cli (1881), 544). The point of this argument was largely to justify England's retention of Ireland and action in Afghanistan.

[1] In this respect, his contribution to the debate on foreign policy compares closely with that of J. R. Seeley, for which see R. T. Shannon, 'John Robert Seeley and the Idea of a National Church', in *Ideas and Institutions of Victorian Britain*, ed. R. Robson (1967), pp. 262–7.

[2] *Q.R.*, cvii (1860), 516. [3] *B.Q.R.*, i (1859), 23.

54

Three years later, he described with obvious approval how Castlereagh had been concerned in his policy not to stir up trouble by intervening abroad to try to further the triumph of particular ideas or institutions, but simply to preserve European peace as the precondition of a tolerable life for the mass of the people.[1] What he had in mind as much as anything was Castlereagh's refusal to pursue the doctrine of nationality. For Salisbury, nationalism was not only largely nonsense – he was sarcastic about the 'philological' and 'poetical or literary' law of nations[2] – but constituted a dangerous menace to European stability and to the interests of England, 'who owns, without any consent of the peoples whatever, more nationalities than she can comfortably count'.[3] He rejected its equation with the cause of freedom, and even represented it as anti-evolutionary:

the splitting up of mankind into a multitude of infinitesimal governments, in accordance with their actual differences of dialect or their presumed differences of race, would be to undo the work of civilisation and renounce all the benefits which the slow and painful process of consolidation has procured for mankind...
It is the agglomeration and not the comminution of states to which civilisation is constantly tending; it is the fusion and not the isolation of races by which the physical and moral excellence of the species is advanced. There are races, as there are trees, which cannot stand erect by themselves, and which, if their growth is not hindered by artificial constraints, are all the healthier for twining round some robuster stem.[4]

With the minding of her own business and the avoidance of commitment to doubtful causes, England must combine a sense of her obligations to 'the European commonwealth of which she is a citizen'.[5] This meant taking a firm stand against any power that might threaten European order, and reinforced the point that even a basically moderate and pacific foreign policy must be supported by adequate force. What as much as anything else brought Salisbury into political prominence was the vigour of his reaction in the sixties to the realisation that that force was lacking and that England's leading role in European affairs could not in the last resort be fully sustained. He saw the root of the trouble in the 'commercial spirit', which declined to pay for the necessary armaments and shied away from any initiative in foreign affairs that might cause interference to trade, with the result that a strong policy had become impossible. The country was reduced to getting its glory on the cheap by bullying weak nations like China or Brazil, while having to give

[1] *Q.R.*, cxi (1862), 234–5.
[2] *Ibid.* cxi (1862), 230.
[3] *Ibid.*
[4] *B.Q.R.*, i (1859), 22. Cf. pp. 371–4.
[5] *Q.R.*, cvii (1860), 529.

EDITOR'S INTRODUCTION

way in humiliating fashion to the strong, the culminating wound to pride being the failure to restrain Austria and Prussia in the Schleswig-Holstein crisis.[1] The contempt aroused in Europe by the combination of big talk and small deeds was not forgotten by Salisbury. When he came to the direction of affairs, it was his concern that the national resolution and the national strength should suffice for the support of the proper objectives of national policy, and that no posture should be adopted that could not be affirmed by action.

As a great imperial power, England was concerned in her external dealings not only with other states but with subject and client peoples. At least until his later years, Salisbury had little taste for colonisation: he could see that all too often it was a convenient pretext for the robbery of the weak, and he was doubtful whether the advantages it brought offset the heavy expense and commitment incurred.[2] He resisted, too, the cruder forms of racial and colour prejudice, and did not think that white men had a right to do as they pleased with the rest of humanity. When he visited South Africa in 1851, he found the Boers a very degraded crew, but evinced some admiration for the Kaffirs, whom he described as 'a fine set of men...an intellectual race, with great firmness & fixedness of will, argumentative, opinionated, clever & horribly immoral'.[3] In his period as secretary for India, he showed some sympathy with the native viewpoint, and backed Lytton, when the latter was viceroy, in dealing severely with cases of brutality by Englishmen towards the native population.[4] All the same, he could not entirely escape the influence of prejudice and of the imperial spirit. He let slip a significant aside when he wrote of the eighteenth-century Polish peasantry: 'these were no negroes, men of an inferior race imported from a barbarous land and incapable of the acute and sensitive feelings of the white man'.[5] As early as 1859, in the attack on nationalism quoted above, he had taken the line that some races needed to tie themselves to stronger ones, and gone on to argue that India and Ireland were better off under English rule

[1] See especially *ibid.* cvii (1860), 529–30; cxv (1864), 481–529 – 'Foreign Policy of England'; *Hansard*, 3rd series, clxix, 1151–8 (March 1863). Salisbury's criticism of British high-handedness towards China, Brazil, and Japan was severe, and went back to his speech on the *Arrow* incident in February 1857 (*ibid.* cxliv, 1538–41). In September 1859, he wrote to his wife on 'this dreadful China matter': 'I shrewdly suspect that – as usual – we were in the wrong' (quoted in Cecil, *Salisbury*, i, 87).
[2] Pinto-Duschinsky, pp. 82–3, 132–5. The white colonists' treatment of the New Zealand Maoris was a particular target of Salisbury's disapproval.
[3] Lord Robert Cecil to Lady Blanche Balfour, 30 Sept. 1851; to 2nd Marquis, 7 Nov. 1851 (Salisbury Papers).
[4] Cecil, *Salisbury*, i, 206–7; ii, 67.   [5] *Q.R.*, cxiii (1863), 478.

SOCIETY AND POLITICS

than they would be on their own.[1] It is not very surprising that when it came to the imperial upsurge of the eighties and nineties, Salisbury felt the contagion, sharing the belief in 'the special vocation of Englishmen for the regeneration of uncivilised humanity', and calling the movement of the European powers into Africa 'a great civilising, Christianising force'.[2] In the end, whatever his moral doubts about the behaviour of some imperialists, he had few about empire itself, and no inclination to yield up any part of the edifice of English dominion.

Salisbury's general views on society and politics were far from amounting to a comprehensive and rigorously worked-out conservative philosophy. They can scarcely be regarded as a major intellectual contribution to the conservative tradition. Expressed, sometimes even formulated, in response to specific events and needs, and with particular political purposes in mind, they contained, as their author would probably have admitted, much that was unsubtle and inchoate. Especially crude were the views of human motivation and of the class struggle that lay at the root of Salisbury's description of political dynamics. Though he chose to explain politics in sociological terms, it is clear that his analysis was not based on any refined understanding or analysis of society.

What his ideas constituted was a working stock of concepts and attitudes by relation to which reality could be organised, founded partly on instinctive feeling and prejudice, as filtered by reason, and partly on observation and reflection. They formed a firm basis for his political conduct and seem to have altered very little in their essentials during his career. They were largely formed by the mid-sixties, and growing age and experience would do more to reinforce than to modify them. It would be wrong to represent them as the 'typical' Conservative creed of the day, but wrong also to exaggerate their idiosyncratic character. Despite the unaccustomed elements introduced by Salisbury's sceptical and utilitarian temper, they contained much that was the common property of the greater portion of the Conservative party.

---

[1] *B.Q.R.*, i (1859), 22. Opposing Irish Home Rule in 1886, he said: 'When you come to narrow it down you will find that this, – which is called self-government, but is really government by the majority, – works admirably when it is confided to people who are of Teutonic race, but that it does not work so well when people of other races are called upon to join in it' (quoted in Cecil, *Salisbury*, iii, 302).

[2] *Ibid.* iv, 227, 310.

EDITOR'S INTRODUCTION

THE POLITICS OF RESISTANCE, 1853-67

In the long political career which began with Salisbury's return for Stamford in 1853, the passage of the second Reform Bill marks something of a dividing line. Up to 1867, Salisbury's main concern was to prevent the coming of what he called 'democracy' in England; afterwards, when it seemed that it had come, his preoccupation was to contain it and to find means of living with it. In the earlier period as in the later, much of the interest of his approach to the politics of the time derives from his analysis of the movements and trends which he saw beneath their surface. Always, he viewed the episodes and issues of current politics in the light of a general schematic interpretation, in relation to which his own political action was conceived.

It did not take him long after his entry into politics to detect a vital shift of emphasis in the conflict of classes which for him constituted the basic reality behind the parliamentary scene. The battle of attrition conducted by urban middle-class radicalism against the traditional structure of authority and privilege represented by crown, lords, Church, and land continued, little abated by the successes of the thirties and forties; but this contest within the propertied classes was coming gradually to be overshadowed by a challenge to them from without. In mobilising as their allies numbers of the urban working classes, and in demanding for them the extension of the franchise which was needed to make their support fully effective, the middle-class Radicals of whom Bright was the outstanding leader were introducing into politics forces which they could not in the long run control. 'His own chief personal object', Salisbury wrote of Bright in March 1859, 'appears to be to exalt the factory and to depress the land: but he is willing to buy the assistance of the mob towards the attainment of this triumph by concessions which will swamp the influence of factory and land alike.'[1] Conscious of their differences of interest with the bourgeoisie, the working men were not likely indefinitely to remain docile political subordinates, and the transfer to them of a large share of electoral power would pave the way for the pillage of property and the dethronement of education and culture by the mass of the poor and ignorant.

In face of the threat to their power and possessions from below, the propertied classes, both landed and commercial, had a strong incentive to compose their feuds. An alliance of property as the basis of government was certainly, for Salisbury, rather less than ideal. An aristocrat at heart,

[1] B.Q.R., i (1859), 27.

THE POLITICS OF RESISTANCE, 1853-67

he would perhaps have been happiest with rule by an enlightened aristocracy. But it was obvious that the time of aristocracy had passed. The House of Lords apart, he declared in 1858, aristocratic privilege was dead in England, and it was with the possessors of property that political preponderance lay.[1] So keen, indeed, was his realisation that the old ruling groups must reinforce themselves from a wider sphere that both at this period and later he wanted to enlarge the representative character and strengthen the influence of the House of Lords by introducing into it some of the industrial and commerical bourgeoisie.[2] He was far from admiring the latter. As a young man, he displayed the utmost patrician scorn for the bourgeoisie, whom he found selfish, narrow, conceited, and even febrile. His Australian experience caused him to write in 1852: 'On reflection, I am convinced that turbulence as well as every other evil temper of this evil age belongs not to the lower but to the middle classes.'[3] Seven years later, he spoke of 'cotton-lords' who were, as a class, 'pitiless to the poor', and, looking at the benches of the House of Commons, was unable to repress a sneer at 'the brilliant geniuses selected by the urban constituencies (who are undoubtedly the best judges) as the truest representatives of their own taste and intellect'.[4] But, like the equally supercilious and sarcastic Disraeli, he could see that the middle classes were increasingly essential allies of the older wealth. He thought that their exclusion from a due part in the pre-1832 political system had been a bad mistake, which, tending to drive them into the ranks of 'democracy', had had enduring consequences, and he criticised the conduct of the Tory party's resistance to the Reform Bill of 1832 from this standpoint:

The great error was the attempt to maintain the exclusion of the commercial and manufacturing classes from the share in the government of the country to which their huge stake in it rightfully entitled them. They were the natural friends of order; their interests bound them by the strongest ties to the side of property in the great social struggle of our century.[5]

The 'crude' and 'one-sided' Reform Act of 1832[6] had gone too far in redressing the balance, but even so the form of government evolved,

---

[1] 'The Theories of Parliamentary Reform', *Oxford Essays*, pp. 76-7.
[2] *B.Q.R.*, i (1859), 27; Cecil, *Salisbury*, ii, 28-31. He supported Russell's bill to introduce life peerages in 1869, and under his premiership in 1888 a government measure for the creation of life peers was unsuccessfully brought in (*ibid.* iv, 167).
[3] Journal, 28 March 1852, quoted *ibid.* i, 32. To Lady Blanche Balfour he wrote on 9 July 1852: 'If there is an evil in a community you will be sure to find it in the middle class – especially if it be in the way of fraud or pride' (Salisbury Papers). Cf. his letter to the Rev. C. Conybeare, 11 July 1852 (typescript copy, *ibid.* vol. 'Conybeare to Dimsdale', p. 4).   [4] *B.Q.R.*, i (1859), 26-7.
[5] *Q.R.*, cxix (1866), 274. Cf. *ibid.* cxvii (1865), 551.   [6] *Ibid.* cxvii (1865), 558.

with middle-class participation, in the succeeding generation had solid merits. 'For some years', Salisbury was to write as he looked back on it in 1871, 'it might be said, without exaggeration, that the accidental equilibrium of political forces which it had produced presented the highest ideal of internal government the world had hitherto seen.'[1] That equilibrium he was anxious to preserve, through the conjoined effort of the classes who were its elements to repel the 'democracy' which otherwise must destroy it.

If the fundamental political struggle was between property and station on the one hand and Radicalism and democracy on the other, the existing division of parties was irrelevant, and must sooner or later be superseded. Discussing what he saw as the 'demoralization' and lack of principle of parliamentary life, in March 1859, Salisbury found the cause in the fact that 'the division of parties does not represent the division of opinions'.[2] Party, indeed, seemed to have become merely a vehicle for securing office, rather than the embodiment of common and deeply felt convictions on the central issues of the day. The reason lay in a sort of political archaism which grew more and more evident as the sixties wore on:

It is one of the misfortunes of our political system that parties are formed, more with reference to controversies that are gone by, than to the controversies which those parties have actually to decide. The Reform Bill of 1832, or the Corn Laws of 1846, are questions of no practical interest to the existing generation ...But the dividing-line which marks out the limits of existing parties far more nearly approaches to that which separated opinions in 1846 than to that which separates them in 1866.[3]

Indeed, between the parties, moulded by the old issues and still only groping towards adjustment to the new, time had done a good deal to blur the apparent differences. Many of the changes formerly striven for by the Liberals had been carried, and had become 'incorporated into the political system which it is the function of Conservatives to defend'. The wiser Liberal statesmen did not want 'further organic change'. 'By virtue of no inconsistency on either side, but by the natural influence of events', wrote Salisbury in 1863, 'the opinions of both the great historic parties have approximated so closely that the dividing line between them is all but imaginary.'[4] This convergence in the centre emphasised the most striking anomaly of existing party alignment: it cut clean across 'conservative' sentiment, leaving a substantial part of it, that comprised by the Whigs and moderate Liberals, in the uneasy

---

[1] *Ibid.* cxxx (1871), 279–80.
[2] *B.Q.R.*, i (1859), 6.
[3] *Q.R.*, cxix (1866), 277.
[4] *Ibid.* cxiii (1863), 260–1.

alliance with Radicalism that now reflected historic circumstance rather than current identity of interest and purpose. The false position of the Whigs and other conservative elements in the heterogeneous amalgam loosely called the Liberal party was a constant theme of Salisbury, who hoped to see them eventually take their natural place on his own side. While Palmerston ruled the Whig-Liberal roost with a conservative policy, their difficulties were, of course, kept to a minimum:

> It is quite true [Salisbury wrote, shortly after Palmerston's death in October 1865] that the principle upon which his government was carried on – the combination of Liberal profession and Conservative practice – represented the genuine state of mind of a large portion of the educated classes, imbued to a greater or less extent with Liberal theories, but unable to conceal from themselves that those theories in the laboratory of the world's experience were working out very unsatisfactory results.[1]

The challenge of democracy would in the end, Salisbury believed, force these people to re-examine their affiliation, and would precipitate the regrouping of parties in closer relation to the real divisions of interest and feeling in the country.

To wait and work for such a regrouping, which alone could bring it real power by giving it something approaching a monopoly of conservative support, was the proper policy of the Conservative party. But Salisbury knew that realignment could not be easy or quick, and until it came the party's main task was simply to oppose a steadfast resistance to Radical and democratic demands. In this conception of the party's role, he perhaps did not differ fundamentally from his parliamentary leaders, Derby and Disraeli. But his was the long-term view, and they were bound, much of the time, to take the short-term. He could afford to wait until the gradual evolution of opinion and allegiance re-established Conservative fortunes. They, and especially Disraeli, already forty-nine in 1853, and longing for power, could not. Professional politicians, constrained by the immediate exigencies of party warfare and party leadership, necessarily preoccupied with day-to-day tactics and the chances of office, they were inclined at moments, in their anxiety to extricate the party from its post-1846 minority position, to engage in manœuvres and combinations which seemed to Salisbury dangerously to compromise the Conservative cause.

By 1859, indeed, Salisbury had come to be thoroughly disgusted with the conduct of the Conservative party. With the abandonment of the 'crotchet' of protection in 1852, he felt, the party had become altogether

[1] *Ibid.* cxix (1866), 251.

EDITOR'S INTRODUCTION

bereft of distinctive policy and principles. Its leaders' opinions at that point had hardly differed from those of their opponents: they consisted of 'precisely those moderate progressive principles, hostile to abuses, but equally hostile to mob government, which had been professed by the Whigs of 1832, and to which the Whigs of 1852, if they were let alone, were perfectly willing to adhere'. In this situation, the party's proper course would have been to bide its time. Instead, it had indulged in mere factious opposition to Whig government, and in bidding for Radical aid as the means to oust the Whigs it had forced the latter into a competition which had lowered the whole moral tone of politics and bred cynicism in the House of Commons.[1] For Salisbury, the culmination of this course of ruin was the decision of the Derby government which had achieved precarious office in a minority in 1858 to take up the re-emergent issue of parliamentary reform. If Reform, pursued by Russell in his bills of 1852 and 1854, and now vociferously canvassed by Bright, was to be resumed, there was a good deal to be said for the Conservatives' dealing with the question. As a party which aspired to govern, they could not afford to allow their opponents a monopoly of the cause of moderate constitutional advance, or to leave them to pass such a measure as would adjust the electoral system in their own interests. The Reform Bill which they produced in 1859 was a very mild one: it left the borough franchise untouched, and reduced the county occupation franchise to £10, which, with the attempt to keep borough freeholders from voting in counties, would probably have strengthened the Conservative grip on the county electorate. But Salisbury did not think that Parliament or the country wanted Reform, or that, in any case, it was the business of the Conservative party to pass it. His party loyalty held, as it had on earlier occasions of difference, to the extent that he voted for the measure and even said what he honestly could for it,[2] but his real feelings came out in his articles for *Bentley's Quarterly Review* in March and July 1859 and for the *Quarterly* in April 1860.

Salisbury had no doubt who bore the responsibility for the scandal of the party's recent course, and it was above all the vehemence of his assault on Disraeli that brought him the journalistic notoriety which he desired. It was Disraeli he had in mind when he described how,

[1] *B.Q.R.*, i (1859), 8–15.
[2] Except on the 1858 bill to enable Jews to sit in the House of Commons, which he opposed as contrary to the Christian character of the assembly, Salisbury had steadily voted with his leader in major matters, even against his better judgement, as he pointed out to his Stamford patron, Lord Exeter, when the latter took him to task over his criticism of Disraeli. Cecil, *Salisbury*, i, 93–4.

deprived of 'its natural leaders' by the departure of the Peelites, the party had had to find new ones: 'It went into the market and bought such articles of the kind as were for sale, – mostly damaged goods of unprepossessing appearance, which other buyers had rejected, and whose subsequent wear has hardly made good their original cost.'[1] Disraeli was 'the Artless Dodger',[2] an unscrupulous opportunist, so obsessed by his own dexterity in manœuvre as to be blind to the loss of character and confidence resulting from it. Far from upholding Conservative principles, he recklessly pursued his own ambitions by the policy of combining with the Radicals to beat the Whigs, a policy which Salisbury later suggested might 'be traced in germ in the teaching of the now forgotten Young England School, and the democratic sympathies which they tried to graft upon old feudal traditions'.[3] To the defence that he was simply adapting the party to post-1846 realities and to the necessity of a more liberal outlook, Salisbury's rejoinder was blunt: the Conservatives, he thought, might 'be inclined to murmur at having been made to undergo this process of dirt-eating for their own good'.[4] Perhaps the worst of Disraeli's faults was that it seemed to be largely distaste for him that deterred Peelites and moderate Liberals from that junction with the Conservative party which constituted 'the only safe bulwark against revolutionary change'.[5]

The force of Salisbury's invective against his leader was such that it is remarkable that no permanent breach ensued. Disraeli, however, liked spirit in young men, and could take a great deal of abuse when he thought it expedient to do so, and in any case the attacks very soon ceased. The failure of the 1859 Reform Bill brought the end of the second Derby ministry, and the return of Palmerston to power. Against the latter's domination of English politics with a safely conservative domestic policy, Derby and Disraeli could for the time being do little, and resigned themselves to a sober course of opposition of which Salisbury was generally able to approve. By Easter 1861, he could write to his friend Carnarvon: 'Dizzy, converted from evil ways, has since behaved like an angel – so that I am beginning to incline to the belief that he really has been baptized.'[6]

[1] *B.Q.R.*, i (1859), 5–6. Perhaps there is a reference here to the use of Bentinck money to set Disraeli up as a country gentleman.
[2] *S.R.*, vii (1859), 709–10.   [3] *Q.R.*, cxxvii (1869), 544.
[4] *Ibid.* cviii (1860), 295. Dirt figured a good deal in Salisbury's imagery at this time: in July 1859 he spoke of the rival party leaders' eating dirt and bearing the device of a rat before the Radicals, and pictured Disraeli as 'the grain of dirt' clogging the political machine (*B.Q.R.*, i (1859), 346, 360).
[5] *Ibid.* i (1859), 360.   [6] Quoted in Cecil, *Salisbury*, i, 98.

EDITOR'S INTRODUCTION

Whether the line of conduct championed by Salisbury was, in the long run, better calculated to serve Conservative interests than that which he felt obliged to attack in Derby and Disraeli is not easy to decide. He was thinking of the Conservative cause, in the broadest sense, which certainly was damaged when its natural supporters, divided by an artificial party boundary, engaged in a struggle for office which involved them in the competitive purchase of Radical votes. Derby and Disraeli were thinking largely of the Conservative party, with which their careers were bound up, and upon whose survival as a fighting force, they might plausibly have argued, the effective assertion of the Conservative cause must ultimately depend. Keeping the party in good heart was not an easy task in the fifties and early sixties. The split of 1846 and the loss of the Peelites had weakened it severely both in personnel and in electoral appeal. The solid core of support which it retained was enough to preserve it as a substantial force, varying roughly between 256 and 306 members in the parliaments of 1852-68, but frustratingly not quite enough to give it a majority; and its ten months of minority office in 1852 and sixteen months in 1858-9 were brief oases in a desert of what came to seem like permanent opposition. Much of its brains and ministerial experience had gone with the Peelites, and its front bench was unimpressive. It depended heavily electorally on its extensive support among the landed and agricultural interest, reflected in its strong grip on the county and small borough seats, in England especially.[1] Among the middle-class voters of the larger towns, its following was sizeable, and in the sixties appeared to be growing, but was insufficient to give it the seats without which a majority could not be achieved. In the general election of 1865, the last under the old franchise, the towns of over 50,000 inhabitants returned only 22 Conservatives out of 100 members.[2] The party's preponderantly rural and agricultural roots are emphasised by an analysis of the economic interests held by members of the House of Commons elected in 1865: the Conservatives had a markedly smaller proportionate representation of industrial, commercial, and financial interests than the other side.[3] This base was clearly too

[1] In the general election of 1865, it secured 64·6% of English county seats, and county seats in the whole United Kingdom accounted for about half its total strength; it secured 47·5% of seats in English boroughs with under 1,000 electors, but only 24·6% in those with over 1,000. Figures calculated from those in R. Blake, *The Conservative Party from Peel to Churchill* (1970), p. 46 (see also pp. 73-5).
[2] H. J. Hanham, *Elections and Party Management: Politics in the time of Disraeli and Gladstone* (1959), p. 92, n. 2 (population according to the 1871 census). The Conservatives took only a little more than a third of all borough seats.
[3] J. A. Thomas, *The House of Commons, 1832-1901: a Study of its Economic and Functional Character* (1939), pp. 4-6.

narrow for a great national party aspiring to power, and with it was sometimes associated a certain narrowness of outlook and sympathy which did not facilitate the task of enlarging it. True, the aura of bucolic obstructiveness clinging around the party in its protectionist phase had been largely dispelled by the sixties, but there was still an impression that the phalanx of country gentlemen who set the tone of the back benches were not eager to supply the cautious progress which the nation might require. The traditional defence of constitution, Church, and social order was not by itself enough in an era of prosperity and stability when none of these things seemed to be in very immediate danger (Salisbury's jeremiads notwithstanding) and Palmerston was there to protect them if they were; and the party's tendency to jealousy of industry and trade, hostility to dissent, and preoccupation with such special concerns of the landed interest as the burden of local taxation on real property, the repeal of the malt tax, and the control of cattle plague did nothing to commend it to the urban voters on whom any electoral advance must partly depend. As Salisbury and others saw, it had no distinctive policies on major issues, and after the failure of 1859 could do little more than dance querulous attendance at Palmerston's court. The words of *The Times*, on 6 June 1865, gave the measure of its impotence: 'Except the question of the Malt Tax, there is probably no question of any importance on which the actual policy of a Conservative Government would now differ from that of a Liberal Government.'

Perhaps, in this dispiriting position, it did the party good to be lectured by Salisbury on Conservative principles, especially if, as he was to allege when trying to explain the *débâcle* of 1867, its ranks were increasingly being recruited from 'men who sought a seat for other than political motives, and were more solicitous for the social rank or commercial influence it conferred than for the success of the cause in whose interest it had been avowedly obtained'.[1] But parties do not live on principles alone, and it is not solely by the consciousness of virtue sustained that their corporate vigour is nourished. Other and more concrete satisfactions are required. While Salisbury acted as conscience to the party, Derby and Disraeli had to lead it and to maintain its fighting spirit, and they knew that what it needed was above all the taste of success and the experience, and rewards, of power. In order to obtain those things, they were ready to take any chance to gain office and to broaden the party's appeal by demonstrating its capacity to govern and to respond to the needs and movements of the time. Perhaps they could do this without

[1] *Q.R.*, cxxiii (1867), 559.

sacrifice of principle; certainly they thought they could do it without betraying any of the interests and institutions the party was committed to preserve. The test was to come in the crisis of 1867. At any rate, there is a case for arguing that their idea of how the party should be conducted was more realistic, and thus in the end more advantageous to the Conservative cause, than that held by the brilliant young gadfly at their backs.

The core of Salisbury's political activity up to 1867 was his resistance to what he saw as a concerted assault on the existing structures of authority and property by the forces of Radicalism and dissent and their working-class allies. To some extent this assault took the form of attempts to sap the position of aristocracy, Church, and land piecemeal; but these were increasingly subsumed under the general challenge to property and the constitution offered by the onset of 'democracy', as embodied in the demand for parliamentary reform.

Salisbury devoted a good deal of energy to the defence of the Church and the landed interest in particular against Radical designs. The threat to land he detected not only in demands for measures to promote its wider distribution but also in the fiscal policies advocated by Radicals and implemented by Gladstone. Bright, he alleged, motivated by class interest, aimed at putting the whole burden of taxation on to real property.[1] This was the point of the policy of switching from indirect to direct taxes, followed in Gladstone's budget of 1860, which simply paved the way for a transfer of taxation from the poor to the rich that would ultimately fall most heavily on the landowner.[2] 'Hostility against the land', indeed, it suited Salisbury to represent as 'the animating principle' of Gladstone's financial career.[3]

The threat to the Church was represented at its most extreme by the militant nonconformist agitation for disestablishment, and in milder guise by the steady pressure for abolition of church rates, legalisation of nonconformist burial services in Anglican graveyards, and reduction of the Anglican grip on the universities, endowed schools, and denominational system of elementary education. It received an artificial stimulus, Salisbury thought, from its usefulness in keeping the Liberal ranks together in the early sixties: attacks on the Church compensated Radicals for Palmerston's denial of Reform, and enabled Whigs who otherwise

[1] *Ibid.* cix (1861), 215-17.   [2] *Ibid.* cvii (1860), 522-4, 541.
[3] *Ibid.* cxviii (1865), 291. Despite his dislike of Gladstone's finance, however, he had to admit that it was not unsound in principle.

had nothing in common with them to retain their support in the constituencies and the House of Commons.¹ On all the points at issue, Salisbury was a stubborn defender of the Church's rights and claims. He stoutly opposed, too, what he regarded as a more insidious danger than any curtailment of the Church's privileges and possessions – the destruction of her spiritual identity through the dilution of her doctrines in the effort to achieve 'comprehension'.²

It was not merely that Salisbury was one of the Church of England's most devout sons. He believed that:

there is no more formidable obstacle than the Established Church to the spirit of rash and theoretic change which we, almost alone among the nations, have escaped. Her atmosphere is poison to the revolutionary growths that flourish so rankly in other lands.

Her cause was inseparable from that of the rest of the country's institutions: 'an isolated assault upon the Church is an impossibility. It has always been simultaneous with a general advance along the whole revolutionary line.'³ 'Democrats' and dissenters were natural allies, and Salisbury visited them with very similar opprobrium. He recognised a difference between the 'conscientious' and the 'political' dissenter, but had no sympathy for either species. The former was 'the true descendant of the old Puritan – sincere, narrow, and fanatical', while the latter simply exploited religion for political ends.⁴ The dissenting chapels constituted a dangerous political machine:

they are earthworks and blockhouses for the maintenance of an untiring political guerilla. A large proportion of the Dissenting ministers are ready-made electioneering agents. They are natural adepts in all the lower stratagems of political warfare, and are unequalled in the art of dressing-out grievances and manufacturing discontent.⁵

Against such enemies, it was necessary for the Church to enter into politics to protect her own interests, and Salisbury urged her members to support the Conservative party, which provided their natural agency of self-defence.⁶

---
[1] *Ibid.* cxiii (1863), 260–7. Without the Church, Salisbury wrote, 'the Old Whigs would disappear from the face of the political earth. They love their party too well to be Conservatives, and their country too well to be Radicals: and the elector knows no middle term betewen the two.'
[2] *Ibid.* cxii (1862), 258–68; cxviii (1865), 202–9; Cecil, *Salisbury*, i, 328–35.
[3] *Q.R.*, cx (1861), 544–5. Cf. *ibid.* cxii (1862), 255.
[4] *Ibid.* cx (1861), 556–7.
[5] *Ibid.* cviii (1860), 270–1. With this went the assertion that the Anglican clergy did not cultivate political influence over their flocks.
[6] *Ibid.* cxviii (1865), 193–200, 210.

EDITOR'S INTRODUCTION

Ecclesiastical and fiscal questions, however, were dwarfed by the fundamental issue of the franchise. Reform, for Salisbury, was not a matter of party tactics or of the technical adjustment of the constitution to suit changing circumstances. It was the hinge on which the fate of the nation turned. He had no doubt that any really large extension of the suffrage must take the control of the political system out of the hands of property and intelligence and lead to the destruction of the society in which he believed. The argument that a large apparent transfer of political power could safely be conceded because old-established influences would continue to exert their sway did not impress him.

The dead level of direct political power [he wrote] which modern Reformers desire to introduce would soon bring down to a similar dead level every social or political influence which rises to a special eminence, except where it is founded on individual qualities.[1]

The advocates of Reform wanted it, he pointed out, in order to be able to remodel the social and political system in their interest. In this, they were merely following what he recognised as the pattern of England's constitutional and political development. 'As each rival class or party saw its opportunity', he wrote, 'it has made of the House of Commons an instrument for establishing its own supremacy.' The net result of successive sectional endeavours had, he allowed, been beneficial to the country, in securing 'that every interest should sooner or later place upon the statute-book the laws which are necessary for its own well-being'.[2] But that it was now the turn of new forces and classes to stamp their mark on Parliament and legislation was more than he could admit. The Radicalism of Bright and his friends, seeking through Reform the means to dismantle the edifice of aristocratic, landed, and Anglican power, must be repulsed, not least because its triumph could be no more than the prelude to a far greater evil – the advent of democracy.

Salisbury's general criticism of democracy has already been outlined. All the evils which he depicted so vividly from the experience of America and France he fully expected to see in England, if the working men were given a preponderant share of the franchise. The plundering of property seemed to him inevitable. The agitation for Reform was 'purely a struggle for material advantages'; the artisan 'cares little enough for democracy unless it will adjust the inequalities of wealth'.[3] To secure their economic demands, working men would act in politics with the unity and discipline

[1] *Ibid.* cxix (1866), 555.
[2] *Ibid.* cxvi (1864), 271.
[3] *Ibid.* cxvi (1864), 267; cvii (1860), 523.

which they already displayed in their trade unions,[1] and this would make them irresistible. The unions, indeed, were likely to become the ruling power in the land. 'The fearful sacrifice which their leaders exact, and the implicit obedience of their members, indicate a vigour and tenacity of combination of which associations of the middle and upper classes are utterly destitute.' Their organisational skills would be applied to the borough constituencies by the politically conscious working men – 'usually the most restless, worthless, and noisy of their class' – and the artisan voters 'would be turned over from one candidate to another at a given order, just as they now, like one man, leave the work of an employer or a set of employers at a given signal'.[2]

It was not difficult to forecast the objects which this disciplined tyranny would pursue. The working men and their Radical friends were explicit enough about them – George Odger, for instance, the prominent working-class leader, delivering in December 1865 a speech which Salisbury thought worth quoting at length:

Give them votes, and they would see that the poor man's daughter, who was worked twelve, fourteen, and sixteen hours a-day, should have time to go abroad and view the face of nature. They would prevent the poor man's child from going in early life into mines and workshops before it was educated. *They would prevent the poor agricultural labourer from working for 8s. per week...* He asserted that *all men who were willing to work should have work provided for them.* (Cheers.) Give working men the suffrage, and that would follow.

Such declarations, wrote Salisbury, 'sweep away whole reams of platitudes about "trusting the people"'.[3] Nor was the legislative regulation of work and wages all that was to be feared. The weight of taxation, swollen no doubt by extravagant expenditure on such things as poor relief, the encouragement of emigration, and even help to oppressed nationalities abroad, would be thrown increasingly on to fixed property, and a graduated income tax – which was 'simply confiscation' – was a definite possibility. An attack on the security of landed property could be expected, through the overthrow of primogeniture and measures to provide labourers' holdings. It would be useless to complain to the working men that such steps violated individual freedom, for, as their taste for collective industrial action showed, 'to them personal freedom has not that sacred character which it possesses in the eyes of the more cultivated classes'.[4] Given

---

[1] *Ibid.* cvii (1860), 540-1; cxix (1866), 543-7.
[2] *Ibid.* cxix (1866), 545-7.   [3] *Ibid.* cxix (1866), 264.
[4] 'The Theories of Parliamentary Reform', *Oxford Essays*, pp. 77-8; *B.Q.R.*, i (1859), 29-31; *Q.R.*, cvii (1860), 524, 541; cxix (1866), 266-70, 548-51.

EDITOR'S INTRODUCTION

Salisbury's picture of what democracy would mean, it is not surprising that he thought anything better than surrender to it:

No evil results of resistance can outweigh the evils of concession. Discontent, insurrection, civil war itself, will, in the long run, produce no worse dangers than absolute and unrestrained democracy. Such commotions can only end in a military government; and the despotism of a successful soldier is a lighter burden than the despotism of the multitude.[1]

Obviously there was a good deal of exaggeration in Salisbury's view of what to expect from the working men. Some of it sprang from the desire of a partisan journalist to paint what he opposed in the blackest colours. Some of it came from a lack of close acquaintance. Salisbury had very little direct contact with working men, and his knowledge of them, like his knowledge of most things, came from reading. Not really knowing them, he invented them: as they appear in his articles and speeches, they are less characters of flesh and blood than mental constructs, treated as the undifferentiated components of a mass, and credited with only the crudest mentality. It is easy in retrospect to see the flaws in the assumptions on which his estimate of their potential political action rested. They did not constitute a homogeneous bloc, informed by a strong class consciousness, and capable of a concerted takeover of political power. They were not, in politics, obsessed with questions of economic and social advantage, or united on them, and many of those who wanted the franchise valued it as much because it was a seal of status, a mark of their acceptance within the national community, as because it could be used for material ends. They did not have the intellectual and social confidence, or, despite their unions, the organisation and leadership, to undertake an independent political role. All the same, in the context of the early sixties, Salisbury's fears were not ridiculous. He was facing the unknown: if working men were already a quarter of the borough electorate, as the Poor Law Board calculated in 1866, that was something very different from their gaining a majority. He did not suppose that they were inherently more prone than other classes to use political power in a purely selfish manner, only that they were not less so, and that in practice the pressures on them to use it to alleviate their economic situation would prove irresistible.[2] His alarmist view of the trade unions as engines of tyranny, so vehemently expressed in his first *Quarterly* article,[3] received colour from a string of acts of intimidation and violence

[1] *Ibid.* cxvii (1865), 570–1.
[2] Above, p. 33; *Hansard*, 3rd series, clxxxiii, 9–10 (April 1866).
[3] *Q.R.*, cvii (1860), 539–40.

by unionists against recalcitrant fellow workers, mainly in the cutlery and building trades in the north, which in the early sixties cast on the unions a stigma that was not to be removed until the Royal Commission of 1867–9 had shown most of them to be respectably conducted.[1] In thinking that a large extension of the franchise would bring eventually a movement to redistribute wealth by legislative means in favour of the poorer classes, he was not wrong. He simply exaggerated the pace and degree of change, as well as misconceiving some of its features, because he misunderstood those whom he expected to be its agents, and undervalued the social and institutional influences which would retard and moderate it. Where his excited vision saw the imminent catastrophe of the society he knew, only a long process of adaptation and attrition was to occur.

An important reason for Salisbury's exaggerations of tone, besides his partisanship, his highly-strung temperament, and his desire to command attention, was the need he felt to dispel the comfortable apathy which Palmerston's régime seemed to encourage among the conservative classes. The economic prosperity of the early sixties went a long way to damp down political excitements. It was 'the material prosperity of the country', Salisbury thought, that accounted for Bright's failure to get up a serious Reform agitation in 1859–60.[2] But admirable though the political calm produced by absorption in getting and spending might be, its tendency to induce a false sense of security among the conservative classes was dangerous. The worst threat to the established order, in Salisbury's view, was the complacency and sluggishness which all too easily overcame its supporters when no obvious crisis loomed:

we know too well [he wrote in 1860] the incurable fitfulness of the exertions which Englishmen make to uphold the institutions which they love...those with whom the world has gone well are naturally indolent, and are slow to believe that political changes can possibly trouble their repose till danger is actually at the door. Unless Providence should in mercy send some awkward demagogue who shows the hook under the bait, they will always be ready to nibble at fine sentiments about confidence in the English people until they are caught and landed beyond escape.[3]

Political quiet was more perilous than political turbulence. In 1860 Salisbury spurned the argument that the ruling calm made the moment

---

[1] Salisbury did, however, allow, in 1866, that 'Injustice as great, and social tyranny as oppressive, might be found abundantly in the conduct of individuals in every class of society.' *Ibid.* cxix (1866), 545.
[2] *Ibid.* cvii (1860), 533.
[3] *Ibid.* cviii (1860), 267. Cf. *ibid.* cxvii (1865), 563; cxxiii (1867), 552–3.

propitious for a settlement of the Reform issue, on the ground that men would surrender more in quiet times than they would in the face of furious assault.[1] For the health of the constitution, the political temperature had to be kept from falling too low, and the fulminations of men like Bright did good service in stimulating the conservative classes' awareness of danger.[2] It was Salisbury's constant concern to remind his audience that the enemy was always at the gate, and to keep them up to the pitch of tension that alone could guarantee a steady and effective resistance to the ceaseless sapping of the Radical activists. The *Grand Guignol* element in his journalism stemmed partly from the necessity of persuading contented and sanguine readers of the *Quarterly* that while Palmerston might be in his heaven all would not necessarily remain right with the world unless they bestirred themselves. There was, he believed, a natural conservative majority in the country. 'If victory could be secured by a mere comparison of forces, moderate Conservatism ought always to be in the ascendant.'[3] But of course victory could not: and it was Salisbury's mission to see that it was not delivered into the hands of the Radical minority simply by the drowsiness of their opponents.

There was no doubt in his mind that if the conservative forces showed vigilance and determination they could win. His habitual pessimism was submerged in the exhilaration of combat, and in the early sixties he was very far from admitting democracy to be an inevitable trend of history. The present generation, he wrote in January 1865, might have seen a movement towards a larger development of 'popular power', out of which democracy might possibly grow, but that had been only 'the flow of a tide, whose alternate rise and fall has been recorded ever since the dawn of civilised polity'.[4] He saw good reason to think that the tide was, in fact, ebbing, as faith in the virtue of democratic institutions was eroded by the exhibition of their deficiencies in America and France.

Across the Channel, democracy had produced first chaos and then 'caesarism' in the person of Napoleon III. Across the Atlantic, it produced, in 1861, a civil war. For years, the Radical prophets of human progress had held American institutions up to admiration, as a type towards which a backward England ought to aspire. Salisbury was quick to use their fondness for foreign example to imply that their ideas were somehow alien to the national character, branding Bright and his friends as 'a cosmopolitan school who love England little, and whom

[1] *Ibid.* cvii (1860), 534.
[2] *Ibid.* cxvii (1865), 563-4.
[3] *Ibid.* cviii (1860), 267.
[4] *Ibid.* cxvii (1865), 267-8.

THE POLITICS OF RESISTANCE, 1853-67

England loves less';[1] and, like many Conservatives, he looked upon the American Civil War with almost indecent satisfaction, as a salutary lesson to public opinion. The war seemed to deal the final blow to the naive faith in progress which he so deeply despised. He wrote, in October 1862:

A few years ago a delusive optimism was creeping over the minds of men. There was a tendency to push the belief in the moral victories of civilisation to an excess which now seems incredible. It was esteemed heresy to distrust anybody, or to act as if any evil still remained in human nature. At home we were exhorted to show 'our confidence in our countrymen', by confiding the guidance of our policy to the ignorant, and the expenditure of our wealth to the needy. Abroad we were invited to believe that commerce had triumphed where Christianity had failed, and that exports and imports had banished war from the earth. And generally we were encouraged to congratulate ourselves that we were permanently lifted up from the mire of passion and prejudice in which our forefathers had wallowed. The last fifteen years have been one long disenchantment; and the American civil war is the culmination of the process.[2]

In three major *Quarterly* articles, in July 1861, October 1862, and January 1865,[3] Salisbury underlined the lessons, using the American experience as a case-study in democratic government. The despotism of the democratic majority had caused the war by driving the oppressed minority into revolt, but had then shown itself incapable of waging war efficiently. The immense difficulties encountered by the democratic North in fighting the South, which was in effect an aristocracy, stemmed from the low level of leadership which the degeneration of political life consequent upon democracy produced. Democracy could neither furnish good government, nor, in the heat of conflict, uphold individual liberty, as the arbitrary tyranny of Lincoln showed. The English Radicals emerged from the great test of democratic institutions with less credit than anyone, as pacifists like Cobden and Bright supported the Northern war effort, and the Federal armies fought to crush Southern freedom with the applause of those who had denounced the suppression of freedom in Poland, Sicily, and Ireland, and now revealed that what they meant by freedom was simply the unfettered rule of the majority. All this was, of course, highly prejudiced. Salisbury was too anxious to see democracy's reputation ruined to be able to view the American conflict with anything like impartiality. He was from the first a passionate partisan of the

[1] *Ibid.* cviii (1860), 276. [2] *Ibid.* cxii (1862), 562-3.
[3] *Ibid.* cx (1861), 247-88; cxii (1862), 535-70; cxvii (1865), 249-86.

EDITOR'S INTRODUCTION

Confederacy, and urged the British government to grant it recognition; and his faith in its victory was hardly overcome until the Yankees were in Richmond.

Under the disillusioning impact of events abroad, Salisbury believed, a reaction towards conservatism was taking place in the early sixties, and affecting many 'who by early pledge or family connexion are Reformers'.[1] But traditional party ties still bound those Whigs and Liberals who had had enough of change and feared democracy to the Radicals, and prevented the formation of a bloc representing the overwhelming conservative feeling of the country. To create such a bloc by persuading Whigs and moderate Liberals to act with the Conservative party was one of Salisbury's most important hopes, and the fact that he did not think it capable of rapid realisation did not prevent his harping on the theme of the humiliations and dangers to which the conservatives on the other side exposed themselves by their continued association with the Radicals. If the growing conservatism of the middle and upper classes could be welded into a united force, Salisbury was convinced that it could not be overthrown by the Radicals and their working-class allies. The latter simply did not have the power to carry Reform against a resolute resistance.

It was a question, in Salisbury's view, how far the 'practical' English workman was really interested in the franchise and other political matters when he was not goaded by economic distress. The educated class, he thought, tended to exaggerate the effect of political arrangements on 'the large section of the community whose minds are fully occupied with the absorbing care for the gain of their daily bread'. If working-class supremacy in the political system could be secured only by a long and doubtful struggle, involving much suffering, the artisans would hardly think the potential gains worthy of the risk.[2] Without very substantial support from the classes above them, they had virtually no prospect of success. Salisbury never believed, even in the tense summer of 1866, that they would or could carry out a revolution, if Parliament and the existing electorate denied them the suffrage. He was rather interested in revolutions – 'such frequent spectacles in later times, that we have learned almost to classify their phenomena into a science'.[3] Those aided by a foreign force aside, they were of two kinds. First, there were revolutions brought about simply by an insurrection in the capital of a state with a highly centralised government, as in France in 1830,

[1] *Ibid.* cxiii (1863), 260-1; cxviii (1865), 287-8.
[2] *Ibid.* cxvii (1865), 545, 571.   [3] *Ibid.* cviii (1860), 285.

THE POLITICS OF RESISTANCE, 1853-67

1848, and 1852. That sort of thing was impossible in England, where even if London fell to a mob, government in the rest of the country would be undisturbed, 'and the example of the capital assuredly would not shake the allegiance of a single English county'. Second, there were revolutions dependent initially on the action or co-operation of a large section of the owners of property, like the Great Rebellion, the Revolution of 1688, and the American and French Revolutions.[1] Unassisted proletarian revolution was a rare occurrence:

> there is no instance as yet recorded in which the multitudes who live by the daily labour of their hands have overthrown or even seriously threatened any government not absolutely centralized, unless some bitter practical grievance has inspired them. Except where fired by genuine oppression, the working-classes alone cannot make a revolution.[2]

Such oppression did not exist in England, and the fortress of the constitution should be perfectly safe from its besiegers, so long as the classes within did not connive at its downfall by treachery or indolence.

Salisbury's opposition to Reform was not, in principle, absolute. He never argued that the existing constitution was a perfect form, incapable of change for the better. On the contrary, measuring it against his own principle of representation according to shares in the common enterprise,[3] he thought that it was grossly defective. But the defect lay as much in its failure to give proportionate weight to property (especially landed property) as in its exclusion of large numbers of the working men; and the kind of reform Salisbury was prepared to contemplate was conceived accordingly.

The representative system, Salisbury pointed out, failed to proportion electoral weight to property, firstly, because the counties were heavily under-represented in proportion to electorate and ratable property by comparison with the boroughs, and secondly, because the 'uniform' suffrage gave small property-holders the same voice as large. In practice, the balance was somewhat redressed by certain other features of the system which Salisbury recognised as 'flagrant' anomalies, but defended as an essential protection. First, the *small* boroughs possessed a representation very much larger than was warranted by their share of the nation's population and wealth, which furnished 'an indirect mode of giving a fair share of political power to the rural districts', compensating for the inadequate representation of the counties. Second, the Chandos clause of the 1832 Reform Act enfranchised a class of county voters – the

---
[1] *Ibid.* cxvii (1865), 562-3. Cf. *ibid.* cxx (1866), 274-7.
[2] *Ibid.* cviii (1860), 285. [3] Above, p. 45.

fifty-pound tenants-at-will – who were generally strongly under the influence of their landlords. Through the small boroughs, often more or less controlled by the major local landowners, and the dependent county voters, and through the well-tried methods of corruption and intimidation, property was able to make its weight felt by the exercise of an 'influence' which might, from the standpoint of political purity, be 'illegitimate', but was nonetheless a necessary means of self-defence.[1]

The only tolerable reform for Salisbury was one which avoided worsening, or better still corrected, the unfairness which he saw in the existing system. A simple lowering of the franchise, coupled with removal of anomalies (e.g. disfranchisement of the very small boroughs), would merely aggravate that unfairness and further jeopardise the power of property – which was precisely what he thought Bright and company intended. But some scheme which contrived to give the working men their fair share of the representation and also secured property its due weight would be a different matter. If property had its safeguards, Salisbury was not in theory unwilling to increase the number of working-class voters. He made that clear in his first major pronouncement on Reform in 1858,[2] and in April 1865, while insisting that any demand by the working men for democracy must be fought to the finish, he envisaged a more likely alternative:

it is not impossible that they may learn to seek, as a point of honour, the concession of rights, to the real enjoyment of which they will be indifferent. They may not ask for supremacy. They will probably be shrewd enough to see that it can never be extorted, save by a convulsion less disastrous to their antagonists than to themselves. But they may ask for a share of political power proportioned to the share which their labour gives them in the country's wealth. Such a claim, if it be advanced, must be met in a very different tone from that which has been justly used to repel the intolerable claim of supremacy.[3]

Both in 1858 and in 1865, he toyed with schemes for reconciling a wide franchise with the continuing predominance of the propertied classes – the combination of universal suffrage and plural voting practised in Victoria, Lord Grey's plan of indirect elections, Buxton's of extra votes according to ratable property. But their attractions, he decided, did not justify the risk involved in changing the institutions of the country in a novel fashion.[4] Despite the logic of his own views, he did not really want to change. 'The representative system', he declared in 1858, 'after

[1] 'The Theories of Parliamentary Reform', *Oxford Essays*, pp. 71–6; *B.Q.R.*, i (1859), 28–9; *Q.R.*, cxvi (1864), 258, 271–2.
[2] Above, pp. 46–7.   [3] *Q.R.*, cxvii (1865), 572.
[4] Above, p. 47; *Q.R.*, cxvii (1865), 565–9.

THE POLITICS OF RESISTANCE, 1853-67

many vicissitudes, has settled itself down into an equipoise.'[1] It worked, and that was the only important criterion. That it was unfair or anomalous mattered little. Salisbury thought like Lowe in 1866: 'Government does not deal with justice. It deals with expediency...We may violate any law of symmetry, equality, or distributive justice in providing the proper machinery to enable us to do what is required of us.'[2] Reform was liable to be a slippery slope: the most dangerous schemes were the moderate ones, which went towards democracy without appearing to, and weakened the conservative position against future advances.[3] Salisbury's fundamental feeling was always the one he expressed in 1858: 'we must either change enormously or not at all'.[4] As the Reform movement regained momentum in 1865-7, he recognised that some attempt at controlled and cautious change might have to be made, but the prospect was a disturbing one.

Reform had been defeated without much difficulty in 1858-60, and Palmerston's essential conservatism had subsequently kept it firmly in check. But Palmerston could not last for ever, and there were signs, notably Gladstone's declaration on the franchise in May 1864, that when he went Radicals and more 'advanced' Liberals would raise the Reform banner anew. Writing in the spring of 1865, Salisbury dwelt on the Radicals' disgruntlement with their lack of reward for helping to keep the Whigs in office, and, while admitting 'no need for legislation at this moment', foresaw the possibility of a strong working-class demand for Reform, to which it might be necessary to consider making some concessions.[5] Three months later, commenting on the general election campaign, he dismissed the apparent absence of serious political controversy as only a transitional calm, and, looking beyond the reign of Palmerston, anticipated the ascendancy of Gladstone, and with it spoliation of the Irish Church and the agricultural interest, and a Radical drive for Reform, to which the Whigs would probably surrender rather than lose power.[6] His expectations were not far wrong, and the death of Palmerston in October brought their realisation much closer.

For the Conservative party, dispirited by its failure to make progress in the 1865 election, Palmerston's removal and the prospect of a polarisation of politics over the Reform issue held out hope of revival. It might at last be able to draw to itself the broad central mass of opinion which

---

[1] 'The Theories of Parliamentary Reform', *Oxford Essays*, p. 71.
[2] Quoted in F. B. Smith, *The Making of the Second Reform Bill* (1966), p. 75.
[3] *Q.R.*, cxvii (1865), 564.
[4] 'The Theories of Parliamentary Reform', *Oxford Essays*, pp. 78-9.
[5] *Q.R.*, cxvii (1865), 543, 570-2.   [6] *Ibid.* cxviii (1865), 280-1, 289-92.

had hitherto found in Palmerston its shield against drastic change. But it was not the only possible contender for the centre ground. The new Russell–Gladstone ministry was another, and in particular Gladstone himself, whose Liberal-Conservatism (the term might have been invented for the man) was well adapted to appeal to moderate feeling on both sides of the political divide. There was a real risk of his creating a centre coalition with some Conservative support, which would have done the prospects of the Conservative party enormous damage. Hence the necessity, in the struggle for Palmerston's heritage, for the party to represent him as the tool of Radicalism, and to prevent his achieving a successful settlement of the Reform question.[1] Salisbury, of course, had long sought to tarnish Gladstone's attraction for Conservatives by accusing him of following a Radical and democratic line, and in July 1865 had taken pains to impugn the soundness of the churchmanship which was one of his most dangerous assets. Gladstone was fighting a stiff contest for the Oxford University seat which peculiarly associated him with the interests of the Church, and Salisbury argued that he and his fellow Liberals had consistently failed to give those interests due protection.[2] In January 1866, correctly judging a Reform measure to be imminent, he tried to discredit Gladstone by insinuating his complicity in the aims of the working-class leader George Odger, whom he called his 'confidant' – a description he must have known was nonsense.[3]

Even if Gladstone's credentials in the eyes of moderate opinion could be damaged, however, it was doubtful whether any of the Whig–Liberal force could be induced to cross over from his side. Salisbury believed that opposition to any Reform measure which could be represented as smacking of democracy would certainly bring the Conservatives aid from many Liberals, but he was sceptical at the beginning of 1866 about the prospects of a thoroughgoing reorganisation of parties: old associations, he knew, died hard, and 'more exciting times than these are necessary for the revision of party boundaries'.[4] The Conservatives would have to look to middle-of-the-road Palmerstonian opinion in the country, rather than to the Whigs and moderate Liberals in the House of Commons, for their reinforcement of strength. In so doing, they had to avoid the pitfall of appearing too negative and unprogressive. Their attraction might lie in their resistance to 'democratic' Reform, but it would be unwise to give the impression that they refused to consider any degree

[1] Cf. M. Cowling, *1867 : Disraeli, Gladstone and Revolution* (1967), pp. 90–5.
[2] *Q.R.*, cxviii (1865), 211–22. Gladstone lost the seat to Gathorne Hardy.
[3] *Ibid.* cxix (1866), 263.   [4] *Ibid.* cxix (1866), 277–8.

of Reform whatsoever, especially as they might find themselves in the future facing a widespread sentiment in favour of a cautious settlement of the question. Salisbury had been careful, in April 1865, to allow that any working-class claim for a due share in the representation would have to be taken seriously, and to state that the doctrines of the Conservative party were 'not adverse to the claims of any particular class, except when that class is aiming to domineer over the rest'.[1] Nine months later, with a Reform bill looming, he declared that the Conservatives 'advocate no finality; they cling to no stationary policy in regard to the representation of the people'. They were not tied to the act of 1832: on the contrary, there could be 'no demur from the side of the Conservatives to any improvement upon it which experience may suggest, or the rise of new interests may demand'. But any change must be 'a development, and not a revolution'.[2]

The intrigues of politicians over Reform had, Salisbury wrote, 'created a fictitious political necessity': many people now felt that dealing with the question was inevitable.[3] The easiest course for the Conservative party would perhaps have been to co-operate with the government in getting rid of the issue by some very limited measure. But it was hard to allow Russell and Gladstone the kudos of a great instalment of national progress, especially if they framed it in such a way as to promote their own electoral interests, and in the event the Conservatives stoutly resisted the Reform Bill of 1866, which went a good deal further than most of them wanted, and promised to do their position in the constituencies considerable harm. The parliamentary contest was fought out on a high oratorical plane, as befitted an issue in which the future of England seemed to be at stake. Salisbury saw it as 'the decisive battle...a battle not of parties, but of classes...a portion of the great political struggle of our century – the struggle between property, be its amount small or great, and mere numbers'.[4] The reluctance of the House of Commons to reform its own base in any large manner was evident, and in June the action of the Whig–Liberal defectors known as Adullamites tumbled the Russell–Gladstone ministry from office, and Lord Derby found himself a third time prime minister, with Salisbury in his cabinet, as secretary of state for India.

The first question for the new Conservative government was what it should do about Reform. It might be difficult to do nothing, given the extensive desire for some kind of settlement, and the size of the working-

[1] *Ibid.* cxvii (1865), 572.   [2] *Ibid.* cxix (1866), 278.
[3] *Ibid.* cxix (1866), 256.   [4] *Ibid.* cxix (1866), 552–3.

EDITOR'S INTRODUCTION

class agitation which had grown up by the summer of 1866. Reviewing the situation in July, Salisbury contemplated the possibilities of a future Reform measure. 'It is in itself', he felt, 'an advantage of no contemptible dimensions to gratify the susceptibilities which a considerable number of the artizan class have betrayed upon the question of the suffrage.' But it must be done 'safely', and a simple reduction of the franchise, overwhelming the existing holders of power, was intolerable. 'Participation without predominance' was the formula which the working men and their allies would have to accept, if a settlement was to be made: Salisbury was clearly thinking in terms of some system of weighted voting, which would preserve the supremacy of propertied interests. The trouble was that, having no majority, the Conservative government could not be sure of getting any proposals it might make through Parliament without drastic amendment. Everything depended for Salisbury on the balance of forces in the House of Commons. If the Conservatives could muster enough votes to carry a moderate measure, it might be wise to act. Much turned on the attitude of the 'constitutional' Whigs, and Salisbury summoned them to help Lord Derby and prevent the return of Gladstone and democratic Reform.[1]

That a part of the opposition might be induced to co-operate with the Conservatives did not seem, at this moment, an unreasonable hope. The recent campaign had brought strikingly into the open the divisions in the Liberal party. It had, Salisbury declared, 'no one informing spirit or aspiration'; it was 'united by the past, not by the present or the future'. The current issues of Church and Reform were ones 'upon which it is impossible that squire and townsman, peer and mechanic, should think alike', and were therefore separating the party into two layers, 'which consist, speaking very roughly, of those who are and those who are not connected with the great territorial interests of the country'.[2] There was much talk of a junction between some of the Whigs and Adullamites and the Conservative party, but in the end nothing happened. Old party ties and antagonisms made 'fusion' impossible under Derby's and Disraeli's lead, and both men were not surprisingly unwilling to try to consolidate the conservative forces by abandoning their own careers. The new government had to go on alone.

The chances of the Conservatives' being able to deal safely with Reform were accordingly diminished, and Salisbury came down against risking immediate legislation.[3] He was relieved when it was decided at the end

---
[1] *Ibid.* cxx (1866), 271–3, 278–82.   [2] *Ibid.* cxx (1866), 263.
[3] For a general outline of the Conservatives' dealing with Reform in 1866-7, see below, pp. 253–6.

of the year merely to test out the ground on Reform by submitting general resolutions to the Commons and setting up a royal commission. The introduction of household suffrage into the cabinet's deliberations on the content of the resolutions was less reassuring, but household suffrage in itself was not inconsistent with Salisbury's principles if it was properly counterbalanced, and he accepted it in conjunction with a scheme of plural voting, conferring extra votes according to ratable value or to house-tax payments. This in theory preserved the power of property, though Salisbury doubted whether it would pass the House of Commons. At this stage, early in February 1867, it was not Salisbury who was the die-hard in the cabinet, but the secretary for war, General Peel, who would not have household suffrage in the government resolutions at any price. When it became apparent, however, that the method of proceeding by resolutions would not satisfy parliamentary and public opinion, and Disraeli took the initiative in promising a bill, Salisbury began to feel that the cabinet was being carried too far too fast. Even so, he was prepared to go on, this time on the basis of a £5 rating franchise, with plural voting to the extent of a second vote only. But Derby and Disraeli were irresistibly drawn back to household suffrage as the most plausible foundation for a settlement, and Salisbury found himself unable to accept their assurances that the limited plurality they envisaged would be an adequate counterpoise. He feared especially the effect in the small borough constituencies, telling Derby: 'it is on the smaller boroughs we depend. Nothing will ever give us real strength in the large boroughs.'[1] Once, on 25 February, the threat of his, Carnarvon's, and Peel's resignations pulled Derby and Disraeli back from the brink, but in the end the attraction of household suffrage, not only for the Conservative leaders but for a substantial section of the party, proved too strong, and rather than surrender to it Salisbury and his fellow dissidents left the government on 2 March. The Reform Bill which Disraeli introduced on 18 March was in intention and fact a cautious and restrictive measure, hardly exceeding in numbers enfranchised Gladstone's bill of the preceding year, but to Salisbury its moderate appearance was deceptive, for he did not believe in the adequacy or permanence of the checks and counterpoises on which it relied to render household suffrage innocuous. The most important of these was the requirement of personal payment of rates, which excluded from the suffrage the half-a-million compound householders paying rates through their landlords. To Lord Exeter,

[1] Cranborne to Derby, 22 Feb. 1867 (typescript copy): Salisbury Papers, vol. 'Stanley', p. 2.

Salisbury pointed out that in twenty-nine boroughs and in part of ninety-eight more there were no compound householders anyway, and that where the compounders did exist the vestries could get them on to the register by stopping compounding, or they could get on themselves by electing to pay rates direct.[1] The bill was, in fact, household suffrage, checked only by the two years' residence condition, and insufficiently balanced by the so-called 'fancy franchises' and the dual vote for householders paying £1 in direct taxation.

Salisbury's behaviour over Reform in 1867 vividly illustrated both his strength and his weaknesses. His strength lay in his adherence to principle. It is easy to justify his conduct from his own point of view. Believing that an inadequately safeguarded household suffrage would be the ruin of the nation, he was bound to resist it, just as he was bound to resist a measure which threatened to become much more radical than the one he and his colleagues had denounced as excessive only a year before. Derby and Disraeli, in seeking to achieve a success by leading their party into an instalment of Reform potentially larger than that which they had gained office by opposing, were displaying a cynical dishonesty reminiscent of their dealings in 1858-9, and for Salisbury the defence that they were acting in response to the practical pressures of national need and party interest was of dubious force. Five years later, thinking back not only to 1867 but to 1829 and 1846, he gave his considered view of this branch of political ethics:

In spite of casuistry the point of honour will, in the long run, with the same men, remain the same for public as for private affairs. Men may be misled on particular occasions into assenting to a policy from which, if asked to adopt it in their private concerns, they would recoil. The plea of necessity, the claims of party fealty, the fear of making bad worse, or the hope of mitigating the inevitable, are motives of real cogency whose proper limits are hard to define; and though after the event they are seen to afford no defence for a shifty policy, they often appear at the time sufficient, not only to justify, but to demand, the successive minute steps of concession of which that policy was made up. Such pleas may serve to excuse exceptional deviations from the consistency which the law of honour requires between the promises of opposition and the performances of office; but only so long as they are exceptional.[2]

As a practical politician, however, Salisbury gave in 1867 a clear demonstration of his deficiencies. He was too inflexible, and too limited

[1] Cranborne to Exeter, March 1867 (typescript copy): Salisbury Papers. Cf. *Hansard*, 3rd series, clxxxvi, 85-8 (18 March).
[2] *Q.R.*, cxxxiii (1872), 575. Cf., on the obligation of party leaders to keep faith with their followers, Salisbury's censure of Peel's behaviour over Catholic emancipation and the corn laws (*ibid.* cxvii (1865), 551-60).

THE POLITICS OF RESISTANCE, 1853-67

in outlook. He became over-obsessed with the details of Reform, and insufficiently sensitive to the general situation. The fate of the country did not depend as much as he thought on the precise definition of the franchise, and the future could not be ascertained by arithmetic, as he tried to ascertain it in the famous all-night statistical study which led him to reject Derby's and Disraeli's proposals. He was lacking in a sense both of the need in 1867 to concede a fairly large extension of the suffrage and of the forces and influences which, without benefit of paper 'checks' and 'counterpoises', would limit and control the impact of that extension. From Derby's and Disraeli's standpoint, he was an impossible colleague. They had not taken office in order to be driven out of it almost immediately, and they saw the necessity and the opportunity to show that the Conservative party could tackle what by 1867 had become a pressing national problem in a moderate yet progressive spirit. Doing so involved some suppleness of response to parliamentary and public feeling, and was not facilitated by sudden threats of resignation when the Indian secretary's sums led him to conclude that they had the wrong answer. Their basic intention, and that of the overwhelming majority of the House of Commons, was the same as his – a 'safe' settlement, preserving the dominance of property and education. The measure of Salisbury's imperfect grasp of political tactics was that in the end he made it more difficult for this to be achieved. Derby and Disraeli wanted to take their stand on the sort of overtly large but practically very restricted measure represented by their bill of 18 March, with the support of their own right wing and of the Adullamite Cave. The refusal of Salisbury and the Adullamites to co-operate made it necessary for them to look for Radical votes instead, and so to acquiesce in the progressive remodelling of their bill, which by mid-May had converted it into a measure of household suffrage virtually without limitation or counterpoise.[1]

Salisbury might still have attained his objects had he organised an effective resistance in the Conservative party to stop the bill. He made no attempt to do so. Partly it was his old diffidence at work: he did not believe in his own influence or capacity for leadership. Partly it was a fastidious reluctance to having to cultivate support from his fellows. But there was also a sort of intellectual remoteness from the real business of politics. He told his friend Shaw-Stewart that in his opposition to the bill he was not 'testifying', he was trying to kill it, 'or failing that to take the sting out of it'.[2] The impression persists, however, that he was

[1] Cf. Cowling, p. 302.
[2] Cranborne to J. A. Shaw-Stewart, 17 April 1867, in Cecil, *Salisbury*, i, 263.

ultimately more concerned to establish his polemical position and to assert his integrity in relation to Reform than to exert himself for any practical success. If the country went to the dogs, that was where he had long thought it was going, and there was a certain masochistic relish in the fulfilment of his forecasts of doom, a sort of enjoyment in hugging to himself a lonely virtue in a corrupt and backsliding world. There was a weariness and disgust, too, with the weakness of those who were deserting from their duty. He had no inclination to grasp at the leadership of a Conservative party whose consent to trail at Disraeli's heels discredited it as an instrument for good:

> I cannot look upon them [he told Shaw-Stewart] as more likely to promote any cause I may have at heart than the other side. The suffrage is gone: they are lukewarm about the Church, and would no doubt give it up, as they have given up other things, for the sake of office. And beyond these two there is nothing, so far as I know, of which the Conservatives are in any special way the protectors.

This was on 17 April, and the Reform struggle was far from decided, but Salisbury was clearly demoralised. 'I am not looking forward', he added to Shaw-Stewart, 'to any political career for myself.'[1] He confined his action against the bill to speeches, powerful but of little avail, and to supporting Gladstone's attempt to move towards a £5 rating franchise. The final crisis of Reform had revealed him as politically ineffective, able to preserve his principles but not to secure their victory. He had fought, but he had not fought hard enough, or in the right way. It was perhaps as well. Had he given a lead to those Conservatives who were dismayed by the government's course, he might have wrecked the bill and destroyed Disraeli's career; but in doing so he would have prolonged and exacerbated the crisis, and demolished the claim of his party to be able to meet national requirements in a generous spirit. As it was, Reform was disposed of, the Conservatives entered the age of mass politics without the stigma of having refused to assist at its birth, and Salisbury gained, in the midst of defeat for his cause, a reputation as the guardian of Conservative principle that was already making men look to him as a future leader of the Conservative party.

In two of his most forceful articles for the *Quarterly*, in October 1867 and October 1869, he tried to explain, no doubt as much to himself as to his readers, how 1867 had happened.[2] He found part of the answer in what he saw as the blatant duplicity of Derby and Disraeli. So inflamed

[1] *Ibid.*
[2] *Q.R.*, cxxiii (1867), 533–65; cxxvii (1869), 538–61.

was his sense of betrayal that he plausibly, though wrongly, accused them of having designed to lead the party into household suffrage all along, perhaps even since 1859. What they had done, of course, was the natural consequence of the disreputable policy of flirting with the Radicals in order to beat the Whigs, a policy in which the bulk of the party had readily acquiesced. The Conservatives had shown themselves more remarkable for their organisation and discipline than for any 'living earnestness'. In 1867 they had been swept along by desire for a settlement, the exhilaration of parliamentary success, and a vague faith in the Conservatism of the class of men they were enfranchising. The propertied classes in general had been too complacent and apathetic to defend their interests, due partly to absorption in 'the keen struggle for material prosperity', and when challenged by the democratic forces had had no stomach for a serious fight. The consequences hardly bore contemplation. The 'new masters' of politics had discovered in overrunning the citadel that the great conservative force, which had looked so formidable, was a delusion. There was nothing to check the enforcement of their will, the less so since the events of 1867 had emphasised that party had become a contrivance for securing office rather than for asserting principles, and that ministers would accept any policy at the dictation of the House of Commons in order to retain power. All these things Salisbury could claim to have foreseen and warned against; and all of them he had been powerless to prevent.

CONSERVATISM AND DEMOCRACY

As he looked back over the session of 1867, Salisbury felt that nothing less than a 'revolution' had occurred. Power had been transferred to the masses, and 'democracy', in his sense of the term, had arrived. Yet even in the immediate aftermath of defeat, he believed that the evils of the Reform Act were 'not necessarily irremediable', if the conservative forces exerted themselves vigorously.[1] That did not mean reaction. The new situation had to be accepted. 'In all conflicts', he wrote in October 1869, 'a time must come when the decision of fortune upon one or the other side is unmistakably given, and when to fight longer is only to waste force and alienate sympathy in vain.'[2] Soon, the verdict of 1867 came to seem, in philosophical retrospect, almost a foregone conclusion. The Reform Act of 1832, with its destruction of aristocratic government, had led inevitably towards democracy: the period between 1832 and 1867 had been merely a transitional phase, marked by the attempt (as

[1] *Ibid.* cxxiii (1867), 533, 553. [2] *Ibid.* cxxvii (1869), 554.

EDITOR'S INTRODUCTION

Salisbury saw it) to create a 'provisional aristocracy' from the middle classes, a compromise between 'the government of caste and the government of numbers', which had failed because the middle class was not cohesive enough to be a ruling class.[1]

Salisbury was dispirited by his defeat and had difficulty in envisaging a role for himself in the democratic politics of the future. 'My opinions belong to the past,' he told a friend in April 1868, 'and it is better that the new principles in politics should be worked by those who sympathize with them heartily.'[2] This was the month in which his father's death translated him to the Lords, and he saw the change as removing him from a sphere in which he was no longer of much use. The Conservative party in the Commons had ceased to be an appropriate agency for the assertion of his political principles: its only real object seemed to be the maintenance of Disraeli (who had succeeded Derby as prime minister in February 1868) in power.[3] The construction of a new conservative bloc was not something Salisbury felt capable of undertaking. As he told Carnarvon: 'My opinions are not such as would enable me to work heartily with the moderate Liberals – and it is only under their lead that a Conservative party in the future could be formed. Pure "squire" Conservatism is played out.'[4] But it was not easy for him to escape a prominent part in Conservative politics. His reputation for integrity and ability, and the prestige of one of England's great peerages, made many Conservatives look to him for guidance. Some of the Tory peers, disgusted with Disraeli, would have followed an independent line under his command. Lord Bath told him in February 1869 that he had been sounding the feelings of members of the Conservative party, especially peers, and 'they one and all look upon you as the eventual leader of the party'.[5] He might well have become leader in the Lords in 1869–70, but for the realisation that this would put the party in an impossible position.[6] Whether he liked it or not, Salisbury had become a sort of leader in waiting, and Disraeli's inertia in the early years of opposition after the election defeat of 1868 made some turn to him as a leader in default. In 1871 both Lord George Hamilton and Henry

[1] *Ibid.* cxxx (1871), 278–9.
[2] Salisbury to John Coleridge, 18 April 1868, in Cecil, *Salisbury*, i, 294.
[3] See a draft letter of Salisbury, 11 May 1868, quoted in Blake, *Disraeli*, pp. 499–500, in which Salisbury referred to the fact that Disraeli was not 'identified by birth or property with the Conservative classes in the country'.
[4] Salisbury to Carnarvon, 24 April 1868, in Cecil, *Salisbury*, i, 294.
[5] Marquis of Bath to Salisbury, 8 Feb. 1869 (typescript copy): Salisbury Papers, vol. 'Stapleton to Wolff', pp. 63–4.
[6] See E. J. Feuchtwanger, *Disraeli, Democracy and the Tory Party* (1968), pp. 5–8.

Drummond Wolff wanted him to take the initiative in defining what the Conservative party stood for.[1] He would give no overt lead, and offer Disraeli no formal challenge. But in his speeches and in the pages of the *Quarterly* he entered again into the political battle, and let his admirers know his mind.

He was no doubt helped in overcoming the impulse to contract out of the politics of the new era by the realisation, as the dust of 1867 settled, that they were not for the time being drastically different from those of the old. The new working-class voters made no thunderous immediate impact, and failed to fall with one accord upon property. Salisbury said in October 1867 that the assumption that the poor would not plunder the rich, on which the Reform Act rested, could be justified only on one of two hypotheses. 'Either the conscience of the working men will be so strong as to outweigh the suggestions of interest and the pressure of poverty, or they will not be clever enough to pull together for the purpose of gratifying their wishes.'[2] He neglected a third possibility: that the working men were somewhat less obsessed with class divisions, antagonisms, and interests in politics than he was. Instead of an onslaught on the comfortable classes by the needy and ignorant, what he found himself facing was a continuation of Radical pressure against the entrenched power of aristocracy, land, and Church, uneasily conjoined with the desire of the moderate majority of Liberals, given expression in the legislation of Gladstone's ministry of 1868-74, for further instalments of religious equality, social, administrative, and legal reform, financial retrenchment, and opening of careers to talent – both made newly powerful by the enfranchisement of a large mass of urban working-class support, with which, however, latent divergences of interest rendered their relations distinctly ambivalent.

Salisbury was nonetheless convinced that the great battle between property and indigence must eventually come, and was constantly on the look-out for signs of its approach. An ill-defined notion of class conflict remained fundamental to his interpretation of politics. In October 1869 he spoke of reaching 'the point at which two great epochs in the history of England will be hereafter seen to join'. Since the Reformation, religious passions had been central to politics, but they were now waning in face of the growing power of class envy, heralding a return to 'the great primeval subject-matter of all human conflict'. 'Henceforth it seems

---

[1] Hamilton to Salisbury, 25 March 1871; Lord Eustace Cecil to Salisbury, 9 Aug. [1871]: Salisbury Papers, Special Correspondence. There seems to have been some notion of a coalition ministry abroad.

[2] *Q.R.*, cxxiii (1867), 533-4.

EDITOR'S INTRODUCTION

likely that classes will have to meet each other face to face, with far less of common feelings to break the shock.'[1] What England was experiencing was, of course, part of a general European trend. Like many contemporaries, Salisbury was deeply impressed, not to say scared, by the Paris Commune of 1871, whose anarchic violence readily recalled the terrors of the Revolution. He saw it as portending a bitter social conflict which was bound to affect England. For the socialist doctrines of the International, with their threat to property, the family, and religion, he had a savage horror, writing:

The conflict between Socialism and existing civilisation must be a death-struggle. If the combat is once commenced, one or other of the combatants must perish. It is idle to plead that the schemes of these men are their religion. There are religions so hostile to morality, so poisonous to the life-springs of society, that they are outside the pale of human tolerance.

With the ruthless and bloody repression of the Paris insurrection he clearly sympathised. Fortunately, he believed, English workmen had no taste for 'visionary' doctrines, being too concerned with the more mundane and probably futile effort to raise wages by union action. But the extremists of the Liberal party, who thrived by fomenting new discontents, were all too likely to set about exploiting 'that ancient and perennial source of animosity which, unhappily, has never ceased, and never will cease, to flow in every civilised community – the quarrel of the poor against the rich', and it was too much to hope that the working men would not respond.[2]

The class war obstinately refused to materialise, but Salisbury went on looking for it with a kind of animated gloom. Pondering the unexpectedly severe Conservative defeat in the election of 1880, after a campaign in which Liberals had made some attempt to represent their opponents as the party of rank, wealth, and sectional interests, he wondered whether the popular movement against the government was 'the beginning of a serious war of classes'.[3] Three years later, seeing class divisions gaining strength in a period of economic difficulty, as the leaders of the masses taught them that the function of legislation was to redistribute wealth in their favour, he considered whether England was yet attacked by the conflict between 'possession and non-possession', which killed nations by eating out 'the common sentiments and mutual sympathies

[1] *Ibid.* cxxvii (1869), 539–40.
[2] *Ibid.* cxxxi (1871), 550, 556–60, 563–4, 567–8, 577–9.
[3] Salisbury to A. J. Balfour, 10 April 1880: British Museum, Add. MS. 49688 (Balfour Papers), ff. 22–3 (printed in A. J. Balfour, *Chapters of Autobiography* (1930), pp. 127–8).

CONSERVATISM AND DEMOCRACY

which combine classes into a patriotic State'. He thought it hard to say, 'for the real living political forces of our people lie habitually so much in repose, that an observer is always in danger of mistaking the professional polemic of politicians for conflicts really involving the great classes of which the nation is composed' - a point he might have remembered more often. If classes were not in actual conflict, he decided, they were at least watching each other in his own spirit of 'vigilant distrust'.[1]

To bring all the fundamentally conservative interests in the country together in face of the impending class struggle remained Salisbury's central political aim. In mid-1871 the gist of a conversation he had had with a friend of the Radical E. S. Beesly was conveyed by the latter to Karl Marx. He thought democratic and social change inevitable, reported Beesly. 'Only he thinks it may be postponed, and he is determined to fight tooth and nail for every inch of the ground. He labours to reconcile and bind together all the propertied classes, mercantile as well as territorial, in resistance to the needy.'[2] An alliance of property, of course, would have to transcend existing lines of party. Salisbury watched with avidity the internal tensions of the Liberals, waiting for the moment when what seemed to him the basic incompatibility between the Radicals on the one hand and the Whigs and moderates on the other would break them apart and bring the latter into a conservative front. He repeatedly harped on the designs of the more extreme Radicals on property and the Church, in order to stimulate the moderates' revulsion from the company which, he suggested, they kept only because of party ties based upon exhausted issues, extinct battles, and slogans whose meaning time had altered. After 1867, it was less at the Whigs than at the bulk of respectable middle-class Liberalism that his insinuations were aimed. Middle-class Liberalism, he argued, had largely succeeded in the struggle for 'enfranchisement' from aristocratic, landed, and Anglican power which had brought it into being. The interest of its adherents in the security of property was now threatened by Radical tendencies, and even more by the claims of those who had in the past constituted its willing reserve of force but were now becoming increasingly conscious of their differences with it - the working men. In October 1871, exploiting the alarm caused by the Commune, he tried to alert the middle classes to their danger:

Their mistake in recent times has been, that they have accepted their political connexions and antagonisms too much from tradition, without noticing how

[1] *Q.R.*, clvi (1883), 563-5, 576-7.
[2] Beesly to Marx, c. July 1871, quoted in R. Harrison, 'E. S. Beesly and Karl Marx', part II, *International Review of Social History*, iv (1959), 219.

EDITOR'S INTRODUCTION

much the world has moved. They have gone on belabouring their old adversaries, the squire and the parson, with all the enthusiasm of their fathers half a century ago; and have not discerned the vast, overshadowing power that is growing up behind them. Their old enemies are maimed and shrunken: the force with which they now have to count is that of the auxiliaries by whose aid their former victories were won. New questions are before the world: new issues are to be fought out, which in importance dwarf the old.[1]

Salisbury's main effort along this line came in his *Quarterly* article of October 1873, written at a time when it was clear that the vigour of the Radicals and the emergent electoral and industrial force of the working men were causing considerable nervousness to many middle-class Liberals whose appetite for change had been sated, or exceeded, by the Gladstone ministry's stream of legislation over almost five years, and who were now preoccupied with the consolidation of their economic and social position. As the government faltered and a general election approached, the Conservative party had good hopes of persuading some of these voters into its fold, and Salisbury's article, designedly or not, fitted neatly into its attempt to demonstrate their community of interest with it.[2] He dwelt on the disillusionment of European Liberalism with 'the people', and on the upsurge of antagonism between the middle classes and their former working-class allies, and urged the need for a reconstruction of 'political geography' which would separate the moderate Liberals from Radicals with whose objects they had no sympathy – though he did not expect them to join the Conservatives.[3]

In all this there was a large element of partisan exaggeration. Salisbury exaggerated the extent to which bourgeois Liberalism had already achieved its socio-political ends: in 1873 the power of aristocracy, land, and Church might be 'maimed and shrunken', but it was far from broken. He exaggerated the menace of the extreme Radical challenge to property and religion: the names he cited, Bright, Odger, Harrison, Dilke, Bradlaugh, Chamberlain, and the objects he placarded, disestablishment, remodelling of land tenure, 'nationalisation' of property, confiscation of 'unearned increment', were a long way from possessing the force necessary to their triumph. He exaggerated the degree of estrangement between the middle and working classes, as the persistence of the links between the Liberal party and the labour movement showed. But the difficulties within 'the party of movement' which he was trying to exacerbate were nonetheless real ones, and offered a genuine prospect

[1] *Q.R.*, cxxxi (1871), 580.
[2] For the situation in 1873, see introductory note to the article, below, pp. 292–4.
[3] *Q.R.*, cxxxv (1873), 543–73.

CONSERVATISM AND DEMOCRACY

of its break-up. In October 1872 he noted that there had been for some years a gradual drift of the well-to-do classes towards Conservatism.[1] He seems to have been right, and he had good reason to think that the social tensions he detected in the opposing army would accelerate the trend.

It followed that the first object of the Conservative party should be to do everything to make it possible for disillusioned and apprehensive Liberal moderates to co-operate with it in checking Radicalism and democracy. The tragedy of its action in 1867, Salisbury thought, was that, in surrendering to democracy, it had discredited itself in the eyes of moderate Liberals who would otherwise have worked with it, thus obstructing the restoration of political equilibrium through the disintegration of the forces of change.[2] Its heavy defeat in the general election of 1868 seemed to show that its gamble on Reform had failed, and that it could not command enough support in the new constituency to secure the defence of established interests on its own, but must operate as part of a wider combination, in which it might possibly have to be content with a secondary role. Salisbury was anxious, immediately after 1868, that it should lay aside thoughts of office for the time being, and not be tempted into tactical manœuvres against Gladstone's government for the sake of another period of sham power in which principle would once more be sacrificed to keep place. The proper course of the Conservatives, as he saw it in October 1869, was the admittedly uninspiring one of backing up the moderates on the government side against the extremists. He wrote:

To act the part of the fulcrum from which the least Radical portion of the party opposed to them can work upon their friends and leaders, is undoubtedly not an attractive future. In the changes of political life it may well end in the moderate Liberals enjoying a permanent tenure of office, propped up mainly by their support. Such a result, constituted as human nature is, would no doubt be irritating. Yet it is the only policy by which the Conservatives can now effectually serve their country and their cause.[3]

Three years later, when the Gladstone government was clearly weak, he again warned against a minority ministry, and urged that the overriding duty of the party was to facilitate a junction with the moderate Liberals (which he now saw as only a matter of time), even if that meant accepting Whig leadership. He was thinking in terms of the sort of centre coalition he had hoped for in 1866-7, and was anxious that it

[1] *Ibid.* cxxxiii (1872), 590.
[2] *Ibid.* cxxvii (1869), 548-52. [3] *Ibid.* cxxvii (1869), 552-4, 557-60.

should not be prevented by distrust of the Conservative party's intentions or by the jealousies of political leaders. 'If', he wrote, 'the Conservative party should ever, in dealing with the larger questions that are impending, come to form part of a larger organisation, it is obvious that many politicians, who have been prominent champions of Conservative opinions, will fall into the background.'[1] The meaning of this, of course, was that Disraeli, who had been a main obstacle to fusion in 1866, would have to go. Perhaps, too, remembering his words in April 1868 about his inability to work heartily with the moderate Liberals,[2] it meant that Salisbury himself was ready to renounce front-rank politics. As usual, his thought was for the interests of the conservative cause, not for those of the Conservatives as a party. The cause was not necessarily best served by the party's being in power. He had no desire to see a new Conservative government unless it could be one strong enough to have no need to compromise its principles. Short of that, he felt, the best thing for the country was a weak Liberal ministry with a strong opposition.[3] It was a point he was to reiterate after the Conservative thrashing in the election of 1880. 'A Liberal Government in office, too weak for violent legislation', he wrote in 1883, when that again seemed to be the state of affairs, 'is, perhaps, the condition of things most favourable to the maintenance of the Constitution.'[4]

Disraeli, by and large, followed in the early seventies a policy which had much in common with that which Salisbury was advocating, though rather because there was little else he could do than because he took his cue from the *Quarterly*. He cultivated moderate support, and echoed Salisbury in suggesting to the middle classes that the issues on which their Liberalism had depended were played out, and that in face of the threat to crown, Church, and property it was time to support 'a great Constitutional Party'.[5] While declining to try to produce a Conservative programme of change to rival the Liberals, he held out in his famous 1872 speeches a prospect of useful and uncontentious social legislation which Salisbury endorsed.[6] He prudently refused to form a minority ministry when he got the chance, in March 1873, preferring to let Gladstone's government stew in its difficulties as long as possible. But he had no intention of sacrificing his personal hopes of power for the putative sake of the conservative cause, and the party's victory in the general election of 1874, its first for thirty-three years, put an end to any question

---

[1] *Ibid.* cxxxiii (1872), 581–2, 590–1.   [2] Above, p. 86.
[3] *Q.R.*, cxxxiii (1872), 592–3.   [4] *Ibid.* clvi (1883), 560.
[5] *Hansard*, 3rd series, ccxiv, 1944 (March 1873).
[6] *Q.R.*, cxxxv (1873), 556.

of its merging itself and him in a Whig-led coalition. The Conservative majority of about fifty, in the first election under the full impact of the new franchise, could be taken to show that the consequences of 1867 were not disastrous to the party after all, and that a strong Conservative government was possible in a 'democratic' system. Much depended, however, on whether the party's purists would so far forgive 1867 as to back the new ministry, and Salisbury's consent to enter the cabinet was a vital point. He came in, with his ally Carnarvon, in order to put Tory handcuffs on the prime minister, for whom his mistrust was as lively as ever. It was not until their co-operation in the Eastern crisis in 1878 that his old antagonism towards Disraeli finally gave way to a close relationship in which the latter came to depend a good deal on him. The government of 1874-80 was the beginning of Salisbury's mature career at the highest levels of politics. Henceforth he was to be a minister or party leader, or both, for almost the whole of his remaining life. He no longer had time for a journalistic commentary on events. He wrote only twice for the *Quarterly* after 1873. But his political action continued to follow as faithfully as reality permitted the precepts of his writings.

He became co-leader of the Conservative party with Stafford Northcote on Disraeli's death in 1881, and sole leader on assuming the premiership in 1885. It was ironic that he should be called to lead under the 'democracy' which it had been the passion of his early political life to resist, but his fundamental ideas required, or at any rate received, no great adaptation to the new circumstances. Democracy had to be treated as a fact of life, and the Conservative party had to strive for its principles within its framework. When household suffrage for county constituencies was brought forward in 1884, Salisbury did not fight to prevent it. For him, the essential battle had been fought and lost seventeen years earlier, and there was no point in a hopeless resistance to what was merely the logical extension of the principles then victorious. Yet, while the Conservative party must grant recognition to democracy, it must avoid unnecessary pandering to it. Its business was to try to guide democracy and to check its more undesirable manifestations, not to give itself over unreservedly to currying democratic favour. Salisbury did not think that it should adopt, or would benefit by adopting, a programme of change and reform designed to rival that of the Liberals in attracting the popular vote. The notion was really absurd, for the two parties existed as representatives of the two alternating moods of the English mind, and it was impossible that they should exchange roles.[1] The point

[1] *Ibid.* cxxxiii (1872), 583-4.

EDITOR'S INTRODUCTION

of the Conservative party and the real strength of its electoral appeal lay in its negative and defensive aspects, and could only be damaged by flirting with ideas that properly belonged to the other side. To Salisbury, with his confidence in the capacity of the unalloyed Conservative creed to command the support of a large section of the nation, and his deep sense of the loyalty he owed as a party leader to the feelings of the mass of his followers, the idea of a more 'progressive' Conservatism, as advanced by men like Lord Randolph Churchill, seemed both politically mistaken and morally dubious.[1] The party's survival and success under democracy must depend not on promising benefits and changes which could be provided only at the expense of the interests it was supposed to protect, but on its claim to embody a national sentiment and a conception of the national interest that cut across all sectional divisions, and to promote the social harmony and economic security on which the well-being of all classes could be held to depend. The theme of the Conservatives as the national, and the Liberals as the anti-national and unpatriotic, party, a favourite of Disraeli, appeared conspicuously in Salisbury's last *Quarterly* article of October 1883, the only one he wrote as party leader.

None of this meant that the Conservatives need adopt a purely stationary attitude. 'The object of our party', Salisbury declared in 1883, 'is not, and ought not to be, simply to keep things as they are. In the first place, the enterprise is impossible. In the next place, there is much in our present mode of thought and action which it is highly undesirable to conserve.'[2] His ministries could not and did not abstain from moderate reforms, most notably, perhaps, in the sphere of social questions, where some effort had to be made to encourage working-class support. But their legislative record was not impressive. Salisbury was not fitted to preside over a great legislative programme. It was partly, of course, that his energies were absorbed in his later years by foreign rather than by home affairs. But it was even more that he had little interest in or liking for legislative change. In 1881, discussing what was then the parliamentary innovation of the closure, he told his nephew, A. J. Balfour:

In my view there ought [to] be a strong distinction drawn between those Parliamentary functions, the performance of which is absolutely necessary to secure the working of the executive machine: & those which, having no other object but to change laws under which we are living quite tolerably,

---

[1] Cecil, *Biographical Studies*, pp. 83–4; *Salisbury*, iii, 277–9.
[2] *Q.R.*, clvi (1883), 562.

can be suspended certainly without serious injury, & often with great advantage.[1]

The prime function of the Conservative party as Salisbury saw it continued to be to consolidate the forces of defence rather than to appease those of change. That the support thus mustered might not be sufficient, in an expanded electorate, to secure the party office was a possibility he faced with apparent equanimity at the outset of his leadership. Office did not matter, provided that the party remained strong enough in Parliament to ensure the effective protection of conservative interests. In the early eighties, he seems to have envisaged, without marked repugnance, a long period of opposition, in which the essential Conservative task would be less to try to unseat the Liberal government than to make it impossible for it to pass Radical measures.[2] As it turned out, the party did not have to live off the dry crust of self-abnegation on which Salisbury was always so ready to feed it. Circumstances brought it a great accretion of strength. It was Salisbury's luck that his years of leadership coincided with (as his personal reputation assisted) the junction of a body of Whigs and moderate Liberals with the Conservatives that he had always been anxious to promote. Electorally, he was the beneficiary of a middle-class drift towards Conservatism that had been gaining strength under the spur of Gladstonian energy, Chamberlainite Radicalism, and the emergence of Socialism, long before it was stimulated by the issue of Irish home rule. He was not slow to recognise this movement and its importance for the Conservative cause, and he was to see it change perceptibly the face of the Conservative party. In 1876 he could still refer to the Conservatives as 'the Country party'.[3] But the landed and agricultural interest was less than ever an adequate base for a great national force, especially under the impact of the agricultural depression which set in in the late seventies.[4] The need of reinforcement was patent, and in the growth of urban middle-class Conservatism Salisbury found it answered. 'I believe', he told Northcote in 1882, 'there is a great deal of Villa Toryism which requires organisation.'[5]

[1] Salisbury to Balfour, 15 Jan. 1881: Add. MS. 49688, ff. 37-40. He thought the closure should be limited to the first class.
[2] *Q.R.*, clvi (1883), 560; *National Review*, iv (1884), 161-2.
[3] Salisbury to Rev. E. S. Talbot, 25 July 1876 (typescript copy): Salisbury Papers, vol. 'Stapleton to Wolff', p. 43.
[4] One serious result of this was lack of money. Writing to Lord H. J. B. Manners, 14 Sept. 1881, Salisbury referred to 'the utter impecuniosity of our party owing to the agricultural distress' (typescript copy: *ibid.* vol. 'Manners', p. 9).
[5] Quoted in J. Cornford, 'The Transformation of Conservatism in the Late Nineteenth Century', *Victorian Studies*, vii (1963-4), 52.

EDITOR'S INTRODUCTION

In 1884 he was very anxious to secure such a redistribution of seats as would enable that Toryism to make its maximum electoral mark,[1] especially in face of the possibility that household suffrage would undermine the old Conservative strongholds in the counties. Succeeding election results seemed to vindicate his faith. In 1885 the Conservatives won a bare majority of the English borough seats. In the next four elections (1886–1900) they actually won 71·8% of English borough seats, compared with 68·6% in English counties.[2] Perhaps the most striking token of their urban vitality was their success in London, so long a graveyard of their candidates. 'When you and I were first in the House of Commons', wrote Salisbury to Lord Cranbrook after the general election of 1886, 'how little we should have expected that you would ever be able to write, "London is really the base of Tory principles".'[3] His explanation of the strong Conservative showing in the great urban constituencies was a complacent one:

> He himself accounted for the fact by the demand upon the reasoning faculties which Conservatism makes. The intellectual activity engendered in great towns arms men both against the economic fallacies and the merely emotional appeals of Radical propagandists.[4]

The accretion of middle-class support was vital to Conservative prospects, and a formal recognition of its importance may perhaps be seen in the fact that Salisbury's first ministry of 1885–6 constituted a turning point in the introduction of men with commercial and industrial connections into the peerage.[5] But the composition and character of the Conservative party altered only slowly, and the landed classes retained a very strong grip on it in Salisbury's lifetime.[6] The attempt of provincial middle-class Conservatism to make its influence effective through the

---

[1] Cecil, *Salisbury*, iii, 105–23. In regard to the disfranchisement of boroughs of under 15,000 inhabitants, he 'repeatedly urged at the time, both in public and in private, his conviction that the traditional view had become obsolete, and that it was to the large centres of population that the Conservative party must henceforth look for its main urban support'. He published an article on redistribution in October 1884, in the *National Review*, iv, 145–62.
[2] Calculated from figures in Blake, *Conservative Party*, p. 153.
[3] Salisbury to Cranbrook, 10 July 1886, quoted in Cecil, *Salisbury*, iii, 309.
[4] *Ibid.* iii, 123.
[5] For the first time, 20% or more of all peerage recipients had such connections. R. E. Pumphrey, 'The Introduction of Industrialists into the British Peerage: a Study in Adaptation of a Social Institution', *American Historical Review*, lxv (1959–60), 8. Salisbury even ennobled a brewer, Allsopp, as Disraeli in 1880 had ennobled Guinness.
[6] See J. Cornford, 'The Parliamentary Foundations of the Hotel Cecil', in *Ideas and Institutions of Victorian Britain*, pp. 268–311.

party's mass organisation, the National Union, was contained, and bourgeois Conservatives tended to find offices and honours, especially at the higher levels, difficult to come by.[1] This reflected to some extent Salisbury's predilection. His need of the middle classes did not increase his liking for them. He had never favoured the throwing open of public life to the unrestrained challenge of their talents, and he kept to the end of his days an instinctive preference for the closed aristocratic and gentry politics into which he had been born. In 1860 he had attacked competitive examinations for the civil service, and defended the role of patronage and favour in public life.[2] Forty years later, his tendency to pick his colleagues from his own narrow circle was sufficiently marked for a Conservative M.P. to remonstrate with him over the rumour that he meant to add his son to the three nephews and a son-in-law then occupying important posts.[3] He knew that the world was changing, but in his immediate vicinity he kept it, as far as possible, the same.

The changing balance of electoral forces caused the Conservatives to do very well under 'democracy' in Salisbury's period of leadership. In twenty-one years, they were in power about two-thirds of the time. Salisbury himself showed a paradoxical capacity for democratic appeal. As his daughter points out, 1867 in some ways benefited his political career. Inept at all but the most intimate or the most impersonal relations, he found it easier to project himself to the electorate at large as the new dispensation required than to exercise the arts of parliamentary and party management which had been the key to success under the old; and his predominance in British politics towards the end of the century came to rest more on his reputation in the country than on his popularity among politicians, which was not remarkable.[4] Perhaps this should have reconciled him to democracy, but there is no sign that it did. Democracy remained the repugnant system under which the circumstances of a silver age forced him, reluctantly, to work. He acknowledged it as the irresistible outcome of 'political evolution', and recognised that 'the

[1] *Ibid.* pp. 268, 289–305.   [2] *Q.R.*, cviii (1860), 568–605.
[3] Cornford, 'Parliamentary Foundations', p. 309. Another Conservative M.P. raised the question of the number of the prime minister's relations in the government of 1900 in the House of Commons (B. E. C. Dugdale, *Arthur James Balfour*, i (1936), 314–15).
[4] Cecil, *Salisbury*, i, 296–7; *Biographical Studies*, p. 24. Lady Gwendolen ascribes her father's success with mass audiences mainly to his 'innate fidelity to type as an Englishman; – an unconscious participation in the mentality, the sympathies, the points-of-view, – it may be the prejudices – which were his common inheritance with the race of men whom he was addressing' (*Salisbury*, iii, 64), He was regarded, however, perhaps with more respect than affection, and it may be significant that, unlike Disraeli and Gladstone, he never acquired a popular nickname.

numerical majority, when it chooses to assert itself, is in effect the living power of our particular time'.[1] But he did not soften towards it, and his refusal to exploit the opportunities which it offered him of popular acclaim[2] cannot be put down entirely to shyness or to his temperamental disinclination to enjoy his own success. It seemed to him to intensify the drawbacks inherent in representative government in general, which became increasingly irksome to him as he grew accustomed to the taste of ministerial office. He was by nature an autocrat, disliking the processes of consultation and compromise necessitated by a parliamentary system. He much preferred the direct exercise of administrative power to parliamentary politics,[3] and believed in a vigorous executive arm, which should not be unduly trammelled by the exigencies of political manœuvre. The whole tendency of representative government was to frustrate him. Democracy made it worse.

It was Salisbury's frequent complaint, especially as prime minister, that the power ostensibly attaching to office was a sham. He told a friend in 1884:

to those who know English politics well, they are not attractive, – their highest rewards confer no real power. Their strongest men – you give me an instance in Mr. Gladstone and the Three F's – have to carry out ideas that are not their own. And they fill up life with an incessant labour which to those who are not blessed with optimism leaves behind it the feeling of an almost unmingled waste of time.[4]

The limitations which fretted him were in part those experienced by statesmen in any form of government. But they were also in part, he felt, those stemming peculiarly from the arrangements of British parliamentary democracy. His personal irritation was subsumed under a general concern about the effect of the subordination of executive to legislature, tolerable in the political context in which it had originally emerged, but producing, under the very different conditions of democracy, a dangerous weakness of government.

Perhaps his most interesting pronouncement on this theme came in January 1871, when he discussed in the *Quarterly* the political lessons of the Franco-Prussian war. War, 'the great test of institutions', seemed to him to have demonstrated the superiority of the Prussian to the French political system, and caused him to wonder how well the English

[1] *Q.R.*, clvi (1883), 570.
[2] E.g., in his 1884 campaign. Cecil, *Salisbury*, iii, 115-16.
[3] *Ibid.* iii. 200-1.
[4] Salisbury to Canon MacColl, 11 July 1884: *ibid.* iii, 111. Cf. *ibid.* iii, 165-6, 313-14.

constitution would stand a similar trial. He was clearly much impressed by the strength and consistency of policy displayed by the Prussian government. He spoke admiringly of the brushing aside of parliamentary opposition, and of the position enjoyed by King Wilhelm, as compared to that of the French emperor:

> He was not forced to submit to the caprice of a season, or the enthusiasm of a passing cry. He was bound to obey the people, by the unwritten but inexorable law which binds every sovereign to heed the will of an instructed nation: but he owed no such implicit obedience either to the mobs of great towns who might affect to speak in the people's name, or to the politicians to whom, under the theory of representation, the people had nominally delegated their authority. The unbroken power of his House enabled him to say that neither the agitations of a capital nor the votes of an assembly should prevent him from submitting his policy, tried and developed by experience, to the judgement of his people. He has been fully justified at the bar to which he appealed.[1]

Very different was the situation in England. Dilating upon the obstacles posed by the system of parliamentary government to an adequate policy of national defence, Salisbury was drawn into far-reaching criticisms:

> It is our political machinery which fails. Unrivalled as an instrument for enfeebling the arm of Government, and therefore hindering an excess of executive interference, it has prevented the oppressions into which the zeal of Continental bureaus constantly betrays them. It satisfies the most imperious want of a free people, which is to be let alone. It is not ineffective for purposes of mere destruction, especially when it is driven by the forces of sectarian animosity. But in matters where it is necessary that Government should govern and create, it lamentably breaks down. All the virtues that are attributed to it – in many respects justly – for the concerns of peace, make it helpless for the purposes of war.[2]

The trouble was that in England the ruling power, the cabinet, had no security of tenure to provide the basis for firm and steady policy. It was completely at the mercy of the House of Commons, without even 'the six months' notice accorded to the poorest tenant-at-will'. The decisions of the Commons were affected by hopes of office, and too much determined by the floating vote of special interest groups, to

---

[1] *Q.R.*, cxxx (1871), 267-9. It should not be thought, however, that Salisbury was an admirer of Prussia in general. He criticised her aggressive tendencies, and thought her conduct in the war had shown that 'if you scratch the cultivated German Professor, you will find the nature which made the lanzknecht of the middle ages, or the "marauders" of the Thirty Years' War' (*ibid.* cxxix (1870), 545-6; cxxx (1871), 270).

[2] *Ibid.* cxxx (1871), 274-5.

EDITOR'S INTRODUCTION

whose susceptibilities excessive attention had to be paid. Weak government was the necessary outcome:

the result of our system is that the Minister in England, like the Emperor in France, is too apt to live from hand to mouth. He eschews large, well-organised plans; knowing that if he proposed them they would be mutilated by the pressure of Parliamentary supporters before they could be adopted, and that if they escaped that fate they would be pared down to nothing in two or three years by the reductions of the Chancellor of the Exchequer. He is content to let alone what he can, and only touch what is forced upon him; as far as possible to break up no established routine, to frighten no vested interest, to spend nothing this year that can be deferred to another. He is obsequious to the House of Commons which can displace him: he shows little thought for the future of a department in which he has so precarious an interest.[1]

The control of executive government by the legislature, Salisbury thought, had been more formal than real under the old political system, when royal and aristocratic influence had a considerable grip on the House of Commons and a strong minister could hope to carry through his policies secure from sudden parliamentary tides.[2] It was another matter now that democracy had become the dominant political force and the legislature was ultimately accountable to popular feeling. A minister had become, on major issues, merely a servant of 'the popular power', his 'not to command, but to obey':

If he accepts and retains what is called power, under the delusion that he can serve the people and yet retain a will of his own, the result will surely be that he will find himself, toiling, arguing, intriguing, entreating, to pass the very measures which it has been his most earnest aspiration from his youth upward to resist.[3]

For the political capacity of 'the great democracy we all have to obey', with its 'ill-informed and unbridled impulses',[4] Salisbury had the deepest contempt. No wise and stable policy could be founded on a mass opinion remarkable most of the time for its political apathy, but subject to unpredictable spasms of misguided excitement.

No part comes out more strongly in the history of this century all over Christendom [Salisbury told Lord Lytton in 1876] than the political lifelessness of the

[1] *Ibid.* cxxx (1871), 275–8.
[2] *Ibid.* cxxxiii (1872), 578–9; clvi (1883), 566–8.
[3] *Ibid.* cxxxiii (1872), 579. He could not even escape by resignation, for he was obliged to cling to office in order to satisfy his followers' expectations of places and honours, the purchase of political support being 'as much an essential part of free Government as terror is an essential part of absolute Government'.
[4] Salisbury to Lytton, 2 Nov. 1877 (typescript copy): Salisbury Papers, vol. 'Lytton II', p. 538.

CONSERVATISM AND DEMOCRACY

'masses' - and that, under the strongest stimulants democratic arrangements can supply. They wake up for a moment from time to time, when you least look for it - roused by some panic, or wounded sentiment, or some sharp suffering which they lay to the door of the wrong person and the wrong law. But for the most part they are politically asleep: and must never be counted upon to resist their real enemies, or sustain their real friends, at the right moment.[1]

Undoubtedly, one of the attractions for Salisbury of foreign policy was that in that sphere his action could be to a large extent, and over long periods, independent of considerations of popular feeling.

His concern about the effect on government of the combination of parliamentary supremacy with a democratic franchise had the ironic result of leading Salisbury to parade the merits of the American institutions which he had castigated in the sixties. America showed that freedom could be reconciled with executive vigour and consistent policy.[2] In her constitution, the dangers of democratic control were curbed. The House of Representatives lacked the unrestricted power of the House of Commons, Salisbury argued, and American ministers, having far greater security of tenure than their English counterparts, were less open to pressure. Moreover, the authority of the Senate, the presidential veto, and above all the written constitution provided safeguards against hasty and 'violent' legislation.[3] But Salisbury did not suppose that the American system could be introduced into England, and without its device of fundamental laws, alterable only by special machinery, there was danger in trying to strengthen a democratically controlled government. 'With us', he reminded Balfour, who had quoted to him a complaint of Chamberlain about the excessive subordination of executive to legislature, 'the feebleness of our government is our security - the only one we have, - against revolutionary alterations of our laws.'[4]

But worse even than the tendency of democracy to impair the independence and efficiency of government was its seeming inability to bind the nation together in a common sentiment and purpose. In his last, and most remarkable, article for the *Quarterly*, in October 1883, Salisbury

---

[1] Salisbury to Lytton, 9 June 1876 (typescript copy): *ibid.* vol. 'Lytton I', pp. 91-2. Salisbury's letters to Lytton in the late seventies are full of remarks illustrating his scorn for mass opinion.
[2] *Q.R.*, cxxx (1871), 275.   [3] *Ibid.* clvi (1883), 568-70.
[4] Salisbury to Balfour, 29 March 1886, in Cecil, *Salisbury*, iii, 297. Cf. 'Constitutional Revision', *National Review*, xx (1892), 289-300, where Salisbury contrasted the checks on constitutional amendment in democratic countries abroad with the situation in England, where only the action of the House of Lords could ensure that the opinion of the nation was properly consulted.

stridently proclaimed the menace of national 'disintegration', the break-up of the Empire and the 'slow estrangement' of classes, due to a decline of patriotic feeling, and to a growing class conflict, stimulated by Radical extremists whose aims ran to 'the equality not only of conditions but of possessions, and the extermination of religious dogma'. What was required in this situation was the impartial arbitration between clashing interests that formed the essence of civilised government. The task of providing it, inherited by assemblies from kings, was not, however, one which the House of Commons was any longer capable of fulfilling. With the widening of the franchise and the growth of its power, the House had itself become 'the very field of battle on which the contending classes fight out their feuds', and settlement by arbitration had given way to settlement by civil war – 'only it is civil war with gloves on'. The only possible arbiter between classes in a modern state was 'the judgment – the cool and deliberate judgment – of the generality of the nation', but it was doubtful how far the Commons embodied it. Democracy attended to public affairs only 'partially and fitfully': most of the time its authority rested in the hands of representatives, and, Salisbury pointed out, the theory of representation rested on a set of completely fictitious assumptions. What was derived from the representative system was not, necessarily, the voice of the people, but 'the utterances of men whose right to speak on their behalf is purely conventional'. The vital interests of the country were committed to the mercy of an assembly whose decisions were too much influenced by impulse and by the struggle for party advantage, and which accordingly risked forfeiting 'the confidence of large classes of the community'.[1]

The whole article could be read as an attack on the British system of representative government, at least as it operated under a 'democratic' franchise, and coming from the joint leader of the Conservative party it was a startling production. The suggestion it conveyed that there was a 'real' national opinion or will external to the workings of the parliamentary system and becoming impatient of them had far-reaching implications. There is no reason to think that Salisbury wished to follow them out. He was doing two things (besides whipping up Conservative zeal against Radicalism and claiming for his party the 'national' cause). First, he was repining at what appeared to him as the dominant influence over the political system of the poorer classes. A legislature controlled by a limited class of property-owners was readily acceptable; one ultimately responsible to the enlarged post-1867 electorate was not, and Salisbury

[1] Q.R., clvi (1883), 562–73.

could not bring himself to allow its acts the status of national decisions. True, he said that constitutionalists need not deplore the passing of power into the hands of the masses, since there was nothing to show that it was incompatible with the government of England on 'sober principles', respecting the rights of all.[1] This was a very different song from the one he had sung twenty years earlier, but it is hard to regard it as much more than a hasty genuflection to 'the living power of our particular time'. Salisbury saw very little security for 'sober principles' under democracy, though the electorate's tendency to return him to power would eventually go far to set his mind at rest. Secondly, in his final article, he was expressing his sense of the practical defects of representative government and parliamentary institutions – in particular, the distortion and injustice introduced into the treatment of national affairs by the exigencies of party struggle. His criticism was sharpened by his personal distaste for many features of the political framework within which he had to operate. He did not really like the apparatus of elections, parties, and debates: rather than a minister responsible to an assembly, he would have preferred to be the trusted servant of a powerful monarch, free from the necessity of persuading, conciliating, cajoling, and circumventing opinion, conducting a serene and stable administration high above the sordid clash of faction. It was an ideal and outmoded concept, derived from his picture of the previous century, and impossible to implement under parliamentary democracy, as he well knew. But he was not rejecting parliamentary democracy, or dreaming of overthrowing it. He was simply grumbling at it, relieving feelings that he had no intention or means to express in any other way. The bark was intimidating; but there would be no bite. Democracy was to be endured.

It is in their illustration of a particular mode of Conservative response to the advent of democracy that the main interest of Salisbury's *Quarterly* articles lies. They are not important as political theory. They were not meant to be political theory; and their generalised remarks on politics do not amount to, or stem from, a systematic body of doctrine. They are, however, important for the insight they give into the mind of a major British statesman, for their embodiment of some typical – and some untypical – features of conservative thinking in general and of British nineteenth-century Conservatism in particular, and for their often incisive analysis of the politics of the day. One can hardly add 'for their impact on contemporary politics': despite the attention they

[1] *Ibid.* clvi (1883), 570.

often commanded, they do not seem to have had much practical effect. What they show us is an aristocrat of great family, highly-strung temperament, and unusually intellectual bent, confronting a period of profound and rapid socio-political change, in which the order of things that placed him where he was and the set of beliefs and values that underpinned his at first precarious stability seemed to be in real and immediate danger. His reaction was a complex mixture of instinctive emotional hostility, pessimistic resignation, and careful rational analysis and polemic.

It is the analysis that is most interesting. Though Salisbury might feel threatened by the trend of events, he did not feel bewildered. He viewed what was happening in a broad historical and European perspective, and made sense of it by reference to a schematic interpretation of history based on a predominantly materialistic model of human motivation and on the idea of struggle for economic and social advantage between classes as the driving force of modern politics. This interpretation was crude and imprecisely formulated, but it brought out very clearly some of the major structural features of the politics of his day, and enabled him to see more quickly than most the rise of new antagonisms and issues that must eventually force a revision of party alignments determined by the old. He grasped that British politics were in a more than ordinarily transitional stage – that the clash of parties deriving their composition and ideology from the past was a surface froth, obscuring the emergence of a fundamental challenge to the rule of rank, property, and education by the forces of democracy. The precise nature and strength of that challenge he did not gauge very finely, because he did not know enough about those who embodied it: he had little interest in human personality and none in trying to understand others' points of view, and tended for polemical purposes – perhaps even in his private thinking – to compress the variety of men and ideas which he opposed into a few crude categories suitable for undiscriminating abuse. But however imperfect his picture of the political scene, it was clear-cut: it showed him his enemies and what he must do.

He instinctively feared and disliked a great deal of what he saw in the movement of his times. He found himself fundamentally opposed to some of the most vital and expansive forces of the age – radicalism, democracy, socialism, even nationalism. If he was not a romantic *laudator temporis acti*, he nevertheless measured, and in large part reproved, the present by the standards of a somewhat idealised past, when royal, aristocratic, and propertied rule stood secure from popular interference,

CONSERVATISM AND DEMOCRACY

and strong ministers could concern themselves with administration rather than legislation and with a diplomacy untroubled by considerations of national self-determination and mass opinion. It would be unfair simply to classify him as a man of the *ancien régime*, but he was certainly in recoil from most of the consequences of the French Revolution. That archetypal attack (as he saw it) on order, liberty, justice, and property was the great modern exemplar and source of the evils which he resisted. He never forgot how much of what he hated came from France. 'Whatever else Bismarck does', he wrote during the German siege of Paris in 1870, 'I do hope he will burn down the Faubourg St. Antoine and crush out the Paris mob. Their freaks and madnesses have been a curse to Europe for the last eighty years.'[1] The example of the American Revolution, or at any rate of the democratic state to which it had given rise, was almost as pernicious. But his attitude to democracy in America was softened a little when he came to believe that it had taken an institutional form which safeguarded it from the dangers inherent in the application of democracy to the existing constitution of England. The English system of representative, parliamentary government was uncongenial to him anyway; placed under democratic control, it threatened to be almost intolerable. He resisted its invasion by democracy as long as he could: when the worst happened, only the democratic willingness to return Conservative governments moderated his dislike of the conditions in which his political life must be lived.

Despite his careful deployment of a weight of empirical and utilitarian argument, the real force of Salisbury's resistance to his political and ideological enemies stemmed from deep emotion. He felt himself personally menaced by them, and attacked them with all the violence and vehemence of outraged self-defence. Even when maturity and success overlaid the acute tensions of his young manhood, it remained a fight to the finish, not a sporting contest, in which he and they were engaged, and he behaved towards them accordingly.[2] Yet there was an ambivalence about his relationship with them. However keenly he might seek their destruction, he was, in a sense, dependent on them. Since he conspicuously lacked creative impulse, since his intellect, though sharp, was sterile, his political drive had to come by antagonism; he had to suck strength from his adversaries. His political persona was largely a function of his fears and antipathies. He existed as a politician and controversialist in virtue

---
[1] Salisbury to G. M. W. Sandford, 26 Oct. 1870 (typescript copy): Salisbury Papers, vol. 'Paget to Smith', p. 67.
[2] Cecil, *Salisbury*, iii, 301; *Biographical Studies*, p. 41.

of what he opposed, and, indeed, recognised the fact: 'I rank myself no higher in the scheme of things than a policeman – whose utility would disappear if there were no criminals.'[1] His success, and that of his cause, depended on the repellent properties of his opponents – hence his own comment that 'Mr. Gladstone's existence was the greatest source of strength which the Conservative party possessed'.[2] He worked essentially by reaction.

He was not, however, in the ordinary political sense of the term, a reactionary. He had a strong enough sense of history to know that it could not be put into reverse. What he fought for was always the maintenance of an existing order, never the restoration of an old, and even the existing order, he realised, must disintegrate in time. Change could not be stopped: all a conservative could do was to moderate and delay such of it as he found repugnant, and, when it had happened, to assimilate it as far as possible. 'So long as the great institutions which are essential to our form of Government are preserved', Salisbury wrote, 'Conservatives are bound by their own principles to uphold as laws, alterations which, as projects, they opposed.'[3] Conservatism for him was not a counter-attack on the opponents of religion, property, and the social order, but a fighting retreat, stubborn and slow, involving constant rearguard actions and continual regrouping, and interspersed with brief periods of rest based on a precarious equilibrium. That this meant the progressive concession of ground was a fact to which his natural pessimism helped him to resign himself. In the short run, he always hoped and tried to win; in the long run, he knew he must lose. The game was to lose slowly and to lose hard.

His tactics in the conduct of battle were not faultless. His equipment as a politician was far from complete. Indeed, in some ways, he was hardly a politician at all: his dislike to having to manage and manipulate men forced him to rely too much on the mere power of argument and example, which was why he proved politically ineffective in the crisis of 1866–7. He fought best and most easily on paper, and even there he had conspicuous weaknesses. The tone of his writings was not such as to make converts. Their aim was too often to sustain, or create, tensions, to exacerbate fears, and to inflame feelings, on the assumption that political calm had a dangerous tendency to corrode the vigilance and energy of the conservative classes, and that the way to get moderates into the conservative ranks was to frighten them there. The result was

[1] *Ibid.* p. 84 (also quoted, with different wording, in *Salisbury*, iii, 167).
[2] Cecil, *Biographical Studies*, p. 84.   [3] *Q.R.*, cxiii (1863), 261.

CONSERVATISM AND DEMOCRACY

a degree of exaggeration and vituperation which some found repellent, and an over-indulgence in eschatological prose – the end of the world figured too frequently as a coming event. Salisbury's range of human and intellectual sympathies was revealed as dangerously contracted for a man who aspired to the confidence of his countrymen. '"A clever, able man but too bitter of speech and narrow of heart and views" I hear people say': thus a friendly correspondent warned him, in March 1867.[1]

It was his class consciousness that was most obtrusive. His whole political analysis and prescription, and evidently much of his political feeling, rested on his awareness of class conflict. It was the demiurge, the imperfectly realised idea, of his political universe. He was so attached to it as the great explanatory and organising principle in politics that he was anxious that the actual lines of party division should more closely reflect it. There was in Salisbury a touch of the doctrinaire mentality which he so contemptuously lampooned in others. He wanted reality to conform to the terms of his understanding of it. The forces of property and indigence, being arrayed against each other in his political schema, must be organised as opposing blocs in fact. This stress on the politics of class antagonism had potential dangers for the Conservative party. To begin with, the grouping of forces which it led Salisbury to pursue was, at least up to 1874, one in which the party might well have found its old identity and its old leadership submerged – an eventuality he was quite prepared to contemplate, and would perhaps have welcomed. Then, it was one thing to proclaim the fundamental importance of class conflict in the pre-1867 era, when the classes which that principle of division promised to rally to the conservative side still had a heavy electoral predominance. It was quite another after 1867, and still more after 1884, when those whom Salisbury's analysis designated the enemy had substantial power. Tactically, as Disraeli, for example, saw perfectly well, Salisbury's harping on class antagonism was a serious liability to the Conservative party after 1867: it could tend only to produce an arrangement of forces which would place the party in permanent antagonism to the most numerous section of the electorate. The need was rather to associate the party with some sentiment which transcended class divisions, and the answer was to appropriate the national cry, and to assert the Conservatives' claim to be the patriotic party, standing for the community of interest of all classes in economic security, social harmony and stability, and external prestige. Salisbury

[1] Henry Cecil to Cranborne, 7 March 1867: Salisbury Papers, Special Correspondence.

EDITOR'S INTRODUCTION

took the point, as his pronouncements showed. But his attachment to class conflict as an organising principle persisted, and it was perhaps fortunate for his party that the themes of Ireland and imperialism swelled to overlay that of class in British politics. If Joseph Chamberlain had succeeded in the early eighties in capturing the Liberal party for his Radical programme, Salisbury might have got something approaching the overt politics of class which he had so long been heralding, and how, in such a juncture, the Conservative party would have fared, under a leader of his provocative outlook and record, is an interesting speculation. Far from being the most successful of Conservative leaders, Salisbury might have turned out one of the most disastrous.

For him, of course, the success of the Conservative party was not the prime concern. What he cared about most was the maintenance of conservative principles and the success of the conservative cause, objects which the victory of the party did not necessarily much advance and might, in certain circumstances, damage, as 1867, in his view, showed. He did not like party much: he had the eighteenth-century preoccupation with carrying on the sovereign's government and the eighteenth-century disdain for the selfish manœuvres of faction (together with a certain capacity for indulgence in them at times).[1] His attitude to party was not unlike Peel's, except that he felt an absolute obligation to keep faith with his followers. He saw the Conservative party as an instrument, not as an object of loyalty or affection in itself. Under Derby and Disraeli he found it an organisation that in the end existed more to achieve corporate victory than to guarantee any interest or vindicate any principle. He never loved it, and it never loved him. It is doubtful how much he contributed to its electoral success. The triumphs won under his leadership reflected trends and circumstances with which he had little to do, though his personal reputation for integrity, wisdom, and knack in foreign policy certainly helped. There is no element in the party's personality, no article of its creed or item of its policy, no turn of its thinking that can be said to have originated with him. He represented – if somewhat more in overt posture than in practical action – an adamant, resistant strain of Conservatism, fundamental in the party's make-up, and powerful in gathering defensive interests around it, but hardly conducive to attracting the moderate centre or the working classes, and

[1] An example of the kind of ardent partisanship of which he was capable is furnished by his conduct in the crisis over franchise reform in 1884, when compromise with the government was virtually forced on him by the efforts of the Queen and his colleagues. C. C. Weston, 'The Royal Mediation in 1884', *English Historical Review*, lxxxii (1967), 296–322.

CONSERVATISM AND DEMOCRACY

one, therefore, whose expression has had to be softened and counterpoised, and whose instincts have often had to be frustrated, for the sake of the party's successful adaptation in the modern era.

Yet his influence on the party and its development was not altogether negligible. He reminded it that it was in the end in conservatism that its basic appeal and strength lay, not in flirting with alien ideas for temporary advantage, though he did not guard enough against the danger that its stance might come to seem too much opposed to moderate progress. He set a tone of adherence to principle that combined usefully with the Disraelian tradition of suppleness and manœuvre. And he set also a tone of rationality which seemed to show that Conservatism could equally well be founded on a logical and informed examination of political issues as on a mystical and reverential attachment to established order, a selfish defence of vested interests, a stupid inertia, or an emotional terror of change. In many ways out of time in the world which he inhabited, he was nonetheless in tune with some of its most powerful intellectual currents in his bent for scientific method and his utilitarianism, both of which he tried to import into his political thinking. Though the fundamental content of his beliefs was not unusual for a Conservative, his style of expounding and justifying them was, and did something to establish that a Conservative outlook could be sustained and expressed in a modern idiom. He resisted modernity with its own weapons: not an insignificant contribution to the intellectual respectability and vigour of English Conservative thought as it confronted the age of democracy.

Bibliographical Note

There is little serious modern writing on any aspect of Salisbury (except his foreign policy, which is not in question here). The standard biography remains that of his daughter, Lady Gwendolen Cecil, *Life of Robert Marquis of Salisbury* (4 vols.; 1921-32), which reaches only to 1892, and is to be supplemented by the same author's *Biographical Studies of the Life and Political Character of Robert Third Marquis of Salisbury* (privately printed; n.d.). A much shorter work is A. L. Kennedy, *Salisbury, 1830-1903* (1953). Salisbury's ideas are the subject of M. Pinto-Duschinsky, *The Political Thought of Lord Salisbury 1854-68* (1967), which contains a very useful annotated list of his published writings and early speeches. His role in the Reform drama of the sixties can best be followed in M. Cowling, *1867: Disraeli, Gladstone and Revolution* (1967), and F. B. Smith, *The Making of the Second Reform Bill* (1966). On the Conservative party in his day, there are R. Blake, *The Conservative Party from Peel to Churchill* (1970), for a general sketch, and, for more specific aspects, E. J. Feuchtwanger, *Disraeli, Democracy and the Tory Party* (1968), P. Smith, *Disraelian Conservatism and Social Reform* (1967), and two valuable contributions by J. P. Cornford, 'The Transformation of Conservatism in the Late Nineteenth Century', *Victorian Studies*, vii (1963-4), 35-66, and 'The Parliamentary Foundations of the Hotel Cecil', in *Ideas and Institutions of Victorian Britain*, ed. R. Robson (1967), pp. 268-311.

'The Budget and the Reform Bill' (Q.R., no. 214; April 1860)

INTRODUCTORY NOTE

LORD ROBERT CECIL'S first *Quarterly* article establishes at once his major preoccupations: with the threat posed by the development of the class struggle and the advance of 'democracy', with the corrosive effects of the financial tenets and idealistic pacifism of the Manchester school upon the nation's capacity to maintain its international position, and with the failure of the Conservative party under Derby and Disraeli adequately to uphold Conservative principles. It centres upon the chief domestic political topics of the spring of 1860, Gladstone's budget and Lord John Russell's Reform Bill, with a side glance at the menace supposedly offered to Britain by the designs of the emperor Napoleon III.

Lord Palmerston had become prime minister in June 1859, after the ejection of Derby's second ministry by that Whig–Liberal–Peelite–Radical amalgam that was ultimately to produce the Gladstonian Liberal party. The action of the Peelites, six of whom, Gladstone, Sidney Herbert, Cardwell, Newcastle, Argyll, and Elgin, entered Palmerston's cabinet, finally destroyed the long-cherished hope of bringing them back to the Conservative fold, and dealt a severe blow to the prospects for Conservative revival, though the Conservative party in the Commons, about 300 strong after the 1859 general election, remained a substantial force. The new government quickly revealed strains: the cabinet was divided on a variety of issues, including finance, parliamentary reform, defence, and foreign policy. Especially sharp was the disagreement over the needs of national defence, Gladstone, the chancellor of the exchequer, finding his plans for fiscal reform threatened by the expenditures demanded to meet what was seen as the danger from France.

'L'empire c'est la paix', Louis Napoleon had declared in 1852, but the fears of European statesmen that the name he bore and the internal necessities of his régime would eventually drive him to emulate the exploits of his uncle and overturn the settlement of 1815 seemed justified when, in 1859, he plunged into Italy in support of the cause of her liberation from Austria, and by defeating the Austrians at Magenta and Solferino made possible the emergence of an independent Italian state under the leadership of Piedmont. They seemed still more justified in March 1860, when he announced, as the price of France's aid, the annexation (subject to plebiscite) of Savoy and Nice, with its implications of reversion to the revolutionary policy of natural frontiers. Napoleon wanted Britain's friendship, and had been her ally in the Crimea, and Palmerston's ministry, unlike its Conservative predecessor, sympathised with Italian national aspirations. But there was deep-rooted suspicion of French intentions, and the events of 1859–60 produced a war scare in Britain. Bright and the pacifist Radicals did their best to combat it, denouncing war as fatal to liberty, democracy, and working-class interests, but with small success. Already heavy naval expenditure was being undertaken to keep pace with the French; now came the volunteer movement and a proposal by a royal commission on national defence for the spending of £11 million on coastal fortifications against a possible invasion. Gladstone, rightly sceptical of the likelihood of war, came into conflict with the more martial members of the cabinet (including Palmerston), as he sought to restrain defence spending.

Yet despite the demands of defence, Gladstone was able to continue with his mission of fiscal reform. It was even possible to associate economic liberalism with the appeasing of Anglo-French tensions. The commercial treaty with France signed on 23 January 1860 was negotiated by Cobden, with Gladstone's and Bright's backing, largely as a means of improving relations between the two countries – a classic instance of the Manchester school's faith in the eirenic properties of international trade. France's rigid protectionism was so far moderated as to allow in the staple British manufactures at a maximum duty of 30%, reducing within three years to 25%, while Britain abolished the remaining protective import duties on manufactured goods and greatly reduced the duty on wine and brandy. The agreement had its critics on both sides of the Channel, especially in France, where it was strongly opposed by many of the industrial bourgeoisie, notably in the textile and iron trades, but it led to a rapid expansion of Anglo-French commerce.

The fiscal changes necessitated by the treaty were embodied in the budget which Gladstone introduced on 10 February 1860. This was the culmination of his work for free trade, following in the steps of Peel and of his own budget of 1853. Repealing the duties on 259, and reducing those on 56, of the 397 articles remaining in the tariff, he completed the reform begun in 1842. Import duties were removed from manufactures of various kinds, including 'fancy' goods, and from foodstuffs, candles, soap, glass, and tallow. But all these remissions, at least in the short term, cost money, and, faced with increased expenditure for defence and for the expedition which had just been despatched against the Chinese, Gladstone was hard pressed to find the revenue necessary to produce his anticipated surplus of nearly half a million. There was no chance of his fulfilling the hopes he had raised in 1853, when he had looked forward to the abandonment of the income tax at the end of seven years. The tax, which he had raised from 5d to 9d in 1859, now went up to 10d. The extra penny was a counterbalance to the repeal of the paper duty, which proved one of the most controversial of Gladstone's proposals, Palmerston openly opposing it and encouraging its eventual rejection by the Lords (it was re-introduced and passed in 1861).

After Gladstone's instalment of fiscal reform came Russell's attempt at parliamentary reform. Having abandoned, in 1851, the idea of the 'finality'

'THE BUDGET AND THE REFORM BILL'

of the 1832 Reform Act, Russell had become the leading purveyor of Reform, which helped to secure him Radical support in his duel with Palmerston, and had introduced bills in 1852 and 1854. Aside from the Radicals and 'advanced' Liberals, deriving their strength largely from the manufacturing and commercial bourgeoisie of the north and midlands, there was little parliamentary support for Reform; nor did it rouse the country, as Bright discovered in 1858-9, when in a campaign of powerful speeches he tried to whip up a popular movement for the franchise extension and redistribution of seats which were to him the vital means to break down the political and social system of the aristocratic and landed classes. Reform was a counter in the political game, rather than a real national issue. Nonetheless, it had sufficient importance for Derby's ministry to try to deal with it in 1859. The Conservative party had no desire for Reform, but Derby and Disraeli knew better than to allow their opponents a monopoly of the question, and could hardly ignore the advantages of adjusting the electoral system to their benefit before the Whigs adjusted it to their detriment. The Reform Bill of 1859 left the £10 borough qualification unaltered (a reduction being thought likely to harm the Conservatives), but made a bid to strengthen the Conservative grip in the counties by reducing the county occupation franchise from £50 to £10, while removing from the county electorate a large element of borough freeholders, and providing for a boundary commission whose task would have been to excise urban and suburban areas from county constituencies. Its failure to lower the borough level or to provide for a substantial redistribution of seats, and its party bias, ensured its defeat. Russell took the lead in destroying it, and once in office attempted for the third time to settle the question himself, despite the reluctance of some of his colleagues, including the prime minister.

The Reform Bill which he introduced on 1 March 1860 embodied a £6 rental qualification in the boroughs and a £10 occupation franchise in the counties. Its redistribution scheme was slight: twenty-five small two-member boroughs were to lose one member each, and with the seats thus gained three new boroughs (Birkenhead, Burnley, and Stalybridge) were to have a member each, Birmingham, Leeds, Liverpool, and Manchester were to have three members each instead of two, Chelsea and Kensington were to form a borough returning two members, the West Riding of York was to have four members instead of two, thirteen other county constituencies were to have three members instead of two, and London University was to have a member. Given the paucity of exact statistics on the existing and potential electorates, it was difficult to gauge precisely what the bill meant. But it was apparent that in the larger towns, at least, where rents were relatively high, a £6 rental franchise would be tantamount to household suffrage; while in the counties, the £10 occupation franchise, not counterbalanced by any provisions for boundary revision and the exclusion of borough freeholders, would tend to increase the urban and suburban element in the county electorate. Neither prospect pleased Conservatives. The bill, indeed, pleased hardly anyone, and met with resounding parliamentary and public apathy. In June it was dropped.

SALISBURY'S 'QUARTERLY REVIEW' ARTICLES

This was the background to Lord Robert's article, and he found it far from heartening. While, as the political commentator of a Tory review, he was often guilty of straining after the partisan point, his criticisms of the budget and the Reform Bill reflected a real apprehension about the trends they seemed to signal. 'Manchester' finance, he felt, was not only of dubious soundness; in conjunction with naive pacifism it was placing the country in a state of weakness which was particularly dangerous when combined with Palmerstonian bluster, and it looked to a redistribution of taxation which, under the democracy hastened into being by Reform, would be the great engine for the spoliation of property – especially landed property – by the lower orders. The most galling thing was the failure of the Conservative party to provide a bulwark against these perils. The culmination of Lord Robert's article is a biting exposition of the right-wing Tory criticism of the policy allegedly pursued by the Conservative leaders, accusing them, with considerable exaggeration, of being themselves largely responsible for the furtherance of Radical aims, by engaging, for the mere sake of office, in a competition with the Whigs for Radical support. Lord Robert had no doubt that the author of this policy was Disraeli, and in his review of the latter's actions he displayed the talent for wounding abuse that was to be so prominent in his polemical career.

The venom of the attack on Disraeli, as in the article for *Bentley's Quarterly Review* nine months earlier, no doubt owed something to its author's feeling that if he was to make money from journalism he must strike a tone which would attract attention. Certainly it ensured the notoriety of his article and provoked some shocked reactions.[1] The party press was indignant, *The Times* reproving, and when Russell referred in debate to the suggestion of 'this obscure writer' that Disraeli no longer had the confidence of the Conservative party, there were cries of dissent from the opposition benches. Lord Robert's father renewed his complaints of the previous year about anonymous attacks on the party leader, threatening to stop paying his son's election expenses, and Lord Exeter also remonstrated. The least concerned of those involved was Disraeli himself, if we may trust the anecdote reported by Lady Gwendolen Cecil of his effusive greeting of his young assailant on a chance encounter at Hatfield. Lord Robert recanted nothing. He insisted that he had 'merely put into print what all the country gentlemen were saying in private', and replied vigorously to his critics in the *Quarterly*'s July number. There was some truth in the argument that he had expressed the tacit feeling of the back benches. Disraeli's popularity in the party was low enough to lead him to make one of his token gestures towards resignation in June. Perhaps Lord Robert's article was a factor in inducing in his leader that reversion to sound Conservative courses which the July *Quarterly* noted with satisfaction; but certainly more powerful was Disraeli's reluctant realisation that in the shadow of Palmerston's ascendancy there was little the Conservative party could do but wait and hope.

[1] For the reception of the article, see Cecil, *Salisbury*, i, 91-7.

'THE BUDGET AND THE REFORM BILL'

Practical Results of the Reform Act of 1832. By Sir John Walsh, Bart. London, 1860.

It is a favourite observation that the halcyon days of parliamentary eloquence are gone by, and that speeches have lost their power of influencing a division. The popular belief is, that the most splendid oratory falls in vain upon minds not only prejudiced but pledged against persuasion, and that, therefore, debates are a vain waste of words. Like many of our self-criticisms, this is more than half delusion. This generation is very fond of telling itself, with a sort of cynical complacency, that its feelings are all dead, and that a material stoicism, not free from selfishness, but wholly devoid of nobler emotions, is the mainspring of its acts. If one were to judge from the current language, one would imagine that the nineteenth century was the absolute essence of prose – that its atmosphere was a sort of moral azote, in which neither romance, nor poetry, nor enthusiasm can live. And yet it is an age in which, for the sake of the shadowy sentiment of nationality, Europe forgets the solid blessings of peace – in which band after band of heroes is found to brave the perils of Arctic exploration, merely that they may give expression to a chivalrous sympathy[1] – in which the greatest financier of the day spends his rare and scanty leisure in maintaining against all comers the spotless purity of Homer's Helen.[2] It is not a bit more true that oratory has lost its spell even over the indurated heart of a Member of Parliament. If speakers of very considerable note often fail of any appreciable effect upon their audience, an abundant explanation of the fact may be found in the quality of the speeches which will now-a-days justify the newspapers in conferring the title of 'eminent debater.' The success of the present Budget supplies an ample proof that when a real orator appears there is no reason to complain that his genius is thrown away. There is more reason for complaining that unassisted common sense has very little chance against it. Well might Sir Francis Baring[3] be amazed and terrified at the aquiescence with which so daring a project was received. He well knew that if he had ever ventured upon half Mr. Gladstone's temerity he would have been hooted down by his own junior Lords of the Treasury.

---

[1] A reference to the successive attempts, culminating in 1859, to ascertain the fate of Sir John Franklin's expedition, which had set out in search of the north-west passage in 1845.
[2] Gladstone had stoutly defended Helen's character in the third volume of his *Studies on Homer and the Homeric Age* (Oxford, 1858).
[3] Sir Francis Thornhill Baring (1796–1866), M.P. Portsmouth, a former chancellor of the exchequer (1839–41).

SALISBURY'S 'QUARTERLY REVIEW' ARTICLES

Undoubtedly such an opportunity for display has seldom fallen to an orator's lot, and has still more seldom been so skilfully improved. The stage effects were so admirably arranged, the circumstances that led up to the great speech were so happily combined, that there were not wanting malicious tongues to suggest that that convenient impressive bronchitis[1] was nothing but an ingenious *ruse*. Certainly never was cold timed so opportunely. If it had lasted longer, Sir G. C. Lewis[2] must have brought the Budget forward; and then the House of Commons would have been unquestionably able to give to it a most dispassionate consideration. If it had not come at all, the orator would not have found his audience predisposed in his favour by the high-wrought tension of their expectations, as well as by their sympathy for the heroic will that mastered even a rebellious uvula in a cause of duty. The very doubt that prevailed whether he could do it enhanced the amiability of his audience. Down to the very moment before he began, nay, down to the close of his glorious peroration, criticism and censure were hushed by a feeling of anxious uncertainty whether huskiness or heroism would have the mastery at last. The House was very crowded that night. The benches were full for a good hour before public business began; for the rules of the House piously provide that no Member shall secure a seat who does not present himself at the preliminary prayers. The result is that this ceremonial is graced by a congregation considerably larger than, perhaps, its own unaided attractions would be able to draw together. The bribe is tempting enough, and the religion of the proceeding is sufficiently unobtrusive, even to occasionally lure in a Jew to take part in what professes to be the worship of the Nazarene. After a while the dreary private business and drearier petitions were exhausted; and Ministers began to assembly on the Treasury Bench to undergo their daily ordeal of questions. But no Mr. Gladstone appeared. The Treasury Bench grew fuller and fuller; but still no Mr Gladstone was to be seen. An anxious murmur began to circulate through the excited, expectant House. He was known to have been in bed on Tuesday, and the doctor was said to have talked of congestion on the lungs. Was it possible that he should attempt a budget speech on the Friday? At last a general cheer arose, as the long-looked-for orator, with his usual stealthy, almost timid, step, noiselessly slid into his place. A few minutes of other business, and he rose to speak. It was impossible for the most embittered

---

[1] 'Congestion of the lungs' had obliged Gladstone to put off his budget speech for four days.
[2] Sir George Cornewall Lewis (1806-63), M.P. Radnor boroughs, the home secretary, and a former chancellor; a rather dull worthy.

opponent to avoid scanning his features with something of sympathy, or anxiously trying to trace in his tones whether it was possible that sheer determination and mental vigour would really carry him through. His face was pale, and he occasionally leant against the table with an appearance of fatigue, as though standing was an effort; but his tones were as melodious, his play of features and of gesture was as dramatic as ever. Throughout the whole four hours of intricate argument neither voice nor mind faltered for an instant. Of the success of the speech there is no need to tell. Looked at from a distance, there does not seem much in a Chancellor of the Exchequer having a bad cold; but, at the time, this vulgar accessory added marvellously to the effect of what was in itself one of the finest combinations of reasoning and declamation that has ever been heard within the walls of the House of Commons.

The best witness to the merits of the speech is to be found in the demerits of the Budget. Nothing but eloquence of the highest order could have procured a reception so enthusiastic for a project, which, together undoubtedly with great recommendations, presented so many points open to attack. In a scheme so complex it could hardly be that there should not be much to praise and much to blame. The prospect of unshackled commerce with France might well intoxicate even the sluggish imaginations of the City of London, and a dozen Chambers of Commerce throughout the country besides. Scarcely any sacrifice seems too costly for the peaceful triumph of breaching those walls of prohibition, which still maintain a 'Continental system' scarcely less fatal to commercial progress than that of the first Napoleon. And above and beyond the mere commercial gain, there rose under Mr. Gladstone's magic wand the vista of an age of security and peace – disbanded armaments, forgotten jealousies, immunity not only from the scourge but from the panic of war; pleasant dreams, constantly belied by experience, constantly renewed by theorists, but too closely linked to the hopes of all who believe either in material progress or in the promises of religion ever to be abandoned as chimeras. But to these advantages, or promises of advantage, the drawbacks are very formidable. The treaty dealt with high political as well as great commercial aims. It might have erred in this or that particular, according to each critic's judgment; it might have yielded too much to France in one point or other of the many bargains it contains; but it was obviously the work of men who reason as other men do, and whose intellects were neither above nor below the average intellect of English statesmen. When we get outside the treaty into that part of the Budget which is external to the treaty, we leave this safe prosaic ground. We find ourselves in the enchanted region of pure Gladstonism – that terrible combination of relentless logic and dauntless imagination. We bid good-bye to the simple City virtues of slow security, of safe investments and well-balanced ledgers. We soar into the empyrean of finance. Mighty schemes, huge revolutions, vast comprehensive systems whirl bewilderingly about us. Everything is on a colossal scale of grandeur – all-embracing Free Trade, abysses of deficit, mountains of income-tax, remissions too numerous to count. No wonder the senatorial minds, accustomed to the *sermo pedestris* of Sir Cornewall Lewis' budgets, stood half spell-bound, half aghast. No wonder it seemed to the timid agriculturist as if, amid the rolling thunder of Mr Gladstone's periods, some universal convulsion of the fiscal elements was overwhelming Customs and Excise in a common ruin, to make way for a tranquil millennium of all-pervading Income-tax.

Mr. Gladstone, however, is not satisfied with the praise of having produced a great financial epic. If there is a point upon which he prides himself, it is the modesty of his predictions and the caution of his measures; and to refute the charge of recklessness and improvidence he quotes the honoured precedent of Sir Robert Peel. We should be very glad if the analogy were close enough entirely to reassure us. It is impossible to resist the suspicion that these accomplished pupils of the great Free Trade minister are following the letter rather than the spirit of their master's policy, and that by running one or two of his isolated formulas to their logical extreme, they are rather showing a slavish deference to his authority than any real portion of his large and calm sagacity. The Budget is charged with improvidence on two grounds. Its remissions waste the revenue of the country for all years, without any adequate prospect of a return; and for next year especially it leaves no better prospect than a wider and deeper chasm of deficiency. The first charge is rather a question of financial theory than of account. There is no doubt that the first effect of Mr. Gladstone's remissions of Customs and Excise will be to destroy about four millions worth of revenue: and nearly as much as three millions without including what is involved by the treaty with France. As the taxes so remitted press much upon the rich and little upon the poor, there is no urgent social call for their remission. But Mr. Gladstone maintains that these remissions are no waste, but only a judicious investment: and that all that he now sacrifices will recoup itself in virtue of the financial laws demonstrated and acted on by Sir Robert Peel. That minister proved by actual experiment that you may reduce the duty upon any article – say coffee – and yet that your receipts upon that article will ultimately rise and not fall in consequence of that reduction. Not only will the buyers of coffee increase when the coffee is made cheaper, but they will increase so enormously that the small duty will bring in a greater revenue than the large duty brought in before. But Mr. Gladstone and Mr. Cardwell[1] go further, and claim him as the demonstrator of a still bolder principle. Not only will each individual duty be improved by pruning it, but the whole tariff will be made to yield more richly by pruning off integral parts of it. Of course when Sir Robert Peel struck off the duty upon Swedish iron, the import of iron became profitless to the revenue; but yet the Customs revenue as a whole did not lose, but gained. For the free import of iron engendered an increase of iron manufactures: more workmen were employed at good wages than had been employed before; and therefore more families found themselves in a position to indulge in tea, sugar, spirits, and tobacco, on each of which articles they indirectly paid a customs duty to the Exchequer. That the commercial legislation of recent years has firmly established these two principles can hardly be denied; but the question that was fiercely debated on Mr. Du Cane's motion[2] was, whether they were fairly available in defence of Mr. Gladstone's Budget. In the first place it must be remembered that these are principles which from their very nature must not be carried out with relentless consistency. It is obvious that though you may have too many taxes for the purposes of the revenue, it is also very easy to have too few. It is obvious that there must be a point in the onward process of reduction at which all benefit to the Exchequer will cease.[*] There must be an intersecting point at which the gain by increased consumption, and the loss by reduction, neutralize each other; and when that point is once passed the commercial reformer becomes the improvident financier. The reductions will still be profitable to trade – for taxation is trade's most formidable enemy; but they will be fatal to the revenue. By pruning your vines you will increase both the size and quality of your grapes; but it will hardly answer to proceed with logical consistency and cut down your vines altogether.

[1] Edward Cardwell (1813–86), M.P. Oxford and Irish secretary; a leading Peelite; later distinguished himself by his army reforms as secretary for war in Gladstone's first ministry, 1868–74; peerage 1874.
[2] Criticising the diminution of ordinary revenue and the 'unnecessarily' high rate of income tax. C. Du Cane was M.P. for Essex North.
[*] It was pointed out by Sir Stafford Northcote, in a very sound and closely-reasoned speech, that the present condition of the duty upon tea is an illustration of this danger. That duty never has recovered, and does not seem likely to recover, the fierce assaults that have been made on it of late years.

There is a general ground, therefore, for distrusting an appeal to the precedent of Sir Robert Peel. It is no disrespect to his memory to say, that the course which he recommended us to steer up to a certain point, may become dangerous when that point is passed. No one recognised more readily than he did that the 'miraculous elasticity' of the revenue has its limits. Even, therefore, if Mr. Gladstone could prove that he was rigorously following the path which his master had first opened out, he would still be bound to move along it circumspectly and slowly, waiting for experience to confirm one step before he ventured upon another. But the path is not the same. There is a vital difference between Mr. Gladstone's budget and the budgets of Sir Robert Peel. Sir Robert Peel's principle was to reduce duty upon every sort of article, so that he might reap increased revenue from the increased consumption of the article itself. But he suppressed the duty absolutely only upon raw materials, such as iron, silk, cotton, and wool. And his reason for making this distinction was very obvious. It is only raw materials that in any considerable degree stimulate industry; and the increased expenditure consequent on the increased wages of the workman, from which alone the financier who abolishes duties looks to be recouped, can only result from a stimulus to industry. Now is there any noteworthy stimulus to industry in Mr. Gladstone's Custom House abolitions? With the exception of tallow, there is not a single raw material used in this country for manufacture in the whole of the long list. The few cases in which he merely reduces duty may undoubtedly be defended by an appeal to the precedent of Sir Robert Peel. But in respect to abolitions of duty he has deserted his master's rule. He has selected for exemption from a just contribution to the revenue precisely that which Sir Robert Peel always refused to exempt – the class of manufactured articles. He has given no reason for thus abandoning the precedent to which he so confidently appeals; he does not even seem to be conscious that he has done so. It is obvious that the reason which induced Sir Robert Peel to admit iron and wool free of duty, in Mr. Gladstone's case wholly fails. Gloves and *objets de Paris* will give no stimulus to English industry. Of course more labour must be employed in carrying two bales of goods than in carrying one; and if more gloves are sold, there must be more young gentlemen with white neckcloths and engaging manners to sell them. To that extent free trade in gloves will stimulate British industry; but we suspect that it will be a long time before the extra railway officials employed in carrying the stimulated importation of gloves, or the extra shopmen employed in disposing of it, will drink enough beer and

'THE BUDGET AND THE REFORM BILL'

smoke enough tobacco to make up to the Exchequer the 53,000*l.* of Customs' duty which the remission throws away. What is true of gloves is true of nearly all the new 'reliefs to industry.' All these abolitions are money absolutely thrown away. The difference between Sir Robert Peel and Mr. Gladstone is, that the one sows in a grateful soil, and the other sows on the sea-shore. The duties sacrificed by Sir Robert Peel were remissions well selected, which brought forth fruit abundantly to the revenue, either in the increased consumption of the commodity whose burden was lightened, or of other articles in the tariff. The duties swept away by Mr. Gladstone are remissions for mere remissions' sake, blindly make in obedience to a formula of financial reform supposed to be extracted from the measures of Sir Robert Peel, but stimulating no consumption and no industry that can in any way repay their loss to the Exchequer.

Besieged as the Treasury continually is by the remonstrances of trades whose operations are cramped and clogged by the pressure of indispensable taxation, purposeless remissions must always be unjust. So long as the land, on which our imposts press with unequal weight, is fettered by the malt-tax;[1] so long as the shipowner, on whose prosperity our empire depends, is hampered by the timber duty,[2] a minister of finance who is lucky enough to have superfluous revenue to dispose of, can never be at a loss for deserving recipients of his bounty. But superfluous revenue is very far at present from forming an element in our calculations. For the coming year it is but barely that the two ends are made to meet by the imposition of an outrageous income-tax, and by scraping together every kind of temporary and exceptional resource. To hunt out exceptional resources, and treat them as if they were legitimate income, is a favourite refuge of financiers in distress. A celebrated railway potentate,[3] who, by the help of his ingenious finance, shone a few years ago like a bright meteor in the firmament of polite society, and has since disappeared into the blackness of darkness for ever, was very great in this line. He used to buy locomotives out of capital, sell them again immediately, and use up the proceeds as income; and thus his accounts, even in the most troublous times, always wore

[1] At 2*s*. 7*d*. per bushel, plus 5%, the malt tax yielded over £6m. in 1860. It was ultimately repealed by Gladstone in 1880.
[2] Gladstone lightened the duty on imported timber in 1860 by taxing all timber at the rate hitherto applied to colonial timber only (i.e. 1*s*. 0*d*. a load; foreign timber had previously paid 7*s*. 6*d*. a load). He repealed the duty in 1866.
[3] George Hudson (1800–71), the 'Railway King', Conservative M.P. for Sunderland, 1845–59; lived mainly abroad after the exposure of his malpractices in 1849.

a cheerful aspect. Mr. Gladstone's proceedings, though much more honest, are not much more legitimate. It is scarcely safe to eke out your year's expenditure by the help of a mere godsend like the Spanish repayments;[1] and the use of the malt credits is a simple anticipation of ordinary income.[2] Now anticipating income, in household finance, at least, is not a much more satisfactory resource than putting off your Christmas bills. To found the adjustment of your prospective balance-sheet on 1,650,000*l.* of mere windfall, is a device that would receive a very hard name indeed if it were found in the proposals of a joint-stock direction. The practical inconvenience of it is, that it conceals for a moment the darkness of the future from our view. If next year's prospects were likely to be more favourable, of course there would be no objection to the operation; but if the prospects of 1860 are discouraging, those of 1861 are absolute despair. There will be no million and a half of windfalls for us then. Crumbs and leavings of abolished duties, with which we may put off our difficulties for the present, will be exhausted then. The wine duties will fall still lower; and the glove and straw-plat duties will be finally swept away. A shilling income-tax will hardly fill the chasm that will yawn before us then. And without taking into the account the prognostics of European disturbance, to which Mr. Gladstone cannot be blind, this diminished revenue will certainly have to encounter many millions of charge for the powerful expedition, which, as he sanguinely phrases it, is bearing proposals of peace to the mouth of the Peiho.[3]

Is it a judicial blindness, or only the irrepressible enterprise of the daring pilot in extremity who steers too nigh the sand to show his wit, that has induced Mr. Gladstone to select a conjuncture so strangely inopportune for his projects of remission? The reasoning which he assigns as his motive for the Budget is almost stranger than the Budget itself. It appears, according to his own account, that he entertains a special view of the covenants conveyed by a Ministerial speech in the House of Commons. Arguing from *data*, which at the time seemed unimpeachable,

---

[1] In 1859 and 1860 Gladstone used for the ordinary purposes of the year nearly £0·5m. obtained from Spain in repayment of debt.

[2] Maltsters had been allowed about six months to pay the malt duty. In 1859 Gladstone shortened this 'credit' by six weeks, and in 1860 by a further six weeks, thus increasing the yield of the duty in the ensuing financial year.

[3] An Anglo-French expedition had been despatched against the Chinese, as a result of their refusal to receive British and French ministers and their severe repulse of a British squadron which had attempted to force the mouth of the Peiho river and reach Pekin in June 1859. It was this expedition which, in October 1860, took Pekin and destroyed the emperor's summer palace.

'THE BUDGET AND THE REFORM BILL'

he told the House of Commons in 1853, that there would be a surplus in 1860; and that with that surplus he should make great financial reforms. Therefore, in his view, the House of Commons is a debtor to the people of England to satisfy the expectations that have been raised and make these promised reforms. But he also in the same year promised to sweep away the income-tax in 1860; and therefore the House of Commons is equally a debtor to effect that most desirable consummation. But having spent all its money, it cannot pay either of these debts. In this dilemma the ordinary morality of the Bankruptcy Court would suggest the duty of attempting to pay something in the pound to each of its creditors. Mr. Gladstone is strong upon the obligation of keeping promises, but he takes no such half-hearted view of this department of ethics. He has a way of paying creditors altogether peculiar to himself. His plan is to pay one creditor in full, and to obtain the money for doing so by plundering the other. He makes his commercial reforms according to covenant, but he not only does not carry out the promised abolition of the income-tax, but he reimposes it twice as heavily as before. This is Mr. Gladstone's own account of the process by which he arrived at the conviction that the present was an opportune year for reductions in the tariff. We do not doubt that this statement is his own sincere estimate of the motives by which he has been ruled; but we have too much admiration for his intellect to believe that that estimate was correct. Perhaps there were motives which he hardly liked to confess even to himself, much less to the House of Commons. He must be conscious that there is no financier but himself bold or talented enough to do as he has done; and possibly the constant contemplation of a powerful Opposition and a divided Cabinet has reminded him of the adage, 'To-day is thine own – trust not to the morrow.'

But there are far weightier objections to be taken to the Budget than those which rest upon the alarms of a prudent and sound economy. It is not merely a thriftless disregard of future needs, it is not merely a pedantic and lifeless copy of the mere formulae of Sir Robert Peel. It has the far graver fault of being deeply tainted with the Manchester manias, with which that long exile from office, passed upon the same bench with Mr. Cobden and Mr. Bright, has unfortunately infected the Chancellor of the Exchequer. The two cardinal doctrines of the creed of Manchester are that armaments are wasteful, and that no worker with his hands ought to contribute to the expenses of the State. Both these doctrines have obviously sunk deep into the mind by which the financial project was arranged. It contemplates disarmament; and it paves the way for the transfer of all burdens from the classes that live by manual labour to the classes above them.

The last of these two grave defects lies upon the surface of the scheme. It was brought out by Mr. Horsman[1] with such a vigour of sarcastic eloquence, as not only to compromise the equanimity of the Finance Minister, but also to spoil the speech in which he attempted to reply. Either he did not dare trust himself to give his tongue the rein in that reply, or he misdoubted the success of his own eloquence when applied to a merely defensive purpose; but for one reason or the other, he thought it better to stigmatize his opponent's warnings as 'wild dreams' and pass them by unanswered. But they were, in sober truth, no wild dreams, but the indication of plain and solid dangers. The substitution of the extra penny for the Paper Duty is in itself a petty change; but it is pregnant with a principle of vast and dangerous application. Once admitted that a direct tax may be laid on for the purpose of taking off an indirect tax which presses hard, or which is much complained of, and there is no reason that the process should not be repeated *ad infinitum*. Inasmuch as all classes alike pay indirect taxation, while only those who do not receive weekly wages pay the income-tax, this change is a direct and simple transfer of taxes from one class of the community to another. We have now entered upon the descent of the smooth, easy, sloping path of popular finance, on which there is no halting-place to check our career short of confiscation. This question of the incidence of taxation is in truth the vital question of modern politics. It is the field upon which the contending classes of this generation will do battle. We have no feudalism to sweep away, no privileges, worth the naming, to contest. Till very lately there have been bitter and protracted struggles for political enfranchisement, but the spell of that chimæra to excite enthusiasm has passed away. The proletariat will not now fight for a barren share in the business of legislation, unless it is to bear to each one of them a substantial and palpable fruit. The issue between the conflicting forces of society is becoming narrower and more distinct. The mists of mere political theory are clearing away, and the true character of the battle-ground, and the real nature of the prize that is at stake, are standing out more and more distinctly every year. It galls the classes who barely sustain themselves by their labour that others should sit by and enjoy more than they do, and yet work little or not at all. Benighted enthusiasts in other lands, or other times, may have

[1] Edward Horsman (1807–76), Liberal M.P. for Stroud; later prominent in the resistance to the Reform Bill of 1866.

'THE BUDGET AND THE REFORM BILL'

struggled for idle theories of liberty, or impalpable phantoms of nationality, but the 'enlightened selfishness' of the modern artisan now fully understands that political power, like everything else, is to be taken to the dearest market. He cares little enough for democracy unless it will adjust the inequalities of wealth. The struggle between the English constitution on the one hand, and the democratic forces that are labouring to subvert it on the other, is now, in reality, when reduced to its simplest elements and stated in its most prosaic form, a struggle between those who have, to keep what they have got, and those who have not, to get it. Across the water the succinct formula, '*La propriété c'est le vol*,'[1] expresses in its most naked form this goal of democratic aspirations. In England we are not fond of general principles, and, therefore, we have not got so far. Mr. Ernest Jones did, we believe, once propose something like an agrarian law for England;[2] and Mr. Bright's celebrated letter to the weavers of Glasgow seems to intimate that a similar measure applied to the Scottish deer forests would be the true remedy for manufacturing distress.[3] But, generally, the champions of democracy are content with smaller instalments of confiscation. They are profoundly impressed with the philosophy of plucking the horse's tail, not in handfuls, but hair by hair. They prefer to operate by means of changes in taxation; for they know that the taxation of the State is an engine which may be used almost without limit for the transfer of property from one class to another. This is what is meant by Mr. Bright's frequent declaration, that a Reform Bill will be worthless unless it shall produce a change in our fiscal system, and by the Liverpool Budget which he proposed in connexion with his projects of Reform.[4] The first consequence, in his

---

[1] The best-known maxim of the French socialist Pierre-Joseph Proudhon (1809–65), appearing in his *Qu'est-ce que la propriété?* (1840).

[2] At the Chartist Convention opened on 31 March 1851, the Radical barrister and *littérateur* Ernest Jones (1819–69) had introduced the programme of the Chartist executive, which envisaged the nationalisation of the land and the settlement of the population on it.

[3] The reference is presumably to the letter of 1 September 1858 to Andrew Cumming, Secretary of the Glasgow Council of Trades' Delegates, read on 16 September 1858 at a meeting in Glasgow to consider working-class emigration to the colonies. Bright encouraged the working men to go 'where land is accessible to you, where there are no great hereditary proprietors, as in Scotland, who dare to outrage heaven and mankind by keeping 20,000, or 50,000, or 100,000 acres of land depopulated, that a handful of men may enjoy the pleasures of the chase' (H. J. Leech (ed.), *The Public Letters of the Right Hon. John Bright, M.P.* (1885), pp. 63–8).

[4] Speaking to the Liverpool Financial Reform Association on 1 December 1859, Bright had attacked the injustices of the taxation system and advocated taxing the whole property of the country at the rate of 8s. *per annum* on every £100, in order to permit the abolition of the income tax and of much indirect taxation.

mind, of a measure that shall confer all political power on the poor, is the transfer of all taxation to the shoulders of the rich. Of course, when that is once done, when one class supplies the revenues of the State, and another class disposes of them, no difficulty will be found in applying freely the expenditure of the Exchequer to the benefit of the working man. A hundred different conduits will be devised for diffusing among the many the beneficent stream inexhaustibly flowing from the inherited or acquired property of the few. But how will this be done? On what principle will the first great step, the exemption of the manual labourer from taxation, be carried out? By the very process, of which the substitution of the income-tax for the paper duty is the first example. The working man pays his share of indirect taxation like the rest of the community. All efforts to bring him within the pale of direct taxation have hitherto broken down. Substitute the one for the other, replace each item of Customs and Excise by larger and even larger income-tax, and the transference of taxation, the first great step of democratic confiscation, will be complete. Wherever democracy has prevailed, the power of the State has been used in some form or other to plunder the well-to-do classes for the benefit of the poor. In America it has taken, and takes to this day, the form of repudiation.[1] In France, twelve years ago, it took the form of nominal workshops, in which whole multitudes were paid for doing nothing out of the taxes of the State. But it is instructive to note, that, in the Great Revolution,[2] in which the type of the democracy was the worst, and in which the results of its excesses were the most hideous, one of the first measures that was forced on the Assembly by the mobs in the pay of Bailly[3] was the substitution of direct for indirect taxation. Mr. Gladstone's change of paper duty into income-tax may seem paltry and innocent enough; but we naturally shrink from even the first easy unsuspicious steps along a path which had led previous travellers into so fearful an abyss.

As one of Mr. Gladstone's loans from the Manchester treasury of crotchets points to internal convulsions, so the other is rife with dangers from without. He has intimated not obscurely that our present large expenditure in armaments is distasteful to him, and that he hopes speedily to curtail it. In Cabinet it had to contend, if rumour speaks truly, with his most stubborn opposition, and he has let no occasion pass of dis-

---
[1] I.e. of debt. British investors had suffered a good deal from repudiations of debts and stoppages of interest payments by American states and private debtors.
[2] I.e. the French Revolution.
[3] J.-S. Bailly (1736-93), first deputy of Paris in 1789, and president of the Constituent Assembly; mayor of Paris, 1789-91.

'THE BUDGET AND THE REFORM BILL'

couraging it in public. When his wiser colleagues had forced him to provide the necessary outlay for the defence of our shores, all that remained to him was to make it as odious to the taxpayer as he could. He has piled up the income-tax to its present height, almost avowedly in the hope that its growing pressure will bend and break the martial spirit of the people. If he is asked when it will abate, he replies, 'Reduce your estimates.' If he is pressed for some assurance that next year it will not grow, still his only answer is, 'Reduce your estimates.' And in order that next year, when a chasm of fourteen millions deficit yawns beneath our feet, we may have nothing but an increased income-tax to cast in, he has carefully swept away the other taxes to which, in an emergency, we might have recurred, so that in a short time not a vestige will survive of the machinery by which they were raised. And an increased income-tax, he doubts not, will do his work. If tenpence in the pound does not damp the nation's ardour, a shilling will; or if a shilling fails, the desired effect will be produced by fifteen pence. It is due to Mr Gladstone's colleagues that the financial project provides the defences for which the people call; it is due to Mr. Gladstone's own ingenuity that it provides also the future instruments for wringing out of the people an acquiescence in that disarmament, which at present no one, except the Peace Society,[1] would condescend even to discuss.

Is this a time for soft Arcadian dreams of peace, and boundless confidence in our brother men? Time was when we fondly loved to fancy that war was a worn-out barbarism, and that civilization was a defence stouter than a shield of steel. Men who, living for a theory, see only through its spectacles and reason only from its assumptions, are found to use this language still. They have commonplaces in abundance at command. Has not the panic of a French war been periodical since Waterloo? Has not your great ally literally showered on you the pledges of his love? Was there not the Crimean war, when he might have deserted you, or the Indian mutiny, when he might have crushed you? Can you forget his frankness in asking the Queen to Cherbourg,[2] or his condescension in answering the frolicsome clerks of Liverpool?[3] Can you doubt this last token of his regard, when, in order to admit your produce

[1] The Society for the Promotion of Permanent and Universal Peace, the main organ of pacifism.
[2] Queen Victoria and Prince Albert had visited Napoleon III at Cherbourg in August 1858.
[3] Four Liverpool brokers wrote to Napoleon III enquiring his intentions towards England, and received a reassuring reply dated 30 November 1859 from his *chef du cabinet*, Mocquard. *The Times*, 5 December, 1859.

into France, he has disgusted the whole *bourgeoisie* of his own country, and made no friend in yours but 'M. Milnes'?[1] Such consolations might be collected by the bushel; nor are we careful to answer whatever of argument they may contain. Far be it from us who live on the plain surface of an honest diplomacy, and in the open air of free discussion, to profess to trace the windings of the mole. He who made his way to a throne through the caverns and crypts of a conspirator's life, is not to be credited with the motives and methods of men who have never left the light of day. A short but eventful experience has given us an obscure and doubtful insight into some few of the secrets of his restless policy. We know that he is never so silent as when he means to act. We know that he fawns up to the last moment before he springs. We know, from the example of Austria, that there is no prognostic of his future aims so dark and ominous as an unusual display of cordiality.[2] But we do not need to formulate or to explain the distrust which pervades the whole atmosphere around us, like the still, heavy foreboding of a storm. If there are men who still trust the assurances of peace that flow so glibly from his lips, let them not ask politicians who may be interested, nor writers who may be prejudiced, but let them inquire of the staggering trade and the benumbed and terror-struck enterprise of every mart in Europe, whether or no this that we are entering on is likely to prove a golden age of peace.

Yet it so happens that just now we are less than usual left to our suspicions, and have more of solid inference to rest upon than his caution commonly permits. The mask of the most adroit conspirator will occasionally slip aside. That word '*revendication*' has disclosed the whole.[3] It has given an authoritative sanction to the worst of the suspicions that Orleanists and Liberals have been struggling, during the eight last years, to instil into England's unwilling ear. It has disastrously proved the prescience of the Congress of Vienna when they placed their ban on the dynasty of Buonaparte. We now know – what before we could only guess – that a Napoleonic throne must drag with it Napoleonic traditions. *L'Empire c'est la paix* was not only an improbable prophecy,

[1] Richard Monckton Milnes (1809-85), later first Lord Houghton; society figure, author, Conservative M.P., and a notable Francophile.
[2] Presumably a reference to the incident of 1 January 1859, when Napoleon said to the Austrian ambassador: 'I regret that our relations with your government are no longer as good as in the past; but I beg you to tell the emperor [Franz Josef] that my personal feelings have not changed.'
[3] Announcing the prospective annexation of Savoy to the French legislative body on 1 March, Napoleon had spoken of 'Cette revendication d'un territoire de peu d'étendue'.

but a sheer contradiction in terms. Every form of Government has some special feeling in the human heart on which it relies for its existence. The ancient monarchy can appeal to hereditary loyalty and men's natural respect for undisturbed possession; the republic can appeal to the vanity which is flattered by a dead level of rank and power; but the military adventurer and those who hold from him can lean only on the sword. To the passion for glory they owe their rise, and when they cease to feed that passion they must fall. The present Emperor was lifted to power by no deeds or merits of his own, but simply because he bore a name associated in the hearts of the French peasantry with a fame which they cherished and a policy they would gladly see revived. He has profited by his uncle's glory: he cannot renounce his uncle's system. He has nothing save the one gewgaw of military distinction to offer as a bribe to the fierce political passions which his bayonets hold in check. It is ridiculous to speak of a sentiment of loyalty to the conspirator of yesterday, who is the Emperor of to-day; and no one but Mr. Bright would talk of social liberties in a land where those blessings are illustrated by a mute tribune and a shackled press and drawing-rooms swarming with spies. He has nothing to give his people in exchange for all he has taken from them, except that martial intoxication for the sake of which they will readily pawn alike their prosperity and their freedom. So long as he heaps triumph on triumph and adds conquest to conquest, so long it is probable his subjects will not murmur at the weight of their well-gilded chain. But, unfortunately, this system of distracting attention from domestic suffering by the glitter of military success, adds to its own exigencies by its own action. Wars, and, still more, rumours of wars, are the deadliest enemies of trade. The Emperor's chief claim on the adhesion of the middle classes was the hope that a strong, stern Government would be able to repress the ever-heaving forces of Revolution, by which all other Governments had been overthrown. But a chronic alarm of war is almost as fatal to the operations of trade as the panic of Revolution. When the operations of trade are materially slackened, and the accumulations of idle capital are mounting higher and higher in the coffers of the Bank of France, it means diminished employment and narrowing sustenance for thousands and thousands of working men. There is but one device, old as the origin of statecraft, for charming away their discontent; its fury must be turned upon some foreign foe. Thus the Emperor is driven into a vicious circle. The more Europe is disturbed, the more trade will slacken and suffering increase in France; and the more suffering increases at home, the more restlessly must he prosecute his aggressive plans in order to avert the danger with which it menaces his throne. He may have struggled hard against the necessity; he may have earnestly desired to pursue a milder policy and enjoy a less troubled term of power; but the imperious exigencies of an usurped dominion, the relentless logic of a false position, are driving him to try again the fatal but fascinating career, in which all his uncle's matchless genius could only secure for him a splendid fall. He follows his precedent faithfully, almost tamely. It belongs to the character of the man, and to the fatalist superstition with which it is notoriously tinged, that he should think to win the favour of Fortune by imitating, in the commencement of his military career, the very details of his uncle's earlier exploits. The great Emperor's first command was on the soil of Italy; his first victory was in Piedmont; the first enemy with whom he tried his strength was Austrian, and Nice was his first territorial acquisition. Up to this point – the last is being accomplished as we write – the second Emperor, with something less of talent and something more of opportunity, has carefully picked out the footsteps of his great exemplar. The anxious, momentous question for Europe and England is, how far will this model be copied – how far will this path be followed out?

There are old men living still to whom the proclamations and the despatches, the sophistries and the falsehoods of the last fifteen months must sound like the echo of a long-forgotten tale. They have heard all about 'geographical frontiers' and 'natural boundaries' before. When they are told that there are populations burning to be annexed to the empire of France, they remember that they have often heard of the same phenomenon in days gone by, and they know precisely what it means. It must seem strange to them now again to hear the first notes of the old song which in youth was so familiar to their ears; stranger still to find that with it have been reproduced the clique of well-meaning simpletons who are deluded by its burden of hypocrisy and fraud. It is indeed a gloomy prospect if we are fated to go again through the same experiences before we shall have learned the lesson which we had only too well by heart some fifty years ago. Savoy first – what next? Is the process of *'revendication'* to stop there? Has France no other expansible frontiers? Will not a river serve as a natural boundary quite as appropriately as an Alpine range? And what is the policy of England to be, when next the Empire gives a practical proof that it 'is peace' and 'fights only for an idea'? If we are to predict the probable course of England from what it has been in recent years, the prospect does not promise much either to our safety or our honour. England had once a traditional

'THE BUDGET AND THE REFORM BILL'

policy which was not very difficult to fathom or to apply. She did not meddle with other nations' doings when they concerned her not. But she recognised the necessity of an equilibrium and the value of a public law among the states of Europe. When a great power abused its superiority by encroaching on the frontier of its weaker neighbours, she looked on their cause as her cause, and on their danger as the forerunner of her own. But a change has come over the spirit of our policy in recent years. It is no longer dictated by any single principle, but it is the confused and heterogeneous resultant of two conflicting elements. The traditions and the habits of the old far-sighted and manly doctrines, which admitted the duties that England owes to the European commonwealth of which she is a citizen, still linger among our leading statesmen. But they have been sadly modified by the maxims of a very different philosophy. The gambling and reckless spirit of trade, which never cares to count up distant possibilities and lives only for the chances and profits of the morrow, has bred a school of politicians whose chief claim to attention is that they cast out as barbarous all the precautions on which our ancestors relied. They have selected an age in which steam has infinitely multiplied our intercourse with Europe and has provided facilities for an invader which none of us are as yet able accurately to estimate, to proclaim, as a new discovery, that we ought to be as completely disconnected from the politics of Europe by the Channel as the Americans are by the Atlantic. They would realize the old Roman taunt and make us more than '*penitus toto divisos orbe Britannos.*' Just as they ridicule all perils of invasion as an old wife's tale, so they inveigh against all active efforts to maintain the peace and public law of Europe as a piece of wasteful Quixotism and an act of treason against trade. They can understand the right of one man to employ force to restrain another man from violence or theft; they admit that in the interests of the community the burglar or the highwayman must be hunted down; but when the argument is raised from the man to the people, from the community of individuals to the community of nations, their logic fails them and refuses to go further. No statesmen has as yet professed this creed in its simple and pure absurdity; but it has, nevertheless, from time to time, exercised some influence in the House of Commons, and, through the House of Commons, on the Cabinet. If its pusillanimity was repulsive to the high spirit of the English people, its remissions of taxation were not the less grateful to their commercial instincts, and to this part of the Manchester faith the House of Commons has occasionally listened. The inevitable result, little as Parliament may have intended it, was to tinge with this miserly and blind philosophy the spirit of English policy abroad; but the statesmen who had been brought up in wider views could not at once narrow their intellects to the measure of their new instructors. The tone of their diplomacy remained as bold and plainspoken as of old. Too often it was not until they came to put their grand professions into action that they felt the effect upon their position of the clipped and starved establishments which the new philosophy had imposed. They dared not lift up their arm to strike, lest its nervelessness should be betrayed. This is the origin of that mixture of brave words and craven acts that has disgraced our foreign policy since the Reform Bill, and on which foreigners have so often commented with scorn. In dealing with smaller nations the fatal weakness was not necessarily exposed – we could still act with vigour and hold our own; but, in dealing with a stronger power, the certainty that bold language was an idle vaunt and that immediate war was inevitable destruction forced us into a tone of concession and humility so marked in its contrast, that it could not escape the host of detractors to whom our former triumphs and present freedom have given birth. They justly hold us up to scorn as reversing the ancient Roman maxim – as subjugating the weak and sparing the proud alone. Lord Macaulay's description of the hated Claudian house, who –

'yelping with currish spite,
Still snap and bark at those that run, and run from those that bite' –

aptly represents the estimate of our degeneracy which, soon after the influence of the new school came into play, began to prevail, and still prevails, at most of the Chancelleries of Europe. The cheese-parings of a few years have almost wholly lost us the *prestige* which it had cost four hundred millions to acquire.

So long as the same poisonous element is suffered to infect our policy, so long the same dishonour will be its result. National ignominy is the logical consequence of Manchester finance. So long as our armaments are weak, the more we meddle the more we shall be disgraced. If Mr Gladstone's aspirations for a return to the estimates of 1852 are to be realised, we had better renounce at once and for ever our position as an European power. If we are to take Mr. Bright's view of war, we had better take his view of diplomacy as well. Anything is better than feeble and impotent braggadocio. To try and secure by vapouring a position which we will not or cannot attain by fighting, is a policy worthy of no potentate above the calibre of the Emperor of China. We must abandon all dreams of watching over and protecting the infant growth of Italian

'THE BUDGET AND THE REFORM BILL'

liberty; we must forget the glorious part we have borne in curbing the unscrupulous and desolating ambition of France; we must publicly renounce, as beyond our strength, the guarantees that we have given to Switzerland and Belgium.[1] We must stand calmly, nay humbly, by, while the frontier of the Rhine is added to the frontier of the Alps, and Antwerp becomes, under French auspices, a standing menace to the Thames. This is the only safe and consistent policy, if we are to return to the skeleton army and mouldering navy of Lord John Russell's administration.[2] It is the inevitable corollary of a renewal of that 'thrift' to which Mr. Gladstone is so fond of pointing with applause, unless we are willing that our diplomacy should become a systematic game at brag. Though it might be ignominious in the eyes of those who set their heart on historical traditions, yet, for a time at least, it would be cheap. But no self-delusion, however resolute, can really convert the Channel into an Atlantic. Once at Antwerp the Emperor might possibly remember his solemn promise that Waterloo should be avenged. Whether his appearance on the coast of Sussex would be held, on sound financial principles, to justify an increase of the estimates, is a point on which the Manchester school have never distinctly made up their minds. Mr. Bright would no doubt impartially balance the profit and the loss. He would have an opportunity of deciding in his own case whether 'social' or 'political liberties' were to be preferred.[3] On the one hand, the 'Morning Star' would assuredly receive an *avertissement*;[4] on the other, Mr. Bright, as *Préfet de la Tamise*, would walk out to dinner before the premier Duke. He would probably set himself to learn French with the consolatory reflection, that an annexation to the Empire of France would be a greater boon even than a commercial treaty, inasmuch as it would imply absolute Free Trade.

That an invasion is no absolute impossibility, this Review has already demonstrated in a paper that will not speedily be forgotten.[5] Few persons will be of opinion that such an event is probable, so long as the people and government of England are on their guard. But everything turns on this condition. It will not be attempted so long as our defences are

[1] By the treaties of Vienna (1815) and London (1839) respectively.
[2] Of 1846-52.
[3] In the Commons on 2 March, Bright had spoken of the possibility of Frenchmen preferring 'the social liberty which we have not' to 'the political liberty which we have'.
[4] The *Morning Star*, founded in 1856, was Bright's organ in the press. The *avertissement* was the formal warning given under the press laws of the Second Empire to newspapers which offended the government.
[5] 'The Invasion of England', *Quarterly Review*, cvi (July 1859), 245-84.

efficient: if they be neglected, the attraction of such a pillage may prove too strong for the most virtuous ally. The responsibility of so appalling a calamity, if ever it should occur, will be exclusively on those who shall have persuaded the tempting prey to lay aside her armour as too burdensome to wear. Much of the guilt will rest, no doubt, on the heads of the fanatic school who for mere greed of gain have forced themselves to believe that the age of Saturn has returned. But a far heavier share will be the portion of that Minister who, with deeper and more successful art, shall have schemed, by a finance ingeniously galling and unjust, to make England fret and revolt against the cost of those defences which are the very charter of her national existence.

All these objections, and more also, were urged against the Budget; and their cogency was rather ignored than disproved. But their weight was as nothing against the bribes which the Chancellor of the Exchequer had adroitly offered to the most active interests in the country. For the purpose of passing a budget, a Minister cannot afford to wait till the genuine and solid public opinion of the nation is expressed. True national opinion is a vast, unwieldy machine, which it takes a long time to set in motion. It is slow of thought, and slower still of speech; and weeks and months must pass before it can be irritated to that point of excitement at which it finds vent in words and actions. A genuine national approval of the Budget could not be elicited until the time for deciding on the Budget had passed by; and a Minister who should frame his scheme with a view to that approval would probably, by the time it came to solace him, be safely installed on the front Opposition bench. A Chancellor of the Exchequer who wishes to drive his Budget through by force of external pressure must rely, not on the most substantial and most numerous interests, but on those which are the most glib and the most alert. Mr. Gladstone has always been fully alive to this maxim of political wisdom. The landed interest of this country is probably the most important of any, both from the magnitude and the specially national character of its wealth; but, though tough and strong, it is unquestionably slow. Mr. Gladstone has long known better than to ally himself with the landed gentry; he fearlessly digs his malt-taxes, and succession duties,[1] and hop adjustments[2] into their unresisting carcases, knowing well that the quick stream of political events will have carried him and

[1] The succession duties were regulated by Gladstone's act of 1853, taxing successions in consequence of death.
[2] The hop duty had hitherto been paid about a year in arrears. In 1860 the time allowed for payment was cut to about three months, but the duty was reduced to 1½d a lb. (it was repealed in 1862).

'THE BUDGET AND THE REFORM BILL'

his measures far ahead long before the assailed land-owners have collected their wits sufficiently to return the blow. He knows it is the wise part to throw himself in full confidence upon the manufacturers and the journalists, who are bred up to agitation, and who are well practised in simulating, by dint of monster meetings and fierce leading articles, the accents and the power of the real public voice. They have answered his confidence and carried him in triumph through his difficulties. Possibly, by the time that Members go back to their constituents next winter, the nation may have found out that an active section has stolen a march upon them in their sleep, and that a promising young income-tax, which is likely to grow bigger year by year, was a nuisance worth averting after all.

Political apathy is so much the prevailing temper of the times, that it was probably only by a direct appeal to their purses that the Budget was able to rouse the earnest attention even of one section of the community. The other great measure of the year – the Reform Bill – certainly has not been so fortunate. Many persons have been interested in creating something like a feeling on the subject; but they have applied the strongest and most approved irritants in vain. Mr. Bright has starred it for two seasons in the provinces, and has done all that could be done by the most splendid fictions encased in the most commanding eloquence to stir up an agitation. The first season he preached democracy, the second season he preached confiscation; but in neither did he find that happy mood of discontent which was necessary to prepare the surface of the artisan mind for the exercise of his art. It was to no purpose that in one year he told his audience that all the wars since the Revolution had been got up to provide out-door relief to the aristocracy:[1] it was in vain that the next year he proclaimed that a ten per cent. tax ought to be laid upon fixed incomes, in order to exempt absolutely all earnings from taxation.[2] As one of his school is said to have expressed it, it was 'like whipping a dead horse'. The material prosperity of the country was too much for him. The mechanic sensibly reflected that time spent in agitation was lost for working; and that the possibility of political advantage was not worth the sacrifice of good wages certain. The apathy

[1] Bright said at Birmingham in October 1858 that the foreign policy which had involved the country in so much war was 'neither more nor less than a gigantic system of outdoor relief for the aristocracy of Great Britain'.
[2] Presumably this refers to Bright's suggestions in December 1859 (see note 4 to page 125 above). His proposed tax on property would have amounted to around 10% on the income.

of the public has naturally been reflected in the House of Commons. While Savoy, whose exchange of liberty for bondage we may pity, but cannot prevent, will at a day's notice fill the benches to overflowing, Lord John could scarcely collect a decorously full house to hear his proposals for transferring the government of England to a new and untried body of men. And the heavy indifference under which the question was introduced seems to linger still about its path as it advances. Most people, if they are pressed, will acknowledge that the change may be dangerous, and that its results cannot be predicted: but the subject has been agitated so long without any practical result that people seem incapable of looking at it as one of practical importance. It has so long been the football of the political game that men find it difficult to persuade themselves that it implies a new form of government. The House of Commons has become not so much calm as callous on this question. The warnings of those who have learned from history the certain issue of democratic change, and look upon the unreal liberty of America and the open slavery of France as danger-signals to England, are not less valuable than they were twelve years ago; but the ear has become dulled to their power by constant repetition. Both to one side and the other the controversy has lost its savour. While the Budget was being discussed, as each debater sat down, some dozen candidates for the Speaker's choice jumped up to contest the privilege of succeeding him. The second reading of the Reform Bill was discussed in a thin House, rarely more than two members rising at the same time; and the second night of the debate was actually postponed by one count out and very nearly terminated by another. This condition of the public and the parliamentary mind has been urged as a ground for dealing with the question without delay. Thin houses and dull debates give an opportunity, it is said, for a calmer consideration than was possible while Bristol and Nottingham were in flames.[1] We are inclined to doubt this plausible reasoning. More fortresses have been lost by heedlessness than by panic. An Englishman half asleep may be coaxed into giving away what the same man threatened and aroused would rather die than yield. The year 1832 was a year of great peril for the constitution. It was menaced by a half-starved and maddened populace, a weak king, and the contagion of neighbouring revolutions; and undoubtedly its danger was enhanced by the undue stubbornness of the ruling class. But yet we greatly fear that it will fare worse in the hands of the mild and honey-tongued languor that

---

[1] Serious riots in Bristol and Nottingham had followed the Lords' rejection of the second Reform Bill of 1831.

'THE BUDGET AND THE REFORM BILL'

ushers in the second Reform Bill, than it did in the gripe of the terrible convulsions that heralded the first. The present Reform Bill is so simple that it leaves little room for discussion. It is exquisitely free from all the complexities and compensations, which were such a stumbling-block to the last. So far as it goes it is a pure and simple approximation to democracy. If this be an improvement, it is the Bill's only recommendation; if it be an evil, the Bill has no counterbalancing advantage. All discussion of this measure therefore must be restricted to the degree of its progression, and to the general question whether progression of that kind is dangerous or safe. There are two ways in which it will give an accession to the democratic party in the House of Commons; it will create new constituencies, and it will metamorphose old ones. It is in the latter respect, undoubtedly, that it will operate with the most effect, for, in point of the destruction of boroughs, Lord John's natural tastes have been put under restraint. Scheduling boroughs is a very fascinating amusement to the arithmetical race of politicians, who believe in the inalienable right of eight beggars to govern seven Rothschilds, and, what is more, to tax them. Small boroughs must stink in the nostrils of those whose ideal of politics is a rule-of-three representation. But a trifling obstacle has hitherto hindered the consummation of these scientific aspirations: the ducks have absolutely declined to come and be killed. The small boroughs cannot be persuaded that the Tower Hamlets, which is the largest borough, is so obviously the wisest, that they are bound in patriotism to immolate themselves, in order that its like may be multiplied in the land. Lord John therefore has been content with a very moderate massacre. He has confined himself to five-and-twenty seats; and, relying on one of the evil precedents of the Bill of last year, he has disarmed half the hostility of his victims, as well as rescued a whole batch of Whig boroughs by dispensing altogether with a schedule A.[1] So far Lord John Russell has made a good bargain for his party. But setting aside the consideration of what he might have been forced to do, and confining our view to what he has actually done, the schedules of the Bill, taken by themselves, will not effect any great change in the balance of parties. Looking at the re-distribution of the seats apart from the question of the lowered suffrage, and estimating the political future of each constituency entirely from its present conduct, the result will be as follows. The five-and-twenty boroughs that are partially disfranchised may be divided under these three heads.

[1] In the Reform Act of 1832, schedule A listed the boroughs to be *totally* disfranchised.

7 Wholly Conservative	6 Wholly Liberal	12 Split boroughs
Devizes	Bodmin	Guildford
Marlow	Ripon	Hertford
Huntingdon	Marlborough	Dorchester
Knaresborough	Richmond	Chippenham
Ludlow	Totnes	Cirencester
Leominster	Thetford	Maldon
Honiton		Tewkesbury
		Andover
		Lymington
		Wells
		Evesham
		Harwich

Seven Conservative and six Liberal seats, therefore, are lost for certain; and assuming that the losses in the split boroughs will be equally divided, the disfranchisement will mulct the Conservative party of thirteen seats, and the Liberal party of twelve. Now let us see in what proportion the enfranchisement will restore them. Thirteen seats go to counties which – still assuming that the tone of the constituencies remains the same – will be divided thus:

7 Wholly Conservative	5 Wholly Liberal	3 Split counties
South Lancashire	Middlesex	North Lancashire
West Kent	South Staffordshire	North Lincolnshire
South Devonshire	West Cornwall	West Norfolk
North Yorkshire	West York (2 seats)	
South Essex		
East Somerset		
North Essex		

This would give a gain of, at most, nine Conservative to six Liberal seats. Of the four boroughs that are to receive additional members, Manchester and Birmingham are purely Liberal, Liverpool and Leeds are split boroughs. With these the proportion stands at ten new Conservative and nine new Liberal seats. The course of the perfectly new constituencies it is naturally more difficult to predict. But we fear that the probabilities lean in every case towards the Liberal side. There can be very little doubt that Chelsea and Kensington will become a metropolitan borough of the purest water, and will return two members, well worthy in point of talent and sagacity to rank with the rest of their

'THE BUDGET AND THE REFORM BILL'

compeers. Considering the origin and traditions of the University of London, we shall be pleasantly disappointed if it returns anything more Conservative in politics and religion than Professor Francis Newman.[1] The decision of the newly fledged constituencies of Burnley, Staleybridge, and Birkenhead, is in the womb of fate; but if they do return Conservatives, we fear that they will be selected from that hybrid class of politicians of whom the last election produced not a few, who voraciously swallowed the plumpest Radical pledges, and the Alpha and Omega of whose Conservatism consisted in voting with Mr. Disraeli on a confidence division. Adding these six votes to the Liberal side, it will appear that, whereas the Conservatives lose thirteen seats, they only regain ten; while the Liberals, losing twelve, receive fifteen. The upshot of the schedules, therefore, is a transfer of three seats. If any sanguine politician should flatter himself that Birkenhead will return a Conservative member, the transfer of seats will be reduced to two.

Unhappily this consoling calculation is nothing but a pleasing dream. Every element on which it is founded becomes worthless under the action of the suffrage clauses. After the democratic addition, which is to be made to the constituencies, but little of their political identity will remain. Of the exact extent and direction of this change nobody can form more than a distant estimate. Even the numerical statistics on the subject are wretchedly superficial. It is a curious proof of the unconcern of the political *pococuranti* by whom we are governed, that they have not even thought it worth while to ascertain the number of the new electors into whose hands the wealth and respectability of each constituency are to be delivered. There is some glimmer of information with respect to the increase which is likely to take place in the Boroughs; but with respect to the Counties we are still absolutely in the dark. Returns have appeared of the number of ratepayers whose annual payments lie within the limits of ten and fifty pounds, and who are, therefore, nominally enfranchised by this Bill. But we have no returns whatever to show how many of them are already on the register by virtue of other qualifications – such as freehold, copyhold, etc.[2] The future condition of the county constituencies, as it appears upon the face of the return, may be summed up in the following manner. Eighteen counties in England and Wales,

[1] F. W. Newman (1805–97), professor of Latin at University College London, friend of Mazzini and Kossuth, and a prolific writer of advanced views on religious, political, and social subjects; rejected historical Christianity.
[2] The 1832 Act gave the vote in counties to men holding a 40s freehold, or £10 copyhold, or sixty-year leasehold at £10, or twenty-year leasehold at £50, and also to £50 tenants-at-will.

including divisions of counties in that term, will have their constituencies more than doubled, viz.

South Chester	Middlesex	Brecon
North Derby	Monmouth	Cardigan
South Essex	North Shropshire	Carmarthen
Herts	East Surrey	Carnarvon
West Kent	West Surrey	Merioneth
North Lancashire	South Warwick	Montgomery

Ten occupy the other extreme of the list, and will have less than half their present numbers added to the existing register, viz.:

North Durham	South Leicester
Dorset	South Northampton
East Gloucester	South Northumberland
West Gloucester	North Wilts
North Leicester	South Wilts

The remaining fifty-three lie between these two extremes, and will be increased by more than fifty and less than a hundred per cent. Happily the probable addition, though formidable enough according to the lowest estimate, is not so bad as it looks on this return. In the Counties, as in the Boroughs, one-fifth or one-fourth must be deducted for females, incapacitated persons, and absentees. But the varied suffrage of the Counties furnishes another ground of uncertainty. The interval between ten and fifty pound rating is a region in which small freeholders may be expected to abound: and these men cannot, of course, be qualified twice over, though they may figure in this return among the number of new electors. The case of the West Riding will furnish an illustration. The electors for this division number 36,000,[1] but the fifty-pounders only amount to 10,400. The 26,200, who make the difference between these two sums, are in the main freeholders, copyholders, or leaseholders. Now the number of electors added to the constituency, as being rated at ten pounds and less than fifty pounds, is 27,400. But this will not be pure addition. The list of ten-pounders will contain to a great extent names that are already on the register among the 26,200 freeholders, etc. No doubt a great number of the freeholders will be residents in Sheffield, Leeds, and other represented towns, and will not, therefore, be included in the ten-pound list. But still a deduction, the exact proportion of which nothing but experience can ascertain, must be made on account of the freeholders from the apparent addition to each County constituency.

[1] Presumably this figure should be 36,600.

'THE BUDGET AND THE REFORM BILL'

Of the Boroughs we have more certain information. After the twenty or twenty-five per cent. for incapacitated persons has been subtracted, the returns may be taken as an absolute evidence of the impending increase.[1] The following list, taken from an exulting Radical organ,[2] of the thirty-four Boroughs in which the Bill will leave the register twice, or more than twice as bulky as it is now, will give an idea of the character of the Boroughs on whom its operation will chiefly fall. We have marked with asterisks the Boroughs which now return each one Conservative member (Yarmouth alone returning two), and in which, therefore, Conservative seats will probably be lost:

Boroughs	Registered electors	Additional houses	Per cent. increase
*Liverpool	18,779	18,835	100
Manchester	18,334	22,592	122
Birmingham	9,222	24,500	254
*Leeds	5,945	5,979	100
Sheffield	7,381	12,752	172
Wolverhampton	4,025	9,346	232
Bradford	3,599	3,991	108
Salford	4,375	6,050	138
*Stoke	2,221	3,646	164
*Portsmouth	3,821	6,082	159
*Preston	2,657	6,609	248
*Bolton	2,050	3,039	148
Leicester	4,207	4,248	101
Stockport	1,420	2,282	160
*Blackburn	1,524	2,302	150
Derby	2,505	3,776	150
*Macclesfield	1,073	2,910	271
Dudley	992	1,253	127
*Ipswich	1,926	2,498	129
*Wigan	858	902	105
Bury	1,246	1,598	128
*Yarmouth	1,393	2,247	161
Rochdale	1,346	1,552	115
South Shields	1,156	1,752	151
*Chatham	1,544	1,677	108
Walsall	1,092	3,841	351

[1] From returns of the number of male occupiers at different values in parliamentary boroughs, the government had calculated that the £6 rental franchise would add 194,000 voters, or about 44%, to the borough electorate. This seems to have been a large underestimate.
[2] It appeared in the *Daily News*, 6 March 1860, in a letter from James Acland, 'Parliamentary and Electoral Agent'.

Boroughs	Registered electors	Additional houses	Per cent. increase
Gateshead	913	1,211	132
Warrington	728	1,070	147
*Whitehaven	571	592	143
Kidderminster	487	1,473	302
*Frome	385	403	103
Poole	547	558	102
Peterborough	568	639	112
Merthyr Tydvil	1,341	4,110	306

It is evident, therefore, that the main increase will be in manufacturing places. But beyond this one result the figures furnish no definite rule. Neither locality nor size furnishes any criterion of the prevalence of the race of six-pounders whom Lord John Russell delights to honour. Of the remaining 165 Boroughs of England and Wales, 53 will enjoy an increase of between fifty and a hundred per cent., while the increase of the remaining 112 will be less than fifty per cent. The smallest Borough, Arundel, is in the first list; the Tower Hamlets, the largest Borough, is in the second. It is not very consoling to find that three metropolitan constituencies have an increase of less than four per cent.:

Boroughs	Registered electors	Additional houses	Per cent. increase
Marylebone	21,031	511	$2\frac{1}{2}$
Finsbury	20,951	698	3
London (City)	19,026	319	2

Is the inference to be drawn that in London we have already sunk as low as we can sink, and that, therefore, the Bill is powerless here; and that the effect of its more energetic operation upon other Boroughs will only be to introduce to supreme political power new batches of the class who have so long ruled us in the metropolis, and have given us so many proofs of their sagacity and enlightenment?

The character of these new depositaries of power it is naturally still more difficult to ascertain. We have no means of knowing anything of them as a whole. Individuals may retail the narrow results of their personal experience; but the means of forming a comprehensive estimate or of predicting the combined result of conflicting tendencies are utterly wanting. The leap which the House of Commons is taking with such philosophic calmness is a leap absolutely in the dark. We are humbly carrying our homage to some new king, but we know neither his name nor character. When the transfer is effected, when the new

'THE BUDGET AND THE REFORM BILL'

reign is opened, when the old rulers are irrevocably dethroned, then the veil will be drawn aside, and we shall see the form and lineaments of the now unknown Power which will thenceforth dispose of the fortunes of England. Until this interesting revelation is made, it is scarcely worth while to speculate. Some say that the publicans will be our masters; others declare that it will be the trades' unions. It is a blessed choice between debauchery and crime. On the whole, we pray for King Publican and his merry rule. If the sceptre is to be wielded for the benefit of one, and that the hungriest, class, the weaker the hands that it falls into the better. Anyhow Elagabalus is more tolerable than Caligula.[1] All the evils that we inveigh against in the constituencies where freemen prevail, the chronic corruption, the sickening debauchery, the wide-spreading fraud and wholesale perjury that adorn the working of our representative system in such places as Berwick and Norwich, would be ill exchanged for the strong, steady, deadly gripe of the trades' unions. These bodies have shown a tenacity of purpose, a vigour, and a pliability of organisation which would make them redoubtable antagonists if they were actuated by the purest morality and guided by the most enlightened wisdom. But the stupid barbarism of their economical creed, the ferocity with which their secret conclaves pronounce the doom of a horrible death against all who thwart their projects, the readiness with which they find instruments to execute their murderous decrees, warn us that, if ever England should really pass under their power, we should welcome the military despotism that should relieve us. The mass of readers pass over with unconcern the paragraphs that from time to time record some mysterious outrage in a manufacturing district. It does not occur to them to notice that the house was blown up, or the man was shot for refusing to obey the rules of this or that trades' union.[2] Perhaps these crimes will attract more attention when the supreme power in England has been surrendered to the class at the bidding of whose elected chiefs they are planned and perpetrated.

Whatever may be the special character of our new constitution, it is, at all events, clear that it will be more democratic than before. Whether its advance be great or small, it will, at all events, be great enough to destroy the power of the only element that can staunchly resist any

---

[1] The reign of the Roman emperor Elagabalus (218-22) was notorious for debauchery and depravity; that of Caligula (37-41) for cruelty.

[2] The use by some trade unionists of intimidation, violence, and even murder against recalcitrant fellow workers was attracting considerable attention at this period. The main centres of the 'outrages' were Glasgow, Manchester, and, especially, Sheffield, where the grinders' unions were the principal source of trouble, and gunpowder explosions were used to terrorise.

further movement. Mr. Bright has assured us, and we do not doubt him, that this bill will not be a settlement of the question, but only the preliminary to further change. If resistance be apparently difficult now, it will be utterly impossible with a Reformed Parliament two sessions hence. The bill, therefore, will bring democracy to us, if not at once, at least by stages. Mr. Rolt[1] truly described the peril that is hidden under the word Democracy when he said that the severance between property and representation is increased by this bill and will increase still more. Mr. Bright, while threatening a further agitation, tries to lull us with the assurance that the class he seeks to enfranchise cannot band together for a political purpose, because their differences are as wide as the differences of those above them. On many points it may be so; nay, possibly, on all points but one. But that one, the question of taxation, is the cardinal question of our day. The object of shifting taxation from their own shoulders to the shoulders of their betters is an object for which poor men will not long scruple to band together. The question whether, in a country where there are few rich and many poor, the poor shall use the power that theorists have given them to bleed the rich, is a question that the very first Reformed Parliament will be called upon to decide. We have already pointed out how Mr. Gladstone, foreseeing, no doubt, that this is the battle-field on which the classes of modern society must fight out their hostile claims, has obligingly rolled and levelled it in readiness. He has provided both the hour and the man. By his Budget he has supplied the opportunity for the conflict; by his Reform Bill he has taken care that there shall be champions to fight it. Next year there will be a colossal deficit, which will cast even the deficit of the present year into the shade. How is that deficit to be met? Democracies, in spite of Mr. Bright, are generally combative, and will not care, for the first year or two at least, to reduce the estimates. There will be nothing for it but more and yet more income-tax. But the traders will not long endure – they scarcely endure now – the income-tax as it stands. How easy it will be to silence all clamours, except those of the rich who will be practically unrepresented, by suppressing Schedule D,[2] and allowing the income-tax to slide into a property-tax. Is there not the Liverpool budget and the word of the great prophet Bright to justify it? And then, when the property-tax has been fairly set to work, what a 'mighty financial engine', as Mr. Gladstone would say, it will prove? It will be a great occasion for a new set of reforms in the tariff. The

[1] J. Rolt (1804–71), Conservative M.P. for West Gloucestershire.
[2] The income-tax schedule covering income from professions, trades, and other occupations.

'THE BUDGET AND THE REFORM BILL'

precedent of the paper-duty will come most appositely to hand. The tea, sugar, coffee, and corn duties have already been condemned by the financiers of the future. Talk not of the state of the exchequer or the difficulties of filling the void. Was the great financier of 1860 deterred by the state of his exchequer? The property-tax is at your elbow, ready and able for any burden you may lay upon it. You have nothing to do but to relieve industry – *i.e.* the six-pound voter; and you may safely burden property – *i.e.* the swamped and out-voted landowner. It will be a halcyon era for Chancellors of the Exchequer. It will be a day of simple and straightforward budgets, free from financial difficulties or the claims of jostling interests. Every deficiency can be filled up, every difficulty made straight, by a single application to the one fathomless resource. Until such a policy shall have lasted long enough to scare capital from our shores, property will always be within reach, rich enough to yield abundantly to pressure, too helplessly overborne by numbers to raise a voice or an arm in self-defence. It will, no doubt, be a consolation to the gentlemen of property, who are now conveying away their political independence with such refined indifference, to feel that they extended a 'generous confidence' to their countrymen, and that, if they sacrificed themselves, they at least redeemed the pledges of their leaders.

It seems as if a mysterious fatality attended on this question of Reform. Nobody wishes for it, and nobody dares resist it. A malign and inexplicable influence appears to have mastered the wills of our politicians, so that they vie with each other in professing objects which they do not seek, and forwarding changes whose consequences they dread. '*Video meliora proboque, deteriora sequor*,' might with truth be said, not now by one frail heroine, but by a whole class of sagacious and practised rulers. Some dark spell, like the spell of a nightmare, seems to be on their tongues, and they are all engaged in promoting and praising an undertaking of which in heart their only wish is that it should utterly miscarry. Lord John notoriously dislikes the change to which he is pledged. His colleagues reluctantly accept it, because they cannot do without him. His adversaries hardly dare resist it, for fear he should outbid them with the Radicals; Parliament sullenly submits to it, because it cannot dispense with the Ministry; and the Conservative majority of the nation wonderingly acquiesce, because every man of eminence is committed to it. The rise and progress of this Reform question – how it was sown, and how it grew and spread, and how every statesman successively was entangled in its withes – is one of the saddest tales in the history of modern

Parliamentary intrigues. It brings to light, more than any other question, the famine of principle that desolates the land. One firm will, one fixed political belief, one hearty preference of conviction before place, among the leaders of parties, would have broken the fatal charm which is now compelling Parliament to march on to its own destruction, with a perfect consciousness of the goal that lies before it. Like bankrupt governments, they have created political capital by an unlimited issue of pledges, and for a time their trade has flourished gaily; but the day of reckoning has come at last, and now the holders want gold for their notes. Perhaps the opposing leaders now see, when it is too late, that insincerity is never profitable but when it is practised only on one side. An antagonism of truth and uprightness, instead of an antagonism of false professions, would have produced exactly the same results on the relative strength of parties.

The origin of the evil is no doubt due to Lord John Russell.[1] Among many qualities which have procured for him a high position, both in the political and religious world, scrupulousness in his mode of obtaining office has never been conspicuous; and he has never observed much ceremony in wafting himself over to the Treasury Bench by the help of a delusive cry. No one suffered from his indifference on the subject of political identity more acutely than Sir Robert Peel. Lord John, in the character of a patron of Catholics, ejected Sir Robert Peel from office in 1835;[2] and in the character of patron of Tipperary Whiteboys, he ejected Sir Robert from office in 1846.[3] But when once the object was attained, and the soft benches of office were pressed again by his congenial form, all allusion to the question that had brought him there was as impertinent in his eyes as an allusion to masks would be when the Carnival was over. Sir Robert Peel's views were in both cases exactly carried out. The Catholics got no Church plunder, and the Tipperary Boys were coerced – the only departure from the original programme being that the Minister who carried out this policy was named Russell, and not Peel. Sir Robert had a great insight into his rival's character. Perhaps it was derived from his actual experience in these cases of the

[1] For an earlier, equally savage, characterisation of Russell by Lord Robert, see *B.Q.R.*, i (1859), 365–9.
[2] When Peel attempted in 1835 to settle the question of the bitterly resented Irish tithe, Russell raised the issue of the appropriation of the surplus revenues of the Irish Church, and Whigs, Radicals, and O'Connell coalesced to overthrow the government.
[3] Peel was defeated in June 1846 over his Irish coercion bill, meant to deal with agrarian disturbances provoked by famine. O'Connell co-operated with Russell to stop the measure. The Tipperary Whiteboys were a species of agrarian terrorist.

tendencies of that character, or perhaps from Lord John's unequalled solution of that difficult problem which most statesmen have tried their hands at, but in which all the rest have sadly broken down, of finding the exact moment at which a conversion on the subject of the Corn Laws could be profitably effected. From whatever source he derived his foresight, certain it is that in 1846 Sir Robert made a very remarkable prophecy with respect to Lord John's future career. Among other speculations as to the measures that the new Ministry might bring in, he was asked if he thought Lord John Russell would have recourse to another Reform Bill. 'No,' was the answer, 'he will not dream of it now; it is his last card – he will not play it yet: but whenever his Ministry shall be on the point of falling to pieces, then he will introduce a Reform Bill.' It is needless to say that the prediction was verified to the letter. So long as there was some sort of majority at his back, so long as the magnanimity of his ousted rival guarded him from his own followers and his own blunders, Lord John Russell was abundantly satisfied with the constitution of 1832. But from the moment that his nominal adversary was snatched away in the prime of a statesman's energies, at the culmination of his great career,[1] from that moment Lord John's fortunes began to wane. He floundered from one blunder into another. The Durham letter[2] and the quarrel with Lord Palmerston[3] laid the foundation of the feuds that have most embarrassed his subsequent course. Since that time the Irish Catholics have never ceased to revile him, and Lord Palmerston has missed no chance of tripping him up. But in proportion as his popularity decayed, his heart warmed again to the friend of his youth. Reform had made a great man of him once, and might possibly save him from sinking back into a small one. At all events, it would be an effective thorn in the side of his successor. Accordingly, when his Ministry was at its last gasp, he launched another Reform Bill.[4] Probably he never attached any serious idea to the proposal; it was only a pastime of debate, a little statesman-like flirtation with a question which he never dreamt of really undertaking.

[1] Peel died in July 1850.
[2] When, in 1850, the Pope decided to establish a regular diocesan hierarchy in England, Russell, falling in with the popular reaction, complained of papal aggression in an open letter to the Bishop of Durham.
[3] In December 1851, Palmerston, who had for some time been an embarrassment to Russell, was forced to resign from the latter's cabinet as a result of his unsanctioned endorsement of Louis Napoleon's *coup d'état*. The following February he retaliated by causing the fall of the ministry, and in 1858 Russell in turn helped to eject him from the premiership.
[4] In 1852.

The Whigs had collapsed, not in consequence of any external blow, but from absolute inanition of ability. It was reasonable to suppose that a grateful country, bearing in mind their super-human efforts to govern the State for the last five years, without a spark of statesmanship, would abstain from laying again upon their shoulders the unequal burden of office for at least five or six years to come. Nothing could be safer, therefore, than a pledge that would act as a convenient missile against his opponents, but could not, for many years at least, rebound upon himself. But he argued hastily from what he remembered of the strength of Conservatives in the days of Sir Robert Peel. He then little knew Mr. Disraeli's unrivalled powers of conducting his party into the ditch. That favourite of misfortune was then only known as a debater, who had risen into eminence by his intense Protectionism and by the virtuous indignation with which he proscribed all statesmen who changed their minds; and his advent to power was looked for more with curiosity than with dread. No sooner, however, was the object of his ambition attained, than he went forth, blundering and to blunder, on that career of disastrous leadership of which the recent majorities on the Budget are the latest fruit; and from that time it became evident that the Conservatives would have a long tenure of opposition, and that Lord John's return to power was inevitable.[1] Perhaps, when Lord John saw the calibre of the adversary with whom he had to deal, it occurred to him to wish that he had not said quite so much about Reform. But the pledge was passed, and could not be revoked. He felt bound at least to propose another bill, like the conjuror who, having in a moment of excitement told his audience that he could cut off his own head without feeling it, felt bound for very shame to give himself a little gash. Unluckily, this liability extended itself to all who might be his colleagues. With them, as with him, the delusion was still strong that Reform was a popular cry. Neither he nor those of his followers who still believed in the divinity that doth hedge about a Russell were to be had without Reform; and, if the leaders of the Liberal party had constructed their political position in opposition to Lord John, on the basis of a distinct repudiation of that unpalatable clap-trap, their chance of a majority was very small. Accordingly, pursuant to the ethical maxim now dominant among the mass of statesmen, that conscious virtue is cold comfort for political ostracism, the Coalition of 1853[2] made up their minds to swallow Lord John and

---

[1] The Conservative ministry lasted only from February to December 1852.
[2] Combining Whigs, Peelites, and one Radical in the cabinet, with Russell, Palmerston, and Gladstone serving under Lord Aberdeen.

'THE BUDGET AND THE REFORM BILL'

his pledges in a lump. There were other motives probably that actuated one portion at least of that Coalition. It is difficult to believe that the auxiliaries borrowed from the Conservative camp could really have believed in the wisdom of a Reform Bill. But, considering how minute was the point upon which, two years later, they threw up their places,[1] it is equally difficult to conceive that they were actuated by mere adhesiveness to office. No historian will be successful in unravelling the political complications of the last fourteen years who imputes their varied vicissitudes exclusively to the convictions or the greediness of the actors, and does not take into account the remarkable influence that has been exercised by mere vindictiveness. The successful counterfeit of Christian forgiveness, which is produced by considerations of personal advancement, and usually makes politicians the most placable race in the world, wholly fails to compose the feud between Protectionists and Peelites. Though Protection is as dead as Peel, the bitterness of the strife survives them both, just as a Chancery suit will last long after the estate that provoked it is exhausted. A succession of injuries inflicted by each upon the other, far from satiating, only renews the rancour of their hatred. So far as successful retaliation can be considered an advantage, the Peelites have hitherto had the best of it. Each party has twice driven the other from office; but beyond that the Peelites have handled murderous weapons, such as Budgets and Reform Bills, while the wrath of the Protectionists has evaporated in words. One would have thought that by this time bygones might be bygones, and that all parties having become politically bankrupt of their old opinions on this matter of Free Trade, might be whitewashed, and start afresh. Lord Palmerston has been abused, as no other man since the days of Catiline, by a third of the colleagues who now sit with him in the Cabinet. The only inference that he drew from their abuse was that the sooner they were his friends the better. If the same tact and wisdom had prevailed two years ago with the Conservative leaders, it is possible that some of the followers of Sir Robert Peel might have returned to the party from which they had been divided by the question of the Corn Laws.[2] All hopes of such a junction are over now. The schism, which represents little real antagonism

---

[1] The Peelites, Gladstone, Graham, and Herbert, left the government in February 1855, refusing to agree to a committee of enquiry into the management of the Crimean War.

[2] On Derby's taking office in February 1858, Gladstone was invited to join him, but declined, as he did again in May, when Graham (to whom Disraeli had offered to surrender the Commons' leadership) favoured the step, but Aberdeen inclined against it.

of conviction, is wider than ever, and the old resentment is kindled anew between Peelites and Agriculturists. Mr. Bentinck[1] still, on the part of the country members, denounces a Peelite as a worse enemy than a Whig; and Mr. Gladstone replies by levying his deadly Budgets and deadlier Reform Bills against the land.

The Peelites would have been more than men if something of this feeling had not influenced them in consenting to a Reform Bill in 1853. To sweep away with the besom of destruction those who were perpetually crossing their path and baulking their career was a temptation too strong to be resisted. Mr. Bright has openly professed in the House of Commons that the main recommendation of a Reform Bill in his eyes is the extirpation of the territorial element in that assembly. Mr. Gladstone's words, perhaps his thoughts, have never gone so far. But a Reform Bill will deluge the House of Commons with minds revolting to his own in point of intellect, of refinement, of religious and political belief, in fact, of every quality than can recommend one mind to another. The prospect of it can have but this one charm for him – that, by thinning the agricultural ranks, it will in some degree clear his path towards the attainment of that financial ideal on which his whole soul is now bent, and in which all the aims of his past life are merged.

If, however, the adoption of a Reform policy by the whole Liberal party – new recruits and all – had been the whole of the evil, we should still be far enough from a Reform Bill. It was a pity that Lord John Russell, thoughtlessly or mischievously, should have accepted two revolutions in a lifetime as the fitting rate of a nation's progress towards democracy. It was a pity that his colleagues should have followed their leader, after the fashion of an electoral club at Gloucester or St Albans,[2] and have put on what cockade he bid them on account of a contract, which, for due consideration, he, and not they, had made. But the Liberal party have often made foolish pledges before this, without any damage accruing from them to the State. A quarter of a century ago they bound themselves to plunder the Irish Church; but to this day the Irish Church remains intact. Lord John was not much less mischievous then than he is now, and the Whig party was much stronger. The only difference was that in the one case the Conservatives helped him to recede from his ill-advised engagements; in the other case they outbid him. Or, in other words, Sir Robert Peel was the Conservative leader on the first occasion, and Mr. Disraeli on the second. The Liberal leaders may have committed many

---

[1] G. W. P. ('Big Ben') Bentinck (1803-86), Conservative M.P. for West Norfolk.
[2] Two notoriously corrupt constituencies. The former was temporarily disfranchised in 1859, and the latter disfranchised altogether in 1862.

'THE BUDGET AND THE REFORM BILL'

errors; but, at all events, it is no fault of theirs that *both* sides of the House are committed to Reform. Lord John's heedless ambition may have been the *fons et origo mali*; but his little stream has been replenished by copious tributaries from a totally different quarter.

When Lord Derby, some two years ago, was explaining to the House of Lords the future policy of his then infant Government, and, among other things, announced in language technically vague, but practically binding, that he intended to consider the question of Reform, a wary old Whig Minister who was looking on, at once the most sagacious and the most upright of his party, muttered in disgust, 'That's a mistake.' He foresaw in it not only the certain fall of Lord Derby's Ministry, for which he probably might have been easily consoled, but a new and ominous aspect of the momentous question on which it bore. Going down a steep hill with a strong drag on is pleasant travelling enough; but the boldest driver may well be alarmed at seeing his drag-chain suddenly convert itself, by some strange metamorphosis, into a propelling power. An organic change proposed by Conservatives, with no one to check it except those who were by profession bound to aggravate it, was a phenomenon hitherto unknown to the Constitution.

The severest censure that could be passed upon this promise was the motive that was currently assigned to it. It was not for nothing that Lord Derby called upon his party to resign their traditional functions, and with their own hands to open, no matter how narrowly, the floodgates of the Constitution to the torrent of democracy. The temporary support of the Radicals was the precious guerdon for which Conservatism was to expose itself to ridicule by masquerading for a season in the motley of Reform. The ill-advised pledge was delivered with Lord Derby's accustomed eloquence and off-hand manliness of tone; but there was no difficulty in divining the real parentage of a scheme that had little in common either with his combativeness of temper or proud impatience of restraint. It was of a piece with a policy which had long misguided and discredited the Conservative party in the House of Commons. To crush the Whigs by combining with the Radicals was the first and last maxim of Mr. Disraeli's Parliamentary tactics. He had never led the Conservatives to victory, as Sir Robert Peel had led them to victory. He had never procured the triumphant assertion of any Conservative principle, or shielded from imminent ruin any ancient institution. But he had been a successful leader to this extent, that he had made any Government, while he was in opposition, next to an impossibility. His tactics were so various, so flexible, so shameless – the net by which his combinations were gathered in was so wide – he had so admirable a knack of enticing into the same lobby a happy family of proud old Tories and foaming Radicals, martial squires jealous for their country's honour, and manufacturers who had written it off their books as an unmarketable commodity – that so long as his party backed him, no Government was strong enough to hold out against his attacks. They might succeed in repelling this sally or that; but sooner or later their watchful and untiring enemy, perfectly reckless from what quarter or in what uniform he assaulted, was sure to find out the weak point at which the fortress could be scaled. For mere partisans no doubt this was exciting work. They were never reduced, as under the Fabian guidance of Sir Robert Peel, to look for their sole hope of office in the slowly swelling aggregate of votes, that indicated year by year the gradual growth of the Conservative reaction. Their new chief kept up their spirit by a less scrupulous and more venturesome game. They did not need to bide their time till their principles had slowly wound themselves into the convictions of the people. For their hopes of success they only waited upon that Providence that maketh Radicals to rebel. Any breeze of Fortune that brought them allies would also bring them place. It was a policy well fitted to the capacities and the temper of the mere professional politician. Watching the turn of every passing incident at home or abroad, and extracting from it the precise blister best fitted to goad to madness the irritable Radical cuticle, was as exciting a trial of ingenuity and skill as a scientific experiment; and it was likely to lead to great results much more rapidly than the mere laborious and honest maintenance of principles and pledges. It was true that the mass of Mr. Disraeli's followers were not professional politicians. In every party, most of all in a party made up chiefly of country gentlemen, the great proportion will consist of men for whom office has no attractions, who would refuse it if it was offered to them, and to whom the chance of refusing it is never likely to be given. These men were far from relishing the political sleight-of-hand of their ingenious leader. They did not enter into the game with any zest. Each time the Whigs were outwitted or outflanked by the help of the Radicals, it was impossible that they should forget that it was chiefly to resist these very Radicals that they came into Parliament, and that approximation to Radicalism was the head and front of the offending which they imputed to their opponents. They naturally protested that this fraternization with Mr. Roebuck[1] and

[1] J. A. Roebuck (1801–79), M.P. Sheffield, one of the most vigorous and advanced Radicals of the thirties and forties, but later much modified his views; his motion

'THE BUDGET AND THE REFORM BILL'

Mr. Milner Gibson[1] might be a very amiable exhibition of Christian feeling; that these smart invectives and clever manœuvres might be a very pretty display of ingenuity; but that these things did not advance Conservatism. Such ominous forebodings were silenced with the assurance that it was all for the good of the party. Only a Conservative Government could carry Conservative measures, and in the divided and apathetic temper of the times it was only by tact and address that a Conservative Government could be restored to office. Mr. Disraeli might fraternize with the Radicals now, for no harm could come of it. He might be all things to all men now; but let them wait and see what he would do when he was once leader of the House of Commons.

His party submitted, waited, and saw. What they beheld during the sixteen months[2] of official servitude which rewarded his restless manœuvres of five years, was not calculated to convince them of the wisdom of trying to base a Conservative triumph on a Radical alliance. It was not a reassuring spectacle at the time, it is not a pleasing retrospect now, for those who wish well to the Constitution, and to the party that should be its chief support. Opponents were wont to speak almost with envy of the laudable discipline of the Tory party. They little knew the deep and bitter humiliation that was masked by the outward loyalty of its votes. The Conservatives could not blind themselves to the fact that their leaders held office not because Conservatism was preferred by the House of Commons, but because the Radicals wished to punish the Whigs for not being Radical enough. Mr. Disraeli owed it to these Radical allies that he was leader of the House of Commons; he knew that he must vacate his position at the first breath of Radical displeasure. Tenants-at-will are not usually proof against political intimidation. It was painfully obvious throughout the short career of the Conservative administration that they were conscious of the tenure on which their power was held, and that the instinctive Conservatism of their course was checked and distorted by a kind of sidelong homage to the kingmaker to whom their transient victory was due. It is needless to dwell on the special instances of an error, which, in spite of Mr. Disraeli's natural inclinations, the Conservative party are not likely to repeat. Many of the concessions were of small practical effect, because they could not

---

in 1855 for a committee to enquire into the conduct of the Crimean War brought down Aberdeen's ministry.

[1] T. Milner Gibson (1806–84), M.P. Ashton-under-Lyne, and president of the board of trade 1859–66; ally of Cobden in the anti-corn law struggle and friend of Bright; moved the vote of censure on which the Palmerston government fell in February 1858.

[2] February 1858 to June 1859.

long have been delayed. In some cases, as in that of the Jews,[1] the position was already half stormed; in others, as in that of the qualification of members,[2] it had long been turned. It was more the moment and the manner of yielding what, when concession was profitless, had been stoutly contested, that damaged the Conservative party in the opinion of earnest and thinking men. But there was one concession of which we are now bitterly rueing the results. The English Constitution is likely to feel, as long as it shall endure, the consequences of Lord Derby's resolution to produce a Conservative Reform Bill. We will not stop to discuss the merits of a proposal whose term of existence was so short. It bore, impressed on every feature, the parentage of the ingenious counsellor into whose hands for these many years past Lord Derby's political conscience has been confided. Two of the staunchest, ablest, and most respected representatives of true Conservatism in the House of Commons broke away from the administration rather than give to such a measure the weight of their approval.[3] And, in spite of the immediate party advantage which the success of the measure might possibly have produced, they could hardly have done otherwise. Its various provisions were nicely balanced, so that the landed interest on the whole would perhaps have profited by the change. But it had that fatal and damning defect for a proposal that was to appear before an English tribunal, that the complication of its details exposed it to the suspicion of stratagem and finesse. It was not statesmanlike – it was only ingenious. The result which followed was so inevitable that it might easily have been foreseen. The measure itself was rejected; but the various concessions it contained were picked out from among the restrictions that were intended to countervail them, and used by the Radicals to force larger promises out of the Whigs. The Bill of 1860 is the logical and necessary corollary of the Bill of 1859. The aversion to Reform, common to both Conservatives and Whigs, has been paralysed and struck dumb by this fatal precedent. It was impossible, when the Conservatives had proposed a ten-pound county franchise, for the Whigs to refuse to go as far. When the Conservatives had consented to begin the disfranchisement of boroughs, it

[1] In 1858 practising Jews were enabled to sit in the House of Commons, from which the form of oath for members had hitherto excluded them. Disraeli had been a strong advocate of this reform, which had several times been accepted by the Commons but blocked by the Lords.
[2] The old property qualification for members of Parliament for England and Ireland was abolished in 1858.
[3] These were the home secretary, Spencer Walpole, and the president of the board of trade, J. W. Henley, who resigned in February 1859, unable to accept the assimilation of the county to the borough franchise.

'THE BUDGET AND THE REFORM BILL'

was no longer open for Lord John Russell to do as he had done in 1852, and omit the schedules altogether. And the Conservative Opposition is fretting in vain against the shackles with which its leaders have embarrassed it. By these fatal admissions, every chance of resistance, every outlet of escape, is cut off. It has been no longer possible to resist the Bill on the second reading on the ground that Reform is needless, for the necessity of Reform has been admitted. It is no longer possible to fight for the rights of old constituencies, for the legitimacy of schedules has been admitted. It is no longer easy to struggle against the ten-pound franchise in the counties, for the ten-pound franchise has been admitted. There remains nothing to which we have not committed ourselves, except the lowered franchise in the boroughs. Is there a chance of a successful effort being made in favour of some franchise that shall not admit the trades-unions in a body? It is impossible to predict what may be done in the committee, or what improvements the Bill may receive from the House of Lords. It is impossible to guess at what late hour the pressing imminence of danger may dissolve the spell which seals the lips and stifles the consciences of those who, if they would only face the facts, know perfectly what the facts imply. There are Whigs as well as Tories who know what this Reform Bill means, and look forward to the consequences with a terror which no party opiates can appease. It means that the whole community shall be governed by an ignorant multitude, the creatures of a vast and powerful organisation, of which a few half-taught and cunning agitators are the head; it means a realisation of Mr. Bright's and Mr. Gladstone's fiscal views – the taxation of the affluent and the educated alone; it means, in short, that the rich shall pay all the taxes, and the poor shall make all the laws. If the votes of the House of Commons could be taken by way of ballot, very little indeed of the Reform Bill would be left. But yet no one member may be bold enough by himself to bell the cat. It is very difficult indeed to induce a House of Commons to resist the details of a Reform Bill. In voting against the reduction of a suffrage whether in county or in town, members feel that if that reduction should be carried they have converted into opponents all whom it enfranchises. No six-pounder in a borough, or ten-pounder in a county, whatever his politics may be, will ever forgive the man who has sought to exclude him from the franchise. With this certainty before their eyes, those who support a higher franchise than the Government has proposed feel that they are voting with a halter round their necks. In the present day such a consideration is quite enough to decide their course. Public feeling is not extravagantly Quixotic with us just now.

SALISBURY'S 'QUARTERLY REVIEW' ARTICLES

The tale of Quintus Curtius[1] is not likely to have any counterpart in modern politics. Of course, they will regret that the British Constitution should be undermined. They will deplore that the selfish competition of public men should have brought matters to such a pass, that they are obliged to confide the terrible power of taxation into the hands of the hungriest and rudest. But they will not the less decline to give a vote that shall convert into a certainty the already probable enmity of their new constituents. Something of the same self-seeking dalliance with a momentous crisis is traceable in the attitude of the two parties. The Whigs abominate the Reform Bill, and see in it, not unreasonably, their own political annihilation. But they hope, and have contrived to persuade themselves, that their opponents will pull the chestnuts out of the fire. Thus they count on being completely hedged. In case of success, they will reap the benefit and escape the odium; in the case of failure, their rivals will be even more discredited than themselves. The Tories see through this shabby policy, and resent it; and, by way of revenging themselves, seem inclined to sit still and let their adversaries choose at their leisure between unpopularity and destruction. Each side seems to be persuaded that the other will come forward to avert the measures which, if carried, will be the common ruin of both. The probable result of this sagacious strife will be, that each will have the dying satisfaction of seeing the other fall a prey to the Radical allies, whom both have for so many years been emulously courting.

It is indeed time – if there be yet time – that the Conservatives should abandon the policy of mere antagonism, which has brought them so much of failure and disgrace. If they would save their party, weakened, menaced, disunited as it is, it must be by looking to their principles alone as the prize for which they are to contend. Their cause is too noble, their struggle is too momentous to be degraded into a mere tout for office. It has worn too much of this character during the latest phase of their political history. An unconcerned spectator might reasonably have inferred from what has passed during the last few years, that the mission and function of Conservatism was fulfilled when twenty new faces replaced twenty old vices on the right of the Speaker's chair. Some improvement of tone, the effect, we will hope, of increasing moderation, is traceable in Mr. Disraeli's conduct during this spring; but the Liverpool speech of last autumn, and the seven years' tactics of which it was the

---

[1] The reference is presumably to the story of M. Curtius, the Roman youth who leaped into a chasm which had opened in the Forum, after the oracle had declared that it would never close until Rome threw into it its most precious possession.

'THE BUDGET AND THE REFORM BILL'

explanation and the defence, are still fresh in the memory of all.[1] The reasoning of that speech, and the spirit of those tactics, might well induce the nation to believe that the 'Great Party' which he led cared for no 'great political principles' to justify its existence; that special political convictions had no more to do with its party struggles than with the contests of the Hippodrome; and that Conservatives registered and organised, and lavishly spent their money and their labour, merely that the ambition of a few, or of one, might be contented. And yet there must be among the party still many whose conservatism is older than Mr. Disraeli's, and will probably last longer, and who look back regretfully to the old days when the fight was for real principles, real blessings, real truths. They must feel that there are objects higher than party victories, the loss of which no success in an election or a division will replace. If the religion, which is the keystone of our social existence is slighted; if the Church is given over to her enemies to be stripped and buffeted; if the main beams of the ancient fabric of our Constitution are being sawn through, it is cold comfort to be told that the party is one step or two steps nearer to the enjoyment of nominal power. If our aristocratic system is being discredited and undermined; if the Radicals, by the alternate aid of Tory and Whig complicity, are able to dictate their policy to each in turn; if Democracy creeps on apace, less by its own inherent strength, than by the treachery of its opponents, we shall not be consoled even though Mr. Disraeli be again gazetted Chancellor of the Exchequer. We cannot look with complacency at the distant but rising storm of Democratic spoliation, even though we see it across a long vista of Tory victories gained and Tory Administrations upheld by Radical assistance. Party loyalty is good when paid to a worthy object, and paid without misgiving. Party discipline is a means to a great end; but in some emergencies, and under some leaders, it may be made to frustrate the end at which it aims. The future before the Conservative party is not a cloudless one, for the full penalty of many a past error must be paid. The nation leans strongly to the Conservative creed, but has little confidence in those by whom it is professed. The party can only regain their position in the nation's trust by practically belying the slur which recent faults have cast upon them. If they jealously shun all crooked paths to power, if, with their leaders, or without their leaders,

[1] At Liverpool in October 1859, Disraeli had claimed to have put an end, in his ten years' leadership, to 'the monopoly of Liberalism', whereby the Conservatives were supposed to be debarred from attempting measures of improvement, and to have brought about a healthier state of parties in which men would be judged by policy and actions, not by traditions, 'which are generally false', or promises.

they resolutely refuse the fellowship of those who abhor their creed, and rely for final triumph on the strength of their own true principles alone, they may yet do as noble services to their country as any of those by which their traditions are adorned. They may promote, more efficiently perhaps in opposition than in office, the great work of arresting the march of Democracy, until the lessons which America and France are teaching every year with increased force shall have exploded the delusion that, in the minds of so many, confounds Democracy with Freedom. But if the past has no warning and no meaning for them, and fidelity to a leader who has been tried and has been found wanting is to be preferred to all other considerations, they will expiate their error in the irretrievable loss of that national confidence, without which no party can exist. If the old strategy is to be renewed, and, during five more years of opposition, momentary success is to be schemed for by all arts and at all hazards, – if triumphs are to be purchased by the sacrifice of all that makes a triumph precious, – the certain punishment of a trust knowingly and wilfully misplaced will not delay to overtake them. There is a curse that cleaves to parties as to individuals – Woe to the blind that lead; woe to the blind that follow!

'The House of Commons'
(Q.R., no. 231; July 1864)

INTRODUCTORY NOTE

THE early sixties were years of remarkable placidity in British politics. In the comfortable atmosphere of mid-Victorian prosperity, the personal position of Lord Palmerston, who reached the age of eighty in 1864, was not seriously challenged, and the genial conservatism which he purveyed seemed for the moment to suit the country's mood. Indeed, it went down so well as to render the competing product, offered by the official Conservative party, something of a drug in the market. With Palmerston in possession of the conservative cause, and of much of conservative sentiment, Derby was virtually compelled to acquiesce in his reign, and to prop him up against the more radical elements in his heterogeneous following. Disraeli's co-operation in this policy was so impeccable that Lord Robert felt no need to refurbish the philippics of 1860. The result was that domestic politics, without major issues or keen party strife, became very flat. Reviewing a year of peace, prosperity, and calm, the *Annual Register* for 1864 wrote: 'The spirit of party, indeed, appeared to have lost nearly all its acrimony, and even a large share of its vitality, both in Parliament and in the country at large; it seemed as if few questions remained to divide in any material degree the opinions of the different sections of politicians.' Perhaps the main focus of attention in this period was less any domestic topic than the tremendous struggle of the American Civil War, which, breaking out in 1861, divided British opinion (Conservatives, including Lord Robert, tending to sympathise with the South), and caused considerable distress in Lancashire and elsewhere by interfering with the supply of raw cotton to the textile industry.

All the same, the lull on the home political front was not total. Lord Robert found special cause for concern in the continuing pressure of the nonconformists against the privileges of the established Church, expressed in the controversies over church rate, burials, and endowed schools, and was active in resisting it, both in Parliament and in the pages of the *Quarterly*. And in the first half of 1864 two episodes ruffled the political calm more than a little: the flaring up of the Schleswig-Holstein dispute, and Gladstone's declaration on Reform.

The struggle between Danes and Germans for the duchies of Schleswig and Holstein, which were personally united with the Danish crown, involved Britain both as a signatory to the treaty of London of 1852, by which the great powers had sought to regulate the question, and because Princess Alexandra of Denmark had recently married the Prince of Wales. Palmerston had declared in July 1863 that if the rights and independence of Denmark were attacked the aggressors would not have to contend with Denmark alone, and the Danes had reason to count on British support. But when Prussia and Austria fell upon the duchies in February 1864, Britain had to stand rather ignominiously aside. She could not intervene effectively without a continental ally, and the terms for French co-operation proved unpalatable. Lord Robert dealt extensively with the question in his *Quarterly* articles of January and April 1864, lambasting in the latter what he depicted as the government's policy of bluster followed by inaction (the few pages devoted to the matter which he tacked on to the end of the present article are omitted as unrelated to its main themes). In July the Conservatives moved censure resolutions in both Houses: the government was beaten in the Lords, and survived by only eighteen votes in the Commons. The Danes surrendered ten days after the latter vote.

Meanwhile, the Reform question, half-drowned in apathy since 1860 (even Russell falling back on the maxim 'Rest and be thankful'), had been sharply resuscitated. Speaking on Edward Baines's bill for a £6 rental franchise in boroughs, on 11 May 1864, Gladstone favoured a large increase in the working-class portion of the electorate, and declared: 'I venture to say that every man who is not presumably incapacitated by some consideration of personal unfitness or political danger is morally entitled to come within the pale of the Constitution.' The reservations as to personal unfitness or political danger could clearly be interpreted very largely, and Gladstone was not thinking of admitting more than 'a select portion of the working classes'. 'What', he asked, 'are the qualities which fit a man for the exercise of a privilege such as the franchise? Self-command, self-control, respect for order, patience under suffering, confidence in the law, regard for his superiors.' Nonetheless, his words were taken as a drastic concession to democratic ideas, and it was in vain that he tried to play them down in the preface to the pamphlet version of his speech, where he remarked that his now celebrated principle had not been 'a deliberate and studied announcement', and that he could more readily have understood criticism on the ground of its narrow limitation by the exceptions attached to it than on the ground of its breadth. Palmerston and the Queen were aghast, but the speech marked an important evolution in Gladstone's public position. It signalised his expanding sympathy with the working classes, and stimulated the growth of that popularity in the country which was to underlie his pre-eminence in Parliament. Increasingly, he seemed the man to fill the virtual vacuum in the leadership of Liberalism.

It is on Gladstone's revival of the Reform issue that Lord Robert concentrates in this article, though he begins with a diverting glimpse of the mid-Victorian House of Commons in operation, followed by some reflections on the basic conditions of its proper functioning. Gladstone's pronouncement provoked him into something that was rare with him, because foreign to his intellectual approach, a discussion of the abstract right to the suffrage, which necessarily obliged him to indicate some general views on the purposes of society and

'THE HOUSE OF COMMONS'

government, and to attempt to offer a logical theoretical justification for the political system which he wished to maintain. Just because he wrote so reluctantly and so seldom on this theoretical level, these pages have a special interest for the study of his outlook.

1. *Speech of the Right Hon. W. E. Gladstone in the House of Commons upon the second reading of the Borough Franchise Bill.* London, 1864.
2. *Debate upon the Vote of Censure moved by the Right Hon. B. Disraeli, July, 1864.* Hansard's Debates. London, 1864.
3. *Rules and Regulations of the House of Commons.* London, 1859.

Whatever may be the course of events, it seems to be scarcely possible that the present House of Commons should survive to see another July. When or whence the blow shall fall which will cut the brief thread of its remaining existence, no one can guess. But a House whose continuance depends upon such contingencies as the votes of some nine men, or the continued capacity of an aged man for an exhausting office, clearly does not hold its life upon any very certain tenure. Whenever its fate shall come, it will pass from existence with a fair title to the gratitude of Englishmen. It has done that which it is most difficult and most salutary for a Parliament to do – nothing. Or, if it has not quite reached to the height of this achievement, it has approached to it more nearly than any Parliament of equal duration of which we have the record. With the exception of a few hasty financial changes introduced by Mr. Gladstone, antedated of their true period by a few years to suit his impetuous disposition, and discounted, consequently, at the cost of a crushing income-tax for the time,[1] the conscience of this Parliament is burdened by the recollection of no statute which the future historian will find it necessary to chronicle. But though it has produced little, it has extinguished much. It has made an end, for the present at least, of the great delusion of Reform, and has released the statesmen on both sides from the suicidal pledges by which they had indiscreetly bound themselves. It has converted the overwhelming majority against Church-rates into a majority the other way, which has at least sufficed to stifle the Parliamentary agitation against that endowment.[2] And in respect to other matters

[1] By now, however, Gladstone had brought the income tax down to 6d.
[2] Sir J. Trelawny's bill for the abolition of church rates had passed its second reading in the Commons by a majority of 70 in July 1859; in 1860 it passed its third reading by nine, but was thrown out by three votes in the Lords; in 1861 its third reading was lost by the speaker's casting vote; and after majorities against the second reading of one and ten respectively in 1862 and 1863, it was not reintroduced in 1864.

of more secondary importance, its negative energy has left equally wholesome traces behind. The Burials Bill, the Endowed Schools Bill, in fact the whole programme of the Liberation Society has disappeared.[1] The House has opposed to its attacks, not an enthusiastic championship of the Church or the of Constitution – for enthusiasm in a body which acknowledges Lord Palmerston for a leader is out of the question – but the stolid and far more effective resistance of a sandbag. Liberalism has vainly buried its shafts in that impenetrable mass. The same inertness has, perhaps, been less favourable to our foreign policy; for it has suffered a feeble Minister to betray an ally, and to persuade the world of England's impotence. But still it has done its best. No harm that has happened can be charged upon its meddlesome interference; and, if it has not always let well alone, it has simply been in the cases where there was no well to let alone. Its fault has been, if any, an Epicureanism or fatalism in politics, which, perhaps, may have allowed many evils to flourish that might otherwise have been cured; but which, on the other hand, has spared us the agitation attendant upon over-hasty progress, or the rude shocks of heedless innovation. It has stood by quietly and watched many a change pass over the face of this unstable world. It has seen Italy thrown into Medea's cauldron, with the full hope of immediate rejuvenescence; and has cynically looked on as the hopes of the operators have been gradually dashed by increasing debt, and ineradicable discontent, and the ever-menacing aspect of a religious organisation which can neither be reconciled nor crushed. It has seen America torn in pieces by civil war; and it has preferred that the industry of its own people should be ruined by the result rather than that the torrent of blood should be stayed.[2] It has witnessed revolutions in Greece and Poland,[3] and the commencement of European war in Denmark. It has

[1] Sir M. Peto's Burials Bill, designed to allow nonconformists to have their funerals celebrated with their own rites and services, and by their own ministers, in Church of England graveyards, was introduced in 1862 and again in 1863, when Lord Robert vigorously opposed it, and it was lost on the second reading by 25 votes. The Endowed Schools Bill, aimed at breaking the exclusive Anglican control of endowed schools not specifically devoted by the founder to nonconformity, received a second reading in 1859, but was lost at the same stage in 1860 by 70 votes. The Society for the Liberation of Religion from State Patronage and Control, the principal nonconformist pressure group, had as its leading object the disestablishment of the Church of England.

[2] The government had declined to attempt to mediate in the American Civil War (a step which would almost certainly have meant hostilities with the North), or to recognise the Confederacy, and Roebuck's motion of June 1863 for recognition of the South, strongly supported by Lord Robert, had been withdrawn without a vote.

[3] In 1862 and 1863 respectively.

'THE HOUSE OF COMMONS'

seen treaty after treaty torn up; and it has stood by while its Government, with a spider's undiscouraged perseverance, has striven to weave new subject-matter for similar operations. Garibaldi has been fêted like a prince;[1] his disciple Stansfeld, with a cruel contrast of destiny, has been hooted out of office.[2] But during all this various drama, and across all these changing phases of feeling, the House of Commons – so far as its journals record its history – has preserved a mute impassiveness, which may pass for dignity or for helplessness, according to the charity of its critics. Its existence has been one long negative. If it were not that its forms occasionally clothe a decision substantially negative in the guise of an affirmative, the Speaker's duty might almost have been performed by an automaton constructed to articulate the sounds, 'The Noes have it.'

Unquestionably its inaction has reflected the cautious temper of the day. So many bubbles have been bursting all around, and so many political theories, which a few years ago passed for sterling gold, have proved themselves to be the veriest pinchbeck, that our rulers may be forgiven for displaying diffidence and scepticism. All honour, therefore, to the Legislature that has expended all its energy in harmless talk which hurts nobody but those who are rash enough to read it. If some previous Parliaments had been equally garrulous and unpractical, England would have escaped some trouble, and more danger. Some people are foolish enough to complain of the length of the Parliamentary debates. They irreverently assert that Parliament attends to the business of every nation except its own, and occupies its time in making and listening to splendid declamations upon events that are passing in countries over which it has not the slightest power. No such ungrateful murmurs shall escape from our pen. Honourable members cannot be better employed. If they were absolutely idle, some mischief, according to the hymn, might still be found for them to do. May their tongues never be less! May they long be disabled from all power of damaging the Constitution by the exhaustion consequent upon their own debates!

This curious machine that governs us is worthy of attentive study. It does the work, undoubtedly, in a fitful, slovenly, accidental sort of

[1] He had visited England in April.
[2] James Stansfeld (1820–98), Radical M.P. for Halifax, and supporter of Italian unity, resigned his post as a junior lord of the admiralty in April 1864, after the Paris trial of a group of men accused of conspiring to assassinate Napoleon III had led to the disclosure that he had allowed his London home to be used as a postbox by his friend Mazzini, who was allegedly implicated in the plot. It was suggested that he had acted as banker for the conspirators.

fashion; but still the result is on the whole successful, and, rough and rude as the machine may be, it is not difficult to see how large a share its peculiarities have had in securing our prosperity and our freedom. There is no doubt that, whatever its merits or demerits, it is absolutely unique. There have been many attempts to imitate it; but the results have borne about as much resemblance to the original as 'Gladstone claret'[1] bears to the vintages of Bordeaux. Those who have set them up have found themselves very much in the position of the enthusiast who bought the 'Automaton Chess-player', and forgot to bargain for the services of the living inmate who lay imbedded and hidden in the midst of the machinery. The forms of the House of Commons, or the laws under which it is chosen, would be of very little use indeed, without the English social system which supplies it with members, and the English spirit and habits of thought that control its deliberations. Considered from a theorist's point of view, the House of Commons does not present very much that is worthy of imitation. The system under which it is chosen is anomalous to the last degree. The various constituencies who return its members have nothing to show that entitles them to the proud privilege which they enjoy, except the fact that they are in possession. The limit of suffrage upon which the representation reposes, owes its existence to no other fact than that it happens to be represented by a round number, and that it presented some unexplained fascination to Lord Russell's mind at a critical period of English history. The elections are deformed by every kind of theoretical defect. Bribery and intimidation are not put down, and never will be, so long as the voters belong to a class which is exposed to those influences. The proceedings of the House itself, and the regulations under which they are placed, would not be more satisfactory to a theoretical politician. They are uncouth, complicated, often unmeaning, founded upon circumstances which have ceased to exist, often defensible by no reasons applicable to the present state of things, and liable at any time to misuse, which would bring the whole business of the country to a standstill. If they work their proper purpose, and promote the well-being of the country, the credit is due, not to their own excellence, but rather to the common sense of those who work them. If the workmen were not good, the tools would be intolerable. Of course, it has been found impossible to export a legislative machine whose success depends upon the political climate in which it has been put together, and the inbred instincts of those who drive it.

[1] Cheap wine imported under the Anglo-French commercial treaty of 1860.

'THE HOUSE OF COMMONS'

The rules of the House of Commons are well worthy of the study of political philosophers; for they contain in miniature an exhibition of the causes which make the British Constitution work so well in spite of the anomalies which perplex and scandalise foreigners so much. We shall select one or two examples of the most trivial kind; and we shall do so purposely, because they are the most trustworthy illustrations of the spirit they represent. It is in small matters, where no great occasion invites to a special exertion of self-restraint, that the temper of both men and nations is most surely shown. One of the first peculiarities of the House of Commons that attracts attention, and one that has proved a stumbling-block to almost every other representative assembly, is the absolute freedom of speech in respect to quantity. The mode in which it is controlled, and the contrast which exists between practice and theory, is a fair specimen of the slovenly but effective fashion in which the whole machinery is worked. The theory of the House is that every Member has a right to speak once upon every question that is put, for as long as he pleases. There are some fifty or more questions put in the course of the evening; and, setting aside the Speaker – the only man who may not speak – there are six hundred and fifty-seven Members in the House. It is easy to calculate what chance there would be of any business being done in the course of a sitting of eight or ten hours, if this right were carried really to excess. Nor is this all. When the House is in Committee – a transformation which it must undergo once in the course of every bill, and twice in the case of any financial measure – every Member may speak as often as he likes. One would naturally think that such a liberty must lead to an inevitable break down. It is evident that the legislators of other countries have thought so. Scarcely any have ventured to imitate the English freedom. In America, what is known as the one-hour system is adopted in the House of Representatives, the eloquence of each representative being limited within those narrow proportions. In France, in constitutional days, it was open to any member, at any period of a debate, to move *la clôture*. A division upon that question was immediately taken without a discussion; and if the division showed that the Assembly had had enough of the debate, it was at once peremptorily closed. Under the Empire, the debates of the Legislative Assembly are brought to a termination in far more simple fashion. Whenever M. de Morny[1] has had enough of it, he simply announces that the Chamber is weary of the debate, and forthwith puts

The duc de Morny, Napoleon III's half-brother, was president of the legislative assembly.

the question. All attempts to introduce similar limitations, even in the mildest form, into the English House of Commons, have always been steadily resisted. The fear of a tyrannous majority, of which Englishmen never lose sight, has always operated to make statesmen prefer the severest punishment which it is in the power of a bore to inflict, rather than place in the way of a majority a temptation to stifle discussion.

But it must not be supposed that the British House of Commons is wholly given up as a prey to bores. It has its own method of self-defence, which, though rude in more senses than one, is usually effective. According to the theory of its proceedings absolute silence is preserved in the House during a debate. But in the working of the British Constitution, theory and practice do not invariably coincide. According to an order passed on the 22nd of January, 1693, and still in force, 'to the end that all the debates in this House should be grave and orderly as becomes so great an Assembly, and that all interruptions should be prevented, no member of this House is to presume to make any noise or disturbance whilst any member is orderly debating, or whilst any bill, order, or other matter is being read or opened; and in case of such noise or disturbance, Mr. Speaker is to call upon the member by name making such a disturbance, and every such person will incur the censure and displeasure of the House.' Such is the ideal. But, like many other ideals, the practice falls painfully short of it. There is an amount of human frailty, that mingles in practice with these high conceptions, and which occasionally produces a result which an intelligent foreigner might have a difficulty in recognising as the practical expression of the order we have quoted. The House has its own way of making known the fact that it desires to hear no more – a mode of expression which, perhaps, Mr. Gladstone would not call 'the highest form of political articulation,' but which, at all events, has the merit of leaving no doubt as to its meaning.

A good specimen of the modus operandi is furnished by one of those annual motions in favour of Radical nostrums upon which members must vote in order to keep their ground with their constituents; but upon which nothing new can be said, and which therefore is to be disposed of in the most summary manner. It stands first upon the paper; that is to say, it will come on for discussion about five o'clock. The House meets at four, but it always spends a preliminary hour in a number of desultory occupations and a good deal of idle gossip. First come the prayers, which, by a curious combination of the practical and the devout, serve the double purpose of sanctifying the deliberations of the

'THE HOUSE OF COMMONS'

Legislature and enabling members to secure their places. After prayers are over, half an hour is spent in a practice which curiously shows the attachment of Englishmen to established forms. Parliamentary labours are classified under the two heads of public business and private business. Public business includes everything that is ordinarily known as legislation. Private business consists of the proceedings necessary to authorise the construction of great public works, such as in other countries are dealt with by the general law. The English Parliament, however, insists on keeping them outside the province of any regular authority or tribunal, and requires that no public work shall be carried out until a special law has been passed to authorise it in each case. The consequence is that each of these proposals has to go through both legislative and judicial forms. It is in substance question for judicial cognizance, and therefore it is referred to a Committee which hears counsel, and examines witnesses, and conducts its proceedings as far as it can in judicial form. But it professes to be a proposal for a new law; and therefore it has to go through all the forms of being introduced, read a second time, committed, reported, read a third time, passed, and sent up to the House of Lords. The half hour between four and half-past four every day is devoted to the fulfilment of this curious superstition, and sometimes it is barely sufficient for the purpose. During its performance the House is abandoned to Mr. Speaker and the clerks, one indefatigable member, Mr. Forster,[1] who is bound over to act the part of mover to all the bills, and the indomitable spectators in the gallery, who are never known to flinch from the task they have undertaken. The trio, Mr. Forster, the Speaker, and the Clerk, gallop through the necessary formulas with an agility that does credit to their organs of articulation. There is nothing that at all approaches to their rapidity of recitation except the pace at which the usher of a court of justice appeals to the Supreme Being. But there is necessarily a limit which cannot be passed. It has been calculated that it takes thirteen seconds and a half to read a bill a second time; and besides that the performers must occasionally take breath. So that when there are four or five hundred private bills waiting to be forwarded a stage, half an hour is a very inadequate allowance for the ceremony.

By half-past four, however, the House has sacrificed enough to the decent fiction of private legislation. The time for public business has arrived, and the seats begin to fill rapidly. The Ministers arrive to submit themselves to the battery of questions by which their constitutional

---

[1] W. E. Forster (1818–86), M.P. Bradford; under-secretary for the colonies 1865–6; vice-president of the council 1868–74, and as such responsible for the Education Act of 1870; Irish secretary 1880–2.

responsibility is supposed to be carried out. Of late this has been the most exciting period of a House of Commons' sitting. The security of Ministers has depended on the skill with which they have been able to keep their secrets from the Opposition, and the hopes of the Opposition have turned upon the possibility of luring or taunting the Ministers into some incautious revelation of their misdeeds. The portion of public business at half-past four has consequently taken the form of a sharp tournament of question and answer, in which a good deal of ingenuity is sometimes displayed. Each Minister has his own peculiar mode of parrying the thrusts which are pointed at him. Mr. Layard[1] gets angry, and stands upon his dignity, which is undoubtedly the worst plan. Mr. Milner Gibson says something wholly beside the question, and at the same time smiles in so bewitching a manner that a questioner who should attempt to pursue his inquiry would feel himself the most brutal of mankind. Mr. Gladstone plunges into a labyrinth of words, through which his listeners despairingly give up all attempt to follow him; and when the torrent stops he leaves them so bewildered and dazed that they are fain to abandon all further questions till their intellects have been tranquillised by a few minutes' repose. But Lord Palmerston is far the greatest master of the foil. A keen perception of what the point really is; a firm determination not to seem to see it; and an audacity in making bad jokes, and returning impertinent answers, which, often as the exhibition of it has been repeated, seems every time to take the House by surprise, as a refreshing novelty – all these qualities constitute him the most perfect adept in the use of language upon Talleyrand's principles that the present generation has witnessed. It is a game in which the Opposition very seldom win. They have no means of testing the truth of the answers they receive; and circumstances now and then occur which would almost seem to countenance the notion – of course entirely erroneous – that the Minister holds himself absolved from any blame in point of morality or honour if he misleads them. At the time when the Treaty of London, which has just come to so unlucky an end, was being negotiated, a question was put in Parliament upon the subject. Probably it did not suit Lord Palmerston's purpose to allow the fact to get abroad, that such a treaty was in contemplation; at all events, he roundly declared that England was keeping herself studiously aloof from any such negotiations.*

[1] A. H. Layard (1817–94), excavator of Nineveh, M.P. Southwark and under-secretary for foreign affairs.

* This specimen of Parliamentary fencing has been noticed more than once in the House of Commons; but still the contrast between the assertion made by Lord

'THE HOUSE OF COMMONS'

The questions once over, the lighter amusements of the evening are over. All that can be known of Ministerial decisions or Opposition plans of attack has been disclosed. The rest of the sitting is formal, and probably dull debating. A marvellous change passes at once over the appearance of the House. While the questions were being asked it was a tolerably decorous representative assembly. It never, indeed, presents itself to great advantage, in point of dignity, before the eyes of a foreign spectator. 'Le sans-gêne de ces Messieurs' is a standing marvel to foreigners who know the enormous authority and the world-wide fame of the assembly whose free-and-easy proceedings they are watching. But at all events, while the questions are going on, it is attentive, and does look like a deliberative body. The moment they are over, and the mover of the first motion gets up to make his speech, it becomes simply a very noisy club-room. It is what the agora was to the Athenians, – the place where each man comes to say and to hear some new thing. It is the great Stock Exchange of political gossip, each member disposing of the

Palmerston in the House and the Despatches is so curious that it may be worth while to reproduce them:

'Mr. Urquhart begged then to ask further whether in this correspondence there had been any negotiation as to the succession to the Crown of Denmark, or in respect to the succession in the Duchies?'

'Viscount Palmerston. – A good deal has passed in regard to these points; that is to say, in regard to the succession to the Crown of Denmark: and as connected with that in regard to the arrangements for the order of succession in Schleswig and Holstein. But her Majesty's Government had studiously and systematically held themselves aloof from taking any share in these negotiations. Her Majesty's Government had confined themselves strictly to the mediation which they undertook; which was a mediation for the purpose of bringing about a restoration of peace between Denmark and the Germanic Confederation.' –*Hansard*, March 20, 1851.

In point of fact, England had been actively negotiating for more than a year upon these questions of succession. The following is the opening of a despatch from Lord Palmerston, dated February 19, 1850:

'I have to instruct you to press strongly upon the Danish Government the great importance of settling without delay the question as to the succession to the Crown of Denmark, which is the key to the whole of the questions pending between Denmark and Germany. If the Danish Government could so settle the succession to the Danish Crown as to insure the continuance of the Sovereignty of Denmark and of both the Duchies in one and the same person, it is manifest that all other questions connected with the government and organization of the Duchies would become of secondary importance, and the solution of them would be rendered much more easy.'

Such was Lord Palmerston's idea of 'keeping studiously aloof from taking share in negotiations upon the succession in Denmark and the Duchies.' It is worthy of remark that this curious contradiction was charged upon the Prime Minister by Mr Bernal Osborne[1] in the House of Commons upon the 19th of April last, but he took no notice of the charge.

[1] Ralph Bernal Osborne (1808–82), Liberal M.P. for Liskeard.

accumulation he has been collecting during the day, and gathering new treasures of small-talk for use during the approaching evening. Speaking in the middle of the buzz which all this conversation causes is like speaking under a waterfall, or in an American frogmarsh. The orator whose address is receiving this irregular accompaniment may possibly be audible to himself, but he is certainly audible to very few besides. It is curious to watch the different effect which this strange ordeal has upon different speakers. It is inflicted almost equally upon all, if the subject they have in hand does not happen to be of pressing interest. Even Mr Gladstone, if his topic happens to be a detail of subordinate importance, is not exempted from the buzz which marks the pet gossiping-time of the House of Commons. But different men take it very differently. Upon ordinary members it has the salutary effect of confusing their thoughts, and bringing their rhetoric to a speedy close. Ministers of State are case-hardened by practice, and do not show many signs of suffering; but even upon them it exercises an abbreviating virtue. Lawyers alone are quite impassible. It is said that they are so accustomed to address auditors who are paid to sit and listen to them, that their hearts are steeled against sympathy or pity for those who may be getting weary; and the inattention of their audience never occurs to them as a reason for shortening their speeches. Be the reason what it may, they are certainly the only speakers whom no amount of interruption can discompose.

Conversation, however, is the slenderest form of rebuke which an impatient House can inflict upon a tedious speaker. It is a mere snaffle-bit, and he does not yield to it unless he has a comparatively light mouth. Some tenderness, too, is shown to the mover of a question even if his subject be uninteresting. Moreover the hours between five and seven must be occupied, and the nature of the material which fills the gap is not a matter of great importance. It is not till the mover has sat down, and a succession of speakers have carried the hour-hand of the clock close up to the mystic number seven, that the House seriously bethinks itself of applying the remedies against prolixity of speech. But as time gets on, and the debate appears likely to continue, solitary cries of 'Divide, divide,' are heard in various parts of the House. At first they come singly, like drops of rain before a storm. The voices that raise them are ashamed of finding themselves alone, and do not persist. Then they begin to multiply, and to come from little groups of impatient hearers. Some decorum, however, is still observed. The members gather in a thick cluster near the door of the House, and the front row stand

'THE HOUSE OF COMMONS'

looking at Mr. Speaker with demure and respectful silence, while a knot of stentorian shouters hide themselves behind. If the Member who is speaking be ordinarily thin-skinned, nay, if he be of Saxon blood at all, these hints are sufficient to convince him that his eloquence has ceased to be acceptable. But sometimes it happens that at that critical moment of the evening an Irishman is in possession of the House; and to his combative temper such interruptions rather act as a challenge to persevere, than as a motive for sitting down. He simply looks indignant, and tries to raise his voice above those of the interrupters. But the only result of his persistence is that the uproar spreads. The dinner hour approaches fast, and the meekest and mildest join in the outcry. At last isolated voices cease to be discernible, and the cry of 'Divide' takes the form of a universal chorus, which rises from all parts of the House except the official benches, each time the luckless orator attempts to open his mouth. If the debate at these points were accurately reported, it would have to be printed somewhat in this form – 'Mr.——: I beg, Sir, to assure the House ('vide, 'vide, 'vide, 'vide, 'vide, 'vide), but one minute ('vide, 'vide, 'vide, 'vide, 'vide, 'vide), I wish to express ('vide, 'vide, 'vide, 'vide, 'vide, 'vide), if the House will only ('vide, 'vide, 'vide, 'vide, 'vide, 'vide, *crescendo*),' and so on indefinitely. All the while Mr. Speaker looks on with splendid unconsciousness, as if it had never crossed his mind that the debate was otherwise than 'grave and orderly as becomes so great an Assembly.' Sometimes the struggle endures for a quarter of an hour, or even more: but at last the most pugnacious Irishman becomes convinced of the inutility of pitting one voice against two hundred, and the House goes to a division, and then to its dinner in peace. Such is the method by which a licence of debate theoretically unlimited is reconciled with a due control upon the part of the House of Commons over its own debates. The plan may be rough and rude, and may sometimes provoke irreverent comparisons with the noises that issue from the dens in the Zoological Gardens just before four o'clock. But at all events it is more effective than the one-hour system, and less open to abuse than the *clôture*. It is a fair sample of the irregular evasions by which the rules of the House of Commons are made to work easily in spite of the theoretical difficulties they seem to offer. But it is quite clear that such a licence of debate upon the one hand, and such a mode of checking it upon the other, would only be endurable in an Assembly which could be trusted, when the need arose, to display moderation and self-constraint.

The whole system of our Constitution is to trust to the good sense of those who have to exercise its powers. A little blundering, a little undue self-assertion in this part, or in that, might at any moment bring the machine to a dead lock. Sovereign, Ministers, House of Lords, House of Commons, are all endowed with powers which might easily be made to clash; and if any serious collision occurred, the whole of our elaborate mechanism of government would be thrown out of gear. That no such catastrophe has occurred now for near two centuries sufficiently indicates the secret of the success of the British Constitution. The House of Commons on a smaller scale is worked upon the same principle. Powers are left in the hands of each individual member which he might use, if he were so minded, to the serious damage and almost to the destruction of Parliamentary government; but trust is placed in the good sense of the members, and in their fear of incurring the bad opinion of their colleagues. It cannot be said that this trust has been deceived, or that the exercise of these powers has been ever, in recent times at least, pressed to an extravagant excess. Take, for instance, the power of indefinite adjournment. It is theoretically open to any two members for ever to prevent the House from doing any business whatever. A great deal has been said of the liberum veto in Poland;[1] and the ills of that unhappy country have been attributed not to the temper of the nobles, but to the accidental vices of the Constitution under which they lived. But the power of adjournment possessed by Members of the House of Commons only differs from it in that the consent of two men is required for its exercise instead of one. The form is for one member first to move the adjournment of the debate, and to take a division upon the question – then for his coadjutor to move the adjournment of the House, and to take a division upon that. The first member may then renew the motion for the adjournment of the debate, and so on indefinitely. For temporary purposes upon matters of detail, the privilege is not unfrequently used. Whenever a minority considers that it has been unfairly surprised into the consideration of a measure which the mass of the House did not expect to come on they sometimes insist upon its postponement to another evening by this means. It is a power against which it is almost impossible to struggle; and after five or six divisions have been taken, the majority generally give way. Of course the charge of factiousness is freely levelled at their opponents by those who have been foiled by the process; but it is never used without a good *primâ facie* reason to justify it. It is easy to see that such rules, worked by different men in a different spirit, would speedily clog the constitutional machine. These are un-

[1] By means of which any member of the old Polish diet could hold up business indefinitely.

doubtedly trivial indications; but they are taken from the ordinary everyday incidents of Parliamentary business, and they show perhaps the temper in which Parliamentary institutions are worked more faithfully than would be done by the conduct of members on great critical occasions, when their patriotism was powerfully invoked.

Proofs of that kind, however, are not wanting. It is often made the subject of a reproach to the House that it is very fond of discussing foreign affairs in which it has no concern, while it carefully abstains from touching those in which England is nearly interested. The debates on Italy have been abundant; though, as it had been fully agreed that we were not to waste a shilling or a man upon Italian politics, our sentiments could not possibly affect the destiny of Italy. But upon America it has preserved a nervous silence, and even upon Denmark it has refused to speak until events had deprived its voice of power. Such a policy may not have been strictly dignified. It may speak more highly for the discretion of the House of Commons than its valour. But still it is an evidence of curious self-restraint on the part of an assembly so large, so bitterly divided in opinion, and recruited from classes and even races so distinct. It is not often that any man or body of men refuse to grasp the sceptre when the very handle of it is within their reach. The House of Commons would undoubtedly be a singularly unfit body to exercise executive power. Its proceedings are too slow, its policy too uncertain, and too dependent on the numerical majority of the moment. And the very publicity which is the breath of life to it would be fatal to functions requiring accurate and often secret information, and in the exercise of which it would be called upon at times to shape its course in such a manner as to humour the feelings of powerful personages in other countries. But it is in the power of the House of Commons to extend this executive authority to whatever it thinks fit. An address to the Crown pointing out this or that policy is practically decisive of the course the nation takes. The control which it possesses, if it pleases to exert it, is quite absolute. By a simple vote it can paralyse any single department or all the departments of the civil service. The possession of such a power confers inestimable advantages upon us. It brings the nation and the Government into so close a connection, that any policy which is approved by the mass of the nation is certain to be promptly adopted by its rulers. Other countries have tried to produce the same result by providing that the ruler shall be periodically elected by the people. The contrivance fails in two ways. It makes no provision for changes of opinion which may take place between the intervals of election; and it takes no note of any public opinion except such as can make itself heard over the din of artificial cries which it is the professional duty of an organized body of electioneerers to raise. No one can at present say whether the genuine public opinion of the Northern States of America is for war or peace. The enormous machinery of corruption which is at the command of the Government may enable them to extort from the ballot-box at the ensuing election a verdict favourable to themselves, while the mass of the citizens are averse to the policy they are pursuing. In England the machinery which carries the will of the nation into the policy of the Government is far more sensitive. No Government could exist in England for three months that was acting in the face of a decided national conviction. But we pay for the delicacy of our mechanism by the danger of disturbance to which it is exposed. The relations between the Legislature and the Executive are not, as in America, defined by rigorous laws. There is no written constitution to protect, however feebly, one branch from the invasion of the other. The boundary line which separates their functions might be easily passed; a short period of passion or imprudence might introduce an irreparable confusion. The safety of the Constitution and all the blessings it confers depend upon the moderation of the House of Commons; and the conduct of the House of Commons can be secured by no legislative provisions, but turns wholly upon the discretion and the patriotism of the men of whom it may chance to be composed.

It is not surprising that the composition of a body upon which so much depends should have become the subject of keen political strife. On the one hand it is full of anomalies of all kinds, as we have seen. On the surface of things, neither the suffrage nor the distribution of electoral areas can be theoretically defended. It is quite intelligible that a working man who happens to have political tastes, and lives in a nine-pound house, should think himself hardly used because so sharp a line is drawn between himself and his neighbour who pays sixpence a-week more rent. He finds it hard to reconcile himself to the constitutional theory which supposes all the gifts of political wisdom to reside in that extra sixpence. It is intelligible, too, that the towns of Huddersfield or Wakefield should feel irritated to think that while they are only allowed one member a-piece, their little neighbours, Knaresborough and Ripon, should be trusted with twice as much political power as themselves. Of course, such objections are merely superficial. If there is to be any inferior limit to the suffrage at all, the dividing line must seem sharp to those who are shut out; and the franchise of the small boroughs is merely an indirect mode of giving a fair share of political power to the rural districts, who without such a reinforcement would be enormously under-represented in the House of Commons. But though the objections can be easily answered, it is not unnatural that they should be felt. On the other hand, those who value the freedom and security we enjoy, now so hard to find elsewhere in a similar degree, are intelligibly jealous of experimental meddling with the body upon whose composition all the political blessings we possess depend. What the effect might be of the substitution of an absolutely new class of persons in the place of those who at present fill the House of Commons, it is, of course, impossible to predict with certainty. All we know is, that the attempt will be absolutely new. The forms may remain the same; the proceedings may be recorded in the same journals; the new assembly may meet within the old walls; but it will not be the old House of Commons. The existing body, with all its faults and merits, is dependent upon the social system out of which it is drawn. A body representing the Trades' Unions may have many virtues. It may display all the qualities with which we are familiar in those organisations which, under the plans that have been proposed, unquestionably will furnish the largest portion of the constituency. It may be energetic and thorough-going; and its vigour may be tainted with no suspicion of cowardice or even of discretion. But if it succeed to its predecessor's self-mastery, and self-denial, and the delicate appreciation of the limits of the position which it has a right to occupy, it will marvellously belie its parentage. Anyhow its characteristics must be a matter of sheer guesswork; for it will be a phenomenon of which we have no experience worth the name. A democratic legislature, sovereign, uncontrolled, in the midst of an aristocratic society, is an experiment of which we have had only one example, and that of a somewhat inauspicious kind. The Constituent Assembly of 1789 is not likely to find imitators of its wild pranks in an English atmosphere; but it is literally the only precedent strictly in point, for a House of Commons transmuted as our advanced Reformers desire. Two months ago we would have said that it was idle to speculate upon a contingency which was simply visionary. It may not be anything more substantial now; but a temporary importance at least is given to the idea by the sponsorship it has recently received. That a great Statesman at this time of day should think fit to raise again the banner of Reform is of itself a phenomenon which cannot be hastily passed by.

Mr. Gladstone's speech upon Reform would have created less excitement if he had not laid down the doctrine that every man was 'morally entitled' to the franchise who was not disqualified for it by some personal unfitness, or by some political danger. It was this dogma which created so remarkable a sensation. The House was prepared for some momentous utterance that was to elevate Mr. Gladstone to the post of Radical leader, and chain the democracy to his standard. Rumours had been rife that some bid on his part for that distinction was to be made in the course of the discussion on Mr. Baines's bill. It was obviously a political necessity of his position. He had no friends to look to except the Radicals. The Tories he had alienated by a succession of hostile measures, and the Whigs, for some reason which it is difficult to fathom, have never been able to persuade themselves to give a hearty welcome to their distinguished convert. Upon the Radicals, on the other hand, he had created a favourable impression by the precipitate changes which he had introduced into the tariff. They were inclined, for the time at least, to condone his Churchmanship, if they could only be assured that he would assist them in the enterprise of ousting the present class of electors from power. It was fully expected, therefore, that he would seize this opportunity of making his profession, and, indeed, he had hinted as much to a deputation of the trades' unions.[1] It was clear enough that a man, whom the sight of the trades' unions, with all their terrible organisation and all their lawless traditions, could not deter from undertaking the advocacy of democratic change, must have made up his mind to bid high for the adhesions which he sought. Accordingly the House of Commons was fully prepared for a startling declaration; and though it was only at the very beginning of a Wednesday morning sitting, a considerable audience was already collected to hear him. But, nevertheless, when it did come it took every one by surprise. Nobody had expected anything so sweeping as the new manifesto seemed to be. That Mr. Gladstone should have supported Mr. Baines's bill for a six-pound franchise was naturally to be expected, and that he should have devised some curious paradox in its support could be no matter of surprise; but that he should at a single bound clear the whole space that separates the existing English constitution from a system of universal suffrage was an event which the wildest imagination had not ventured to forecast. The Radicals shouted with delight; a murmur of consternation ran through the rest of the House. Mr. Gladstone saw how acute was the impression that

---

[1] Meeting a deputation of the London Trades' Council, headed by its secretary, Odger, on 16 March 1864, Gladstone said (according to the *Bee-Hive*, 19 March) that he thought the franchise ought to be extended to the working classes, and that he should soon have an opportunity to express his opinion on the subject in the House.

'THE HOUSE OF COMMONS'

he produced, and made a floundering attempt to retrace his steps. But he mistook the cause of the dismay he had aroused. He fancied that it was only the prospect of immediate change which terrified the House, and he hastened to assure them that the results to which he pointed were not to be the consequence of any sudden revolution, but were only to be reached by gradual stages. He did not succeed in reassuring his astounded hearers. The rapturous cheers of his Radical allies accompanied him to the end of his speech; and he left upon the minds both of friends and foes the undoubting belief that a leader for the revolutionary party had been found.

The alarm created by this conversion, apparently so sudden of a statesman who had once been described as 'the last hope of the stern and unbending Tories,' has prompted Mr. Gladstone to offer an explanation in the shape of his celebrated Preface. That remarkable document cannot be said either to have tranquillised or to have enlightened those to whom it was addressed. It conveyed, indeed, a general impression that its distinguished author desired to draw back a little from the position he had taken up, and did not exactly know how to do it; but it did not leave upon the public mind any distinct idea of the limitations, if any, by which he was willing to restrain the stupendous changes he had recommended. It is probably true, as he broadly hints, that the sweeping formula he constructed was struck out in the heat of debate, and was not the fruit of deliberate reflection. It will be evident to any one carefully tracing the course of his ideas, that he stepped into it unawares in the heat of a search after some proposition that should be a logical reply to the argument of his opponent. Mr. Cave[1] had challenged the supporters of the bill to produce either a substantial grievance or any evidence of discontent. If the existing system was evil, it would bear evil fruit; if it was unpopular, it would have called forth either an agitation, or at least a considerable number of petitions against it. As neither evil results nor unpopularity could be shown, the *primâ facie* case in favour of the bill absolutely failed. Mr. Gladstone seems to have felt the necessity of meeting this argument; but his mind was not entirely satisfied with the ordinary commonplace that the change should be made at a time when the working-classes did not wish for it, in order that, when they did wish for it, they might have less to wish for. Nor was he likely to betake himself to the curious theory that they are like the parrot in the story, which, because it did not speak, thought all the more. It was evident from the mode in which he approached the argument

[1] Stephen Cave (1820-80), Conservative M.P. for Shoreham.

to which he had to reply, that it embarrassed him. He floundered from one line of reasoning into another, manifestly not satisfying himself any more than his audience with the fallacies which he successively picked up and threw aside. At last in despair he saw that there was nothing else for it but to throw the whole onus upon his opponent. He could not make a case out for extension, and he concealed his difficulty by challenging his opponent to make a case out for exclusion. And thus to effect this argumentative manœuvre, he laid down, without thinking where it would lead him, the tremendous proposition that every man has a natural right to a vote, except those against whom a special disqualification could be charged.

There is little doubt that Mr. Gladstone did not intend to propound a system of universal suffrage. There is still less doubt that he practically did so. The unlucky contradiction between his meaning and his words, in the mouth of so great a master of language, is due to a style of reasoning which is peculiar to himself, and which the English of all nations in the world are the least capable of understanding. During the whole of his varied mental history the passion for sweeping general principles has steadily adhered to him. Widely as his intellectual position differs now from that which he occupied when he wrote his essay upon the 'Relations of the State and the Church,'[1] this habit of thought retains as strong a hold over him as ever. He is not comfortable unless he can base his proposed action upon the foundation of some simple, large, grand first principle, which, applied to the existing condition of the world, would turn society upside down and revolutionize every existing institution. But this result is in no way his intention. His actual objects are often moderate enough. Accordingly he proceeds to cut down his great first principle by limitation after limitation, until, for practical purposes, the merest shred of it is left behind. Even in a scientific point of view this mode of proceeding is very unphilosophical. It involves a forgetfulness of the object for which general propositions are used at all. At best the whole apparatus of rules and exceptions are merely figments of the human mind, devised by it to aid itself in picking its way through the endless variety of Nature. To lay down, therefore, a rule which is swallowed up by its own exceptions, or a rule which applies to fewer actual facts than those which must be classed under the exceptions from it, is to pervert a nomenclature which is intended to act as an aid to thought, and to make of it an element of confusion. When Mr. Gladstone laid down that all men are morally entitled to the franchise, and only

---

[1] Gladstone published *The State in its Relations with the Church* in 1838.

'THE HOUSE OF COMMONS'

excepted from that rule the cases of those who were personally unfit, or whose admission would involve a political danger, it appears that he intended to make an exception so large as to leave little of the rule remaining. It would surely have been more accurate in that case to lay down that only those had a claim to the franchise whose admission was politically safe. But the scientific error of putting his rule where his exception should have been, and stating as the exception what in reality was to be the rule, was trivial compared to the political blunder which it involved. The mass of Englishmen do not understand logical gymnastics. When a great performer makes a jump, they cannot be brought to comprehend that it is only the beginning of a summersault which when completed will leave him standing much as he was before. They will conclude that when he throws himself upon his head, it is upon his head that he means to remain. They have no patience to wait out the upshot of that internecine struggle between general propositions and particular limitations, which issues, like the battle of the Kilkenny cats, in leaving only the tip of the tail of one of them behind. When a man says that every one is morally entitled to a vote, they conclude that he means it, and that if he accompanies his statement with any exceptions the cases to which they are to apply are really to be exceptional. If Mr. Gladstone is generally supposed to have taken up the battle-cry of manhood suffrage, he has only himself to thank for it. It was a construction that was not put about by the malice of his enemies, but was adopted as confidently by the working men whom he desired to conciliate as by the party whom he was advisedly deserting. It was the natural sense of his declaration, according to the standards of interpretation by which men usually give meaning to each other's words. And after all, the sense of most political importance was not that in which the author uttered it, but that in which hearers and readers received it. It raised as many groundless hopes and bred as much perilous discontent among the small portion of the working class who are inclined to agitation as could have been done by the most revolutionary manifesto. The speech throughout incited the working-men to consider the existing state of the law as not only an injustice, but an insulting imputation of personal unfitness. If the effect of the speech has been insignificant, that happy result has been due to the wise apathy of the working-men, and not to the moderation or carefulness of Mr Gladstone's language.

The short time that has elapsed since the speech was made is happily sufficient to enable us to predict that it will be devoid of practical consequence. It evidently strikes no responsive chord in the national feeling of the day. Nobody wants Reform – except the few who think they have ground to hope that the constituency of the future will not display so mortifying an ignorance of their merits as the constituency of the present. To the mass of the nation the existing form of government has this inestimable recommendation, that it succeeds. Those outside the electoral pale who are capable of political reflection are not inclined to believe that either they themselves, or the country to which they belong, will derive any notable advantage from the privilege of possessing the ten-thousandth part of a right to return a Member of Parliament. But as the Chancellor of the Exchequer's new political creed does not seem likely to pass out of the domain of speculation, it may be worth while to examine it a little in that point of view. It professes to rest upon a basis purely theoretical: it may be worth while to ascertain what the speculative value of that basis is. It is not likely that so practical a people as the English will ever consent to abandon institutions which work well, in order to satisfy a philosopher's ideal. But still, as the matter has not come yet to be the subject of practical agitation, there is leisure for the harmless pastime of political metaphysics. In the real business of life no one troubles himself much about 'moral titles.' No one would dream of surrendering any practical security, for the advantages of which he is actually in possession, in deference to the *a priori* jurisprudence of a whole Academy of philosophers. But as a matter of literary controversy the subject is as interesting as any other. Theories, moreover, though they probably never inspired with enthusiasm any considerable mass of human beings, are yet prized for the purpose of throwing a veil of decency over the naked passions by which political convulsions are brought about. The 'rights of man' have already served as the pretext for many an orgy of bloodthirsty frenzy, at the memory of which nations now recoil: and they always have this interest about them, that, if opportunity serves, they may be put to the same use again.

In conducting the discussion upon the abstract rights of the population of this country to the suffrage, it is the habit entirely to avoid all reference both to the nature of the suffrage and to the object which it is designed to serve. The laws of nature, whatever they may be, do not contain any allusion to representative assemblies. Writers upon them usually lay down that mankind have a natural and inalienable right to their freedom – that is to say, to doing what they like with their own muscles and their own bodies, so long as they do not therein interfere with the similar right possessed by their neighbours. Then they lay down another right, subject to a similar limitation, that every one has a right to do what he likes with his own property, so long as he does not interfere with his neighbours' rights. The community of men, which we call a State, exists, or is theoretically supposed to exist, in order that these two rights may be adequately protected, and also that their exercise may be rigorously kept within the boundaries of these two limitations. Every political right which a man can be said to possess by natural law, according to any received interpretation of that vague term, must arise from one of these two fundamental rights – from his right to the free control either of his own body or of his own property. It is obvious that if men enter into a community, this unfettered control must be to a certain extent abandoned. It must needs be that the decisions of the whole would constantly be at variance with the decisions of individual members; and that in such a contingency the former must overrule the latter, unless the organization of the community is to be arranged upon the model of the Diet of Poland, in which case it might as well not be a community at all. Many a man has to pay taxes, very much against his will, for objects whose value he does not recognise. Many a man has to serve on a jury who had much rather not do so: and in other countries may be forced, with most genuine reluctance, to go as a conscript and stand to be shot at in a quarrel with which he does not sympathize. His free control over his person or his property in such cases is a very imaginary quantity: but for the convenience of having a theory of some kind to go upon, writers on these subjects have agreed to assume that that free control is not compromised so long as the constraint to which he is subjected is approved by the community to which he belongs. To the unlucky man who is sold up for not paying taxes which he dislikes, or is shot for running away in a war in which he had rather not take part, it may very possibly seem a mockery to tell him that he is nevertheless a free man. But he must console himself with the reflection that it would be impossible to put together a coherent theory on any other terms. Perhaps he may be of opinion that being shot or ruined by order of a despot, or of an officer appointed by a representative assembly in which a man whom he once voted against at the hustings has a seat, is very much the same thing to him. But that only shows that he is unacquainted with the elementary principles of freedom. What seems a very practical fallacy to him is an indispensable postulate in the construction of a representative system. It is very desirable, on the one hand, to be able to tell everybody that they have an inalienable right to be free. On the other hand, it is indispensable for the interest of their neighbours, and in some degree, perhaps, for their own, that large inroads should be made upon that freedom. The only chance of reconciling these two divergent objects is the invention of a doctrine that a man is free so long as he has (if he be in the majority) a practical part, and (if he be in the minority) a theoretical part in the selection of the governors under whose authority he lives.

But then, the question is, what part? If everybody came into the common concern with an equal contribution, it would be just that he should possess an equal share of power over the whole. So far as Government has to do with the disposal of life and limb, each man stands before it with a tolerably equal claim, and may demand an equal voice. The Teutonic constitution of ancient times, giving to each man an equal share in the election of the chief, was reasonable enough at a time when the amount of accumulated property was insignificant, and one man was nearly as rich as his neighbour. But the problem we have to consider is a very different one. We have to divide political power among a people to whom anything approaching to equality of property is unknown. In such a case, is an equal share a just share? The chief object of Government, in England at least, is the protection of property. For with the protection of life and limb Parliament has not now very much to do. It is part, undoubtedly, of its duties, and a part which is not, even now, wholly free from difficulty. But still, the main business of Parliament is to make laws to define and to secure in some form or other the distribution of property. The Church controversies, which occupy so large a share of its attention, are in essence only a struggle between different sets of persons for the possession of certain rates, or tithes, or lands. Finance, which has been the battle-field of so many conflicts, is a contest between various classes waged for the purposes of resisting the imposition of what each considers an unfair proportion of that contribution from property by which the service of the State is carried on. Even foreign policy, so far as the mass of the nation is concerned, is more a question of property than of anything else. Here and there, with individuals or among certain classes, sentimental considerations predominate. But with the large bulk of the inhabitants of this country the course towards foreign nations which they desire their rulers to take is traced out by material interests alone. And so it is throughout. If all that business were to be withdrawn from Parliament which directly or indirectly affects the distribution of property, its occupation would be gone. If it were not for the complex interests which the existence of property creates, the machine of civilized government would be far too cumbrous for its work. If it were not for the guard which those who own property must

'THE HOUSE OF COMMONS'

keep over their possessions, representative assemblies would scarcely be needed, and assuredly no one would care to dispute over their composition. Countries where property is slender in amount or equal in distribution seldom find the necessity of an elaborate form of government, and, still more rarely, of violent political agitation. As property is in the main the chief subject-matter of legislation, so it is almost the only motive power of agitation. A violent political movement (setting aside those where religious controversy is at work) is generally only an indication that a class of those who have little see their way to getting more by means of a political convulsion.

Here lies the fundamental fallacy of those who press for a wide extension of the franchise. They tell us that every man has a right to a share in the government of the community to which he belongs. But they persist in forgetting that 'the suffrage' means something very much more than a share. It means an equal share. To give 'the suffrage' to a poor man is to give him as large a part in determining that legislation which is mainly concerned with property as the banker whose name is known on every Exchange in Europe, as the merchant whose ships are in every sea, as the landowner who owns the soil of a whole manufacturing town. An extension of the suffrage to the working classes means that upon a question of taxation, or expenditure, or upon a measure vitally affecting commerce, two day-labourers shall outvote Baron Rothschild. This is the result to which we are brought by vague declamations about 'moral titles' or 'natural rights'. The best test of natural right is the right which mankind left to themselves to regulate their own concerns naturally admit. Now, the idea of representative government is not confined to governments. It is well known in commercial enterprises. Joint-stock companies, like States, find themselves too numerous to undertake in person the management of their own affairs; therefore they elect representatives to do it for them; and they confide to those representatives, subject to certain constitutional limitations, all the powers which they themselves possess. How do they settle this thorny question of the suffrage? They have no mediæval traditions to prejudice them. They have no powerful aristocracy or intriguing Court to beguile them. They are not rude mechanics or impressible peasants. In their keen rivalry, in their perfect freedom from prepossession, in their enlightened perception of their own advantage, they are as happily placed for forming a trustworthy judgment upon any point affecting their common or conflicting interests as any persons the world has ever seen. How then do they settle this knotty controversy upon the distribution of the franchise? Is it upon the principle that the two day-labourers are to outvote the one Rothschild? If such a proposal were made to them, would they exhibit a very complimentary appreciation of the common sense of the man who proposed it, or be inclined to take him as their guide upon the question of natural rights? Men's minds are confused upon this question of the franchise by the controversy which it has excited for two or three generations. If they came to look at it for the first time, the theory of the English suffrage, even as it stands, and still more as the Reformers propose to alter it, would be thought to be the dream of a lunatic.

It is quite true that a higher view of the State may be taken. It may be looked at as something grander than a Joint-stock Company for the preservation of life and property. Undoubtedly, with the East India Company's career in our recollection, the logical division between the two may be hard to state in words. But there are sentiments and emotions attaching to the idea of a State which have nothing commercial in their nature. The self-sacrifice and heroism that it can evoke when it is threatened show that it is the object of emotions far higher than self-interest. The glory which it has won, or hopes to win, centres round it affections and aspirations which would not be felt for an organization that only existed to foster the material well-being of those who belonged to it. But this sentimental aspect is not the one in which our advanced school of Reformers love to look at it. Their efforts are unceasingly directed to the task of stripping off these poetical trappings. They tell us that such follies are the heritage of darker times; that it is a delusion to give a personality to the State; to attribute to it moral duties, or to employ its powers for the gratification of lofty aims and feelings. Their constant struggle is to present it nakedly as a Joint-stock Company for the preservation of life and property; and they are estopped by their own philosophy from appealing to the loftier views of it which have descended from less business-like times. But in any case these loftier views have nothing to do with the agitation for the extension of the franchise. That is purely a struggle for material advantages. It is only as an instrument for dealing with property that the agitators desire to obtain for the lower classes greater influence in the Legislature. Political power is recommended to the working-classes as a worthy object of their desires and their efforts, almost entirely by a recital of the changes in taxation, or in the laws affecting property, which that power might be used to bring about. They are told that the taxes are unjustly distributed, and that if they obtained a Reform in Parliament they would be able to

'THE HOUSE OF COMMONS'

lay a larger proportion of them on their richer neighbours; that the law which regulates the relations of employers to their workmen[1] will be in such a case made more favourable to the latter; and that such marvellous changes would be made in the laws affecting land, that the working men of England will possess, like the peasantry in some other countries, each his own plot of freehold. To agitators acting with such objects, the State is obviously nothing more than a machine for regulating rights of property and claims upon it. They simply regard themselves as shareholders in the great Joint-stock Company, whose interests are unfairly treated, and who therefore wish for a more powerful voice in the conduct of its affairs. They are demanding that each one among them, with only the very smallest stake in the concern, shall have as much influence in its management as the largest holders. Their proposals are about as reasonable as those of a body of shareholders would be, who, having only one share a-piece, should demand that each of them should have as many votes as the holders of a thousand shares.

The constitutional system under which Joint Stock Companies are managed, we believe in every country, is that which is dictated by common sense, viz. that each man should have as many votes in the government as he has shares in the concern. It is a system whose justice has never been disputed. The question has never even been matter of controversy. The wildest dreamer never suggested that all the shareholders should each have a single vote, without reference to the number of shares they might hold. But let us indulge for the moment in an extravagant hypothesis. Let us suppose that some wild delusion came over the minds of commercial men. Let us imagine them to have discovered in their internal consciousness, or other source of philosophical revelation, that it was one of the elementary rights of man that the shareholder of one share should enjoy an equal suffrage with the shareholder of a thousand shares, and that every Joint Stock Company in which this rule did not prevail was a community of tyrants lording it over slaves. Assume further that one or two Companies were weak enough, in a moment of panic, to endorse these doctrines and to introduce this reform into their constitutions, – would it require any gift of prophecy to conjecture the result? The shareholders of one share, especially if they happened to be comparatively very numerous, would soon discover that it was their interest to act together. They would find out that it was possible to manage the concern entirely to their own profit, without

---

[1] I.e. the law of master and servant, whereby an employee breaking his contract of service with his employer was guilty of a criminal offence and liable to imprisonment with hard labour.

burdening in any degree that modest portion of the capital which was represented by their own shares. If they were cold and strictly logical in the pursuit of their own interests, they would at once resolve that all the calls should be made upon the shares of the larger holders, and that all the profits should be divided amongst themselves. It is possible that a remnant of morality might hinder them from formulating robbery in terms so naked, at least for some time; but such a result would be the point towards which all the measures they resolved upon would most assuredly tend. It is quite true that when once the deluded theorists, whom we have assumed to make this experiment, had found out by actual experience the folly of which they had been guilty, no more Joint Stock Companies would be formed upon such terms, and that if such a constitution were imposed upon such associations by the law of the country, capitalists would betake themselves to some saner and happier land. But it is equally certain that, unless rescued from the faults of its own organization by some strong external power, the Joint Stock Company that had tried the theory would be irreparably ruined.

What hinders the parallel from being applied to States? Can any one deny that the same rule governs the gigantic finance of a State which governs the smaller finance of a Company? The bestowal upon any class of a voting power disproportionate to their stake in the country, must infallibly give to that class a power *pro tanto* of using taxation as an instrument of plunder, and expenditure and legislation as a fountain of gain. As the disproportion becomes greater, the power increases in dimensions; with each new admission of working men to the privileges of an equal franchise, it would become more uncontrollable; and when universal suffrage was reached, it would be a simple despotism. It is not necessary to assume that that despotism would at once, or necessarily, be used for an evil purpose. No despotism, no oligarchy, has been invariably bad; and though the despotism of the multitude would be free from the political fears that keep aristocracies and autocrats in check, still it would be liable to all the influences which do modify human selfishness, and prevent the world from being nothing else than a battle-field of rival self-interests. It is not to be supposed that the working-classes, more than any other classes, would commit an act of glaring robbery unless they had some very strong motive to do so, and something in the nature of a pretext to cover from the eye of their own consciences the nudity of the operation. But this reservation, though edifying and necessary to make, is wholly beside the question. Political systems have only been devised because these restraining influences have been found

'THE HOUSE OF COMMONS'

to be imperfect. As despots are liable to individual temptation, and aristocracies sometimes give way to class selfishness, so the pressure of want or the intoxication of passion will overpower the conscience of a democracy. It is to provide against these exceptional aberrations on the part of the depositaries of power that constitutional checks have been invented. If there was no danger that any one would ever desire to take what does not belong to him, politics would be an extinct science, and law would be reduced to a system of friendly arbitration. It may be conceded, therefore, that the working classes, if they obtained that monopoly of power, which any considerable extension of the suffrage would secure to them, would not consciously rob the classes above them. But no one in politics ever need be conscious of the wrong he is doing. In political morality it is easier to gloze over guilt with a varnish of good intention, even than in other ethical departments. Political rights are so complicated, and often so ill-defined, that there is no difficulty in persuading people that they are doing right to violate them, especially if their stomachs applaud the argument. No political crime has ever been committed for which it would be difficult to discover a defence specious enough for a hungry crowd. A demagogue will always be found to furnish the necessary sophisms, if the presence of distress or the vehemence of class-hatred be there to drive them home. The good intentions or the good feeling of the multitude are of precisely the same value as the good intentions or the good feeling of a despot – and no more. They may serve for ordinary times, and in the absence of special temptation; but they will not stand a strain.

Natural right, then, cannot be made to justify an equal suffrage, so long as there is not equal property to protect. The common consent of mankind, expressed in the management of their own concerns, has agreed that in the government and administration of common property, men should vote in proportion to their shares. But it may be said, that even according to that view of the case, the working classes have reason to complain. There is a very large proportion of the population who have no votes at all. Now they all have some share in the commonwealth, however small. An amount of influence in the government of the country, equal to that of his richer fellow-citizens, may be more than a working-man has a right to claim; but, surely, no share at all is by the same rule much too little. Such an objection to the existing state of things would be unanswerable, if our representative arrangements professed to be based upon any kind of theory. That is very far from being their character. They are not the result of any calculation. They do not record the labours of any one man's brain, nor of any number of brains working in any one direction. They cannot be said to be the issue of any kind of intellectual operation, individual or collective. They are a collection of the trophies of centuries of conflict – an accumulation of the deposits which have been left behind by the varying tides of political sentiment that from age to age have flowed over our island – the resultant of all the political forces, which, working in harmony or in antagonism, have combined to propel England along the track in which it has been her destiny to travel. Ever since the House of Commons assumed even a small importance in the State, the efforts of various competitors for political power have been directed to the task of arranging its composition for their own ends. Sometimes they have done it by the direct transfer of electoral rights, more constantly by the slower process of operating upon the constituencies themselves; but it has been done according to no theory. As each rival class or party saw its opportunity, it has made of the House of Commons an instrument for establishing its own supremacy. The combined results of these sectional efforts have been salutary to the whole country. They have secured that every interest should sooner or later place upon the statute-book the laws which are necessary for its own well-being; and the general consequence has been the enormous prosperity and material power which England enjoys. But the process by which this desirable consummation has been achieved has been necessarily irregular, because it has been thoroughly natural. With the exception of the unhappy adoption of a uniform suffrage of 10*l*. – one of the most infelicitous ideas that ever issued from Lord Russell's brain – not a single line in our representative institutions betrays the stiff hand of the theorist. They are all the more elastic, and all the more suitable to the capricious, unstable world we live in on that account. But it is simply impossible to defend them before a jury of philosophers.

We should be very sorry to substitute any amount of theoretical symmetry, for an efficiency which has been tested by experiment. But if it is to be so, it must be done completely. If we are to import Mr Gladstone's 'natural rights' and 'moral titles' into the discussion, they must be accepted without reserve. It is very possible to find theoretical objections to the English Constitution in its present shape. Its only defence is its practical success. But the extension of the suffrage Mr Gladstone desires would only make its worst theoretical error more flagrant than before. According to the letter of our present law, the influence which the possessors of property enjoy in the government of the country is utterly inadequate to their pecuniary share in the concern.

'THE HOUSE OF COMMONS'

It is true they contrive to get it back in a variety of irregular ways; but it is very far from desirable that the necessity for this self-compensation should be increased. Mr. Gladstone's proposal for the extension of the suffrage would enhance this anomaly. He would bring in more and more of the needier classes to outvote the owners of property. The large shareholders would be reduced to a still slighter share in the administration of the concern. They might, or they might not, be able to indemnify themselves by the irregular means to which we have referred. They might, or they might not, be able to buy up, or frighten the crowds of poorer voters at whose mercy they would legally be placed. If they failed to do so, the security for their rights of property would be gone, and they would sooner or later realize, in unfair taxation and profligate expenditure, the ruinous helplessness of their position. If they succeeded in saving themselves by bribery, the scandals which at present attach to the working of our elections would be increased tenfold.

This is the true answer to Mr. Gladstone's proposals – that, unless he will recast the whole system upon the plan of a graduated suffrage, every extension of the franchise only aggravates the anomalies and the disregard of 'moral titles' with which our present law is chargeable. But there are other practical evils which the present state of the world forces upon our notice. We have already pointed out how little the House of Commons is indebted for its success to its own rules, and how much it depends upon the common sense and good feeling of those who compose it. It is an instructive fact that, at this moment, we should have in two different quarters of the world specimens of two States that have been brought to ruin by the want of moderation displayed by the politicians who rule them. We have before this expressed our opinion upon the merits of the quarrels that have originated the Danish and the American wars. But, setting the merits aside, there can be no question that the disputes were pushed to the last terrible arbitrament of war chiefly in consequence of the impracticable temper in which they were handled by the statesmen of the moment. If Mr. Seward and Mr. Sherman had not issued the celebrated declaration in favour of Helper's book,[1] the advent of their party to power would not have been, as it was, the signal for

---

[1] H. R. Helper's *Impending Crisis of the South* (1857) was a violent attack on slavery in the southern states of America from the viewpoint of free labour, which was exploited by the Republicans for party purposes, notably in the election of 1860, to the alarm of the South. Among those who endorsed it were the Ohio representative John Sherman, whose action cost him the speakership in 1859, and the New York senator W. H. Seward, who, after failing to secure the Republican presidential nomination in 1860, became Lincoln's secretary of state.

immediate secession. If the earlier stages of the rebellion had been dealt with in a more conciliatory spirit, it is likely that Virginia and North Carolina would never have seceded. Again, if M. Hall[1] had insisted upon the rights of Denmark in a less pugnacious spirit, such fearful consequences would never have resulted from a controversy which the great German Powers, in its earlier phases, at least, were not anxious to embitter. In each of these cases the constitution of the country is democratic, and the Minister who has done the mischief was the nominee of universal suffrage. The same phenomenon – the connection between a democratic constitution and the political recklessness of those whom it brings to the surface – is equally traceable in the history of the democratic period of ancient Rome and modern France. And the cause is not difficult to perceive. The moderate and calm-judging type of politicians consists of those whose resources are independent of politics, and whose minds are formed, and whose tempers are restrained by the public opinion of an educated class, among whom they live. Such men a democracy excludes from power. It loves them not; and the aversion is reciprocated. Be they right or wrong, educated men do not like going round, hat in hand, begging for the votes of a mob. It may be pride, or finery, or undue fastidiousness. The name which is given to the feeling is of small importance. The material point is, that it exists. Educated men generally, in the present age, dislike begging for anything. They dislike it still more when that for which they beg is, or is supposed to be, for their own advantage. But their aversion becomes almost insurmountable when those from whom they have to beg are their inferiors in the ordinary concerns of life, are rough and coarse in their manners, and delight in humiliating a 'gentleman,' and require him to swallow the most claptrap pledges as the condition of their support. The consequence of this feeling has shown itself both in Denmark and the Northern States of America. The higher class refuses to enter upon political life. Politics ceasing to be the pursuit of the richer men of the country, loses its position as a vocation. It is no longer a liberal profession. It becomes the refuge of educated men who have lost their character, and of ready-tongued adventurers. The man of easy means, who in England would betake himself to politics, at once as a means of making his life useful and as a mode of increasing his own social consideration, in America flies to art, or science, or travel, or commerce. He abandons politics, as an Englishman abandons professional betting, to the offscourings of his own class. The reaction upon the government of the country of this

[1] The Danish prime minister.

'THE HOUSE OF COMMONS'

change in the elements out of which it is formed is direct and inevitable. The politician pursues a public career, not out of patriotism or party feeling, or under the pressure of his friends, or as a path to honour, but simply that he may live. It is his livelihood – his wherewithal to obtain meat and drink. Viewing his election in that light, it is naturally his only object to propitiate those by whose favour he is enabled to pursue his vocation with success. He consults their fancies with as much care as a confectioner displays in suiting the palates of his customers. He is no more scrupulous of changing his politics to suit them, than the confectioner is of changing his sweetmeats. He will speak for war or peace, for slavery or abolition, for protection or free-trade, for extravagance or parsimony, according to the views of his constituents, with as little compunction as the confectioner would display in obeying orders for cream-ice or water-ice; or, if he is of a more honest type, it is because his character is in unison with that of the multitude, and secures their sympathy by hard, pig-headed, unreasoning obstinacy. As long as easy times last, in which nations prosper without guidance and even in spite of mis-government, the recklessness of such men does no harm. But when the tempest comes, their country is left upon the rocks such a wreck as America or Denmark.

This law, by which a gulf is dug between democratic constituencies and the better kind of the candidates, would be of small importance to us, if signs were not showing themselves that it had begun to operate among us. The evil, if it exists, has not gone very far. But there is, even now, an enormous difficulty in finding good candidates for the larger constituencies; and there is an uneasy feeling abroad that the race of public men is deteriorating – that there is a gap in the succession, which is but scantily and unsatisfactorily filled up – and that when those who attained to manhood before the passing of the Reform Bill shall have died out, they will leave their posts to a race of statesmen of an inferior and less capable type. The career of politics is not sought out, as it once was, by the cleverest men of the upper class of society. The feeling is gaining ground that the solicitation of a constituency's votes is so degrading a task, that a man has a right to decline it without any slur upon his patriotism. Whether these anticipations are exaggerated or not, there can be little doubt of the effect that would follow if all constituencies were to become large and democratic. If Mr. Gladstone were to have his way, the aversion which clever men are apt to show to politics would become unmanageable. The sacrifices required of an English politician are heavy enough as matters stand. It is surely enough that he should give his time, his money, and his health to his country, and devote himself to an exhausting labour without reward. To require of him, in addition to all this, that he shall seek the privilege of being permitted to do it by solicitations and compliances which he feels to be degrading, is a heavier trial than the patriotism of the better spirits among the educated classes will bear for any length of time.

[The article concludes with seven pages on the Schleswig-Holstein question, criticising the government's policy.]

'The Reform Bill'
(Q.R., no. 238; April 1866)

INTRODUCTORY NOTE

DESPITE Gladstone's May 1864 speech and the encouragement offered by the success of Northern democracy in the American Civil War, the cause of parliamentary reform seemed destined to frustration as long as Palmerston endured. But the limits of his endurance were clearly approaching, and there was a general expectation that when he went the unleashing of pent-up Liberal energies would bring rapid movement on the political scene. Writing in the *Quarterly* just before the general election of July 1865, Viscount Cranborne (as Lord Robert had just become) gloomily envisaged the succession of Gladstone and a new onrush of Reform. At least, however, as Derby told Disraeli, a Radical trend under Gladstone might, by causing a reaction, do something to reinvigorate the Conservative party, which emerged from the 1865 election slightly weaker (about 290 seats) than in 1859.

Palmerston died at last in October 1865, and was succeeded by Russell, with Gladstone as leader in the Commons. The new ministry, needing Radical backing, could hardly dodge the question of Reform. At first there was some disposition to procrastinate by taking up the Palmerstonian Lord Elcho's suggestion of a commission of enquiry, but the insistence of the Radical W. E. Forster on a bill instead of a commission, as a condition of his joining the government, precipitated the decision to produce a definite measure. At the same time, the demand for more information was appeased by setting the Poor Law Board to work on the compilation of extensive electoral statistics. The formulation of the bill emphasised the divergence in the cabinet between reformers and Palmerstonians, and was not made easier when the Poor Law Board's researches began to reveal some startling facts – notably that working men already comprised more than a quarter of the borough electorate. Nonetheless, the government was able to introduce its measure on 12 March 1866.

It was a franchise bill only. This was because Gladstone had not had time to produce a redistribution scheme, but it looked like a surrender to Bright, who wanted the franchise dealt with on its own in order to avoid the opposition likely to be roused by redistribution, which he preferred to tackle in a reformed Parliament. The borough qualification was to be reduced to £7 rental, supposedly adding 156,000 voters (144,000 of them working men) to the existing 488,000 (including 126,000 working men). Compounders (i.e. occupiers paying their rates not personally but through their landlords, and so excluded from the franchise under the 1832 act) were to be allowed to claim enrolment in the rate books and hence the vote.[1] The county occupation franchise was to come down from £50 to £14, and possessors of copyhold and leasehold property in parliamentary boroughs were to be enabled to vote in the counties (the point of this being to give county votes to urban dwellers who were expected to be predominantly Liberal). There was a £10 lodger qualification in boroughs, and one for a £50 savings bank deposit in counties. The bill was intended to enfranchise altogether about 400,000 men, 172,000 in the counties and 204,000 in the boroughs, plus 24,000 under the 'fancy' franchises.

The Conservative party was not committed to oppose all Reform. Some opinion in the party favoured co-operation with the government in making a moderate settlement, and as late as 8 March Derby advised his followers not to declare outright against Reform. But on the same day Disraeli, Cranborne, Northcote, Heathcote, and Walpole agreed to oppose whatever measure the government brought forward, and a party meeting on 16 March heard that the bill was to be resisted. This decision was almost inevitable. It was not only that much of the party felt with Cranborne that any substantial concession to 'democracy' must entail the progressive ruin of the country. The Conservative leaders could not readily allow their opponents to settle the question on their own terms and to their own advantage, and in the need to extricate the party from twenty years of minority and almost permanent opposition they could not afford to neglect the chance which Reform offered of breaking up the uneasy Palmerstonian coalition and securing for themselves new sources of strength. By taking up the defence of the constitution and the social order against Radicalism and democracy, as allegedly promoted by Gladstone and Bright, they might hope to detach from the opposing force a considerable body of Whigs and moderate Liberals, and, by bringing in much of the Palmerstonian middle class, to achieve that enlargement of their party's social base which was a precondition of its advance to power. Already there were signs of disruption in the heterogeneous government bloc. It was no secret that Whig magnates inside and outside the cabinet disliked the Reform Bill, and in the Commons the nucleus of the Adullamite 'Cave' which was ultimately to wreck the measure had been in existence for some time, and was co-operating with the Conservatives – their joint pressure had its first success in obliging the government to promise the introduction of a redistribution bill, which was bound to make the passage of Reform more difficult. By the time that Cranborne wrote his April article for the *Quarterly*, shortly before the Reform Bill's second reading, a crisis was approaching which gave serious prospect of Liberal disintegration.

Not only strategic considerations impelled the Conservatives to resist the bill. Its specific proposals held much to alarm them, and it was on those that Cranborne dwelt in the first part of his article, using the statistics just made available. The £7 franchise threatened to place well over a hundred boroughs

[1] The Reform Act and Clay's act of 1851 did allow compounders to get on the register by claiming to be rated directly, but not very many had done so.

'THE REFORM BILL'

under working-class control. Worse still was the way in which the bill deliberately sought to loosen the grip of the landed interest and the Conservative party on county representation by providing for an influx of voters who would be largely urban and suburban in origin and probably mostly Liberals (though this was far from certain, and the statistician Dudley Baxter told Derby and Disraeli in June that the new county franchise would *improve* Conservative chances). The measure, Cranborne had no doubt, portended the triumph of democracy and the subjection of property to the tyranny of labour. He drove home the point he had already stressed in his January *Quarterly* article: that the working men would carry over into politics the mass organisation of the trade unions, and would use it to enforce their economic and social demands, notably the redistribution of taxation and the revision of the land laws. But there was still the possibility of resistance if the Whig aristocracy would realise that it was facing a class not a party issue, and would cease to connive, for party reasons, at the destruction of the political system on which its own position depended. The whole article, with its highly coloured picture of what Reform must mean, and its appeal to Whig instincts of self-preservation, was a carefully calculated attempt to muster the votes necessary to defeat the Reform Bill's second reading.

1. *Electoral Returns: Boroughs and Counties.* Parliamentary Paper. London, 1866.

2. *Debate on the First Reading of the Reform Bill.* London, 1866.

3. *Parliamentary Reform.* By Edward J. Gibbs. London, 1866.

The story about the live fish that could be put into a full jar of water without causing it to overflow, with which Charles II. puzzled the Royal Society, has lately been regarded as a myth, chiefly on account of the impossibility of attributing such extreme simplicity to so philosophical a body. Whether common repute did them injustice or not, it can hardly be asserted by the present generation that they were guilty of any incredible or unique absurdity. Several Cabinets and more than one House of Commons have become competitors for their fame. For nearly twenty years the question has been before Parliament, Why are the working-men, as a class, excluded from the franchise? It has been discussed at endless length, and with immeasurable warmth. It has split up parties, it has lifted up Governments and cast them down, it has torn asunder statesmen previously united by the closest ties, it has been the battle-cry of divisions, the ground of dissolutions, the subject-matter of innumerable pledges extorted from reluctant candidates by imperious Radicals; – in short, it furnishes the only clue to the almost inexplicable vicissitudes of party-struggles during the last sixteen years. At last it occurred to some original genius, as in the case of Charles II.'s fish, to enquire whether the exclusion, which politicians were expending so much ingenuity and animosity in denouncing or justifying, really was a fact or not. Lord Elcho,[1] we believe, has the credit of first suggesting this seemingly elementary inquiry. But, like all great ideas in advance of the intelligence of those to whom they are unfolded, it was at first received with scorn. It was all nonsense, people said, for Lord Elcho to ask for a Commission; the exclusion of the working class was a matter of common notoriety. Mr. Bright had proclaimed it upon fifty platforms; it had been the theme of five Queen's speeches and four Government Reform Bills, besides a countless host of smaller abortions produced by private members: and it was ridiculous to suppose that so many authorities could be wrong.

However, Lord Elcho persevered with his demand: and more, apparently, to take a plea out of his mouth, than from any suspicion of the real state of the case, the Government resolved that a partial inquiry should take place. It is clear that they could not have expected that it would result in any reversal of preconceived notions: for at the same time that they set the inquiry on foot, they announced the measures to which they intended it should guide them. Before they proceeded to examine into the malady, they relieved the patient from embarrassing suspense by announcing what the remedy would be. It is easy to conceive that when the returns which they had ordered began to pour in, the consternation of the Government must have been extreme. In most cases, and under most leaders, the unexpected information would have produced not only a revulsion in feeling, but also a change of policy. But Reform had not been proposed to meet a public necessity, and was, therefore, not discredited by the proof that that necessity was imaginary. Grounds of pure policy never made men Reformers of the constitution in any country in which contentment is so general as it is in this. It is an insult to the intellect of the present Cabinet to suspect them of being influenced by a genuine belief that the quality either of our legislators or our legislation would be improved by admitting a needier class to the franchise. Nor, again, would it be fair to impute to them any sincere acceptance of Mr Gladstone's dreamy sentimentalism. The considerations which have impelled them to the fatal step which may possibly be their

[1] Elcho (1818–1914), later tenth earl of Wemyss and March, was Liberal–Conservative M.P. for Haddingtonshire, and one of the principal opponents of the Reform Bill, being prominent in the 'Cave' which finally destroyed it.

'THE REFORM BILL'

ruin, have been of a far homelier character. The pressing necessity of purchasing by some concession the votes of the American school in the House of Commons was the first consideration with which Lord Russell had to deal when he succeeded to power. So long as the American war lasted, the path of the Government was smooth enough. Do what they would, Mr. Bright dared not overset them; for they might have been replaced by a Government which would have consulted English interests, rather than democratic sympathies, in its conduct towards the contending States of North America. Just as in 1860 and 1861 the reforming zeal of the Radicals was bought off by the sacrifice of the Paper Duty, so from 1861 to 1865 it was appeased by the sacrifice of the gallant Confederacy. But, with the fall of Richmond,[1] Mr. Bright's heart was set at ease concerning the fate of the Government to which his true allegiance is given, and which he has represented in the House of Commons for so many years with such unflagging devotion. His tone changed at once. Even in September, in his letter to a friend at Bradford, he denounced those to whom he had given his vote in the confidence division of the previous year as the perpetrators of the greatest fraud of modern times.[2] As long as Lord Palmerston was alive, it was less material to the Ministry whether Mr. Bright threw off his allegiance to them or not. The old man's enormous popularity was a sufficient shield to them. But the moment he was removed by death they instinctively felt that the time had again come round for buying off once more their insatiable ally. This time there was nothing for it but to reproduce a Reform Bill.[3] There remained no taxes to which he had a special aversion, no foreign crisis in which he took an absorbing interest. Accordingly, Mr. Gladstone tells us, they had no sooner lowered down their stout Anti-Reforming Chief into the earth, than they set about preparing themselves to pay the next instalment of the tribute which they were well assured would be immediately demanded by Mr. Bright. It is evident from the varying tone of his speeches, as one opinion or another gained the mastery in

[1] The Confederate capital fell in April 1865.
[2] The letter in question was that of 10 September 1865 to George Newton of Glasgow (not Bradford), in which Bright attacked Palmerston's ministry for failing to carry a Reform measure (Leech, *Public Letters of Bright*, pp. 99–100).
[3] Gladstone was so galled by these charges that the government's actions in 1860-6 had been dictated by the desire of appeasing the Radicals that he referred to them while moving the second reading of the Reform Bill on 12 April 1866, the day the article was published. He relieved his feelings by quoting *Henry IV*, part 1:

'These lies are like the father that begot them –
Gross as a mountain, open, palpable.'

the Cabinet, and from the information which he was always able to give to his hearers as to the sentiments of different Members of the Cabinet, that his communication with them was close and constant. They seem to have shrunk at the last moment from admitting him into it, as was at one time intended.[1] But he has exercised over their decisions a greater influence than would have been exerted by any one inside it. The form of the measure was the most important question for those who looked mainly to a Parliamentary triumph. Mr. Bright, almost alone among Reformers, entertained the view that the franchise question ought to be dealt with independently of any proposals for the redistribution of seats. That, contrary to the tradition of all former Reform Bills, and to the views of all other Reformers, this particular plan was followed in the construction of the Reform Bill, is sufficient to establish the real parentage of the measure.

Men who came in this spirit to their task were not likely to pay much heed to statistics. Indeed, it needs no proof that a resolution taken in November could not have been taken with much regard to statistics, which were to be procured by the end of February. The only use to which the returns could be applied was to furnish arguments for a predetermined theory; and Mr Gladstone must have mentally echoed the Frenchman's ejaculation, '*Tant pis pour les faits!*' when he found how little they were adapted for the use for which he had destined them. To those, however, who look upon the proposal to change the ruling class of England as something of more importance than a mere party struggle, these returns will furnish matter of the deepest interest. They are, indeed, terribly defective. All the conclusions based upon them must be to some extent precarious, because there are gaps in their figures which can only be bridged over by conjectural computations. Still, such as they are, they have a value which no other statistics upon the same subject can boast. They furnish a glimpse of a country hitherto wholly unexplored. They tell us something definite about the working man, of whom we have hitherto heard so much that is declamatory and vague. They lift up just one corner of the veil which hides from us the future destiny of this country when a Reform Bill shall have passed. They furnish the first answer that has been given, though it is still faltering and indistinct, to the question that has been so often asked, and has always been asked in vain, – Who are the rulers to whom our

[1] Russell considered having Bright in the cabinet in December 1865, but Gladstone pointed out that this would 'sink' the government and its Reform Bill, given the critical state of feeling on the Liberal side about the franchise. Cowling, p. 86.

submission is to be transferred, and on whose pleasure our future fate is to depend?

Unfortunately these statistics, so far as they are of any value, only extend over one portion of the wide area which it is proposed that Reform legislation should cover. In respect to the boroughs, some kind of trouble has been taken to make the information perfect; and Mr. Lambert,[1] to whose care was entrusted the administrative duty of collecting and preparing the returns for which the Government determined to ask, deserves every praise for the care and skill with which his task has been performed. Even in the borough returns, however, several highly important links are wanting. But in framing the scheme of the county returns, the Government appears to have been guided by no other desire than that of decorously filling the pages of their Blue-book with a sufficient array of figures. No effort has been made to ascertain the social position either of those who at present have the suffrage, or of those who under any conceivable form of franchise are likely to possess it. There is no information as to the nature of the large freeholding constituency – no intimation how far it is to be ranged with the middle or the lower class, or assigned to the rural or the urban interest. No attempt is made to divide the 50*l.* occupiers who live in towns from those who live in agricultural districts. But if the information with respect to the existing constituency is imperfect, it is ample in comparison with that which is vouchsafed to us concerning the constituency that is to be. An elaborate table has been prepared, showing the numbers that would be added to the present electoral body if a ten pound, or a twelve pound, or a fifteen pound, or a twenty pound franchise were adopted in counties. But there is no hint whatever of the results that would follow if the fourteen pound franchise which has been proposed by the Government were adopted. The Minister who prepared the order for these returns appears never to have dreamed of so eccentric a proposition. It has been demanded by nobody; it has been suggested in none of the countless schemes for the reconstruction of the House of Commons which have appeared in Parliament or in the press. Mr. Gladstone seems to have worked it out arithmetically. Auguste Comte's mind was deeply infected with the idea of constructing institutions according to certain numerical relations; and the present Ministry appear to have been studying his philosophy. The borough franchise is placed at seven pounds because it is the exact arithmetical mean between the proposal

---

[1] John Lambert (1815–92), poor law inspector and electoral statistician; later first secretary of the local government board.

of Mr. Walpole,[1] who was in favour of eight pounds, and of Mr. Bright who has been pressing for six; or, symbolically,

$$b = \frac{\text{Bright} + \text{Walpole}}{2}.$$

The county franchise is ascertained with equal facility. Mr Walpole has proposed twenty pounds for the county franchise. Mr Bright has proposed ten pounds. Then

$$\frac{\text{Walpole}}{\text{Bright}} \times \text{borough franchise} = \text{county franchise}.$$

Unless the Ministry had resorted to pitch and toss, it was impossible for them to have fixed their franchise upon a simpler principle. But the result of their having followed their formula with such mathematical precision is that the figures collected to illustrate the Reform Bill have no connexion with the franchise which it proposes.

To a great extent therefore we are in the dark as to the mere number of the addition which Mr. Gladstone proposes to make to the county constituency. The figures which he gave in his speech were founded on his own conjectures, and did not represent facts officially ascertained. Nor again had any pains been taken to discover to what class these additional votes, whatever their numbers, will belong. Mr. Gladstone assumes that they will belong to the middle-class. But how he arrived at that satisfactory assurance he does not tell us. It may have been supernaturally revealed to him: he may have evolved it from his inner consciousness, as Schelling[2] used to evolve what he called his facts in chemistry and geology; but assuredly he did not obtain them [sic] from the statistics collected so elaborately, and laid before Parliament so ostentatiously. There is another point yet about these added county voters upon which the Government do not even profess to give information. Do they, in truth, belong to the county or to the town? Any one casting his eye over the Census Returns for this country will see that large numbers of the population, who for electoral purposes are included in the counties, are thoroughly urban in their character. All the counties which contain great centres of population within their borders have to struggle with a disadvantage of this kind; for though most of the great towns themselves are taken out of the county, and return members of their own, they are always surrounded by widely extending suburbs which, in character, belong to them wholly, but which are separated

---

[1] Spencer H. Walpole (1806–98), M.P. Cambridge University, home secretary 1852, 1858–9, and again in Derby's third ministry, 1866–7.
[2] Friedrich Schelling (1775–1854), German philosopher and pseudo-scientist.

'THE REFORM BILL'

from them for electoral purposes by an arbitrary line. Thus Stratford goes far to swamp the representation of South Essex; Chelsea and Kensington and the northern suburbs of London make Middlesex little better than a metropolitan borough; while Woolwich and Wandsworth seriously modify the balance of parties in the western division of Kent and in the county of Surrey. A similar influence is exercised in the North by manufacturing towns, such as Darlington, Burnley, and Staleybridge, and numerous others, which, being of comparatively recent growth, have as yet obtained no special representation.

Combined with the influence of the freeholders, who, though their qualification lies inside the boroughs, possess yet a vote for the county by virtue of it,[1] this state of things places the rural interest in the counties in a position of serious disadvantage. Their representation is becoming less and less rural in its character, and growing to be but a pale copy of that of the towns. London, Brighton, and the great seats of manufacturing industry, in addition to their own members, are coming to have an influence over the representation of the counties to which they belong which is most unjust to the agricultural population. The case is well put in Mr. Gibbs's able pamphlet:

> It is usual to say that in the country districts 70,000 people, and in the boroughs 25,000 people have a member – that a million people in the towns return thirty-nine members, and a million people in the country only fourteen members. It is concluded from this that the towns are nearly three times as well represented as the rural districts. But this is only half the truth. The 25,000 people in the towns not only return their own member, but have a large and yearly increasing share in the county member. The thirty-nine borough members represent a million people who are to a man townspeople, the fourteen county members represent partly the rural population, but also to a very great extent the townspeople over again. Looking at this double voting, it is tolerably clear that the inhabitants of parliamentary boroughs have, in proportion to population, not three times only but four or five times the weight in the legislature that is given to country districts and unrepresented towns.

But the land is not sufficiently crippled yet in the eyes of the Radicals; and therefore it is proposed, by reducing the occupation franchise further, to make the urban populations more completely masters of the counties. The rural voters will not be largely increased, for small holdings of agricultural land are not common in this country; but the voters out

---

[1] Under the 1832 Reform Act, a freeholder in a parliamentary borough might register in the county in which the borough was situated, if the specific property for which he claimed a county vote did not qualify him to vote in the borough. The Conservatives' Reform Bill of 1859 would have altered this.

of the unrepresented towns, and from the suburban fringes of the larger boroughs, will come in in troops. The balance will be utterly destroyed. For electoral purposes, county will only become a name for a less compact kind of borough. It is not much justice that agricultural interests now receive from a Parliament chiefly composed of borough members. It is owing to no other cause than the inferiority of their numbers that they must submit to be taxed upon principles which the other classes of the community have successfully resisted. The extreme injustice which the counties suffer in the apportionment of the representation is far the most flagrant anomaly of our present system; but it is one that Reformers generally find it convenient to ignore. The following figures will show how great this disproportion is:

BOROUGHS IN ENGLAND AND WALES			COUNTIES		
Population	Electors	Members	Population	Electors	Members
9,326,709	514,026	331	11,427,655	542,633	159

We have already pointed out how deeply the injustice is aggravated by the intrusion of urban votes even into this scanty representation. But if what remains of the county representation is to be taken from the rural districts by a new inroad of townspeople, they will be erased from the political register altogether. They would cease to constitute an element of political power of sufficient importance to claim even a respectful consideration from the Chancellor of the Exchequer. The weight of his hand falls ever upon the weakest. The poll-book is a foreshadowing of the budget. Woe to the interest which fails at the elections when the annual adjustment of financial burdens takes place. Office is the blue ribbon, the mere decoration, that awaits a victory at the polling-booth; but it is the budget that distributes the substantial booty. For twenty years the landed interest has been in a minority; and for twenty years, while financial changes have brought relief to every other industry, agricultural alone has not benefited by one single change that has been made. The country gentlemen will naturally draw their inferences from these patent facts, and, by the light of their past experience, will have little difficulty in casting the horoscope of their class if such a measure as Mr Gladstone's should ever become law.

With respect to the boroughs the case is a good deal clearer. The information given, though still fragmentary, is extensive. We do not know exactly how many of the artisan class the future borough constituency may contain; but we do know how many it contains at present, and we can form an estimate, rough and imperfect, but probably approximate, of the numbers of that class it will include when it is enlarged. There are two difficulties in the calculation, which are due to the defective plan of the statistics. We know how many seven pound occupiers there are in each borough, and we also know that those who inhabit houses of value between ten pounds and seven pounds belong almost exclusively to the artisan class. But there are two material points which we do not know. Certain causes of incapacity – non-residence, non-payment of rates, receipt of relief, employment by the Government, composition[1] by landlord – do in the existing constituency reduce the number upon the register considerably below that of the actual occupiers of houses of the value of ten pounds. It is not, however, safe to calculate the deduction for the new constituency upon the average percentage furnished by the experience of the old, inasmuch as one of the most potent causes of incapacity – the non-payment of rates – is abolished by the Bill. Again in several boroughs a number of working men who live in houses of value between ten pounds and seven pounds are already on the register in the capacity of freemen. They must clearly be deducted from the number of working men whom the new measure will add to the constituencies. But unfortunately their number is absolutely uncertain, and no effort has been made to remove our ignorance upon this head. These, then, are two items of deduction to be made from the number of the seven pound occupiers whom the Bill will add to the register, and whom we may look on as a pure reinforcement of working men. But the uncertain elements do not appear only upon one side of the account. No estimate whatever is furnished of the number of working men whom the lodger franchise, the repeal of the rate-paying clauses, and the enfranchisement of compound householders will add to the electoral body in each borough. These numbers, however, must be very large, and will bring an addition to the strength of the working class more than sufficient to outweigh any deduction from it due to the causes we have specified. Mr. Gibbs, in a letter to the 'Times' of March 31st, states that the constituency of Birmingham, with which he is acquainted, will be doubled by the operation of these provisions, and that the new Bill will more than double the borough constituencies. His authority is as good, probably, as any that can be obtained upon a point that is purely conjectural. It would be very desirable that accurate information should be obtained of the exact value of all these items, whether of addition or of deduction. But in the mean time the safest course is to treat them as balancing each other, and to strike them out of both sides of the account. Such a mode of computation

---

[1] I.e. for the rates.

is much more favourable to the Government than that of Mr. Gibbs, and by adopting it we shall certainly not be overrating the strength of the artisan contingent that is to be added to the constituencies.

Disturbing elements, then, being struck out on both sides, we may assume that the number of seven pound occupiers is identical with the number of working men that are to be added. The following will then be the list of boroughs in England and Wales in which the working-men will be absolute masters of the representation:

	Boroughs	Percentage of working class	No. of members		Boroughs	Percentage of working class	No. of members
1	Beaumaris	52	1	33	Leicester	56	2
2	Beverley	60	2	34	Lincoln	57	2
3	Birkenhead	57	1	35	Liverpool	50	2
4	Birmingham	59	2	36	Macclesfield	51	2
5	Bridgewater	64	2	37	Maidstone	63	2
6	Bristol	52	2	38	Maldon	64	2
7	Bolton	58	2	39	Manchester	65	2
8	Bury	53	1	40	Marlborough	50	2
9	Cambridge	52	2	41	Marlow	51	2
10	Canterbury	59	2	42	Monmouth	52	1
11	Cardiff	51	1	43	Newark	54	2
12	Carmarthen	51	1	44	Newcastle-under-Lyme	61	2
13	Chatham	67	2				
14	Cheltenham	52	1	45	Newcastle-on-Tyne	52	2
15	Chester	54	2				
16	Colchester	57	2	46	Newport	54	2
17	Coventry	80	2	47	Northampton	68	2
18	Derby	62	2	48	Nottingham	56	2
19	Devonport	52	2	49	Oldham	69	2
20	Dover	50	2	50	Oxford	56	2
21	Dudley	57	1	51	Pembroke	67	1
22	Durham	50	2	52	Peterborough	60	2
23	Gateshead	53	1	53	Preston	60	2
24	Greenwich	66	2	54	Portsmouth	64	2
25	Guildford	55	2	55	Reigate	56	1
26	Hastings	50	2	56	Rochester	59	2
27	Haverfordwest	50	1	57	Rye	55	1
28	Hertford	52	2	58	Salford	65	1
29	Hull	53	2	59	Scarborough	56	2
30	Hythe	50	1	60	Shrewsbury	50	2
31	St Ives	66	1	61	Sheffield	58	2
32	Lancaster	54	2	62	Southampton	56	2

'THE REFORM BILL'

Boroughs	Percentage of working class	No. of members	Boroughs	Percentage of working class	No. of members
63 South Shields	54	1	71 Warrington	55	1
64 Southwark	59	2	72 Westbury	62	1
65 Stafford	69	2	73 Wigan	60	2
66 Stoke	61	2	74 Winchester	55	2
67 Sunderland	55	2	75 Wolverhampton	68	2
68 Swansea	56	1	76 Worcester	61	2
69 Tamworth	50+	2	77 Yarmouth	50+	2
70 Walsall	68	1			

Total number of members in whose constituencies the working men would have a majority, 133.

The result will be that in about two-fifths of the existing boroughs of England and Wales working men will be in a majority. Considering their power of combination, their ignorance of economical laws, their strong taste for the despotism of numbers, this result is far from reassuring, even if it went no further. A very slender reinforcement from theorists of the upper or middle class, or any slight freak of fortune, might place them in absolute command of the boroughs. Of their position in the counties it is difficult to speak with certainty. The forty-shilling freehold costs about fifty pounds; and to judge from the enormous sums which the working classes are able to collect whenever they are on strike, it is probable that a very large number of them have accumulated savings which do not fall far short of that amount. How large their influence in counties is or is likely to become we have obtained no statistics from the Government to tell us, and therefore we are incapable of accurately judging.

But even these calculations do not represent the full danger to which the balance of the Constitution is exposed. Every calculation is merely provisional until the Bill for redistributing seats has been produced. No one can tell how far the new county franchises will overwhelm the rural interest until we know how many unrepresented towns and suburbs are to be taken out of the county representation. No one can tell how many boroughs will return members elected purely by the working class until we know what boroughs are to return members at all. We have been told nothing as to the views of the Government in reference to the question of redistribution; we know still less what will ultimately be the view of Parliament. Mr. Bright, in the only Reform Bill he ever produced,[1] proposed to transfer to larger constituencies no less than ninety-six of the seats which under this Bill would remain to the upper and middle classes. He appears to be keeper of the conscience of the Government; and if, in their scheme of redistribution, they follow him as faithfully as they have hitherto done, it is needless to point out how overwhelming will be the preponderance of the working class in the boroughs. But here again we are left to pure conjecture. This time it is not from the ignorance of those who should enlighten us. The Government, of set purpose, withhold the information which they have in their hands. They require the House of Commons to work out this political problem, and they refuse to it and to the country the most important of the elements upon which its solution depends. It seems impossible to conceive a more hopeless calculation than that which we are called upon to make. Elaborate data have been furnished us, difficult to master, and insufficient, when we have them, to support any reliable conclusion. But for the sum we have to do these data are simply worthless; they might as usefully have remained among the archives of the department that compiled them. The one and only thing we know with certainty concerning the future structure of the House of Commons is that it will not be founded upon the state of things which these statistics portray. Be the balance between town and country, lower class and middle class, what it may, no sagacity can discover it from the statistics of constituencies of which a quantity quite uncertain is to be destroyed in order to be replaced by substitutes absolutely unknown. Whigs as well as Conservatives could hardly do otherwise than rebel at a plan of legislation at once so humiliating and so unsafe. In the smallest matters no one is fond of unlimited liability. Men do not willingly embark on an enterprise without knowing the chances on both sides. They do not undertake contracts of which they do not know the subject matter, vouch for statements of which they have not seen the wording, nor sign deeds of which the contents are hidden from them. But any of these follies would shine out as wise and far-seeing proceedings compared with the infatuation of consenting to alter the ancient constitution of a mighty empire by enactments of which the most experienced of those who vote for them cannot even distantly guess at the result.

Mr Gladstone, however, sturdily declines to furnish any more statistics. Like a burnt child he dreads the fire. He has had enough of statistics; he weakly made a concession last autumn to the cry for information, which he would now gladly recall, and consented to the collection of a volume

[1] In 1859.

'THE REFORM BILL'

of figures, which, imperfect as it is, has already struck a deadly blow at his Bill, and bids fair to upset his Ministry. He is fond himself of the Rule of Three, and loses no opportunity of impressing its value on the House of Commons; and, by its aid, he has no doubt already worked out in his head the answer to the question: 'Given a Ministry jeopardised, and six Whig magnates alienated,[1] by one volume of statistics; what will be the result of half-a-dozen?' So far as he is concerned, he is resolved that the answer to that question shall remain a matter of calculation, and not become a matter of experience; therefore he prefers to urge any argument, no matter how puerile, rather than yield another inch to the demand for more accurate information. He even condescends to urge on us that we ought not to count those whom he proposes to admit, because they are 'fellow-Christians and our own flesh and blood.' It does not appear to have occurred to him that this novel qualification for the elective franchise will admit every man, woman, and child in the United Kingdom, with the solitary exception of the unlucky Jews. It seems, however, to be on the strength of this consanguinity and fellow-Christianity suffrage that the House of Commons is to be asked to take its 'leap in the dark' on the 12th of this month.[2] If it looks for better arguments to encourage it in venturing upon this great experiment, it does not seem likely to obtain them.

It is, in truth, the absolutely experimental character of this undertaking which brings into the strongest relief the imprudence of the course which is now urged upon the House of Commons. Even in enterprises which have often been undertaken before, and of which the conditions are well known, men do not ordinarily put any important interests to hazard, without procuring all the available information that can be necessary for their guidance. The most experienced seamen upon the best known sea will not willingly set out without lead, or chart, or compass. If the operation of placing supreme power in the hands of the poorest section of the community had been a common one in the history of the world, and had often been performed with success, the House of Commons would still be justified in asking for the most abundant information on the subject before it moved a step. But there are no such precedents to encourage us in this case. The experiment is absolutely new. The ancient republics are put out of the question by the existence of slavery, which acted as a very effective restriction of the

---

[1] It is hard to know which particular six Cranborne means. By this time the list of great Whig malcontents included Clarendon and Somerset in the cabinet, and Cleveland, Grey, Halifax, Lansdowne, Lichfield, Spencer, and Sutherland outside it.
[2] The Reform Bill was down for its second reading on 12 April.

franchise. In modern times the United States and our own Colonies are the only instances in which supreme political power has been given to the masses upon any considerable scale. In them the experiment is for the most part so recent as to furnish little ground for inductive reasoning. We know little of the result of the experiment as yet, and what little we know is far from reassuring. But this at least we know, that the experience of a new country, blessed with a boundless expanse of unoccupied land, is no guide for an older country in which that happy period of national infancy has long gone by. The great danger of democracy is, that it places supreme power in the hands of those who may be misled by hunger into acts of folly or of wrong. In an old country, no excellence of institutions can ensure that such periods of maddening want shall not occasionally occur. Where the bounty of Nature is wellnigh exhausted, and multitudes exist upon no other resource than the prosperity of trade, it must be that sometimes that one precarious resource will fail. When such periods of distress do come, it is vain to hope that argument will restrain hungry men from relieving their own and their children's misery by any measures which the institutions of their country give them power to take. But there can be no danger of this kind in countries where unexhausted natural wealth makes it impossible that large multitudes should ever be in want, except through their own misconduct, for any length of time.

The examples, therefore, of Washington and Melbourne, even if their political condition were far more inviting than it is, are not relevant to our case. Whatever they may do, the fact will still remain the same for us, that no old country of any considerable population has ever yet abandoned political supremacy to the working class. If we do it, it may be right or wrong, wise or foolish: but at all events we shall be doing something of which the world never heard before. It is a new thing in the history of man. We may guess *a priori* as to what the results will be; but until we have tried, we can only speak of them hypothetically, as men discuss the nature of the country in the centre of Australia, or the state of the temperature at the top of the Himalayas. And the nervous part of the experiment is, that if it does not answer it can never be undone. It is an experiment made once for all. If it fails, other lands may study and profit by our error; but to us nothing will be left except hopeless remorse. We shall be in the condition of the Prussian doctor who ate trichinose bacon in order to prove that the disease was a chimæra. His courageous experiment has been of great service to the rest of mankind, by establishing the reality of the danger of which he was warned in vain.

But this involuntary benefit to his species probably comforted him little when he was dying in agonies.

Before, then, we take this tremendous plunge it is reasonable that we should inquire, by the aid of the little light that *a priori* reasoning can shed, what its results are likely to be. It is natural that the House of Commons should ask whether the new arrangement will give to the working class a power absolutely without restraint; and, if it does so, what use they will probably make of it? It is idle for Mr. Gladstone to tell us that they are fellow-Christians, our own flesh and blood, and so forth. The depositaries of absolute power have often been fellow-Christians, and have generally been composed of flesh and blood akin to that of those over whom they ruled. The Emperor Paul,[1] Robespierre, Ferdinand of Naples,[2] were all baptised, and all of the same race as their subjects: but those circumstances did not make the absolute power which had been lodged in their hands less of a calamity to their fellowmen. It is not likely that the particular misdeeds of these monsters will ever find any parallel on English soil: but men can keep at a very respectful distance from these great archetypes of wickedness and yet be the authors of a very fair quantity of wrong and ruin. If Mr. George Potter,[3] and his like, are to rule us absolutely, it seems natural to ask for some better security that he will be a beneficent despot than the certainty that he is an Englishman, and the probability that he is a Christian.

What the working men would do if they came to have an actual preponderance in such a country as this is difficult to prophesy, because, in point of fact, they have never been placed in such a position before. We can only dimly guess by the conduct they have pursued in their present position. The inference is not conclusive, because power changes much in the nature of men, and according to their characters develops in them a recklessness of passion, or a zeal for their duty, never traceable before. They may prove, when they are clothed with their new powers, much better or much worse than we can now forecast. It is one of the gravest evils of this desperate venture that even the amplest information will not reveal to us all the risks that wait upon a change never fully tried before. But it is at all events worth while to make use of all the knowledge we now possess, and see if the light it throws on the path

[1] Paul I of Russia; reigned 1796–1801; possibly insane.
[2] Ferdinand II ('King Bomba'); reigned 1830–59; his brutal treatment of political opponents provoked a celebrated outburst by Gladstone in 1851.
[3] 1832–93; prominent trade unionist and working-class leader; edited the working-class newspaper the *Bee-Hive*; the leading figure in 1866–7 in the primarily political London Working Men's Association.

along which we are being hurried discloses a prospect fitted to console and cheer us on. The first thing which the friends of this Bill tell us is, that the working class will not act politically *en masse*. This goes to the root of the matter: for if they do not act together their preponderance will be neutralized. But it is so important a point that we cannot be content to take it on the unsupported assertions of Professor Fawcett[1] and Mr. Arthur Peel.[2] We had rather ask what they do now; and draw our estimate of their tendencies from their own actions, and not from the panegyrics of their friends. Do they act *en masse* at the present moment? Professor Fawcett tells us that they do not go entirely with the Liberal party; and that many of them were very enthusiastic upon the question of going to war for Poland,[3] and upon several other equally important points, in respect to which they were at issue with the advanced Liberals. Other speakers declared that they were frequently divided in opinion upon questions of foreign policy. But no one was bold enough to assert that they were divided in opinion in matters upon which their pecuniary interests were concerned. Probably no class in this country, or in any other, have ever exhibited such a perfect party discipline, or so well drilled a contempt for ruin and hunger incurred by obedience to their elected chiefs. The spectacle of the Trades' Unions, and of what they can do and suffer, has not been lost upon employers of labour. It has effected a profound modification of political opinion upon this question of Reform. Mere exhibitions of ignorance on the part of the working men, or even of ill-will toward their superiors, such as those with which politicians were familiar thirty or forty years ago, would not have produced misgivings so serious as the steady, well-matured action of these exacting and despotic organisations. There is something appalling in the severity of the sacrifices which these combinations demand from the workmen over whom they claim to rule, in the readiness with which their commands are usually received, and the deadly promptitude with which punishment is measured to the daring offender who disobeys. He may be commanded to leave a good master, to squander the savings of years, to watch in idleness while his wife and children starve, though work at good wages is within the reach of his hand; but he may not accept it. He must obey, though the policy pursued by his Union be one that he disapproves, and

---

[1] Henry Fawcett (1833–84), though blind, was professor of political economy at Cambridge, and Radical M.P. for Brighton.
[2] A. W. Peel (1829–1912), youngest son of Sir Robert Peel and Liberal M.P. for Warwick; later speaker of the House of Commons.
[3] At the time of the Polish insurrection against Russian rule in 1863 there was much pro-Polish feeling in England.

though it be enforced by men whose motives and character he despises. If he rebel, he knows well that there is no limit to the vengeance which his fellow-workmen will inflict upon him, except their power. The barbarous assassinations with which this illegal tyranny has been enforced in Sheffield and other manufacturing towns within a very recent period, are unhappily too notorious.[1] It may be justly urged, indeed, that the artizans of the whole kingdom ought not to be made responsible for the crimes of a few localities, and the Trades' Unions in most places have undoubtedly shrunk from this terrible corollary upon their assumed dominion over their class. But short of this extreme, no limit is placed to the ferocity with which the rebellious 'knobstick' is persecuted. He is not only driven forth from the society of his class, but every effort is made to reduce him to pauperism. If he tries to find work with a master who is accessible to the threats of the Union, every workman in his employ throws up his work, and remains on strike till the offender is dismissed; and if there be any brisk demand or heavy contract to be fulfilled, the master generally prefers to make his peace cheaply with the Union, by driving the outcast forth upon the world again. If the master is obstinate, or the slackness of trade deprives a strike of its terrors, then the knobstick is waylaid on his road to and from his work, insulted, hustled, and maltreated, as far as the appointed executioners of the decrees of the Union think that they can go without incurring legal punishment. Occasionally, in the ardour of their task, they overstep this line, and then the existence of this systematic tyranny is brought under the public eye in the shape of a case at the police court.

It is not the moral guilt of these proceedings that gives them their peculiar bearing upon the question of the extension of the suffrage. Injustice as great, and social tyranny as oppressive, might be found abundantly in the conduct of individuals in every class of society. It is not the criminality, but the tremendous power of these associations which gives them momentous interest in a crisis like the present. The fearful sacrifice which their leaders exact, and the implicit obedience of their members, indicate a vigour and tenacity of combination of which associations of the middle and upper classes are utterly destitute. Armed with political privileges, these organisations would wield a power against which no other political influence could make head. The power of any organised body of men depends upon the fidelity with which they obey

---

[1] The long series of acts of violence (even extending to murder) by trade unionists against recalcitrants in the Sheffield cutlery trades reached a peak in 1865–6, and there was similar trouble elsewhere, notably among bricklayers in the Manchester area.

their leaders. Even if the numbers on both sides were equal, the working men will always have the best of it, because the obedience to which they have been trained in their Unions far exceeds the obedience which in the ranks above them any one Englishman will pay to any other. Of all the arguments that can possibly be used to reconcile us to the preponderance of the working men in the constitution, the plea that they will not act *en masse* is the most absurd that can be devised. They act *en masse* with a success which no class or order of men not bound together by religious ties has ever succeeded in attaining to before.

But then we are told that these organisations exist only to secure the private interest of their members, and would never be applied to political purposes. It may be so; but the mere assurance of those who have a controversial interest in making it, is not sufficient to dispose of all apprehensions upon this head. Certain it is that at a time when Mr. Bright had not awakened to the necessity of keeping in the background the probable results of working-class supremacy, he looked with complacency upon the idea of using the Trades Unions as engines of political agitation. The language he used at Birmingham, towards the beginning of the last parliament, shows that in his eyes the machinery of the Trades Unions was perfectly applicable to the purposes of politicians:

Working men have associations; they can get up formidable strikes against capital, sometimes it may be upon real and sometimes upon fancy grievances, sometimes for things that are just, sometimes for things that are impossible. They have associations, trade societies, organisations, and I want to ask them why it is that all these various organisations throughout the country could not be made use of for the purpose of obtaining their political rights.*

We may assume he did not recommend to his followers a mode of agitation which was impracticable or absurd. He knows enough of them to know what they can do and what they cannot. We have his testimony that the vast organisation of the Trades Unions, which is becoming wider and more powerful every day, may be applied without difficulty to the purpose of obtaining whatever the working men may deem to be their 'political rights.' If they do not, then, act *en masse*, it will be no fault of Mr. Bright's. And countless other agitators will take up his advice, and will repeat it for objects from which he himself would recoil. Everywhere the maxim will be pressed on the working men that union is power, and that their political desires can only be obtained by rigorous obedience. And gradually the teaching will work into their minds, and they will accept it. When they do accept it, we may be certain, from all

* Speech of Mr. Bright at Birmingham, Jan. 6, 1860.

that we have seen of their proceedings, that they will follow it out with all the fearless self-sacrifice, and all the reckless disregard for the rights of others which they have hitherto shown in their battles with their employers. Every other tie that binds them will be broken, every other motive that might restrain or deaden their zeal will be resolutely given up, every consideration of personal interest, or convenience, or affection, or esteem will be ruthlessly put aside. Have they not abandoned all these things at the bidding of their leaders for the sake of extorting a trifling increase of pay from some small number of employers? and will they not do that, and more also, to win the far higher prizes that may be wrung from the nation at large?

Take, upon the authority of Mr. Bright, that the Trade Union mechanism can be worked to secure a political result, and it is not difficult to conceive the plan of tactics that will be adopted. The working class will have a majority of the boroughs absolutely at their disposal; and even in those boroughs in which they will not be supreme, they will still be an important and powerful interest. In every borough a working man's Political Union will be established in connexion with the principal Trade Unions. It will be established and maintained by those mechanics who form a constant per centage, though not a large one, among the working men – who take a keen interest in politics, and are usually the most restless, worthless, and noisy of their class. Antecedently, one might hope that the working men would be too sensible to be governed by these busybodies; but the deplorable experience of the Trades Unions demonstrates past controversy how enormous is the influence for evil which men of this stamp possess. They would be all-powerful in the Political Union as they now are in the Trades Unions. On general political questions it might be that these Unions and Political Unions would be agreed neither among themselves nor with each other. But upon questions which affect the pecuniary interest of the working men they would work together against the classes above them with all the unanimity they now show in working together against individual employers. The artisan force would be handled in the conduct of elections as they are now handled in the conduct of strikes, with as much promptitude of action and as much exactness of drill. The whole body of artisan voters would be turned over from one candidate to another at a given order, just as they now, like one man, leave the work of an employer or a set of employers at a given signal. The fate of a dissentient artisan who dared to give his vote for the wrong man would be exactly what the fate of a 'knobstick' is now. In Sheffield and other towns of the North, he would find cans of gunpowder hidden under his hearthstone, or have a bottle of vitriol thrown into his face as he walked the streets. In the milder South he would be cast out like a leper from the society of his class, and by the exertion of terrorism upon employers driven out of every employment he might enter. Either way the number of dissentients would be very small; for if they now yield to the pressure of their Unions in questions of strike, where obedience is often utter ruin, how much more readily would they yield in political disputes, where there would be nothing to be sacrificed except a principle or a friend. On the other hand, unless the nature of the working class undergoes a sudden metamorphosis, it is equally certain that such pressure will be pitilessly applied. The Trades Unions and their agents have done these things systematically, when the only object in view was such extra wages as the employers could afford to give. What is to make them less bold, less dexterous, less unscrupulous, where the national treasury, or the rights of property belonging to the whole middle and upper class are the objects of 'loot'? No such political organisation exists at this moment, for the very good reason that it would do no service to the views of the Trades Unions, but rather harm. In the present distribution of political power, any such attempt would alarm other classes, without effecting any practical result. It would be very different when the demagogues of the Unions knew that political supremacy was within their reach, if they but stretched forth their hands to seize it. They only attempt what is in their power; they do not waste strength or influence upon impracticable enterprises. If we wish to know how they would behave in a state of things which made them politically predominant, we must look to their conduct, not in political disputes, where they are at present feeble, but in trade disputes, where they know their power. As they use their strength, now, in one field, so would they use it then, in another.

   What might in such a case be the objects of their efforts it is difficult to predict. That they would ultimately be more practical than the objects set forth by some of their orators at recent meetings may be readily granted. When they came actually into possession of political power they would probably convince themselves, sooner or later, that wages could not be raised by Act of Parliament. How much injustice and oppression would be committed before that salutary lesson had been learnt – how far trade would be paralysed and capital driven from the country would, of course, depend on the rapidity or the reluctance with which the prejudices which they entertain at the present moment were abandoned. But their desires may be confined to the most purely practical objects, and yet they may not cease to be mischievous to the nation and absolutely destructive to some classes in it. There are two points in respect to which a Government representing purely or mainly the lower class would have interests at variance – or which at least would seem to them to be at variance – with those of the classes who even in the most moderate degree are the owners of wealth. One of them is taxation and the expenditure of it; the other is the disposition of landed property. Upon both these points Mr. Bright has taken great pains to impress upon the masses to whom it is now proposed to transfer the representation that they have special interests to serve by a violent change of policy. In regard to taxation he has advocated the scheme of the gentlemen who call themselves Financial Reformers. According to their plan, taxes are to be levied solely on fixed property, and taxes on fixed property will fly entirely above the heads of the mass of the seven-pound voters. Unless human nature is strangely altered by some miraculous attribute of this Reform Bill, the seven-pound voters will be very enthusiastic for the finance of the Financial Reformers. Cheap tea, cheap sugar, cheap spirits, cheap tobacco, and no drawback at all to this catalogue of blessings, except that your neighbour in the big house has four times the income-tax to pay that he ever paid before. Taxation ever falls lightly on the depositaries of absolute power. The magnates of Hungary, the noblesse of France, and many another privileged class, have left us a warning that, even to cultivated minds, self-exemption from taxation is one of the most valued results of irresponsible power. What ground have we for the fond belief that if we trust the English working class with so perilous a gift, they will be proof against a temptation to which every other class that has been exposed to it has succumbed? When alarms are expressed at the possible result of such an experiment, it is vaguely replied that the English working class are deeply attached to our institutions. Speaking of the present moment, when they have been comparatively exempt from the solicitations of demagogues and have not been tempted by the possession of supreme power, the statement is in the main correct. But specific dangers are not averted by vague declamation. The question is, how will the temptation of getting rid of all taxes work at an election? Supposing two candidates go into the cottage of a seven-pound voter to canvass him. One of them declares that he will sustain our institutions, of which the seven-pounder is no doubt enthusiastically fond; but he says nothing about taxation. The other says that he will vote to abolish all indirect taxation, and thereby give the voter cheap tea, sugar, spirits, and tobacco; but he says nothing about our institutions.

Is there any sane man who doubts for an instant which way the seven-pounder (unless he is bribed) will vote? When men are living on from fifteen to twenty shillings a-week, money or money's worth stir the depths of the human soul with a force which 'loyalty to institutions' or attachments of any kind cannot hope in the long run to rival. Great stress, however, we admit, must be laid on the reservation we have made. The seven-pounder will vote for the candidate who promises the remission of the most taxation to him, unless he is bribed; but he is very likely to be bribed. It may well be that the plan of making mere numbers supreme, and leaving no direct representation to wealth, so outrageously unjust in theory, may also prove to be so intolerably oppressive in practice, that wealth, driven to bay, may be forced to defend itself with any weapons that come to hand. The world has seen in America how far popular government can be modified by a wholesale distribution of 'good things.' And here, where the differences of fortune are far greater, and the proposed depositaries of power far needier, the practice will find a still more congenial soil. It may take the form partly of the bribery of individuals, by direct gifts, partly of the bribery of constituencies, by a promise to procure in some shape or other the expenditure of public money upon the locality. Neither form of corruption is unknown to our existing system, and the extent to which it prevails shows the facility with which it might be committed if the will were co-extensive with the opportunity. Now, however, it only or mainly represents the desire of a few wealthy individuals to obtain by purchase the social honours of a seat in Parliament. The case would be very different if it represented the efforts of a powerful class to secure themselves against oppressive legislation. That wealth, if forced into such an enterprise, might succeed in it, is very possible. But no one can believe that a House of Commons, of which the majority was known to owe their seats to corruption, could maintain its credit for an hour, or even its existence for any length of time.

The other prize with the hope of which Mr. Bright and several other democratic politicians have tried to stimulate the working-men is the possession of land. They are not very definite in their offers. They do not say what legislation they would apply to land if they had the power. They content themselves with dwelling upon the fact that the working classes do not own the land, and urging a Reform Bill as the remedy. In what way the remedy is to act upon the disease, they do not say. They have the fear of exasperating the great Whig landowners before their eyes; for they know that until a Reform Bill has made the Whig landowners powerless, it is not possible for Reformers to dispense with their aid. Mr. Bright and his friends therefore do not tell the working men how a Reform Bill is to bring within their reach the promised blocks of freehold land. But they have allies who are not so cautious. The Radical writers of the day dwell much upon this grievance about land, and make no secret of the remedies they desire to see applied. Mr. Stuart Mill goes so far as to maintain that landlords only hold their land on sufferance of the State, and may be discarded in a body, on compensation given, if the State should see fit to do so. He also desires to enact that no owner of property shall be allowed, in any case, to leave to any one individual, more than a small amount to be fixed by law.[1] There are few, however, who, at present, entertain views so extreme. The change which seems to be most in favour with the advanced school of politicians is some law which should apply the provisions of the Code Napoléon to the case of land at least, and should force a father to divide his real property equally among his sons. Such a law would of course make large estates impossible, and by making land comparatively valueless to persons of large fortune, would force it in large quantities into the market, and so bring it within the reach of peasant purchasers. There is no law that Radical theorists upon the Continent prize so earnestly as the law of equal division; for they know it as an instrument of matchless efficacy to ensure absolute equality, and to destroy the possibility of a class of landed gentry growing up. Their brethren in England fully appreciate its value, and are beginning to recommend it as openly as they dare. But for the present they speak to deaf ears; for no change probably would be more odious to the classes that now rule in this country than any interference with the freedom of testamentary disposition.

It is not necessary now to examine the causes of this aversion, or to defend the prevalent feeling of the upper and middle classes. The point which it is at present of importance to bear in mind is, that the affection with which the existing law is regarded by those who have any property to dispose of does not necessarily extend to the classes below them. On the contrary, there is every reason to believe that some law of compulsory division would be acceptable to the working men. All accounts represent them to be desirous of possessing land. The great success of the Building Societies can only be attributed to the prevalence of such a feeling; and the demagogues to whose guidance they surrender

---

[1] These views are expressed in Mill's *Principles of Political Economy*, 6th edition (1865), book II, ch. ii, §§ 4 and 6.

themselves would not dwell upon the subject so pertinaciously if it were not one to move the enthusiasm of their audience. If they have these feelings, the compulsory division of property will undoubtedly be the only mode by which it [sic] can in any degree be gratified without resorting to absolute confiscation; and it will not be difficult to persuade them that its effect will be far wider and more rapid than will actually be the case. They will therefore have every motive to induce them to press for it; and the consideration which ought to be most potent in restraining them will have no effect upon their minds. It will be vain to tell them that such a law is a violation of individual freedom. Their great disqualification for any large share of political power is an entire inability to understand the idea of individual freedom. Their conduct to each other in the management of strikes, the cry for such measures as the Maine Liquor Law[1] which has arisen from them alone, the extravagant doctrines concerning the rights of employers and the rights of landowners which are always propounded at their meetings, show that to them personal freedom has not that sacred character which it possesses in the eyes of the more cultivated classes. No consideration of that kind would prevent them from insisting on the testamentary provisions of the Code Napoléon. They would be told then, as they are told now, that in France and Belgium the working men are in the universal enjoyment of freehold property, from which they are debarred in England; and they would naturally infer that to obtain such blessings it was only necessary to liken the law of England to that of France. Whether the English working classes will take a fancy for this policy is of course purely a matter of conjecture. It seems improbable that what is so dearly cherished by the proletariat abroad will long remain a matter of indifference to their brethren in England. Whether they do or do not introduce it into the legislation of this country, will depend, as in all other political questions, absolutely upon their good will and pleasure. Whether freedom of bequest is or is not to be left to testators will be decided finally and without appeal by the classes who have nothing to bequeath. If in their own interest they think fit to take this liberty away, their decision cannot then be averted by those who are now resigning political supremacy into their hands. It will be a supreme consolation to the great families who are now abetting this transfer of power that the law dismembering their properties has been passed by 'fellow Christians' 'of their own flesh and blood.'

We have dwelt upon this part of the subject because of the peculiar

---

[1] The 'Maine Law' of 1851 (repealed 1858 but reenacted 1885) prohibited the manufacture and sale of intoxicating liquors in the state of Maine.

'THE REFORM BILL'

position which is occupied in reference to this question, by a section of community, on whose conduct at the present crisis very much will turn. In no true sense of the word can the present Reform Bill be termed a party question. It is not one upon which the political success of either party immediately depends. If the opinions of some calculators are to be trusted, its first effect would be to give a majority to the Conservatives, who are foremost in opposing it. But its vast moment raises it above the level of the party battle-field. The interests it puts to hazard belong to a more important category than the prospects of individual politicians. It is a battle not of parties, but of classes. It is a struggle to decide whether the payers of direct taxation shall tax themselves, or shall be taxed at the will of those who do not pay it; whether the laws of property shall be made by the owners of property, or by those who have everything to gain and nothing to lose; whether the country shall be governed by those who have the most stake in it to stimulate them, and the most culture to guide them, or by those in whom both these qualifications are nearly or wholly absent. In short, it is a portion of the great political struggle of our century – the struggle between property, be its amount small or great, and mere numbers. Whether this particular measure will at once place property under the control of numbers, or whether one more advance will be necessary to complete the process, is a point upon which men will form different opinions according to the interpretation they place upon the fragmentary statistics of the Government. But no one who has studied the present balance of political forces can doubt that, if this Bill passes, the same goal will still be reached, whether the journey is performed in one stage or in two. If the democratic power is strong enough now to make resistance a matter of the utmost difficulty, it will be utterly irresistible when this Reform Bill shall have brought in a huge contingent of democratic votes. This is, therefore, the decisive battle of the long campaign – not because the assailants will win by it all they hope to gain, but because when this position is carried, and this reinforcement obtained, the disparity of force will be so great that all further resistance will be hopeless.

But there is one strange feature about this struggle. It is fought for objects which deeply concern all who, by their own industry or by inheritance from others, have property to lose; and by all thoughtful politicians its course is watched with an intensity of interest that the mere oscillations of party conflict never command. If those who dread the advance of democracy are right in their apprehensions, the success of the series of measures, of which the first is now before us, will imply results which every class, every industry, and every holder of property will feel; and those will feel them most whose stake in the welfare of their country is largest. It means Government by men of less independence and lower culture: it means laws which will fetter capital to favour labour, and will trammel the freedom of the owners of property to make it cheaper and more accessible to those who have it not: it means taxes levied and spent by the men that contribute to them least. The inexplicable thing is that, on such a subject, the conflict is not entirely sincere. There is no small proportion of the combatants who deprecate and dread the success of the banner under which they are fighting. The peculiar disadvantage with which the adversaries of democracy have to contend is, that a large section of those who by position, by inclination, earnestly sympathise with them, yet give their votes, though not their wishes, to the other side. With the sincere friends of democracy we of course expect to have to struggle. There can be no permanent peace, there can be nothing but a hollow and delusive truce, between those who wish that property should go for something in political arrangements, and the devout believers in the abstract rights of man. For the votaries of the new religion, who have set up Humanity for their God, – for the enthusiasts who declare that the material progress of our age has carried society beyond the reach of human passion and folly, – for the youthful politicians who think that it indicates 'large-heartedness' to profess an unbounded belief in the working man, – for the more sober demagogues who find their account in fostering the delusions and weaknesses of others, – for all these antagonists we must be prepared. They are formidable enough. In a languid age the cheap distinction conferred by novelty of opinion will attract many recruits to their standard. And the feeling which was so prevalent ten years ago, that democracy was the winning side, and that submission to it was a mere question of time, has not yet, in spite of adverse appearances, entirely died away. All this was to be expected. But what was not to be expected was that this combined band of enthusiasts and adventurers should count among their allies men of property and position, who cherish no delusions upon the subject, and are perfectly sensible of the fatal results that would follow the projected enthronement of the working man. Party allegiance and a blind obedience to tradition have done many wonderful things; but they never achieved a more remarkable triumph than that of driving into the ranks of Mr. Bright's battalions the representatives of some of the leading houses of the English aristocracy.

There never was a position more paradoxical than that which is

'THE REFORM BILL'

occupied by some of the great 'revolution families' at the present moment. They know perfectly well the direction of the road they are treading, and the end to which it leads. Some of their younger members may be misled by the fashionable sentimentalism of the day, and may believe that Mr. Gladstone's wordy declamation represents intelligible and trustworthy ideas. But such delusions do not infect the hard-headed representatives of families which have never been hitherto guilty of sentimental or visionary abnegation. They, the heads of the English aristocracy, the owners of boundless wealth, the lords of enormous territory, the representatives of centuries of accumulation, are not inspired by any burning ardour for the importation of American ideas. They have an uneasy misgiving, which no disclaimers and no blandishments can lull, that if they once allow the 'working man' to put his heel upon their necks, the political career of the great Whig houses will belong to history. And beyond these considerations of individual interest and ambition, they are well aware that they are the foremost representatives of English wealth, and the spokesmen of that peculiar form of culture which the social organisation of England has produced. On them, they cannot forget, rests the responsibility of guarding it from assault, and transmitting it to others in principle as unimpaired as it has come down to them. They are fully convinced, if rumour does not much belie them, that the result of any American experiments will at best be doubtful, and will probably be disastrous. The rule of mere numbers is absolutely antipathetic to the social system of which their fathers were the founders, and of which they are the natural guardians. The dead level of direct political power which modern Reformers desire to introduce would soon bring down to a similar dead level every social or political influence which rises to a special eminence, except where it is founded on individual qualities. The graduated social influence, the pyramidal form of constitution, which the great Whig houses did so much to establish, is utterly inconsistent with that *primâ facie* title to an equal share of political power which Mr. Gladstone in his famous manifesto[1] ascribed to every individual British subject. If the multitude once comes to rule, the Whig aristocracy will, so far as political influence is concerned, be laid in that historical burying-place to which Mr. Bright in imagination has already consigned it. They will be fortunate if they escape legislation which will dissipate their vast accumulations, and shatter their historic families into a multitude of indistinguishable fragments.

These are facts which, in their secret thoughts – nay, in their private

[1] I.e. his franchise speech of May 1864.

conversations – they freely recognise. On them it depends whether the movement which this Bill inaugurates goes forward or not. If they manfully spoke their real thoughts, there would be an end of all further controversy upon the 'vertical' extension of the suffrage. Reformers would then be reduced to the alternative of either abandoning their scheme for Americanising our institutions, or else procuring its adoption by means of one of those 'accidents', for which it may be that in 1832 the country was prepared, but which they know well to be a simple chimæra now. What is it that prevents the Whigs generally standing by the institutions to which their traditions bind them, and repudiating the novel and distinctive elements which a Radical alliance has introduced into their creed? There seems to be only one cause for the acquiescence and seeming approval which they are giving to a measure which will not be less fatal to their position than to the cause of good government generally in this country. They are afraid that it will involve division within the ranks of a party, or entail upon that party a temporary loss of political supremacy. We do not desire to underrate the importance of fidelity to party obligations. There is no doubt that, for ordinary purposes, they constitute the only machinery by which Parliamentary liberties can be reconciled with executive vigour. But their acceptance does not involve an entire sacrifice of political freewill – a surrender into the hands of any one political leader of the right to independent thought, even in the most momentous national conjunctures. We cannot admit any such extravagant interpretation of the great principles of party government. For ourselves, we have never, in theory or in practice, recognised any such subservient doctrine. Party allegiance is but a means to an end; it can never determine the decision of questions more important than itself. No true patriot can become a party man without reserving to himself the liberty of independent action upon measures by which our national life, and the very continuance of our form of society is [sic] affected. There are few probably who, upon a question so momentous as that of Reform, would profess to prefer his [sic] party obligations to his duty to his country. But a delusion appears to have gained ground that, in reference to the division which will take place on the seventeenth or nineteenth of this month,[1] it is possible to reconcile the two. The old Whigs have generally preferred to trust to the efforts of their opponents, to the opportunities of delay, to any accident that might happen, rather than to their own straightforward votes, to prevent

---

[1] The division on the second reading of the Reform Bill did not actually take place until 27 April.

'THE REFORM BILL'

the Reform which they detest. It is said that the same strategy is to be pursued on the present occasion, and that if the Reform Bill passes the second reading, it will be by the help of a considerable contingent of Whigs, who hope that the chapter of accidents may enable them to destroy or postpone it in Committee. Thus they hope that they may at once save their allegiance to their party, and yet avert a measure they sincerely dread. It is a miserable policy; and, like all such cunning devices for avoiding a manly performance of public duty in a great national crisis like the present, it will probably bring those who have planned it nothing but discomfiture and shame. If the Bill once passes the second reading, the opposition to it will be broken and disheartened. The difficulty will be insuperable of combining members to offer effective resistance in Committee to particular provisions, each of which will probably affect the constituencies of a great number of those who vote upon it. In 1860, when the leader of the House[1] was notoriously averse to Reform, it was not difficult to trip up a Reform Bill in Committee. In 1866, when the leader of the House is not only eager but fanatical for the reduction of the suffrage, such a manœuvre will be all but impossible.

If the Reform Bill passes the second reading, it will probably reach the House of Lords. What its fate will be in the hands of that assembly, which in recent years has been more remarkable for circumspection than for intrepidity, the boldest prophet would find it difficult to forecast. It is a possibility, perhaps a probability, that, mindful of the events of 1832, they will not venture to dispute the decision of the House of Commons; and in that case the majority for the second reading in the Commons will be responsible for its ultimate success. If by the agency of some half-dozen Whigs this fatal measure is placed upon the Statute Book, we trust that the reflection that they have been true to their leader Mr. Gladstone will be a great consolation to them. They will need the consolation, for there can be no doubt which section of the political world will suffer most by the surrender of the polling-booths to the multitude. The Conservatives will suffer much; but in a country like England there must always be a certain amount of Conservative opinion, and the party will have the benefit of whatever reaction so extreme a measure may produce. The Radicals will not lose at all, but largely gain: for the change will be all in their interest. There is no class in England with whom their views are more closely in unison than the class of artizans. But for the Whig party, under the new system, there can be no future. Unless they descend to compliances from which

[1] Palmerston.

any but mere adventurers would shrink, they must give way to politicians more advanced and socially more congenial to the working class. The dwellers in the large boroughs have no taste for aristocrats, and most of them have never heard of Lord Somers.[1] The seven-pound dwellers in the small boroughs – if any small boroughs remain – will follow the precedent set by most of their class who have the franchise now, and will present their votes to the most lavish millionaire. Whether Mr. Bright will be inconsolable at the erasure of the great Whig families from the political race may be fairly doubted. It may be equally open to a doubt whether they, on their part, will be well satisfied with their own past policy when they discover that they have performed the 'happy despatch' mainly for his benefit.

At least, if the Whigs make up their minds to follow Mr. Bright to their own undoing, they cannot complain that he has deceived them as to his intentions. He has not flattered them with insincere praise or lulled them into a false security by soothing promises. He has very distinctly told them that a Whig Ministry belongs to a political species as extinct as the dodo, and that no great harm would be done to the country if the whole Whig party were deposited in Westminster Abbey. He has never concealed his hostility to the great landowners, or his desire for measures that would divide their estates. He professes his contempt for 'worn-out royal and noble stocks,' warns the House of Peers, even while he is asking for its aid, that it cannot be 'a permanent institution,' and makes no secret of his universal preference for the institutions and social arrangements which prevail on the other side of the Atlantic. If the Whigs labour under any delusion as to the estimation in which he holds them, or the fate to which he destines them, it has certainly not been because he has withheld that information from them, or has conveyed it with undue delicacy or reserve. From his bearing upon this Reform Bill, they may learn what its probable operation will be in the judgment of one who has devoted a lifetime to studying the political tendencies of the large centres of population. From the intense enthusiasm with which he has thrown himself into the support of this Bill, it is easy to see that he believes it will fulfil the aims he has so frequently avowed. He evidently thinks that the object of his life is within his reach – that the downfall of his aristocratic and landowning enemies is at hand. So eager is he to finish with them that he has lost all control over his language. He will not stop to conciliate, or temporise,

---

[1] Somers (1651–1716) was one of the principal heroes in the Whig pantheon for his part in the 1688 revolution and the ensuing settlement.

or treat. If the recalcitrant Whigs are not convinced, they must be browbeaten and bullied. Their resistance to a scheme of Reform, which will simply annihilate them, is a 'dirty conspiracy.' The Parliament which shows signs of reluctance at passing a Bill which will probably unseat two-thirds of its members is 'the offspring of landlord power in the counties, and tumult and corruption in the boroughs.' He can see but one remedy. 'Parliament-street, from Charing Cross to the venerable Abbey,' is to be 'filled with men seeking a Reform Bill,' who will 'beat down as by one blow the power that threatens to bolt the door of Parliament against the people.' He does not condescend to argue the matter or to deprecate on public grounds the opposition that is being offered to the Bill. He knows that the Whigs are deeply apprehensive of it, and that a considerable number of them will certainly resist it. He is not surprised, for Parliament is elected by 'landlord power,' which to his mind is the earthly embodiment of the spirit of evil. But he thinks it as base as it is vile. If only sufficiently threatened, it will hasten to pass the measure it detests. It remains for a few days to show whether he wrongs it by this estimate of its courage. If the second reading of this Bill should pass a House of Commons which utterly abhors it, Mr. Bright will have deserved his victory, for it will prove that his menaces were well aimed, and that he has learnt that greatest secret of success, the art of knowing whom to despise. The votes of some half-dozen Whig members will probably decide whether the aristocratic constitution, upon which their historic party has been built up, is or is not to be sacrificed to the tactics or the blunders of the hour. If, moved by the importunity with which they have been beset, or by some paltry personal fear, they are false to their real belief, the step they take can never be retraced. We shall only have the melancholy consolation of reflecting that if the classes who now hold political power have not courage enough to uphold their own convictions, at a juncture so momentous, against the threats of demagogues or the entreaties of placemen, they have lost the moral title to rule and are fit only to be cast aside.

'The Change of Ministry'
(Q.R., no. 239; July 1866)

INTRODUCTORY NOTE

BY THE time the next issue of the *Quarterly* appeared, in July 1866, the political scene had changed sharply. Gladstone's attempt to drive Reform through a Palmerstonian House of Commons had collapsed, taking the government with it, Derby had come into office, and Cranborne was a cabinet minister at the age of thirty-six. His July article surveyed the convulsion, and the prospects which it opened up.

The struggle over the Reform Bill had been a classic contest. The debates produced some of the finest parliamentary oratory of the nineteenth century, with Robert Lowe's anti-Reform speeches taking the first place. The determination of Gladstone to carry Reform was matched by the determination of the Conservatives and the Whig and Liberal dissidents who were dubbed 'Adullamites' to stop it. In conjunction with the Adullamites, among whom Lowe, Elcho, Grosvenor, and Horsman were especially prominent, the Conservatives waged a steady guerilla campaign against the progress of the government bill. The first major challenge came when the Whig Earl Grosvenor, M.P. for Chester, was persuaded to move an amendment on the second reading postponing discussion of the franchise bill until the promised redistribution measure was also before the House. The point of this amendment, seconded by Derby's son, Lord Stanley, was to intensify the government's difficulties by bringing into play against it the fears of those whose interests redistribution would threaten, and it was persisted with even after Russell decided to introduce the redistribution bill before the franchise bill reached the committee stage. The government won the division only by 318 votes to 313, thirty-five Whigs and Liberals voting against it and six abstaining. The fissure in the Liberal ranks which Derby and Disraeli aimed to exploit was now wide open.

Nonetheless, the ministry battled on under Gladstone's impulsion, and brought in its redistribution bill, which grouped single-member boroughs of under 9,000 population, removed one member from double-member boroughs under 8,000, and reallocated 49 seats. The measure necessarily upset those Liberals whose seats it affected, and was unacceptable to the Conservatives, whose interests it was in fact so devised as to damage. The Reform Bill tottered from ambush to ambush, with the government holding on by small majorities, and Gladstone incurring much unpopularity by the high-handed manner in which he sought to impose Reform on a House most of whose members strongly

'THE CHANGE OF MINISTRY'

disliked it. Finally, the opposition concocted an amendment substituting rating for rental in the borough franchise clause (thus greatly restricting the proposed enfranchisement). It was moved by the Adullamite M.P. for Galway, Lord Dunkellin, and on 18 June the government was beaten by 315 votes to 304. Russell resigned eight days later, and the Queen summoned Lord Derby.

For some time the possibilities of fusion between the Conservatives and the Whig–Liberal dissidents had been canvassed, and the moment seemed to have arrived for the formation of a mixed ministry combining all shades of anti-Reform opinion. But fusion never came, probably because Derby and Disraeli did not really want it. It would have destroyed their personal positions, since neither was acceptable as a leader in a coalition. Derby did formally try to secure Whig and Adullamite support for his new government, but met with no success. Clarendon and Somerset refused cabinet seats, and the Lansdowne–Clanricarde group also declined office. The Adullamites in the Commons held aloof, too: they had not fought to put Derby and Disraeli into power, and would really have preferred a Whig-dominated stand-pat coalition, perhaps with Clarendon as prime minister and that very liberal Conservative Lord Stanley as leader in the Commons. Pushed by Disraeli, who was determined not to lose the chance of establishing the Conservatives as a party capable of governing, Derby took the premiership for the third time with a purely Conservative ministry, in a minority in the lower House. Cranborne entered his cabinet as secretary of state for India. How long, and on what terms (especially in regard to Reform), the new government could survive remained doubtful. The hope of enlarging the base of its support was not given up, and in his ministerial statement on 9 July Derby looked forward to 'a new arrangement of parties', which would concentrate defenders of the constitution on the one side and exponents of Radicalism and democracy on the other.

Cranborne's article reflects his satisfaction at the repulse of Reform, and not least at the discomfiture of Gladstone, that tool of Radicals and arch-enemy of the landed interest, on whose capacity for self-deception he has a trenchant passage. The events of the last few months seemed to Cranborne to have demonstrated that Parliament would not accept any Reform measure threatening a large alteration in the balance of political power, and, by bringing out the incompatibility of the heterogeneous elements on the Liberal side, to have hastened an eventual realignment of political groupings, corresponding to the real divisions of interest and opinion in the country. Now that radical Reform had been disposed of, he was ready, as he had been now for at least a year, to contemplate an instalment of conservative Reform, giving the working classes 'participation without predominance'. But this, he felt, the new ministry should undertake only if it could command sufficient strength in the House of Commons to prevent the remodelling of its proposals in a democratic direction.

SALISBURY'S 'QUARTERLY REVIEW' ARTICLES

1. *A Bill to Amend the Representation of the People in Parliament in England and Wales.* London, 1866.
2. *Act for the Re-distribution of Seats.* London, 1866.

The history of the Session now drawing to a close has been marked by a unity which rarely distinguishes the prosaic labours of the English Parliament. It is the history of the beginning and end of Mr. Gladstone's career as Reforming leader of the House of Commons. In the perfect order and symmetry of its parts, in the completeness of its action, in the brightness of its first promise, and in its tragic close, it would be a fitting subject for an epic. The Muse could not be more fitly invoked than to tell of the versatile man, who after having known many political creeds and the ways of many Parliaments, contrived to ruin one of the finest majorities ever enjoyed by minister, in the shortest space of time ever allotted to any statesman for such a task. And the theme will have this further fitness, that, throughout, the mind is never distracted from the figure of the hero. Every vicissitude in the eventful plot is due to his immediate action. His impetuosity forces the perilous enterprise upon his friends; his passionate resolution sustains their wavering zeal during its chequered course: and it is to his peculiar tactics alone that the disastrous catastrophe is due. *Qualis ab incepto* is a rule of art never departed from for a moment. Those great qualities which alone could have forced a democratic Reform Bill on a constitutional party, and alone could have changed a majority of 75 into a minority of 11, are as conspicuous at the end of the drama as at the beginning. Fortunately the display of them was more agreeable to bystanders, than their effects are to those whose political fortunes they have ruined. They have redeemed Parliament from the dulness that had become native to it under Lord Palmerston's uneventful rule. Some of Mr Gladstone's efforts were not unworthy of the imperious attitude he had assumed; and Mr. Lowe's[1] three speeches would alone be sufficient to make this session conspicuous in the annals of the House of Commons. The sustained interest of the close and constant contest, carried on upon both sides with unflinching tenacity and resolution, has not been equalled in Parliament probably since the time of the great Reform Act.

The session, however, has another interest besides the pleasure caused by good debating or the excitement of a well-fought battle. To all students of our system of party Government, it furnishes rich material

[1] Robert Lowe (1811–92), M.P. Calne; later chancellor of the exchequer and home secretary in Gladstone's first ministry.

'THE CHANGE OF MINISTRY'

for investigation and reflection. The remarkable issue of a contest in which the two sides were at the outset apparently so ill-matched seems, at first sight, difficult to explain. There was no doubt that Mr. Gladstone came to Parliament with a nominal majority of seventy-five; and that when the last decisive division came the casualties of the session had left him rather stronger than when he started. It was true that the majority had been elected during the lifetime of Lord Palmerston; but it had never shown any aversion to Mr. Gladstone. During the last Parliament, the same majority, less strongly reinforced, had supported Mr. Gladstone through some of his most questionable measures, such as the repeal of the Paper Duty, in spite of Lord Palmerston's known aversion to the course of his colleague. In 1864 they had voted in a body for the maintenance of peace in the Danish controversy, which was certainly more Mr. Gladstone's than Lord Palmerston's policy. It cannot, therefore, be said that, when Parliament assembled last February, there was any foregone conclusion against Mr. Gladstone's leadership; nor again, could there be said to have been any fixed determination to resist every proposal of Reform. A great portion of the Liberal majority had voted in favour of Reform in 1859 and 1860, and many members of the Conservative party were known to wish for what is called 'the settlement of the question.' It should have seemed that a campaign began under such auspices was already half won. How came it to issue, after many months of even fighting, in an ignominious defeat?

Undoubtedly, both faults of manner and faults of tactics contributed to this result; but the effect of the faults of manner has perhaps been exaggerated. They certainly exist; and as soon as the contest becomes warm they show themselves prominently. Nor is their effect at all neutralized by an extravagant affectation of humbleness during the intervals of the conflict. The imperiousness which is so irritating to an assembly of English gentlemen has been ascribed by Mr. Gladstone's devoted admirers in the press to a virtuous indignation and a consciousness of superior purity, which will not suffer him to treat with forbearance the meannesses or the follies of his opponents. Perhaps, if the House fully realized this superiority, it might take his rebukes more meekly and kiss the rod that smites them. But they are a sceptical body of middle aged men, not believing much in virtuous indignation, and strongly inclined to suspect all claims to special purity of purpose. And then Mr. Gladstone has a peculiar infelicity in the occasions he selects for delivering what he calls his 'rebukes.' He does not keep them for set speeches of solemn exhortation, but brings them out at the moment when, if you were listening to a less celestial being, you would say that he was in a rage. The threat that the House should be kept during an autumn sitting to pass the Bill, the announcement upon the night of the final division that the Government would not yield a single iota of the enfranchisement they had proposed, were made, not in moments of serene reflection over the follies of inferior beings, but in moments of most terrestrial and unmistakeable irritation. And the consequence was that the House did not submit to them as 'rebukes,' but resented them as attempts to dictate.

Yet it was no fault of manner that singly or mainly brought the Reform Government to the ground. No doubt Mr. Gladstone's singular dexterity in giving offence to waverers on the eve of critical divisions, may in the case both of Lord Grosvenor's and Lord Dunkellin's motions have sent two or three votes into the wrong lobby. But the House of Commons is not an assembly of women: and whatever the chances of this or that vote may be, its choice of a policy in the long run does not depend upon the personal graces of those who advocate rival propositions. It has been a succession of tactical faults, affecting the whole plan and object of his operations, that has brought Mr. Gladstone's campaign to a disastrous close. His conduct of the Reform question was a capital instance of an error to which ingenious party leaders are specially prone. It was that of appraising the value of support, not in proportion to the fidelity with which it is given, but, on the contrary, in proportion to the difficulty with which it is obtained. Every party is constructed on the plan of a comet, with a fixed nucleus, and a floating tail. On ordinary occasions the votes of the nucleus can be counted on securely, and no thought or trouble is necessary to make sure of them. The chief solicitude of those whose duty it is to marshal the troops, is for the stragglers – to keep them in the right line of march, and prevent them from becoming deserters. No party was ever free from this difficulty, or could boast of a perfectly well-defined and compact phalanx. Men will follow their standard or their leader with varying fidelity, so long as caprice or gregariousness preponderate variously in different minds. But the necessity of incessantly looking after these stragglers is apt to produce a pernicious habit of thought in any leader who is not controlled by hearty political convictions of his own. He comes at last from thinking of them oftener, to think of them as more important than his steady, untroublesome followers. He is engaged in working out problems which always depend on the voting value of a set of variables, and he speedily forgets his constant quantities altogether. But the constant quantities, in

'THE CHANGE OF MINISTRY'

spite of their constancy, have beliefs and objects of their own: and after much endurance, some day their patience is tried a little too far, and then they become variables in their turn.

All combinations of men for carrying out any special set of opinions are liable to this embarrassment. But it has been the special affliction of the Liberal party in Parliament, especially during the last ten years. The nebula in this case is not only particularly large, but it has always had a tendency to condense into a separate nucleus, and to go off upon an orbit of its own. It has always therefore been a subject of more than ordinary solicitude to Liberal chiefs. For it is sufficiently evident that the Liberal party, though it still has a common organisation, has no one informing spirit or aspiration. It is united by the past, not by the present or the future. It fought together earnestly for the admission of the middle classes to political power, for the destruction of every form of religious disability, for the reconstruction of our fiscal system. Upon these questions it has been completely victorious; but with its triumph the conditions of its unity are at an end. With the exception of one or two points of detail, it is not agreed as to the policy of disendowing or disestablishing the Church of England. It is still more hopelessly divided upon the question of transferring supreme political power to the wage-earning class. Nor is this difference accidental or temporary. It is one that in the nature of things must continue to exist: for the points in issue are points upon which it is impossible that squire and townsman, peer and mechanic, should think alike. They are separating the party, therefore, into two layers, which consist, speaking very roughly, of those who are and those who are not connected with the great territorial interests of the country.

The guidance of such a party, or rather of such a disorganised band of politicians, was unquestionably no easy task. But looking at the subject merely as a question of tactics, it is very obvious that the policy adopted towards them by Lord Palmerston was the judicious policy to pursue. It was, on the face of the matter, hopeless to gratify two sets of men who were animated by diametrically opposite desires. It was necessary, especially in regard to this matter of Reform, to select the policy of one section or the other; for they were too antagonistic to be combined. Lord Palmerston boldly cast in his lot with the 'Old Whigs' – the moderate and constitutional successors of Mr. Burke. He was probably impelled to that choice by his own strong convictions. The requirements of his later political career never quite drove out of him his early Tory training. But if he had been wholly without personal convictions upon this, as he was upon many subjects, the selection he made was the one which, as a matter of tactics, he was forced to make. The constitutional wing of his party was not only the most numerous and the most powerful, but it had another recommendation, which will always induce a judicious party leader to lean on the less extreme portion of his followers. It can desert. The Radicals are active, noisy, turbulent. They can be profuse with menaces of obscure disaster; they can give trouble upon critical divisions: but so long as the Whigs choose to tolerate their alliance, they cannot permanently desert. For a deserter must have some other army to which he can desert. Moderate politicians can incline their weight to one side or the other, according as the exigency of the time seems to require. But extreme politicians, if they are dissatisfied with the moderate men who are nearest to them, have no one else to whom they can go. If the Radicals quarrel with the Whigs, they cannot take their services permanently to any other ally – unless they choose to go to America. They might injure an individual minister for a time, by factious votes upon by-subjects. But, as has been proved by experience more than once, their discontent can do no permanent harm to their more moderate allies.

Mr. Gladstone has acted on an entirely different theory. He has treated the radicals with a consideration, almost with an awe, that was never shown to them by any minister before. The form of proceeding which they adopted[1] was originally suggested by Mr. Bright, and he risked the fate of his bill and his government rather than consent to depart from it before the second reading of the bill. When it was proposed to adopt for the counties a less extensive franchise than that contained in the bill, he refused on the ground that it would be a breach of compact between Parliament and the Reformers, as though they constituted an independent power, competent to negotiate with Parliament on equal terms, and to bind it, as a matter of compact and good faith, to the provisions contained in any bill that had been read a second time. On the other hand, the idea of any 'compact' between Parliament and the Whigs who sat behind him never entered into Mr. Gladstone's head. Still more marked was the tenor of his arguments. To some extent the provisions of his bill recognized the fact that his party were not entirely democratic. The bill, no doubt, had to meet the approval of his colleagues, and did not express Mr. Gladstone's opinions without mitigation. But in his speeches, where no colleagues could check the free flow of his language, he has framed every principle and every argument to please

[1] I.e. the introduction of a franchise bill without a redistribution scheme.

not the moderate but the extreme wing of his party. He was arguing nominally in favour of a seven and fourteen pound franchise; but in doing so he was careful to lay down principles which would cover not only those suffrages, but even household or manhood suffrage. He proposed a lowering of the line of extension; but he argued against any line at all. The relationship of 'flesh and blood,' the similarity of religion, did not cease at the limits of a seven-pound rental. When he asked the audience at Liverpool[1] whether they thought the figure of 10*l*. could be permanently maintained as the boundary, when there were millions whom it did not admit, he must have been perfectly aware, that the same argument would apply with almost precisely the same force to the limit he was at the time proposing to adopt. When he summed up, according to fancy estimates of his own, the wages of all who lived below the ten pound line, and contrasted them with the income of those who lived above, trying, out of their imaginary excess, to construct an argument in favour of the supremacy of the poorer classes,[2] no one knew better than he did that his reasoning was worthless unless it extended to the whole of the population who do not possess the franchise. This scarcely disguised purpose of furthering to the utmost the views of the democratic party in the House was at last distinctly revealed by his two chief law-officers, the Attorney-General and the Lord-Advocate, who shortly before the bill was defeated announced their adhesion to Household Suffrage.[3]

From the beginning of the long argument to the end, Mr. Gladstone did not indicate a single principle that would enable the Legislature to stop short at the limits which the bill contained, and refuse to be pushed further. His proffered favour was not unrequited. The politicians to whom he offered to give up, not only the opinions of his past life, but the party to whose leadership he has so recently been raised, were not ungrateful or unappreciative. They have hung upon his speeches with the well-drilled cheers of hearty partisans. From above the gangway, from the immediate supporters of the Government, Mr. Gladstone's most fervid eloquence could rarely elicit any expression of sympathy. Throughout the whole discussion their morose and distrustful silence

[1] On 6 April 1866.
[2] This seems a misunderstanding of Gladstone's argument at Liverpool. His contention was that the working classes were not represented in the electorate in a fair proportion to their income, and he estimated that with perhaps three-sevenths of total income they had only about one-seventh of the total votes.
[3] In debate on 31 May, the attorney-general, Sir Roundell Palmer, envisaged the eventual adoption of household suffrage, and the lord advocate, Moncreiff, used words implying support for it the next day.

during his speeches furnished a curious contrast to the tumultuous applause with which every point was received below the gangway. In the press the same contrast has been apparent. The papers which a year ago were enthusiastic supporters of Lord Palmerston have followed Mr. Gladstone's course with hesitation and alarm; while those that a year ago only upheld Lord Palmerston's government as the least of two evils, have been almost abject in their flattery of Mr. Gladstone. There is no formal mode by which a Minister can announce his adhesion to one section rather than to another of the party that follows him. But short of such a formal declaration, every indication combines to prove that Mr. Gladstone having been offered a choice between the moderate and the extreme politicians of his party, discarded the Whig, and chose the Radical.

What could his motive in doing so have been? His friends will tell us that it was sincere conviction. It is difficult to use such a phrase in reference to Mr. Gladstone's mind. It assumes an analogy to other minds which has no true existence. Many men allow their interests to overbear their convictions. A still greater number are biassed by their interests in forming their convictions, and half-consciously drive their reason to conclusions to which it would not otherwise guide them. But such a description is not applicable to Mr. Gladstone. He is never, even half-consciously, insincere. But he is not, on that account, exempt from the action of the temptations which generate insincerity in other men; nor is his conduct free from the results which it produces upon the conduct of other men. His ambition has guided him in recent years as completely as it ever guided any statesman of the century; and yet there is not even a shade of untruth in the claim made for him by his friends, that he is guided wholly by his convictions. The process of self-deceit goes on in his mind without the faintest self-consciousness or self-suspicion. The result is that it goes on without check or stint. Other men's convictions follow after their ambition coyly and coquettishly, and with many hesitations and misgivings: but in Mr. Gladstone's mind the two are inseparably wedded. He was much nettled at an assertion we made in our last number that he had sacrificed the paper-duty at a moment of great financial pressure, and to the disadvantage of worthier claimants for remission, in order to gain the votes of Mr. Bright and his adherents. The statement irritated him so much that he began his speech, on moving the second reading of the Reform Bill, by designating it as a 'lie,' with a frankness which he hardly cared to qualify.[1] We have no intention of retorting his courtesy. We are quite

---

[1] See above, 197 and n.

ready to admit that he fully believes that the proposal to remit the paper-duty in the face of a deficit, in 1860, was not dictated by any wish to conciliate the Radicals. Probably he believes further that no such notion had any part in impelling him to make a sudden declaration in favour of universal suffrage, in 1864.[1] He no doubt persuades himself, with perfect success, that he has introduced the late Bill in a purely impartial spirit, and that in the course of its discussion he has not sought to make political capital by inflaming the passions of the lower class. No one who has closely watched the progress of his political career can doubt that the sudden development of vehement opinions, where they existed only faintly or not at all before, had some connection with the political advantages which at the moment of their appearance they seemed to promise. If Mr. Gladstone really felt as keenly as he now speaks concerning the honourable obligation that has lain upon Parliament since 1860, to enfranchise the working-class, his career is quite inexplicable. We should be forced to conclude that the conscience that actuates him, though a very active organ, is, like some diseases, intermittent in its activity; and that its energy at the time of the paroxysms is fully made up by a singular torpidity during the intervals that come between. How his intense conviction that Parliament has been pledged to a large measure of enfranchisement permitted him for four years to suffer in silence while that pledge was being dishonoured, or again in 1865, to sit by while Sir George Grey, in his name, refused to recognise that pledge at the elections,[2] is an insoluble mystery, if we believe that Mr. Gladstone's mind is constructed upon the ordinary plan. The only mode of reconciling his sincerity with the facts, is to assume that the process by which the mind is made to accept the most advantageous or the most convenient belief, is with him automatic and unconscious.

Certainly the course which he pursued, though hardly explainable by a keen sense of Parliamentary obligations, was one that would have commended itself to a reckless and far-sighted ambition. There is something unsatisfactory in an ordinary Parliamentary triumph. Its advantages are purely for the moment. It contains no guarantee, no promise for the future. Parties are too evenly balanced to suffer any statesman, however large his majority may seem to be, to indulge in the dream that his tenure

[1] Gladstone's celebrated May 1864 speech had not, of course, advocated 'universal' suffrage, or even manhood suffrage, which is what Cranborne means.
[2] Speaking on his re-election for Morpeth in July 1865, Sir George Grey, the home secretary, contended that Palmerston's government had fully redeemed its pledges on Reform, and that it was not its duty to press the question forward when Parliament was reluctant to deal with it and the country was apathetic.

of office is secure. For him the fight is never over. He lives in a beleaguered city, and must sleep always under arms. At any moment, from the quarter in which he least expects it, the 'difficulty' may appear which is to be fatal to his power. Mr. Gladstone has suffered more than the average share of these vicissitudes. In one who had so suffered, the idea of seizing a favourable moment to secure once and for ever his own power, and that of those who thought with him, may have been especially inviting. A lasting occupation of office, such as the Whigs enjoyed after the death of Queen Anne, and the Tories after Fox's India Bill, in which the schemes of an all-powerful Minister would not be menaced or impeded by the struggles of an opposition, would be a golden dream to him. If only the territorial interest could be laid so low that it could be safely despised, how easy finance and legislation upon property would be for the future! How pleasantly and smoothly all such Radical theories concerning the non-existence of any true property in land, as Mr. Mill delights to propagate,[1] would speed forward to their fulfilment, if once the power of the Squires could be broken! What glorious budgets might be produced, if only the great enigma of finance could be solved by putting all taxation upon the land!

It would be worth while incurring a very considerable risk in order to realise such a dream as that. But it can only be attempted with any chance of success under peculiarly favourable circumstances: for governing classes are not easily persuaded into suicide. The elections of 1865 seemed to offer a most unexpected opportunity. The popularity of a Minister, nominally Liberal, but really Conservative, had created a heavy majority in favour of the Liberals. The popular Minister died before he could make use of the weapon his name had forged; and it fell 'by seniority' into the hands of a fanatical Reformer. Such a piece of good fortune as a large Reforming majority elected upon Conservative pretences seemed to be a chance not to be neglected. Whether such reflections actually passed through Mr. Gladstone's mind of course it is impossible confidently to affirm. He may have acted under their implicit guidance, in that condition of complete unconsciousness as to the real nature of his own motives, which distinguishes him so peculiarly among the prominent men of his time. Or such calculations may have been reserved for the less exalted schemers to whom he has in the last few years given so much of his confidence, and whose venomous hostility to the land disdains even the pretence of moderation. We cannot decide between these alternatives: we can only judge of the result. The measure

[1] Cf. p. 217 above.

which was produced was unquestionably the work of a very ingenious and very zealous enemy of the influence of property in general, and of landed property in particular. It was 'made to pass,' as Mr. Goschen[1] somewhat cynically informed the House: and to that extent it was a moderate measure. Only just enough was asked to make it certain that the artisans of the large towns could have more whenever they chose to demand it. The balance was just upset, and no more. Enough was taken for complete mastery; but beyond that point everything that could obstruct the passage of the bill was left for a more convenient season. What was done, however, was done effectually. The working men were placed in secure possession of the boroughs. The supremacy of the large towns over the country districts was carefully preserved. The redistribution of seats was so arranged as to extinguish members of small boroughs which were essentially rural in their character, and to increase the representation partly of large towns, partly of those counties, which, owing to the unjust state of the law, were little else for electoral purposes than groups of large towns. With a good boundary bill, and with the admission of unrepresented towns to the right of separate representation, additional seats to the most populous counties would be a real boon, and an act of justice to the ill-represented land. But until those measures of relief are in some degree granted, the bestowal of new seats upon the divisions of Yorkshire, or Cheshire, or Lancashire, or Durham is merely another device for increasing the already extravagant influence of the great towns. Even the boons, therefore, that the bill seemed to contain were injuries in disguise. If it had passed, no financial caprice or injustice of Mr. Gladstone's would ever again have met with any obstacle from the resistance of the landed interest. Probably the Conservative party would have lost at the first ensuing election about a hundred seats. The attack was well planned: if it had been successful it would have struck a deadly blow. It was worth while to risk a good deal both in reputation and in influence, in order to succeed. It is easy to understand why Mr. Gladstone drove on his reluctant and frightened colleagues, strained every tie by which his party was held together, exhausted every resource of argument, of declamation, of menace, upon the House of Commons, in order to attain a victory which would relieve him for ever from the necessity of such efforts in the future. It was a great opportunity of crushing his adversaries, never likely to recur:

[1] G. J. Goschen (1831–1907), M.P. City of London, and in the cabinet as chancellor of the duchy of Lancaster; after serving in Gladstone's first ministry, was to become a leading Liberal Unionist and ultimately a Conservative.

and their narrow escape justifies the boldness and the dexterity of the attempt.

It failed because Mr. Gladstone, in spite of his boast to the contrary, did not know with whom he had to deal. The ties of party will in the end prove too weak to induce Englishmen to use their political power for the purpose of destroying it. From the very first the House of Commons was thoroughly averse to the bill: and if any fairy could have revealed to Mr. Gladstone what was passing in the hearts of his own supporters, he would have known that it never could pass. Indeed, it is more than probable that Mr. Brand[1] to an imperfect extent performed the part of that fairy for him. But Mr. Gladstone chose rather to trust in the apparent acquiescence, than to believe in the concealed hostility. To some of the members on the Liberal side of the House there was great temptation to get rid of the Bill if possible, without any precise declaration of their opinions upon its principle. Any such declaration would involve them in a gratuitous conflict of opinion with a portion of the electors who supported them. It would either force them to look for support to some who had hitherto opposed them; or it would put their seats in hazard. So long, therefore, as there was any ground for hoping that Lord Russell's Reform Bill would be, like Lord Palmerston's, a mere demonstration, the hostility shown to it from the Liberal side was not sufficient for its overthrow. Mr. Gladstone appears to have imagined that when once he had complied with the proposition contained in Lord Grosvenor's resolution,[2] the main danger of his bill was passed. But as it advanced its path became more and more encumbered. Hostile amendments, friendly additions, dilatory motions, criticisms of a most exhaustive character met it at every turn. The numbers of the divisions varied every evening; but every one of them showed that discontent was eating more and more deeply into the Ministerial ranks. The supporters of the Government were clinging to the belief, which rumour avers to have been conveyed to them upon no mean authority, that the bill would not ultimately be pressed.[3] As the increasing vigour and vehemence of Mr. Gladstone's language dissipated this hope, the support of the bill became more and more wavering, and Mr. Brand's labours more and more unavailing. Towards the end Mr. Gladstone's object

[1] Henry Brand (1814–92), M.P. Lewes and parliamentary secretary to the treasury, the Liberal whip; later speaker of the House of Commons.
[2] I.e. that redistribution should be considered alongside the franchise bill.
[3] In May Lord Halifax, anxious to hinder Reform, had been persuading backbench Liberals and the editor of *The Times*, Delane, that the government would eventually drop its bills. Cowling, p. 103.

appears to have been to pledge the House to the borough franchise which he had selected, so as to leave a basis for operations next year in case he was obliged, by stress of time, to abandon his bill for the present. He vaguely intimated that he had this end in view, and the newspapers in his interest urged it openly. But to the demand for this pledge members of the House had an insuperable objection. If taken it would have committed them to what was in effect an abstract resolution, which might have been mischievous at a future time: if refused, it would have given needless offence to a considerable number of persons. The conflict between the House and the Government as to whether an abstract vote should or should not be taken on this particular point was an animated one for some time; but it needed no prophet to predict how it would end. The Government forced the House to the very brink of the pledge they wanted; but on the words just preceding the fatal words 'seven pounds,' the critical division was taken,[1] and the bill was destroyed. In their desperate efforts to save it the Ministry had entangled themselves in unnecessary pledges, from which they could not afterwards escape: and, in consequence, though possessing on a question of mere confidence an undoubted majority, they were compelled to resign.

Peace to their memory! Mr. Gladstone has told us that an '*ultor*' will arise out of their remains. It may very possibly be so. No one can foresee the freaks of fortune. It may be our destiny to live under a Government in which Mr. Gladstone and Mr. Bright shall lead a willing majority to the 'revenge,' to which he looks forward. Even if that should be the result of the struggle of this spring, we shall see no cause to regret what has been done. The Government whose existence has been terminated was more perilous to the Constitution than a Government professedly far more violent would have been. It combined with names that seemed to be a guarantee for moderation, a measure pregnant with revolution; and, therefore, it beguiled many into the support of its measures to whom the measures themselves were repulsive. Such a phenomenon is happily rare, because it is transitional. It can only happen during the troubled period which marks the development of differences that have been long in germ and the final rupture of old-standing ties. There is a time during which men, who have been reluctantly convinced of the danger of tendencies which they formerly thought innocent, are waiting

---

[1] I.e. the division on Dunkellin's amendment, which, substituting the words 'rateable value' for 'clear yearly value' in the borough occupation franchise clause, forestalled a division on the following figure of seven pounds.

for some chance to set them free of their old engagements, and in the mean time refuse to proclaim by any decided step their real belief that those engagements are practically at an end. Such a confusion of forces will not repeat itself at any future period of the conflict. Men who take office under Mr. Gladstone for the future, with a Reform programme, will do so with a full knowledge of what they are undertaking; especially as it is probable that, pushed by his Reforming allies, he will propose a more violent bill next time. They will know exactly what agitation they are supporting, what rule they are beginning to set up. The line between the opponents of democracy and its adherents will be sharply drawn. This service at least will have been performed by those who have pressed the late Ministry to the ground. There is no such dangerous decoy as the reputation of a moderate man who has abandoned his moderation. This session will have extirpated a whole brood of such deceptive reputations, and that alone will be a larger good service than any single session is generally privileged to perform.

It will also have accomplished the task of making out the conditions under which alone in the future any Reform Bill is possible. The most important characteristic of any measure really 'made to pass,' must be, that it shall not involve the abdication of a class. The day is gone by when it was practicable to urge upon Parliament the deposition either of the middle and upper classes generally, or in particular of that portion of them which is dependent upon the land. If any Reform Bill can be devised which shall not involve such a result, it may have a good chance of passing. It is in itself an advantage of no contemptible dimensions to gratify the susceptibilities which a considerable number of the artizan class have betrayed upon the question of the suffrage. If there were only a thousand persons who felt themselves slighted because until they got richer there was no chance of their possessing, even in the most indirect and limited degree, any formal share in the government of their country, it would be profitable, so far as it could be done safely, to remove that cause of discontent. It is obvious that the feeling extends to a very much larger number, though it is by no means general even within the limits of that class; and therefore, still subject rigorously to the same reservation, it would be in the same proportion more desirable that their wishes should be gratified. But the number of persons whom it would be necessary to admit, in order to cover these aspirants by a simple reduction of the franchise, would leave the classes at present in power in a condition of hopeless inferiority. If such an end, therefore, is to be attained it must be done by some other means than a simple reduction of the franchise.

'THE CHANGE OF MINISTRY'

This is the test which will decide the sincerity of those who clamour for Reform. If they really mean what they continually say; if they are only asking on behalf of the working class for a share, and not for a monopoly of power; if they are willing to recognize that in our social state, where a dense population and the accumulation of a long history have produced a vast contrast of conditions, precautions must be taken that poverty shall not become supreme – they will consent to the provisions which are necessary for carrying such an object into effect. They will not shrink from such provisions because they are new in principle or complicated in detail; for they well know that great changes cannot be wrought in one portion of a well-balanced machine, without requiring corresponding changes throughout the whole. But if they are insincere; if their clamour for a share covers a design upon the whole; if they intend to ignore property in the distribution of power; if, under pretence of breaking down exclusive barriers, they contemplate setting up the rule of numbers – then we must be prepared for every objection that ingenuity can suggest against any plan for so extending the franchise as not to disfranchise those who hold it now. They will, in that case, insist without compromise or modification upon a blank reduction of the suffrage. If any balancing provision is proposed, by which the value of the vote so conferred shall be sufficiently modified to prevent it from enthroning the multitudes, whom it admits, as masters of the whole community, we may expect our Reformers to cast out such a plan with scorn as something which does not coincide with the 'ancient lines of the Constitution.' But the events of this session have sufficiently established that to Reform understood as they understand it, the present depositaries of power will not consent. To say that this Parliament, or any party in it, is opposed to the admission of the working-man to the polling-booth, is studiously to falsify the facts. But it is as little consistent with facts to dream that in this or in any other Parliament, the present depositaries of power will put his heel upon their necks. They are not yet reduced so low as to dream of abdication. When the working-man and his advocates have become so practical and sincere in their demand for Reform that they will accept participation without predominance, the 'settlement of the question' will have been attained: but not till then.

There are two fallacies that must be cast aside, before any real progress can be made. The first is that the mere passing of any measure, great or small, will of itself secure the 'settlement of the question.' It is not very easy to get at the exact meaning of that familiar phrase. To some minds it seems to indicate a future state of absolute repose, in which Reformers shall cease from troubling, and all struggles for political power between classes shall disappear. We might as well hope for the termination of the struggle for existence by which, some philosophers tell us, the existence or the modification of the various species of organized beings upon our planet are determined. The battle for political power is merely an effort, well or ill-judged, on the part of the classes who wage it to better or to secure their own position. Unless our social activity shall have become paralyzed, and the nation shall have lost its vitality, this battle must continue to rage. In this sense the question of Reform, that is to say, the question of relative class power, can never be settled. But those who take the trouble to define the words they use, generally apply the phrase to an object more limited and transient. They merely mean by it a respite from agitation for twenty or thirty years. This is an object, no doubt, capable of attainment. There have been much longer periods in our history during which a truce in the struggle of classes has been observed. But it has been due to causes more potent than the passage of 'a satisfactory measure,' 'with a view to the settlement of the question.' An absence of pressure among the more numerous classes, or a consciousness on their part of inability to extort any advantage from the propertied class has often indisposed them for the attack, and made them deaf to the ever ready exhortations of agitators. But it is in their own state of mind, and in that alone that any hope of such a truce is to be looked for. The condition of things which will induce them to abstain from aggression is one that it is impossible to command and not very easy to foresee. It is due, when it happens, to a combination of causes, whose working is obscure. It certainly cannot be made the subject of a Parliamentary arrangement. Mr. Bright and half-a-dozen of his followers may undertake that if such and such a measure is passed, all movement upon the question shall cease for thirty years; but they are making a covenant whose performance they have no power to secure. They may close their own mouths; but what power have they to silence hundreds of others who may be eager upon this question, and who, if there is any widespread feeling in respect to it, will infallibly be pushed to the front to occupy the places of those who may think themselves bound in honour not to agitate. Nothing can be more futile than the attempt of temporary leaders to impose permanent pledges upon a class. A glance at the history of the last Reform Bill will dispose of the delusion that in a downward movement the leaders of one agitation can bind the leaders of that which comes next after it.

'THE CHANGE OF MINISTRY'

In passing the Reform Bill, Lord Althorp,[1] the recognised leader in the Commons of the movement by which it was carried, announced that it was to be 'a final measure.' How was his pledge respected by those that came after him? Scarcely three years had elapsed before the Chartist agitation was commenced by O'Connell's celebrated campaign in the North,[2] and culminated in the insurrection of Frost.[3] So far, therefore, from a period of repose having been produced by the concessions of the first Reform Bill, in spite of the pledges of its authors, its concession was immediately followed by an organized and dangerous agitation for far more sweeping changes. In 1839, however, the question was settled in a different manner. The failure of the insurrection, and the punishments that were inflicted, convinced the authors of it that their cause for the time was hopeless; and for nine years the land had peace. It was not till the outbreak of 1848 raised the drooping spirits of the party of action that the question of Reform was revived in England. Even this revival taken by itself shows how little value can be attached to the promises of the leaders of Reform agitations. It was but sixteen years since Lord Althorp's pledge, yet the question was mooted again by one of those who had sat in the Parliament to which he made that pledge:[4] and in four years more it was taken up by Lord John Russell, who had been Lord Althorp's colleague at the time. Since that time further democratic change has been kept off, not by the tenacity of Reformers' pledges, but by the vigour of the Conservative resistance. It is an argument commonly used, that the Reform Act has lasted for five and thirty years, and that, therefore, if another were passed now the question would be settled for an equal space of time. But it is forgotten that the question was not settled, in the sense of procuring a respite from agitation, even for four years after the passage of the Reform Bill. It is only for the purpose of staying agitation upon the subject that the settlement of the question is to be desired. If that welcome armistice could not be procured for more than three years even by the great changes contained

[1] Viscount Althorp (1782-1845), chancellor of the exchequer and leader of the House of Commons in Grey's ministry, 1830-4.
[2] Cranborne seems here to confuse the leader of the Irish parliamentary party, Daniel O'Connell, who campaigned in the north and elsewhere against the House of Lords in 1835, and the Chartist leader Feargus O'Connor, who agitated the north from 1835 with nearly all the demands that were to be embodied in the Charter. Chartism proper began with the publication of the Charter in May 1838.
[3] The draper John Frost attempted to seize Newport at the head of a small Chartist band in November 1839.
[4] The reference is to the Radical Joseph Hume, who, in 1848, brought forward a motion for household suffrage, ballot, triennial parliaments, and more equal electoral districts.

in the first Reform Bill, how is it possible to expect that a less sweeping measure will secure it now?

The other delusion is that the danger of insurrection enters in any degree as an element in the consideration of the question of Reform. Of course the Radical orators threaten it freely. In 1858 Mr. Bright told us that a reduction of the franchise would soon be demanded in rougher tones than his; and in 1866 he has told us that unless we granted it, an 'accident' would happen to our institutions, such as drove Charles X. from his throne.[1] Orators of less distinction than Mr. Bright, and the writers in his daily organs, follow in the same strain more boldly, and tell us a great deal about 'the people rising in their might.' This form of political reasoning for the guidance of doubting legislatures has during the last two generations become a favourite commonplace in political argument upon the rabid side. Discussions upon questions of organic change are carried on as it were under the shadow of revolution, and the possibility of an appeal to physical force is referred to with a frankness which would never have been dreamed of a century ago. Issues between the legislature of a country and the lower classes in the great towns are quietly assumed by Radicals and believed by timid Conservatives to be mere questions of the patience of the latter. The resistance of a government to any ill-advised project alleged to be popular among those classes is merely a resistance upon sufferance. When once they are piqued by their enemies, or persuaded by their 'friends,' to 'rise' – *cadit quæstio* – the ultimate tribunal of the nineteenth century has spoken. No one who has watched the recent tendency of political discussion can have failed to observe how deeply this theory has tinged our political philosophy, and to a certain extent modified our political action. Yet it is a very curious doctrine to have lifted itself so high, especially in this country. No one can say that our history gives the slightest countenance to it. Its whole course is a chronicle of constant concessions to enlightened public opinion; but it does not record a single instance of concession to mob violence. The case most nearly in point in recent times is the agitation under which the Reform Act of 1832 was carried. There is no doubt that the circumstances were remarkably favourable to mob dominion. A feeble and fanciful King, a Home Secretary[2] who certainly was not prejudiced against disturbances by any strong political interest in repressing them, and the powers of legislation practically consigned to the hands of a narrow class, bitterly

---

[1] Charles X of France was deposed by the revolution of 1830.
[2] Lord Melbourne.

divided against each other by polemical hostility, were eminently conditions under which popular license ought to thrive. Yet, as a matter of fact, the movement derived its strength from something much stronger than the lower class, and it was not to insurrectionary violence that the Legislature yielded. The movement proceeded mainly from the middle class. *Is fecit cui prodest.* The middle class, before the Reform Bill, possessed little, if any, direct political power: after the Reform Bill it enjoyed the largest share. The middle class, reinforced by the discontent which intense distress had produced among the lower, presented a formidable combination, which any Government might well fear to encounter. The House of Lords actually yielded to the extraordinary pressure put on them by the King; but it is more than probable that had they been able to surmount his opposition, they must have given way to the resolute demands of the middle class. They were fighting a battle in which almost every element of social power was ranged on the other side. Those who compare those times with these, and threaten the opponents of this Reform Bill with the rout that befell the antagonists of its greater prototype, forget the material fact that the middle classes were on the wrong side of the 'pale' then, and that they are on the right side now.

It is not, however, from any English experience that the popular notion of the invincibility of the lower urban classes, if roused, has arisen. The political history of our neighbours across the channel has always produced a strong effect on the imaginations of all classes here; a stronger effect, perhaps, from the slight distance and the strangeness of the surrounding circumstances, than would have been produced by similar events if they had happened at home. And it would be worth while, did time permit, to examine the real bearing of the French revolutions upon the question of insurrectionary power, because they have tended to instil into the minds of the present, and the last generation, a belief in the irresistibility of the lowest class, which is new in the political history of this country. But these cases are precedents for us in no other sense; and they are only worth referring to because they have been perverted. It is well known that the artisans of the large towns – the 'people,' as they are called by a strange perversion of words – have a factitious importance in France on account of the power which an extreme centralization has given to the artisans who live in the capital. Those who master Paris master France; and, therefore, in the presence of an irresolute executive, the barricades are, or at least have hitherto been, a tremendous power. Neither London, nor any other great town possesses such an ascendancy. But in a country ruled as England happily is, by public opinion, and by the general pervading sense of what is best for the whole community, we can never arrive at such extremities as France has so often and so lamentably witnessed. No doubt if the *real* people of England – the large masses of the population in country as well as town, whom our experience entitles us to regard as the friends of law and order – if they were to rise in favour of Reform, or of any other measure, their action must be successful; but long before any such unanimity could come to pass, the change of public opinion it implies would have told upon the Legislature, and made any rising unnecessary. But it is a mere dream of timidity that the town artisan class, the only class whose alleged discontent is in question now, can ever be so formidable, that the Legislature, in discussing their demands, should have need to take counsel of fear, and be debarred from considering calmly what is best for all classes.

The most difficult question which the new Government will have to decide, will be whether they ought or ought not to introduce a Reform Bill. Its course will have been simplified to no inconsiderable extent by the events of the past session. No future Government can venture to present any such measure which shall involve a large transfer of power, or which shall be constructed under fear of the artisan classes, in order to satisfy the agitation their advocates have made. The most liberal Parliament ever assembled during the reign of the present sovereign has declined to pass a Reform Bill of this type. This fact, however, by no means necessarily disposes of the question. There are other types of Reform still possible. There are numberless irregularities and inconveniences in the present arrangement that may well be corrected. Few impartial persons will be disposed to deny that, considering the large transfer of wealth and population that has been made to the north by the progress of mechanical discovery, the balance of legislative power inclines too heavily toward the south-west of England; although a good deal is to be said, too, for Cornwall, which is teeming with wealth, and in a high state of progress. No one, again, can deny the advantages of what has been well called the 'lateral' extension of the franchise.[1] Whether the vexed question of vertical extension ought to be entertained at the

[1] I.e. an extension so devised as to bring in men of the same class as those already possessing the vote, rather than those of a lower class who would be reached by 'vertical' extension. Disraeli had talked of 'lateral' extension in relation to the Conservative Reform Bill of 1859, with its 'fancy' franchises, copying those proposed by Russell in 1854 (votes for university graduates, for the payment of 40s in direct taxation, for a £50 savings bank deposit, etc.).

same time, to any material extent, must depend, as we have said, on the tone in which it is claimed by those who are to benefit by it. They will never induce the present depositaries of power to agree to it unless they accept the guarantees that are necessary to prevent the preponderance of mere numbers. There are, moreover, many points of minor moment in which our electoral system might be advantageously improved. The principle affirmed by Lord Dunkellin's motion[1] is in itself of inestimable value. A self-adjusting machinery, which shall dispense with the intolerable expense of voluntary registration, and shall get rid of the costly and sometimes partisan tribunal of the Revising Barrister, will be a great boon.[2] Some remedy is also required for the costliness of elections, especially county elections. It is an evil that is growing every day. It threatens, if its development is to continue at the present pace, to confine the choice of candidates to the relatives of wealthy landowners, or else to mercantile or manufacturing men of the class that find it useful to them in their vocation to have a seat in Parliament. A Parliament so composed would be a poor representation of the varied interests of the country. Some measure that would put a stop to the necessity of paying travelling expenses for the voter – some adaptation of the system of voting papers, which has answered so well at the Universities, would go far to meet the evil.[3]

Many other changes in our electoral system, which are small in extent, but which still it would be desirable to make, might be suggested. But they must all be subject to the far more momentous question, whether it is desirable for a Government formed from the ranks of the Conservative party to undertake the question of Reform at all. There is a genuine desire in the minds of many persons that something should be done in order to release the numerous persons in all orders of society, from Cabinet ministers down to pot-house politicians, especially upon the Liberal side, who have pledged themselves to the passing of some measure that shall bear the name of Reform Bill. Beyond this, there is undoubtedly the consideration, that both electors and non-electors have heard the question of Reform so much discussed, and know that so many promises have been given on the subject, that if nothing is done,

---

[1] The basing of the borough franchise on ratable rather than rental values.
[2] Registers of electors were drawn up in the first instance by the overseers of the poor, and specially appointed barristers held revising courts annually to hear and decide applications for the erasure or addition of names. Making or defending a claim to the vote could be very expensive.
[3] Cranborne had favoured the idea of voting papers, enabling electors to vote without personally appearing at the poll, at least since 1857, and they had been proposed in the Conservative Reform Bill of 1859.

they may retain a vague feeling that some one has kept from them what authorities, which they think good, told them they had a right to possess: and though they may entertain no very distinct idea of its precise value, a certain amount of resentment may be left behind in their minds. Some of this feeling must undoubtedly be created by any Reform Bill which could be accepted by the Conservatives, or the moderate Liberals: for it must of necessity leave a large number of persons without the franchise for whom it is now claimed. Yet there can be no doubt that if some enfranchisement were made, the feeling of soreness even in their minds would be diminished. They would not have won anything for themselves; but still they would have won a partial triumph. Half, or more than half the earnestness of a political struggle, belongs to the *sporting* category of feelings. Men are sore when they lose, and satisfied when they win, not for the value of the thing at stake, but for the value they set on winning in the abstract. Therefore it is that any termination of a struggle in which either side wins nothing is unsatisfactory. It is not that one of the extremes may not be perfectly right. In times of great excitement the mean between two extremes may be anything but moderate in reality. But a complete victory on either side leaves a wound that will not heal. It gives earnestness to the defeated, while the victors are apt to lose it: and earnestness, no matter in what cause, exercises a fatal charm often upon whole generations as they pass through the sentimental age. If legitimacy had not conquered so completely in 1815, that strange ultra-Liberal superstition, which so deeply tinged and fired the growing minds of the country for a whole generation after that time, would never have been more than the eccentricity of a few enthusiasts. It would not, therefore, be an unmixed good to conquer completely in this matter of Reform.

Such are some of the principal arguments which might be urged in favour of a Conservative Reform Bill. We do not deny that a certain weight might be assigned to them, if the Conservatives were in a position from which they could secure the passing of a fair compromise. But it is not for combatants to offer terms of compromise unless they are certain that they are strong enough to hold their own in case of need. Otherwise, to offer a compromise is to sue for peace. The attitude which the Conservative party ought to assume in reference to the question of Reform must depend on the strength which they find they possess in the House of Commons. If they can command an assured support which shall enable them to secure that the terms of any compromise adopted shall be really moderate, it may be wise to close the controversy, so far as it can be closed by any action of theirs. But to bring forward any measure affecting the representation of the people in the presence of adverse forces strong enough to engraft democratic amendments on it, would be to throw away all the advantages which the labours of this session have secured.

On this subject we are tempted to refer to Lord Derby's most impressive speech in the House of Lords on the 9th of this month, when he first met the present Parliament as Prime Minister:

My Lords, I must in the first place say that I hold myself entirely free and unpledged on that great and difficult question of Reform. I have in reference to that question experienced certain dangers of my own – and I shall certainly consider well and carefully, before I again introduce a Reform Bill, the wise advice given by the noble earl, my predecessor, that no government is justified in bringing in a Reform Bill without having a reasonable prospect of carrying it; and also the remark of the noble earl upon the cross benches [Grey], that a Reform Bill cannot be carried, or the constitution amended, except by a mutual understanding between the two great parties in the country. On the other hand, I am afraid that that portion of the community who are the most clamorous for a Reform Bill will not be satisfied with any measure such as can be acceded to by the great parties of the country, and I greatly fear that any measure of a moderate character would not satisfy those persons, but would lead to further agitation and be made a stepping stone for further measures. I reserve to myself entire liberty as to whether the present Government shall or not undertake in future sessions to bring in any measure for the amendment of the representation of the people: but of this I am quite sure, that if there be no reasonable prospect of passing a sound and satisfactory measure, it will be an unfortunate thing and a great disadvantage to the country that session after session should be lost, and measures of useful legislation should be put a stop to, by continued contests over a Reform Bill.

It is, in truth, impossible to forecast the course which the Conservative party will preserve upon this momentous question until the position which is likely to be occupied by the constitutional Whigs is more clearly ascertained. That they have resolved not to aid Lord Derby in assuming the government of the country, as they aided him in repelling an attack upon the Constitution, will be matter of earnest regret to every friend of the Constitution. It can in no sense, however, be a matter of complaint; for the honour of public men is too precious to be hazarded lightly, and every man is the best judge of the course which a regard for it prescribes to him to follow. In such matters precipitate action might lead to misconstruction of motives. The recasting of political associations, however imperatively the exigency of the times may demand it, should not be the work of a momentary impulse. The time, however, it may be hoped, is not far distant when merely personal and traditional ties will cease to keep apart those who are of one mind upon the most vital question of our generation. In the meantime their refusal leaves the House of Commons divided in effect – though not very distinctly – into three parties. It is obvious that no one of those three parties can command a majority without the help of one of the other two: or, to put it more practically, neither the Conservatives nor the Radicals can retain the government of the country for any length of time except by the assistance of the Whigs. On the heads of this central party, which holds the balance between the other two, a heavy responsibility rests. It is clear, from what has passed this year, that they will not consent to an alliance with the Radicals except upon terms which the Radicals refuse to accept. They will not take Mr. Gladstone, in his present mood, as their leader. Rather than do so they have helped to drive a Liberal Ministry from power. It will lie with them to decide whether Mr. Gladstone shall remain powerless for evil until either he shall have abandoned his Radical allies, or until a broad Constitutional party shall have been formed strong enough permanently to baffle his designs, – or whether he is to come back with a stronger Reform Bill and increased power to pass it. That they should look to the ultimate – perhaps the early – formation of a party whose course they should have their just share in guiding is natural enough. But it lies with them, by giving a general support to the Government which has just been formed, to render the formation of that party possible.

There can be no doubt – so far as the subject matter admits of such an expression – that Mr. Gladstone intends to adhere to the democratic policy he has already announced. It is doubtful whether he intends now to head the movement for suffrages still lower than those which he proposed. He does not disdain apparently to act as the recognised leader of Mr. Potter and Mr. Lucraft.[1] To what extent he has by that act accepted their doctrines may be a matter of dispute; but he clearly sees in them nothing to repel him. It may, therefore, be assumed that if he moves at all from the seven pound limit, it will be to go lower and not higher. He is evidently in no mood to win back by concession those who have left him, or to calm those, who, though they voted for him, watched his proceedings with undisguised alarm. Opposition, as is usually the case with him, has made him more bitter and more extravagant.

[1] Benjamin Lucraft (1810–97), cabinet- and chair-maker; an old Chartist and a leader of popular politics in London, active in 1866 in the Trafalgar Square and Hyde Park Reform meetings.

He is trying to put himself at the head of a great democratic agitation. It is quite clear that if he comes into office again he comes in as the nominee and champion of the Radicals – pledged to their measures, accepting their principles, and relying upon them to inflame the populace out of doors against his antagonists. And he will come in again as the inevitable Minister: as a last resource after all alternatives have been exhausted: not upon his trial, as this year, but in triumph. In such a position it is needless to point out how terrible his strength will be. He will then level again the blow, which this year he has narrowly missed, and which will hardly fail again. He will introduce, and, supported by the belief that no other Ministry but his own can exist, he will pass a Reform Bill that shall build up his future power on the attachment of the Trades Unions of the great towns, and shall rid him for ever of aristocratic opposition.

It is for the Constitutional Whigs to consider how far they will be partakers in this enterprise. If they allow Lord Derby's Government to be thrown out upon any vote of confidence, no other result can follow but that Mr. Gladstone will come back again. We will not urge the title Lord Derby's Cabinet has to their confidence – the agreement upon the one vital point, the paucity of subjects on which any difference can be found, the real identity of interest and of sympathy in presence of the movement which Mr. Gladstone leads, and which Mr. Potter and Mr. Lucraft represent. We will content ourselves with pointing to the inevitable result of their defeat. There may be members of that Government of whose appointment they disapprove, or to whose views on particular subjects they are opposed. Questions may arise on which they may dislike the course of the Government, or may feel inclined to censure the bearing of some particular member of it. If they could replace it by something which they liked better there would be nothing unreasonable in their giving effect to their objections. From their own point of view they would be acting logically and consistently, if they could replace a Conservative Government by a moderate Liberal Government, free from the reproach of any democratic leanings. But they are bound in this momentous crisis to take all the elements of the calculation together, and to work out from the whole the result which according to their views will be most beneficial to the community. They must not sacrifice to their feelings upon a secondary question, or their dislike to this or that individual, the issues of the one all-important conflict. It is not a moment to quarrel about party badges, when the common enemy is at the gate. If Mr. Gladstone comes back upon the shoulders of the politicians who hold their debates in Trafalgar Square, the personal controversies that are keenly canvassed now will become matter of faint but melancholy historical interest. The classes who now are divided among themselves upon differences merely personal, or on questions of altogether subsidiary importance, will have leisure in the retirement of absolute political annihilation to reflect on the wisdom and opportuneness of their mutual distrust.

The decisions that are taken within the next two or three years will determine in all probability the future character and complexion of our constitution. The public apathy upon all questions of domestic policy is profound. The nation is too intent on other matters to point out to its rulers the course it would have them take. Our destiny is in the hands of a score or so of influential politicians of various schools. If they sufficiently understand the supreme importance of the crisis to forget awhile for their country's sake old antipathies or personal aspirations, the men who really love our ancient constitution will be gathered under one banner, and their united force may defy democracy. But if the opportunity is squandered in personal self-assertion or sectional bickering, they must fall before an enemy who at least may claim the praise of never suffering private ambition to impede the attainment of a great end. Our system may fairly be said to be on its trial. If the virtue of our public men is not equal to an exigency which for objects so precious asks for sacrifices so small, the world will think we have little cause for boasting over the less pretentious selfishness of more democratic communities.

'The Conservative Surrender'
(*Q.R.*, no. 246; October 1867)

INTRODUCTORY NOTE

CRANBORNE could hardly have foreseen in July 1866 the extraordinary course of events which he was to review when he next wrote for the *Quarterly* in the autumn of 1867. Having come into office by resisting Gladstone's moderate Reform Bill, Derby and Disraeli, in the space of a year, led the House of Commons step by step into a measure of more than twice the size, which, by establishing household suffrage in the boroughs, seemed drastically to alter the balance of electoral power in favour of the urban working man. As a feat of dexterity and impudence, their successful conduct of the Reform Bill of 1867 was a triumph; as an act of moral tergiversation, it seemed to Cranborne to mark a new nadir in their leadership of the Conservative party.

The *volte-face* of 1866–7 was the product of political expediency. Neither Derby nor Disraeli wanted Reform as such: they were driven to accept it by the dictates of party and personal advantage. Their overriding concern was to make their ministry something more than a mere interlude between the last Liberal administration and the next; to show that the Conservative party, almost permanently out of office for twenty years, was capable of giving the country sound government, and, far from being reactionary and obscurantist, was sufficiently flexible in outlook to provide such instalments of moderate, constitutional progress as the nation might require – including, if necessary, parliamentary reform. It would have been hard for them to ignore Reform, which was, by mid-1866, what it had not been since 1832, a major national issue. The debates of 1866 had roused feelings and expectations, and a considerable popular agitation was under way, manifesting itself most forcibly in the riots of 23–25 July, when Hyde Park was invaded by a mob which had pushed over the railings, and producing, in the course of 1866–7, massive demonstrations in the great towns. If the government, in a minority in the Commons, tried to evade the Reform question, it was likely that the other side would compose their divisions sufficiently to combine behind some reforming motion and eject it. The Conservatives would then face the alternatives of a Liberal revision of the franchise calculated to damage their interests or a general election which would place them in an anti-popular posture. By taking the question up, on the other hand, they could hope to secure solid advantages. They might demonstrate their capacity to implement necessary but cautious change, and so underline their fitness for government. They might deepen and exploit the divisions in the Liberal ranks which the Reform issue bred, and hasten the realignment of forces which would enable them to grasp the heritage of Palmerston and engross all the really conservative elements in the country. With a cleverly devised measure, they might at the same time satisfy the desire of moderates for a 'safe' settlement and appeal to the working men as friends of the people; and by keeping the details of the change in their hands, they might make it more favourable to Conservative electoral interests than a Liberal bill would be. Whatever happened, Derby and Disraeli felt, they must keep office and keep the initiative, in order to establish the capacity of their party to govern and to deal with great national issues. But in determining to do this without a Commons' majority, they in effect bound themselves to accept whatever measures were necessary to prevent their being beaten – exactly what Cranborne had warned against in July.

Derby concluded in September 1866 that Reform would have to be tackled, and it was decided to move gradually towards legislation by first putting general resolutions before the House (which would sound out opinion and stimulate Liberal dissension) and by setting up a royal commission. What the resolutions should contain and what the commission should do led to considerable disagreement in the cabinet in the first weeks of 1867. Cranborne was worried about the path the ministry was taking, especially when the idea of household suffrage, albeit restricted, began to figure prominently in its discussions. However, he assented at the beginning of February to the insertion in the proposed resolutions of rated household suffrage in the boroughs, safeguarded by plural voting. Plural voting at this juncture was understood to mean giving householders extra votes according to ratable value (as had long been the practice in most parochial elections) or according to the house-tax paid, so proportioning their voting power to their material stake in the country. Cranborne said later that he had considered this a just principle, while not expecting the House to accept it. The scheme also satisfied another cabinet minister troubled by misgivings, the young Earl of Carnarvon, secretary of state for the colonies, but it foundered on the refusal of General Peel, the secretary for war, to swallow household suffrage, and as presented to the Commons on 11 February the resolutions simply put forward the principle of plural voting as a means to facilitate an unspecified extension of the borough franchise.

It was immediately apparent, however, that the resolutions alone would not afford the government an adequate standing-ground. There was strong pressure to cease temporising and make a settlement, and Disraeli, suddenly, and without his colleagues' sanction, committed the ministry to the production of an outline bill. It was at this point that Cranborne became convinced that the chancellor was trying to hustle the cabinet into an unpalatably large measure. He suggested a £5 rating franchise as the basis of the proposals which had now to be concocted, and this was accepted, but three days later Derby and Disraeli reverted to household suffrage. The attractions of household suffrage for the Conservative leaders were powerful. It offered a simple and permanent resting-point for

'THE CONSERVATIVE SURRENDER'

the borough franchise, which the Liberals could hardly outbid, and, while seeming to provide a sweeping and generous enfranchisement, could be so qualified and counterbalanced as to have a very limited impact in practice. But the counterbalance provided by plural voting did not seem adequate to Cranborne when he got down to detailed examination of the statistics of the new measure. In the smaller boroughs, he calculated, it would not equal the addition made by household suffrage, so that some three-fifths of the constituencies would fall under 'democratic' control. Reaching this grim conclusion on 24 February, he obliged Derby to hold a cabinet next day, less than two hours before the prime minister was due to outline the proposed bill to a party meeting, prior to Disraeli's presenting it in the House. Under threat of his, Carnarvon's, and Peel's resignations, ministers hastily botched up a plan on a £6 rating basis, but the Commons received it badly, and it was obvious that it was not substantial enough to be the foundation of a satisfactory settlement. A settlement was what M.P.s wanted most, and even in the Conservative party there was a good deal of feeling that household suffrage must be its basis – feeling reflected in the Carlton Club meeting of the 28th. Derby and Disraeli agreed, and went back to household suffrage at the cabinet of 2 March, whereupon Cranborne, Carnarvon, and Peel resigned.

The Reform Bill introduced by Disraeli on 18 March subjected household suffrage to large checks. It was made conditional on two years' residence and on personal payment of rates, a provision which excluded some half-a-million compound householders paying a reduced rate through their landlords, though they could get on the register if they elected to pay the full rate. It was counterbalanced by the 'fancy franchises' – votes for educational qualifications, for possession of £50 in the funds or the savings bank, and for payment of £1 p.a. in direct taxation – and by the dual vote, i.e. a second vote for householders meeting the £1 direct taxation qualification. The county occupation franchise was reduced from £50 to £15, and there was a small redistribution scheme. The measure would hardly have enfranchised more new voters than the 400,000 of Gladstone's 1866 bill, and was carefully devised to look generous while being practically very safe. It represented the sort of moderate settlement, adapted to split the Liberals and give the Conservatives a sound platform in the event of an election, which Derby and Disraeli wanted.

Ironically, the refusal of Cranborne and his friends to co-operate in it was a factor helping to force the Conservative leaders to greater concessions in a Radical direction than they had probably intended. Committed as he was to staying in office and settling the question under Conservative auspices without a Conservative majority, Disraeli had no choice but to acquiesce in the measure's progressive expansion. He preferred almost anything to defeat in the House, and, as Cranborne had feared, the bill's safeguards were removed one after another. The fancy franchises and the dual vote disappeared, the residence requirement was reduced to one year, a lodger franchise was inserted, the county occupation franchise came down to £12, with £5 copyhold and leasehold franchises, and the redistribution was enlarged. Most drastic of all, Disraeli accepted the tenor of an amendment from the Liberal Hodgkinson, abolishing compounding in parliamentary boroughs, and so removing the obstacle to the enfranchisement of the compound householder. As finally passed, the Reform Act added nearly a million voters (about 90%) to the electorate of England and Wales, and gave the working men a majority in the borough electorate, which it increased by perhaps 700,000, or around 138%.

The bulk of Conservative backbenchers followed their leaders quietly enough through this transformation scene. They were not without misgivings, especially when the exclusion of the compounders, upon which many of them had relied to make household suffrage safe, was abandoned. But they felt the need to make a settlement, had no desire to provoke a costly dissolution, and enjoyed the excitement of a great party triumph which Disraeli gave them as he slid eel-like out of every difficulty and cleverly frustrated the challenge of the detested Gladstone. They could hope, too, that household suffrage might in the end produce a constituency more favourable to them than that of 1832: Cranborne was to give an acid sketch of this feeling when he surveyed 'The Past and the Future of Conservative Policy' in the *Quarterly* of October 1869. Despite his desire as expressed to his friend Shaw-Stewart, to 'kill' the bill, Cranborne did not attempt to organise opposition to it within the Conservative party, an exercise which would have required arts of management that he felt himself to lack. But in debate he did not disguise his opinion of the government's course, and on 15 July he moved the rejection of the bill's third reading with a stinging accusation of betrayal against Disraeli.

'Betrayal' was a common theme among those Conservatives who had regarded their party as pledged to resist a sweeping enfranchisement at all costs. Some of them felt that their leaders must have schemed from the outset to gull them into 'democracy': Disraeli, in particular, was suspected of deliberately setting out to realise that junction between the Tory party and the people which he had preached in the thirties and forties. The conspiracy theory of Derby's and Disraeli's conduct was given scathing expression by Cranborne when he considered the events of the session in an article which – its authorship being no secret – created a sensation and necessitated several reprints of the number containing it. In charging Derby and Disraeli with plotting to introduce large-scale Reform even while they were gaining office by appearing to resist it, Cranborne relied heavily on two statements: Disraeli's that the cabinet of 1859 had been unanimous for household suffrage, should the borough franchise be reduced, and Derby's that on taking office he had determined not to be a mere stop-gap and to do what he could to turn his minority into a majority. The first of these was a typical piece of Disraeli's cheek, designed to give some appearance of consistency to his course, and Cranborne must have known that. The second proved only what it said: it did not prove that Derby, in July 1866, had intended to carry household suffrage. It is hard to believe that Cranborne really supposed the Conservative chiefs to have been bent on household suffrage when they took office. In his anger at what had been done, he was simply exploiting their words so as to place the worst possible construction on their

'THE CONSERVATIVE SURRENDER'

conduct. Yet if there had been no premeditation, Cranborne was, in a sense, justified in alleging treachery. Derby and Disraeli had, in order to keep office, abandoned the positions by whose defence they had obtained it, to the dismay of many who had sincerely supported them in 1866. They had put place and tactical success before what Cranborne regarded as Conservative principle. That they had done so in the best interests of the Conservatives as a political party was not an argument which he could admit in their defence. Indeed, he felt that they had denatured party by turning it into a mere contrivance for securing and retaining office, and had opened the way for the total subservience of ministries to the whim of an uncontrolled House of Commons.

Perhaps the worst aspect of the whole train of events for Cranborne was the lack of will to resist which it had revealed in the 'comfortable classes'. The Reform League had blown its trumpets, and the walls of the constitution had promptly collapsed. Power had been transferred to the urban masses, and, with the demoralisation of the Conservative party through its leaders' cynicism, there was no reliable agency of resistance to Radical schemes. Cranborne had little doubt where those schemes would begin: as the first fruits of the Reform Act he foresaw a massive assault on Church and land, in which Ireland would act as the proving-ground for measures later to be applied in England.

1. *Speech of the Right Hon. B. Disraeli on the Motion for the Second Reading of Mr. Baines' Bill*, 1865. London, 1865.

2. *Speech of the Right Hon. B. Disraeli on the Third Reading of the Representation of the People Bill*, 1867. London, 1867.

3. *Speech of the Earl of Derby on the Second Reading of the Representation of the People Bill, in the House of Lords*, 1867. London, 1867.

Now that the heat of the conflict is over, there is very little dispute as to the nature of the revolution that the year 1867 has seen accomplished. Fantastic computations intended to soothe Conservative apprehensions were in vogue in the early part of the session; but they have served their purpose, and are forgotten now. No one at present doubts that as far as figures go, the transfer of power has been complete. What the result of that transfer may be, must of course be a question of conjecture. Many are sanguine that a great and salutary change in our legislation is at hand: many more affect a hopefulness which they are far from feeling. Few care by injudicious frankness to incur the wrath of the new masters, whose rule is inevitable now. It is, indeed, scarcely worth while to guess at results which experience must soon reveal to us. The question of our destiny is one of extreme simplicity, and comparatively few years of trial will enable us to judge how it will be answered. A clear majority of votes in a clear majority of constituencies has been made over to those who have no other property but the labour of their hands. The omnipotence of Parliament is theirs, wholly and without reserve. Subject to them is a minority possessed in various degrees of a vast aggregate of accumulated wealth. If he were to set all considerations of conscience aside, each member of the poor but absolute majority would naturally desire so to use this new power as to make some portion of this wealth his own. We have legislated on the assumption that he will not do so. That assumption can only be justified on one of two hypotheses. Either the conscience of the working men will be so strong as to outweigh the suggestions of interest and the pressure of poverty, or they will not be clever enough to pull together for the purpose of gratifying their wishes. The measure of this session has been recommended by nothing but vague declamation; it is not easy to discover to which of these two securities it is that our legislators look to be the bulwark of property in this country. Both sides were singularly silent upon the principles of the vast change that was being made. The general tendency among those who were responsible for the measure appeared to be, in public to rely upon the virtues of the working class, in private to draw what consolation they could from a belief in its unbounded pliability.

We do not intend to speculate upon the answer which events will give to this interesting question. No past experience can help us to discuss it. The experiment, stupendous as are the interests it puts in hazard, is yet absolutely new. Great cities have before this been placed, for a brief and troubled period, under the absolute control of the poorest classes of their population. Large empires have been governed, and are governed still, with considerable success, by a democracy of petty rural cultivators. But the idea of placing a great empire under the absolute control of the poorest classes in the towns has never until the present year been entertained by any nation. We have nothing, therefore, but *a priori* considerations to guide us in a forecast of our future fate. What we know of the fallibility of human nature, of the proneness of mankind to shape their conduct by their desires, and to devise afterwards the code of morality necessary to defend it, is not reassuring. We still think, as we have always thought, that to give the power of taxation to those from whom no taxes are exacted, the supreme disposal of property to those who have no property of their own, the guidance of this intricate machine of government to the least instructed class in the community, is to adopt in the management of the empire principles which would not be entertained for a moment in any other department of human

'THE CONSERVATIVE SURRENDER'

affairs. But it is futile to argue *a priori* now. The decision of this issue has been remitted to the test of experience. For us its teaching will be valueless; for we have taken a step that can never be recalled. But before another generation has passed away, other nations will have learned by our success or our disasters how far the rule of the poorer urban multitudes is favourable to the freedom of property, or to the maintenance of wise and stable government.

Had this revolution been accomplished in fair fight we should have been content to lay aside the controversy at this point. It is the duty of every Englishman, and of every English party, to accept a political defeat cordially, and to lend their best endeavours to secure the success, or to neutralise the evil, of the principles to which they have been forced to succumb. England has committed many mistakes as a nation in the course of her history; but their mischief has often been more than corrected by the heartiness with which after each great struggle victors and vanquished have forgotten their former battles, and have combined together to lead the new policy to its best results. We have no wish to be unfaithful to so wholesome a tradition. As far, therefore, as our Liberal adversaries are concerned, we shall dismiss the long controversy with the expression of an earnest hope that their sanguine confidence may prove in the result to have been wiser than our fears.

But there are other questions of public interest which do not belong to the Reform controversy, but to which a melancholy prominence has been given by the passing of this Reform Bill. It has been attended by political phenomena of no ordinary kind. It has been the result of manœuvres, singularly skilful and successful, but in their character wholly new to the history of our party conflicts. Whatever may be the issue of the momentous constitutional experiment we have been trying, the nation will not pass by as matter of no account the tactics by which the change has been brought about. The strange morality which has guided public men, the unexpected results to which parliamentary discipline and faith in party leaders have conducted us, will awake in the minds of thinking men a deeper solicitude than even the adoption of a hazardous form of government. The tone of public opinion, and the character of institutions undoubtedly react upon each other; but not with equal power. If it be not absolutely true of governments that 'that which is best administered is best,' still the form of the machine is indeed of slender importance compared to the manner of men by whom it is worked. The patriotism and honour of statesmen may force the worst institutions to yield a harvest of prosperity; but no political mechanism will restore the tone of a public opinion that has been debased. The marvellous termination of this Reform controversy will exert a powerful influence upon the future spirit of public men; but whether that influence is for good or evil will depend very much on the judgment which the nation ultimately forms of the conduct of those who have brought it about. It is a critical case. The decision pronounced in it will rule our political moralists for many a year to come. If the practice that has been recently pursued shall be sustained, it is difficult to believe that our system of parliamentary government can long survive. The interests involved are so important that it is worth while to examine carefully what the precedents are which the conduct of the leader of the present Government has established, and what their bearing upon the future working of our institutions is likely to be. That the Reform Bill has been carried by one of the most rapid and sudden changes of front ever executed by a Government is undoubtedly true. But if only a change of opinion were in question, the charges that have been made against them would be destitute of any great importance. Such changes are, so far as they go, a slur on the reputation of politicians. In regard to questions that have been much discussed, and the elements of which have not materially altered, they imply either prejudices pertinaciously cherished, or professions thoughtlessly made. It is fair to infer that those who have changed lightly once may do so again. But a mere change of opinion cannot be reproached with dishonour or breach of faith. If the Conservatives had come into power as they did in 1852, through the mere weakness of their opponents, or as in 1858 by an accidental victory on a passing issue, they would have been free to deal with the question of Reform unfettered by their own previous action. Even then a sudden conversion, made in view of a hostile majority, and under the threat of losing office, would have exposed their motives to suspicion. This species of 'obloquy' Lord Derby experienced in 1852 upon the subject of Protection, and again in 1859 on the subject of the county franchise: and by the readiness with which he has executed a still more startling change this year, he appears not to have disrelished the sensation. But the charge recorded against him by recent events is far graver than that of any change of opinion however rapid. It is that he obtained the votes which placed him in office on the faith of opinions which, to keep office, he immediately repudiated. It is that – according to his own recent avowals[1] – he had made up his mind to desert these opinions even at the very moment when he was being raised to power as their champion.

[1] See below, pp. 272–3.

'THE CONSERVATIVE SURRENDER'

Of the real facts of the case no one outside the innermost ministerial circle affects to have any doubt. That up to the beginning of this year the Conservative leaders were stoutly opposed to any very large reduction of the franchise, and especially to household suffrage; that Mr. Gladstone last year was defeated at their instance by a majority largely composed of men of these opinions; and that this year, with the help of the Radicals, they have passed a bill of household suffrage, are facts which can only be contested by denials of the hardiest kind. Courageous efforts in this direction have, indeed, not been wanting. In the early part of the session, and even after the compound householder had been slain, Mr. Disraeli boldly denied that he was introducing a household suffrage bill. The facts were unfortunately too plain for him. As Mr. Forster immediately pointed out, the new franchise is simply the old occupation franchise with the 10*l.* limitation struck out; and of late even Mr. Disraeli has accepted the phrase as the proper description of his measure. On the third reading of the bill, he tried to extricate himself in exactly the opposite direction. He declared that not only had the Conservative leaders not opposed household suffrage in the previous year, but that they had come to a decision in favour of it, even so far back as 1859.[1] No one else has been sufficiently master of his countenance to repeat this wonderful defence; but efforts have occasionally been made to argue that the opposition to Mr. Gladstone's bill of last year was not caused by its going too far, but by its not going far enough; that the Conservatives never objected to the class of workmen, but only to the class of skilled workmen; and that they would at any time have patiently submitted to the enfranchisement of the artisans, if they had been allowed to enfranchise the residuum at the same time. It is needless to say that this theory is of very modern date. It did not exist even in the spring of the present year. At that period it was the fashion to believe in the compound householder, and, on the strength of his exclusion, to represent the ministerial bill as a very moderate measure. It was not till that troublesome stalking-horse had been removed that it was found necessary to discover the antiquity of a Conservative belief in household suffrage. But the discovery is too new and too opportune to have had much weight with the public. It could only challenge a moment's attention from those who had either never watched, or had wholly forgotten, the events of 1866. Roman Catholics tell us that recent developments of their

[1] Disraeli said on the bill's third reading, on 15 July 1867, that the cabinet of 1859 had been unanimous that if they reduced the borough franchise they would have to go to household suffrage.

faith, which to an ordinary reader of ecclesiastical history seem very novel indeed, were in reality held by the ancient Fathers; and that the entire absence of any mention of such things from their writings, and, indeed, the occurrence of many observations of a totally different complexion, were due to the fact that the Fathers held these beliefs implicitly and unconsciously.[1] Conservative belief in household suffrage, previous to last Easter, must have been very similar in character to the Patristic belief in the Immaculate Conception. It is not very difficult, either in the one case or in the other, to show how wholly unconscious this belief must have been. The speeches of Lord Derby, of Mr. Disraeli, of Lord Stanley,[2] of Sir Stafford Northcote,[3] of Mr. Hardy,[4] of Sir Hugh Cairns,[5] even during the last two years, will furnish, to any one who cares to refer to them, abundant materials for a catena of Conservative authorities against a large reduction of the franchise. They have been quoted again and again in the course of the last few months both in Parliament and in the Press, and it is not necessary to repeat them here. Any one who cares to refer to 'Hansard' will find that the danger of lowering the franchise even to 6*l.* or 7*l.*, because it would give to the working classes a preponderating power, was one on which the Conservative speakers constantly dwelt; and that no hint ever escaped them, that a still larger reduction, and the bestowal of a still more preponderating power, would have in any degree diminished their objections. The most pointed statement of the Conservative view that can be found was given by Mr. Disraeli in his speech on Mr. Baines' bill for introducing a 6*l.* franchise, in May, 1865.[6] As it was delivered just

[1] Cranborne is referring to the doctrine of the immaculate conception, declared an article of faith by Pius IX in 1854, despite the feeling of some bishops that it was not sufficiently prominent in scripture or tradition to be so dignified.
[2] Edward Henry Stanley (1826–93), Derby's son; M.P. King's Lynn and foreign secretary; later, as 15th Earl of Derby, foreign secretary under Disraeli, 1874–8; left the Conservatives in 1880 and served as Gladstone's colonial secretary, 1882–5, but then became a Liberal Unionist.
[3] Stafford Henry Northcote (1818–87), M.P. North Devon and secretary of state for India; later chancellor of the exchequer under Disraeli, 1874–80, joint leader of the party with Salisbury, 1881–5, first lord of the treasury, 1885–6, and foreign secretary, 1886–7; created 1st Earl of Iddesleigh 1885.
[4] Gathorne Hardy (1814–1906), M.P. Oxford University and home secretary; later at the war and India Offices in Disraeli's second ministry, and lord president of the council under Salisbury; created 1st Viscount Cranbrook 1878, and earl 1892.
[5] Hugh McCalmont Cairns (1819–85), since February 1867 1st Baron Cairns (earldom 1878); solicitor-general, 1858–9, attorney-general, 1866, lord justice of appeal 1866–7; later Disraeli's lord chancellor, 1868 and 1874–80.
[6] May 8th. Disraeli warned strongly in this speech against democracy.

'THE CONSERVATIVE SURRENDER'

before the general election which was then impending, it was accepted generally as a manifesto of the opinions of the leaders of the party. But, in truth, the case would not be materially altered, even if these strong expressions of opinion did not stand on record. Even if Mr. Disraeli had carefully abstained from uttering a word against the reduction of the borough franchise, the delusion encouraged would not have been less real, though it would have been less flagrant. There was no doubt at all as to the nature of the resistance offered by the Conservative leaders in 1866 to Mr. Gladstone's bill; there was no doubt of the nature of the support they received in doing so. The division which carried them to power was won by the votes of half-a-dozen men. Numbers of those who voted with them on that occasion would have supported any leader and have accepted almost any bill rather than have promoted a measure of household suffrage. The Conservative leaders knew this perfectly well. They were not ignorant of the motives which inspired the enthusiasm with which the eloquence of Mr. Lowe was received, or of the sentiments which animated the majority of the speeches delivered from their own side of the House. Both in public and in private they were stimulating those feelings to the utmost of their power. Not a single hint escaped from any of them which could damp the ardour of their anti-democratic supporters and allies. By every means at their command they not only allowed but encouraged and sanctioned the belief that they were resisting as excessive the admission of the lower classes to the franchise, proposed in Mr. Gladstone's bill. Their supporters were fully hoodwinked. They voted in blind reliance on the assurances they had received. In order to defeat a proposal which they feared might ultimately result in household suffrage, they ousted Mr. Gladstone from power; and when they greeted that victory with tumultous applause, no presentiment crossed a single mind of the utter ruin of their hopes and their cause which by that very victory they had accomplished.

And yet at this very time, by their own avowal, the Conservative leaders had made up their minds to propose an enfranchisement of the poorer classes far exceeding anything contained in any bill that had yet been presented to the House of Commons, and falling in no degree short of the utmost that Mr. Bright or Mr. Forster had ever demanded in their speeches. Mr. Disraeli has told us that household suffrage had been the secret aspiration of the chiefs of the Conservative party ever since 1859, and Lord Derby has never said a word to repudiate the indiscreet confession of his lieutenant. On the contrary, he boldly stated in the House of Lords that when he accepted office, after Lord Dunkellin's motion, he did so with the full intention of outbidding the Liberals on the subject of Reform.[1]

But, though they had thus made up their minds, they kept that determination to themselves. They knew that large numbers of those on whose aid they counted were acting on an entirely opposite belief. They knew that if they had breathed a hint from which their real intentions could have been gathered, their expected victory would have been turned into a shattering defeat; and therefore they kept their counsel, and encouraged the profitable delusion which was conveying them to power. They kept it, apparently, even from their colleagues in opposition, or those colleagues would hardly have plunged so deeply into pledges which they have since been forced to shake off. They certainly kept it, after the critical division, from their colleagues in office, as we know from the disclosures of the three seceding Secretaries of State, – not only during the remainder of the Session of 1866, but during the whole of the ensuing recess and for many days after Parliament had met in the beginning of the present year. Indeed, it was not till the earlier struggles of the session were over and majorities had been obtained by apparent restrictions upon the compound householder, that the project of Tory democracy, which had been so long and so sedulously concealed, was at last given to the world.

What defence is it possible to offer for tactics of this kind? The world politely speaks of the 'reticence' of last year. To encourage your friends to believe that your intentions are exactly the opposite of what they really are – to watch them acting for you in that belief and thereby ruining the cause they cherish most, and yet to sustain them in their error – is not 'reticence' a flimsy euphemism for such proceedings? Lord Derby told his audience at the Mansion House[2] that he was indifferent to obloquy upon this subject; and others of his Ministry have used similar language. It was hardly necessary to tell us so. If he was indifferent to the moral character of the course he was taking, he would hardly trouble himself about the language in which he would be described by others. But that audience were familiar with reticence of this kind; and some of them occasionally suffer from its effects. We have heard much lately of a case in which some merchants practised upon the general public reticence of this peculiar nature. They invited the public to become shareholders in a concern, which they represented as likely to be lucrative, though they knew it to be insolvent; they did not *say*

[1] See below, pp. 272–3.
[2] On 7 August 1867.

'THE CONSERVATIVE SURRENDER'

it was solvent, only they were reticent on the subject, and allowed their silence to lead others into risk and ruin. But there was this difference between them and the politicians who subsequently imitated them – that while the politicians gained the object of many years' ambition by the delusion into which they had lured their allies, the merchants lost all they had. Lord Cranworth, delivering judgment in the House of Lords, reprobated the reticence of the ruined merchants in language stronger than we care to reprint;[1] in what terms will the calm judgment of posterity estimate the manœuvres of the successful politicians? If they wish to seek for an historical parallel, they will have to go far back in our annals. They will find none during the period for which parliamentary government has existed. Neither the recklessness of Charles Fox, nor the venality of Henry Fox, nor the cynicism of Walpole will furnish them with a case in point. They will have to go back to the time when the last Revolution was preparing – to the days when Sunderland directed the councils and accepted the favours of James, while he was negotiating the invasion of William.

But it is said on their behalf that the offence was condoned because the party pushed them on. The assertion has undoubtedly been frequently made. It was advanced with especial emphasis by Mr. Disraeli in his speech on the third reading, in which he represented the country gentlemen behind him as a band of buoyant and untameable Reformers who were perpetually dragging old-fashioned Conservatives like himself somewhat faster than they cared to go. The description was humorous; but it was purely an effort of imagination. There was no general expression of opinion on the part of the Conservative party in favour of the bill. Nothing was more remarkable than their general silence in the debates. No division, indeed, was taken against the bill, because, the Liberal party having decided to support it, the Ministers would have obtained with their aid an overwhelming majority. The only critical division that was taken was upon a Liberal amendment involving as the immediate and primary issue the question of the personal payment of rates.[2] It was

---

[1] The lord chancellor, Cranworth, gave judgement on 15 August 1867 in a case arising out of the failure in the previous year of the great discount house of Overend, Gurney & Co. The firm had tried to extricate itself from insolvency by forming a joint-stock company whose prospectus concealed its true position, and Cranborne himself had lost a good deal of money in the ensuing collapse.

[2] This was the division of 12 April 1867 on an amendment by Gladstone which would have enfranchised borough householders paying their rates through their landlords – i.e. the compounders. Disraeli having committed himself to the principle of personal payment of rates as a condition of the vote, the amendment was a fundamental challenge to his bill. Gladstone was aiming ultimately to establish a £5 rating

taken during the period when the restrictions upon the compound householder were believed in Conservative circles to be a genuine security. How little the division of the 12th of April can be taken as evidence of Conservative approval of the bill is evident from the fact that such men as General Peel[1] and Sir R. Knightley[2] and others who have denounced both the bill and the Ministers in the strongest terms, may be found in the Ministerial majority on that occasion. The position of the unofficial members of the party was undoubtedly very much changed by the Ministerial surrender. From the moment that a household suffrage was promised from the Conservative Treasury Bench it became certain that a Reform Bill and a strong Reform Bill would be passed. The hopes of deriving any advantage from further resistance were consequently much weakened; while the danger of quarrelling with the new constituency, whose advent to power was assured, grew into alarming proportions. Many thought the position hopeless, and submitted in silence to a disaster which seemed inevitable. But their perplexity, created by the Government itself, in no way absolves it. No one will pretend that the Conservatives, if consulted on the first day of the Session, would have advocated household suffrage. An attempt was made by the agents of the Government to obtain some such expression of opinion from a meeting at the Carlton; but it signally failed. No resolution could be carried; and the meeting broke up in confusion.[3] Still less would the Conservative party, or any considerable fraction of it, have followed Mr. Disraeli in June last year, if they had guessed, what he has since informed them, that he and his nominal chief had already resolved upon household suffrage as their policy. And that, after all, is the real question when we are inquiring how far their studied and successful reticence *at that time* did or did not sin against the laws of honour.

qualification with no exclusions above it, and in this he was supported by Cranborne, who voted for the amendment, together with five other Conservatives. But large Liberal defections from Gladstone meant that the government won by 310 votes to 289.

[1] General Jonathan Peel (1799–1879), brother of Sir Robert Peel; M.P. Huntingdon; secretary of state for war 1858–9 and 1866–7.
[2] Sir Rainald Knightley (1819–95), later 1st Baron Knightley; M.P. South Northants.
[3] The Carlton Club meeting of 28 February 1867 was organised by a group of Conservative backbenchers, Laird, Graves, Goldney, and Jervis, who favoured household suffrage and, encouraged by Disraeli, wanted to give proof of the support for it in the party. Though the meeting was not unanimous, and Laird and Graves did not press their resolutions, a large majority of the 150 or so Conservative M.P.s present seems to have favoured household suffrage, qualified by three years' residence, personal payment of rates, and plural voting. Cranborne does not mention the party meeting of 15 March, when the government bill was presented to backbenchers and apparently well received.

'THE CONSERVATIVE SURRENDER'

But personal questions are among the least of those which are forced upon us by the events of the last few years. The statesmen whose conduct we have been discussing, take them at their worst, are but the effects of a cause. One or two of them have shown a freedom from scruple surpassing all former example, others have shown a feebleness of conviction which it is difficult to understand. But their unscrupulousness and their facility alike have only borne testimony to the working of some strong external cause, by which the one has been attracted and the other has been coerced. It is true, as the Duke of Argyll[1] observed, that Lord Derby, in his determination not to become a stop-gap, has become a weathercock: but the nimblest weathercock does not turn upon its pivot unless there is a breeze to turn it. No one can now affect to doubt that there is a democratic power which, either relatively or absolutely, is a most potent factor among the political forces of our time. No one can be blind to the ease with which it has swept down all the bulwarks, political or social, which were trusted to obstruct its progress. A few bold speeches upon platforms, a day's holiday-making among the populations of a few large towns, has sufficed to bring every opposing power to its feet. The party whose proclaimed mission it was to restrain it, the class whose power it aims to strike down, and whose resistance in other days was manful and tenacious, have been the foremost to bring in their submission, and eager to sue for its favour by the most unreserved concessions. Whatever the cause of this pitiable humiliation, whether the democratic force is in itself really stronger, or whether its present power merely proves that the classes which should have restrained it have lost heart and nerve, the triumph of the present year, won so easily after so many brave announcements of resistance, must equally suggest disquieting forebodings of the future that lies before us. They are a presage of assaults, probably of victories, compared to which that which has been achieved this year will be looked upon by posterity as trivial. A transfer of power which last year was generally denounced as revolutionary, has this year been passed – as far as the principle went – hurriedly and with little debate. Such a sudden change cannot be attributed to calm conviction. The inference must be either that the system of parliamentary party as a machinery for representing opinions widely prevalent, has failed to act, or that the classes in this country, whose interest is opposed to democracy, have no heart to fight. In either case we may be certain that these facts, newly ascertained by the world,

[1] George Douglas Campbell (1823-1900), 8th Duke of Argyll; lord privy seal in Russell's late ministry.

will go a good deal further in their effect than the Act which has just been placed upon the Statute Book.

When the troops run away at the first charge, it is of course difficult to decide whether they have lost because they could not win, or because they dared not try to win. But, for practical purposes, the world generally assumes that when an army does not discover its hopeless inferiority of strength until the powder begins to burn, its nerves are more to blame for the result than its numbers. A school, however, has arisen in recent days which formally denies that the bloodless conflicts of the political world have any analogy, either in the feelings of honour that should animate them, or the rules by which they should be judged, with the conflicts of the field. According to their teaching, nothing ought ever to be fought out. It is legitimate to show a bold front, and use brave language, and proclaim strong opinions in precise words: but it is equally legitimate, or rather it is a sacred duty, the moment that a determined resistance shows itself, practically to give those words the lie. It is hot-headed, it is dangerous, it is Quixotic, to terminate a Ministry, or imperil a party's prospects, or risk a single jolt in the progress of the administrative machine, in order to uphold deep convictions and to be true to a cherished cause. The desperate resistance which our fathers made to the last Reform Bill is blamed, not so much because their views were mistaken, as because it was madness to defend those views against so formidable an assault. It is said, – and men seem to think that condemnation can go no further than such a censure – that they brought us within twenty-four hours of revolution. Their successors boast that their prudence will never go so near to the heels of danger. No one will suspect them of it. But is it in truth so great an evil, when the dearest interests and the most sincere convictions are at stake, to go within twenty-four hours of revolution? Did the great classes whose battle had been so fierce, respect each other less when it was once lost and won? Did Sir Robert Peel, who fought it to the end, lose by his tenacity in the estimation of his countrymen? Did the cause he represented suffer through his temerity? He was indeed beaten down in 1832, vainly struggling for a hopeless cause. But before six years had passed he was at the head of half the House of Commons: and before ten years had gone by he led the most powerful Ministry our century has seen.

We live in other days. It may be doubtful how far the more modern plan of yielding every political citadel on the first summons, in order to avert the possibility of disturbance, really springs from the peace-loving

'THE CONSERVATIVE SURRENDER'

sentiments on which it is sometimes justified. There can be little doubt that it tends to screen timidity or foster self-seeking in politicians according to their temperament; and that they are beginning to look on principles which may be upheld with so little danger, and abandoned with so little shame, as mere counters in the game which they are playing. But there can be no question that this view of political duty is widely held among the classes who have always governed this country, and who until the next election will continue to govern it. They value our institutions, they dislike organic change, they object to a large transfer of power. But it is now well established that whatever these objections may be, they are such as a very moderate display of physical force is quite sufficient to remove. This spirit is so different from that which the governing classes of this country have shown during the long period of its history, that it is not easy to estimate the full consequences of the change. But it must inevitably affect largely not only the working of the ordinary machinery of parliamentary government, but the existence of our institutions themselves.

We have been for so many generations accustomed to government by party majorities that we have learned to look upon it as the most natural contrivance in the world. We admire it: and our admiration is justified hitherto by its practical success. But any one who attempts to analyse it theoretically will not be surprised that foreigners, who can only see it on that side, should be unable to share our enthusiasm. As it now exists, it differs utterly from any other system existing in the world; and even from its own self as it first sprang into existence shortly after the Revolution. Its original object was to organise the opinion of the House of Commons, in order to enable that opinion to work smoothly with the enfeebled but still considerable power of the Crown. It still serves that end in a limited degree. The greater part of the power still practically retained by the Crown depends upon the influence it can exercise on individual statesmen, and through them on the dominant party of the day. But the centre of power has shifted: and politicians have long looked for their advancement not to the Crown but to the constituencies. From the outbreak of the French Revolution Ministries have depended more and more for their existence upon the policy they pursued and the legislation they recommended. Simultaneously the mutual relations of statesmen forming a Ministry have become more strictly defined; and a curious theory of constitutional responsibility on their part has been evolved, at which the world would have laughed very much if Swift had put it into his 'Laputa', but which is enforced with perfect gravity, and no little acrimony, by politicians against each other. The theory is that every act of any member of the Government is the act of the Government as a whole; and that as a whole they are jointly and severally responsible for it. Of course, if responsibility meant anything serious – if members of the Government were held mutually responsible in their fortunes, like partners in trade – the theory would not live for a session. It ignores the fact that each member of the Government is fully occupied and has no time to look into the conduct of his colleagues; and that moreover each member of the Government, except upon the largest questions, acts in perfect independence of his colleagues. Still more it ignores the fact that fifteen men wholly of one mind are not to be found upon earth in these evil days, and that for the conduct of public business it is as necessary to acknowledge the sway of a majority in Cabinets as in Legislatures. On the one hand, it would be intolerable that Lord Stanley, while engaged in reconciling France and Prussia, should be held, in any practical sense, to be responsible for the answers the Duke of Marlborough[1] might be giving to a country clergyman; on the other hand, no reasonable man could be expected to believe that two men like Lord Palmerston and Mr. Gladstone were cordially agreed upon every decision to which the Cabinet had arrived. No well-informed person actually believes in these assumptions. It is well known that the *moral* responsibility of a Minister for acts of administration ends with the department he actually conducts; and that his silent adhesion to a proposal made by his colleagues in Parliament need mean no more than that he does not consider his objection sufficiently important to justify him in breaking up a Government. But for every parliamentary purpose, the responsibility is insisted on as if it represented an actual fact. Not only at that time, but at any future time, the Minister is held to be estopped from criticising the action of his colleagues, however much he may have disapproved of it at the time: nor can he in debate repudiate any censure that may be passed upon him as one of the authors of the obnoxious measure. If he be a man who values the expressed opinion of others, this responsibility for the acts of others in which he took no part, and which he heartily condemns, may be a heavy burden upon him: for he is absolutely precluded from publicly revealing his freedom from any real share in the error committed. It is strange that in a day when so little mercy is shown to fictions or anomalies of any kind, however venerable their origin, this one of modern creation

---

[1] John Winston Spencer Churchill (1822–83), 7th Duke of Marlborough, the lord president of the council.

'THE CONSERVATIVE SURRENDER'

should have shown so much vitality; but in proportion as all others are crumbling away, the House of Commons clings to it with a more and more tenacious affection.

To men without distinct opinions, and mainly careful about the material advantages and social promotion conferred by office, such an arrangement must be eminently satisfactory. It is a kind of insurance against individual blunders. Like the rope in Alpine climbing, it forces the colleagues who have not slipped to pick up the one who has: and as it is unlikely that the slip of any one should pull the whole body down, or that many of them should slip at the same moment, it practically prevents the Government being injured by administrative mishaps, unless they are of the most momentous kind. But the arrangement has for numbers of years been cheerfully accepted, not only by the limpets of place, but by high-minded and independent men. The explanation of their submission is to be found in the objects for which party exists. The consideration that has reconciled them to accepting so largely the responsibility for other men's acts and thoughts, has been that the great cause, in the support of which their party was banded together, could not be successfully defended without such sacrifices. But for such a motive the compliances of office and the unquestioning obedience exacted by party discipline would be alike without justification. It is the great end on which all are in common bent, which contributes all that is noble or even innocent to party warfare. The tactics of parliamentary parties are often hardly to be distinguished from faction: the agencies by which they operate upon the wavering or the wayward are far from exalted: the temptation to purchase allies by concessions of principle is enormous. The one ennobling element, the palliation, if not the atonement, for all shortcomings, is that all the members of a party are enlisted in common to serve one great unselfish cause, and that it is in that service that their zeal, even when least scrupulous, is working. Take this great end away, and parties become nothing but joint-stock companies for the attainment and preservation of place.

It is clear that the system of party will become beneficial or noxious according as it approximates to one or the other standard. As an instrument for giving expression to great principles, and insuring for them a full hearing, it has been of singular value. Moralists, reasoning on abstract grounds, may demur to a plan which to so large an extent utilises the meaner principles of human nature for good ends. But no one who looks at the course of English history for the last fifty years can doubt that a system which makes it the interest of politicians to mass themselves in one or other of the two great camps into which human thought is divided, and, so opposed, to compete with each other for the nation's good will, has been marvellously efficient in securing cautious and regulated progress. But its whole utility depends upon the elements which distinguish it from a mere tout of place-hunters. The vigilance of interested opposition is ill purchased by the necessity of entrusting the destinies of the empire to men who rule in the spirit of adventurers. To which of the two standards does the conduct of the present Government approach?

Up to this time party leaders have observed with substantial fidelity the conditions under which alone parliamentary parties can be prevented from becoming instruments of organised corruption. Hitherto they have always borne a banner; they have been the votaries of a special principle. If their principle has been in favour with the nation, they have held office: if the fashion of the time has been against them, they have remained in opposition. Some leaders have occasionally strained the rule. We have often expressed the opinion that Sir Robert Peel, when he had become convinced that Free Trade was a necessity, acted wrongly in himself undertaking its introduction, instead of leaving the task to those who were less pledged against it. But he protected himself from all imputation of selfish motives by taking the earliest opportunity of resigning. Lord Palmerston, again, was far too fond of combining a Conservative inaction with a great warmth of Liberal professions. But it has been reserved for Lord Derby and Mr. Disraeli to break formally with the traditions of the past, and openly to accept the more ignoble view of party obligation. In this matter we have no mere inferences to deal with. Lord Derby, with perfect candour and with characteristic clearness of language, has recently described his own motives, and his own mode of proceeding:

> My Lords, I have upon former occasions, unfortunately, occupied the position of a Minister on sufferance. I have upon two previous occasions attempted to carry on the Government with a minority in the House of Commons, and upon both occasions I have failed. It was, therefore, a very hard, and, I will say, a very sincere triumph of duty and public over private considerations, when I felt myself for a third time called upon, under peculiar circumstances, to take the important and responsible duty of First Minister of the Crown. I did not do so without feeling fully the responsibility of the duties which devolved upon me, and the whole burden which I had to undertake. I did not intend for a third time to be made a mere stop-gap until it should suit the convenience of the Liberal party to forget their dissensions, and bring forward a measure which should oust us from office and replace them there; *and I determined that I would take such a course as would convert, if possible, an existing majority into*

'THE CONSERVATIVE SURRENDER'

a practical minority.[1] – LORD DERBY'S *Speech on Second Reading of Reform Bill*.[2]

Not a word about the cause of which he was the champion, or the principles which his party existed to defend. Not a word about his pledges and professions, or the tactics by which his lieutenants had ousted Mr. Gladstone from office. When summoned to power his ambition was not to struggle for the Conservative principles which he had up to that moment advocated, or fall in the attempt. He did not welcome the opportunity of showing the sincerity of his Opposition professions by his practice when in office. The simple standard he proposed to himself to reach was to bring forward such a measure as would save himself from being 'ousted from office,' and would convert the majority of his opponents into a minority; and, as he subsequently informed the House of Lords,[3] he was well aware that that measure was 'a leap in the dark.'

Lord Derby does not pay the homage of hypocrisy to the virtues he is renouncing, and the very frankness of his avowal shows that he knew that his doctrines were shared by his colleagues, and by a considerable portion of his supporters. It is quite clear that if they find any general acceptance, they must transform the whole nature of parliamentary government. The great common end, the ennobling cause is gone. If it is still professed, it no longer exists in the first place. To please majorities, to prevent his opponents from uniting, to avert ousting divisions, is avowed to be the leader's highest aim, his first thought on taking office. It may of course be that these great objects are compatible with adhesion to the principles professed in opposition. But in the case of a leader taking office with an avowed minority, the probabilities are strongly the other way. If the two come in conflict, which master will he serve? Will he adhere to the principles, and disregard the 'ousting' majority, or will he bend to the majority and renounce the principles? The events of this session furnish a melancholy proof that Lord Derby had fully counted the cost, and had made up his mind, whatever the price might be, not to be ousted a third time.

If he had avowed this plan at the close of the session of 1866, instead of last July, we should have confidently predicted that it must break down for want of instruments. We should have said that it would be impossible to find a sufficient number of competent statesmen inclined

---

[1] *Hansard* gives: 'an existing minority into a practical majority'.
[2] 22 July 1867. In December 1866 Derby had written to Sir John Pakington: 'I accepted office very unwillingly, but having accepted it, I mean to keep it as long as I can...' (quoted in Cowling, p. xi).
[3] On 6 August 1867.

for such a service. But after the present year's experience we must not count too confidently on this security. We must face it as one of the probabilities of the future, that one at least of our great parties will work, at all events for some time, upon Lord Derby's principle. They may for convenience sake retain old names, but they will carry no banner, and will be attached to no special cause. The necessity will still be on them of conciliating the majority, and of avoiding the supreme calamity of being ousted by their opponents. Having abandoned so much for this object, they will not shrink from the further sacrifices it may require. If the House of Commons should turn out for the time to be Conservative they will be very brave defenders of our ancient institutions. If, as is more probable, the House of Commons calls for somewhat drastic legislation upon Ireland or upon the Established Church, they will see the necessity of 'removing all cause for agitation,' and 'settling the question upon a permanent principle;' and will concede all that the most extreme of their opponents is demanding. As the wind blows, so will they point. Any minister who takes it as his first principle that he will not be 'ousted,' renounces all pretension to independence. He becomes the slave of the majority of the House of Commons. He is a leader in no other sense but that in which the first horse in a team is called a leader: he is the first to be driven. He will probably be paid in the coin which he has selected for his guerdon. The House of Commons, like all popular bodies, is avaricious of power; and so long as he does its bidding without shrinking, his minority will be converted into a majority, and he will not be ousted by the re-united Liberals.

This will of course, except in the name, be no longer party government. Whether it can be worked for any length of time by statesmen of the existing stamp remains to be seen. It is possible, we hope it is not probable, that the classes who have hitherto furnished the mass of our statesmen, will accept this new definition of the word. They may look upon it as an honourable function to act as the mere index of popular pressure, as a piece of mechanism for recording in the form of statutes the ideas and convictions which others impose upon them. They may not shrink from combining with such an office the external demeanour of independence, the profession of real opinions, and a pretension to individual consistency. This may be the course of events; for the feeble and halting policy which the classes who now govern have pursued for some years past, may well suggest a doubt whether the indifference to principle which has infected our statesmen so remarkably, has not eaten deep into the stratum of society from which they come. We cherish the

'THE CONSERVATIVE SURRENDER'

hope, however, that they will choose a course which better becomes the character they have inherited. If the social battle is for the future to be fought by mercenary troops, it is probable that the more independent classes will retire to a great extent from the service; and that a very different description of men from those who have hitherto been prominent will come to the front. In the lower ranks of the party organisation a similar change must follow. The army of professional electioneerers will not diminish. The example of America assures us that these industrious labourers grow both in numbers and in power in proportion as parties become more mobile in their principles, and more interested in their aims. But these have hitherto not formed the main strength of English parties. The enormous patronage, which in America constitutes the chief apparatus of their handicraft, is almost wholly wanting here. Parties have mainly been worked by volunteers; and it is obvious that volunteers will receive a severe discouragement under the new principles. They cannot be expected to feel as lively an interest as Lord Derby does in the question whether he is 'ousted' or not. The intrigues of politicians, the succession of office-holders, the vicissitudes of individual careers, have had for them but little interest beyond what by-standers may feel in a game which they are watching. They, and their fathers before them, have loved their party and worked for it, not for the fame or power it might bring to particular men, but for the cause which it has represented. They have valued it for its pledges, guaranteed to them by its past performance – for the institutions it has upheld, or the legislation it has promised. In the long run, when the effect of long habit has worn off, their attachment to it must depend on its fidelity to some principles which command their allegiance. If it should become, as it now seems in danger of becoming, merely a banner round which adventurers, greedy for political loot, can rally, it will no longer be served by the invaluable because unselfish zeal of those who have no loot to gain.

These changes in the character of the men by whom the party system is worked, evil in themselves, will be specially mischievous in their tendency to suspend the mediating influence which party government has hitherto exercised in the working of the constitution. The House of Commons was certainly never made, by those who devised it, to do the work of an executive. Its size, its instability, its swift obedience to every changing breath of opinion that sweeps over the popular mind, its lack of any special provision to secure within its body the presence of trained administrative talent, all unfit it for such a function. It has been the great danger of our constitution, visible so far back as a century ago to the keen eye of Montesquieu, that the course of events was tending to place the House of Commons in this position. Generation by generation it has been growing in strength, while all around it has been losing ground. By dint often of straining its prerogatives far beyond their first intention, but still persistently and successfully, it has acquired a complete control over every portion of the executive. In every matter within the competence of the Crown, the 'humble' addresses of the House of Commons have all but the force of law. And it is no slight aggravation of the danger of this usurped prerogative that these addresses are not, like bills, subjected to repeated reconsideration, but are introduced, discussed, and finally passed in a single sitting. Up to this time, however, no serious mischief has ensued, because one important check has remained. The one thing that has hitherto controlled the capricious omnipotence of the House, has been the organisation of parliamentary parties, and the independence of party chiefs. It has been well understood that a parliamentary leader would not endure to be overruled on any important point of policy; and that he could not concede this claim without a loss of personal honour. The House, therefore, has always been compelled to act with caution, under pain of bringing the whole machine of Government to an immediate dead-lock. The majority has been forced into fidelity to its leaders, under penalty of losing its own political supremacy.

But, upon Lord Derby's new principles, this check is at an end. The independence of the Minister, his refusal to accept a policy from others, is essential to its existence. As long as his chief object is to uphold his avowed principles, the House of Commons must choose between an acceptance of his policy or a change of ministry. But when the Minister's chief object is that he shall not be 'ousted,' and his measures are framed mainly to secure a majority, the House of Commons ceases to be under any check at all. Ministerial resignations in consequence of parliamentary defeats will have become an antiquated superstition. The Minister will be there simply to do its bidding. He will no more think of resigning because that bidding is not agreeable to him than if he were the Sergeant-at-Arms or the door-keeper. The last check to the executive supremacy of the House of Commons will be removed. Such a result would be formidable enough with a House of Commons practised in its duties, and chosen from classes who are used to the responsibilities of power. It is no trivial addition to the dangers of our present situation that it is to a Parliament thus disorganised and leaderless that the representatives of the vast masses of new electors are to be introduced.

'THE CONSERVATIVE SURRENDER'

How badly such a system works may be learned from the experience of the session which has just expired. The Ministry have acted conscientiously up to Lord Derby's teaching. They have laid it down as a vital principle, from which they would suffer no departure, that they should not be ejected from office. But on every other point they have been willing, and something more than willing, to defer to the House of Commons. Whatever the majority of the House desired to do, they were willing to accept. The consequences of this abdication of leadership we have seen, and its effects the nation will feel for a long time. It showed itself in many minor matters; such as the strange vacillation of the Government upon the question of Hyde Park,[1] and upon the punishment of the Fenian convicts.[2] But the Reform Bill was the capital instance. A session in which all parties began with the intention of passing a moderate Reform Bill, has ended in the adoption of household suffrage. So unforeseen were all the changes it underwent, so entirely independent did its progress become of the politicians who impelled it, that the form in which it emerged from Committee was diametrically opposed to the descriptions given of it, and the pledges contracted in regard to it by at least three of the Cabinet Ministers who defended it in its earliest stages. A measure of mild change, strictly guarded, was put in at one end of the hopper, and after a due lapse of time, a revolution came out at the other end. The agency of no one man or set of men was apparently responsible for this result. The action of a popular assembly emancipated from its leaders, is not the result of any distinct volition. It represents no plan or idea. It moves along, by inscrutable laws of its own, now obeying an impulse from without, now expressing the resultant of the conflicting forces within it, in consequences which surprise and perplex all the disputants alike. Its movements are as impulsive and irresponsible as those of a crowd. To call it rash or reckless, would be to attribute to it an informing spirit and a capacity of perception which it

[1] Ministers were much exercised by the attempts of the Reform League to hold mass gatherings in Hyde Park. The refusal of entry to the park in July 1866 had resulted in the celebrated riots; and in May 1867 the League did hold a Reform meeting there, in defiance of a prohibition issued by the home secretary, Walpole, who was widely blamed for weak handling of the question and resigned in consequence. The government was advised that it had the legal right to prevent such meetings, but was reluctant to risk a clash by trying forcibly to do so. A Royal Parks Bill introduced in May 1867 to deal with the problem was abandoned in August.

[2] After the failure of the insurrectionary nationalist Fenian movement to carry out an armed rising in Ireland in March 1867, the government showed uncertainty in dealing with those convicted of participation and sentenced to death. The cabinet decided against reprieving one of the principals, Burke, on a Wednesday and changed its mind under pressure of opinion the following Saturday.

does not possess. But because careful and moderate legislation is often, of necessity, complicated, and must always depend on a multitude of detailed and balanced considerations, the legislation of a leaderless assembly will generally be violent. Extreme measures are simple, easily stated and understood. Their lack of restrictions and reservations saves time and spares thought; and, therefore, they offer an overwhelming recommendation to a body of men with whom leisure and mental power are equally limited. For making startling changes in a fearless manner, there is nothing to compare with an assembly which follows and trusts no leader. But history must be rewritten if we are to believe that such a body can conduct for any length of time the ordinary government of an extensive empire.

We do not think so meanly of our countrymen as to believe that a House of Commons, working on the system that has prevailed this year, would long enjoy their confidence or be permitted to exercise supreme power on their behalf. If the new doctrines are to prevail, and Ministries are to be formed on the mere principle of not being 'ousted,' we do not doubt that far more extensive changes are at hand. The House of Commons will decline in authority, and supreme political power will find some new depositary. But we dwell on the matter rather for the purpose of calling the attention of the classes in this country who dread violent change to the position in which the recent course of events has placed them. Most of them have been accustomed to take politics very easily. They have pursued their business and made their money, and enjoyed their success without much solicitude as to the future of the system under which they have prospered. They know that no serious change has happened in their time, or their father's time, or for many generations before that; and they have an abiding faith that, whatever Parliament may resolve, business will go on much as it did before, and that those institutions of the country which are material to their own comfort and enjoyment, will thrive on as they have hitherto thriven. But the results of these two last years concern them more nearly than they think. It is not merely that our institutions have changed – that their development has made progress in a direction which we think the wrong one. It is not merely that the power of a class once great has been shaken; it is not merely that the poorest have been made supreme. The issues of this conflict are far more momentous. The very conditions under which our institutions exist have been changed; the equilibrium of forces by which they have been sustained is shaken. The defences on which we have been wont to rely have proved utterly rotten. They have

'THE CONSERVATIVE SURRENDER'

broken down absolutely before they were even subjected to serious pressure. The breakwaters that were to protect us from the fury of popular passion have crumbled away in fine weather. What seemed to be strong and durable has proved worse than worthless. Those who have trusted to the faith of public men, or the patriotism of parliamentary parties, or the courage of aristocratic classes, must now find other resting-places on which to repose their confidence. The supports on which they have hitherto relied will pierce the hand that leans on them.

If the Conservative surrender of 1867 be considered, not in its results but in the state of things that it reveals, it is a phenomenon of tremendous import. The evils of the measure itself, dangerous as we think it, are not necessarily irremediable. If the probability arises that the newly-admitted classes will combine to abuse their power, the classes who are threatened may combine on their side in self-defence; and, if their mettle were equal to that of their assailants, the conflict would be far from desperate. The hopelessness, if hopelessness there be, lies in the spirit and feeling on the part of the Conservative classes which the vicissitudes of this conflict have disclosed. To appreciate the full significance of this great surrender we must not look to the mere clauses of the Act which it has produced, or even content ourselves with scrutinizing the conduct of individual statesmen. To understand what a headlong rout it has been, we must take into view the earlier as well as the later movements of the struggle, the manifestoes that were put forth, the claims that were made, the positions that were occupied during the years which preceded and led up to this last fatal campaign. Let any one who wishes to form a just conception of the feelings of the middle and upper classes upon the subject of Reform during the last few years, devote himself to the ungrateful but instructive task of reading not only the past parliamentary debates, but the speeches to constituents and the articles in periodical publications on the subject. There were many differences of opinion as to whether it would be wise or not to reduce the borough franchise in some degree, and there were many discussions as to the degree of reduction that was desirable. But there was an overwhelming preponderance of opinion that no enfranchisement ought to be admitted which should enable the working classes to take the whole political power of the country into their hands. Household suffrage was the cry of a few isolated Radicals. In 1863, at a Reform meeting held at Leeds, Mr. Forster was asked how many men in the House of Commons would vote for a proposal of household suffrage. His reply was that there were not fifteen. Even as late as last year, when Sir Roundell Palmer[1] volunteered a profession of household suffrage, there was a general outcry at the eccentricity of his declaration, and no one pledged himself more strongly in opposition to it than the present Secretary of State for India.[2] And the opinions which are thus publicly recorded were only a faint echo of those which might be heard in every private circle.

Less than twelve months passed and all was changed. When household suffrage, after much preliminary manœuvring, was at last openly proposed by the Minister, it was received with much murmuring indeed in private, but externally with almost universal acquiescence. Only a few scattered men here and there in Parliament ventured to oppose it. The Ministers who were most deeply and most recently pledged against it swallowed their pledges in silence. The Peers accepted obsequiously what they were known to detest. The country gentlemen, scared, hustled, perplexed, 'supposed it was inevitable,' and made no effort to move. The middle classes sent up but one cry, and that was to 'settle the question.' They said that the agitation of it had a tendency to disturb trade, and to prolong the monetary crisis. Few people approved, but all, or nearly all, bowed their heads in humble submission.

It was certainly a startling change, and one that naturally perplexed those who had adopted their opinions after calm consideration, and did not see what had happened to refute them. Suddenly the whole of the forces of resistance that had rallied so numerously, and had fought with so much apparent resolution last year, disappeared like Rabshakeh's army, in a single night. As Mr. Disraeli remarked in one of his speeches against Sir Robert Peel[3] –

What a compliment to a Minister, not only to vote for him, but to vote for him against your opinions, and in favour of opinions which he always drilled you to distrust. That was a scene, I believe, unprecedented in the House of Commons. Indeed, I recollect nothing equal to it, unless it be the conversion of the Saxons by Charlemagne, which is the only historical incident which bears any parallel to that illustrious occasion. Ranged on the banks of the Rhine, the Saxons determined to resist any further movement on the part of the great Cæsar; but when the Emperor appeared, instead of conquering, he converted them. How were they converted? In battalions, the old chronicler informs us: they were converted in battalions, and baptized in platoons.

[1] 1812–95; Liberal M.P. Richmond; solicitor-general 1861–3, attorney-general 1863–6; later lord chancellor and 1st Earl of Selbourne; ended as a Liberal Unionist.
[2] Sir Stafford Northcote.
[3] On the third reading of the Corn Law Bill, 15 May 1846.

'THE CONSERVATIVE SURRENDER'

But what was the cause of this strange phenomenon? Why did the household suffrage that was so hateful, so dangerous in 1866, become in 1867 the fitting and proper settlement of the question? It can scarcely have been a change of conviction. Educated men are not really 'converted in battalions,' either in politics or religion. The question had been thoroughly discussed; and everything that was possible to be said on either side was well known to all who had paid any attention to the controversy. Nor can we afford much more credence to the motive on which Lord Derby, and many humbler apologists of the Ministry, are constantly dwelling, 'that it was necessary to settle a question which was standing in the way of all useful legislation.' We doubt if any previous orator has attained to the courage of offering such a reason for consenting to the deposition of one class, and the enthronement of another. Those who seem so anxious to promote useful legislation, had ample opportunity of showing their zeal in 1860, and again in 1866. But it did not occur to them to accept a revolution in order to facilitate the progress of public business, until it became necessary to avoid being 'ousted by the re-united Liberals.'

There can be no doubt that, as far as those who had no official reasons for passing a Reform Bill were concerned, the one dominant feeling of the present year has been a feverish anxiety to 'settle the question.' Mr. Henley,[1] with cynical candour, betrayed the ignoble secret, when he acknowledged that a fear lest 'the pot should boil over,' was the motive that animated his friends. The meetings in the manufacturing towns, and the riots in Hyde Park, had had their effect. The comfortable classes had no stomach for a real struggle. Their hearts misgave them, indeed, about Reform: they saw in it ugly visions of the future – labour giving law to capital, Trades' Union rules supreme, democratic Parliaments contriving a graduated income tax, the poor voting supplies and the rich finding ways and means. In past years they have not concealed their apprehensions. But they did not hold such opinions as owners. They only occupied them as tenants-at-will, ready to seek others as soon as the physical force of the multitude should give them notice to quit. They had no heart to fight for the rights they had inherited or won. They had beguiled themselves with the belief that it was possible to hold their rights without a struggle; and under that impression they had talked bravely for a time. But when they discovered their mistake, they took their overthrow meekly and gave up at once. All they entreated

[1] J. W. Henley (1793-1884), Conservative M.P. for Oxfordshire, and president of the board of trade in Derby's first two ministries.

was that the agitation should be got rid of, and the question settled without delay. And Ministerial speakers boast of it as their great achievement that they have satisfied this one longing. 'They have settled the question in a manner so liberal as to leave no room for further agitation.'

Now we do not deny that in this precipitate capitulation the comfortable classes may possibly have judged rightly – so far as this one question is concerned. We quite agree with Lord Derby in his estimate of his own measure. It is a leap completely in the dark; and, it follows, that it would be as conjectural to predict destruction as to promise safety. It may be a bed of roses upon which we are now swiftly descending; but even if that be the issue, the surrender will scarcely be less disastrous. If the upper and middle classes had made up their minds to this tender trust in the people with which they have become suddenly inspired, seven years ago, or even one year ago, no harm would have been done beyond that which might result from the particular measure they were passing. It would have been a concession – possibly a foolish one; but it would have displayed no weakness, and would not necessarily have provoked further attacks.[1] But they have just fought long enough to betray the weakness of the garrison and the poverty of the defences. The dullest of their antagonists perfectly understands that they have not yielded to argument or to sentiment; that the apostles of Reform who have the real credit of their conversion are the mobs who beat down the palings of Hyde Park, or went out marching with bands and banners in the towns of the North. Any one who reads their organs in the press will be satisfied that there is no mistake among them upon this point; and indeed, they would hardly deserve credit for the ordinary sagacity of Englishmen if there was.

Now, this appears to us the most dangerous lesson which it is possible to teach to the possessors of physical force. The present holders of power appear, after the fashion of decaying and feeble rulers, to imagine that it is possible to buy off those who threaten their security with donatives. They seem to fancy that the appetite for political power is like the natural appetites, which lose their edge when they are gratified. They will find that the meal they have afforded is but a mouthful, and that the appetite will regain its vigour after a very brief repose. Invaders have never yet been repelled by the discovery that their antagonists were running away. The innovating classes for years have imagined that a great Conservative force stood opposed to them, and that they could only win the victories they coveted at the cost of risks they did

[1] Cf., however, Cranborne's argument in 1860 (above, pp. 135ff.).

'THE CONSERVATIVE SURRENDER'

not care to run. They have now discovered that this force is a pure delusion. The guns are painted wood; the soldiers, like a Haytian army, think they have done their duty gallantly if they abstain from running away until the few first shots have been fired. Will this discovery induce them to suspend their operations and abstain from further demands?

There can be no finality in politics. Whatever the actual state of things in any state may be, the spirit of innovation always must exist. The world would grow very stagnant if it disappeared. The appetite for change can never be glutted. If the old leaders of the movement are made Conservatives by their own conquests, others, unsatisfied, will step forward to supply their place. What fulfils the ideal of the agitator of today is only 'a step in the right direction,' in the eyes of the aspirant who is preparing to be his successor. When Mr. Bright is preaching moderation and caution, Mr. Beales[1] will be just girding himself for the battle; and doubtless Mr. Beales already numbers among his lieutenants politicians who look upon him as absurdly behind his age. The Girondin always has a Jacobin behind him ready to trip him up; and further back still stands a Hébertist anxious to perform the same service to the Jacobin. The long periods of political repose which communities enjoy from time to time, is [sic] due, not to the disappearance of the *rerum novarum cupidi*, but to the establishment of an equilibrium between the Conservative and the innovating force. Of course the impulse of each force differs widely in each successive generation, according to the teaching of events. The pressure of abuses which have been bred by stagnation, or the memory of the disorders which have been caused by change, will alternately depress one or the other extremity of the balance. But it is idle for the Conservative classes to think that the innovating force can be held under salutary control without labour or risk on their part. The two forces are complementary to each other; the paralysis of either makes the other ruinously strong. The idea that we can retain the blessings we possess by any other guarantee than our own ability to defend them – that trustfulness or philanthropy can be our security – is a delusion which in some minds may be Utopian and amiable, but in most is a mere screen for selfish love of ease. In our history, at all events, it is quite new. It was not so that our fathers won the liberty they have handed down to us. It will not be so that we shall hand down to our children that scrupulous respect of individual rights without which political liberty simply means the tyranny of the many.

[1] Edmond Beales (1803-81), lawyer and political agitator; president of the Reform League and a supporter of manhood suffrage and the ballot, but a relative moderate.

The great danger of the Conservative classes at the present crisis is, that they shall cultivate too highly the virtues of quietness and confidence. It is an opinion generally entertained that the nation is on the whole 'Conservative;' not in the party sense of the word, for that meaning has disappeared, but in the sense of a general preference of our institutions to those of any other nation. We believe this general impression to be true: but it is a most misleading truth. It does not follow because the mass of the nation is Conservative, that therefore our institutions are secure. Political forces must be estimated by their intensity, as well as by their quantity. The feeble preferences of even a large and powerful majority are no protection against the hearty and vigorous hatred of a few. Our institutions at present are likely to fare much as the Bishops did at the outset of the great Rebellion: those that hate them, hate them worse than the devil; those that love them, do not love them better than their dinner. It is quite natural that men should not disquiet themselves about the safety of blessings which they have enjoyed for a long time without interruption, and which have successfully withstood so many assaults. That to-morrow will be as yesterday is the ordinary reasoning of mankind; and they will hardly admit the possibility of a new danger, until it is impressed upon them by some sharp experience. It is no matter of surprise, therefore, that during the last few years the feeling of security should have grown in proportion to the general contentment of the nation. The belief gained ground that the educated classes were becoming more and more averse to organic change; and simultaneously there grew up a disinclination for efforts in support of what seemed unassailed. Other causes, no doubt, have contributed to the apathy which has prevailed. In the keen struggle for material prosperity less value has been set on the more distant advantages promised by the triumph of this or that set of political ideas. For the last twenty years, again, politics have been less attractive to men of independent minds than they used to be. A different spirit has crept into parliamentary warfare. Politicians have traded more and more upon the profession of sentiments they did not really cherish, and which were distasteful to the class to which they belonged; and they have seemed eager to avail themselves of excuses for delaying from time to time to give effect to their professions. The calculation of the value of 'cries' has assumed a prominence in party arithmetic which it did not possess before. Changes of opinion among public men became more and more frequent, especially of those who leant towards the Conservative side, or actually belonged to it: and these conversions, instead of bringing damage to the personal interests

'THE CONSERVATIVE SURRENDER'

of those who were converted, were timed so as to be judicious and opportune. All these things tended to repel the better class of Conservative thinkers from the active field of politics, and to react with a mischievous effect upon the composition of the House of Commons. The Conservative party became famous for its organisation and prompt discipline: and yet that discipline did not seem to be the result of any unusual admiration of its leaders. Its ranks were being gradually recruited from a class eminently fit to exhibit the virtues of parliamentary discipline; men who sought a seat for other than political motives, and were more solicitous for the social rank or commercial influence it conferred than for the success of the cause in whose interest it had been avowedly obtained. Elaborate and successful electioneering became one of the attributes of the party: and that is a species of excellence which, while it leads to brilliant results for the moment, is of evil omen for the moral vitality of the party which has attained to it. Destitute of the living earnestness which can only be developed in average politicians by contagion from the classes who support them out of doors, and led by a chief whose Conservative connections were an accident of his career, when they arrived at the year 1867, having just tasted the first fruits of office after a long and dreary fast, they were not in a condition to withstand any severe temptation. The urgent question which lovers of the constitution have to ask themselves is, whether, unless the balance of fears which acts upon their leaders is materially altered, they are likely to be proof against a second temptation of the same kind.

Whatever the result may be, there seems to be little doubt that their virtue will be tried. Mr. Forster, in a recent speech at Bradford, gave to his constituents a sketch of the result which, according to the hopes of his party, a Reformed Parliament will enable them to attain. He did not enter much into detail, but he indicated as the first objects of attack the laws which regulate the ownership of land in Ireland and in this country, the endowments of the Established Church, and the present system of education. This declaration is in conformity with all his previously expressed opinions, and was to be expected. But the remarkable portion of the speech is that in which he explains the plan of operations he intends to adopt for this purpose. It is creditable to his sagacity, but a melancholy illustration of the character which the Conservative party has earned, that he thinks that the objects he seeks will be best secured by not disturbing the present Ministry. The following are his words:

By what means are we to attain these things? Do I look forward to an immediate change in the Government for the purpose? I do not: and I do not wish for it until Mr. Disraeli has exhausted the Radicalism of his Conservative followers. (Laughter and applause.) During the last days of the late Session I had some fear that we were getting to the bottom of this store of Radicalism; but I daresay that during the recess it will be again added to: and I have great hopes that Mr. Disraeli will be able to persuade his followers to settle as we could wish one or two of those questions. So long as he is able to do so, by all means let him remain in power; for it is far easier that good reforms should be passed by Conservatives than by us 'Reformers', if they are willing to do it, for then we have not to contend with their opposition. – *Speech at Bradford*, Sept. 18, 1867.

A stranger unused to the ways of English politicians might have imagined that these words were bitterly sarcastic, and that they would be resented as unjust by the friends of the Government. But any one who formed such an opinion would entirely misjudge the spirit in which the Government and its friends look upon overtures from the more advanced Liberals. A week afterwards the 'Globe,' a paper which during the session has acted with great ability as an exponent of Mr. Disraeli's views, commented upon Mr. Forster's speech in the following strain:

Mr. Forster knows that every right-minded Minister, when called upon to legislate, *must think of many things in addition to the prejudices of his party*... He thinks that the Conservatives can and will give good government; and his patriotism is strong enough to welcome it by whomsoever bestowed...The fact is too plain to be contested; the feeling is now rooted that the Conservatives can and will give such an administration of public affairs which the country feels that it needs. Mr. Forster is welcome to call it a vein of Radicalism in the Ministry; he only expresses thereby a truth now generally recognised that in the region of pure politics most Englishmen are now alike. Education, Trades' Unions, Army Reform, the Dwellings of the Poor, Ireland, Foreign Affairs, are as open to Conservatives as to Liberals, are encumbered with no greater pre-existing prejudices on one side than on another. A coalition of Conservatives and Radicals for the mere purposes of office would be as bootless as it is impossible: a concurrence of all parties in dealing with the many, and in many cases difficult, problems of our social state is feasible, and contains the best promise for the future. – *Globe*, Sept. 24.

That the conduct of the Radicals in adopting this policy is wise, and from their own point of view patriotic, we have no wish to dispute. It is but just to admit that much of their success is owing to the simplicity of purpose with which they have pursued the objects they had at heart. 'The Lamp of Sacrifice' has not been extinguished among them. While Tories and Whigs have been quarrelling for place, they have only studied to bend to their purposes the ambition of each in turn. The result has been what might have been expected. The Tories and Whigs have enjoyed the offices; the Radicals have secured the victory of their principles. It is but natural that Mr. Forster should be anxious to continue the practice of a policy which has the merit of being at once so honourable and so fruitful in results. But the astonishing part of the article we have quoted, is the view that all Englishmen are of the same political creed as regards the problems of the future; that it is not only not impossible, but probable and very desirable, that the Radicals and the Conservatives should act together; and that in regard to such questions as Ireland, and to those Irish questions to which Mr. Forster referred – the Established Church, and the tenure of land – the Conservatives are as unembarrassed by previous opinions as the other side. If these be the views encouraged in high quarters, we may well ask what the Conservative party is doing, and where it is going? or rather what the Conservative party is? Has it any opinions of its own? Does it labour and spend to carry any particular principles into practical effect? Or will it have attained the *summum bonum* of political desire when it sees Lord Derby and Mr. Disraeli, permanently in power, carrying out Mr. Forster's policy?

No one who is not gifted with second sight could attempt to predict the course which the ministerial leader will take upon the many thorny questions which will be the next subjects of agitation – especially those which concern the Church and the ownership of land. Least of all would those eminent persons venture upon such a prophecy themselves. Men who take a leap in the dark naturally refrain from determining the nature of their future movements until they know the kind of bottom upon which they are descending. As the leap itself was taken purely in obedience to external influences, the movements which result from it are not likely to be independent. But it is a poor prospect for the Conservative classes, the classes whose interests and whose affections are bound up with our existing institutions, if their future course is to depend upon the estimate which an electioneering expert may make of the prospects of the political share-market of the day. They at least ought to be guided by larger principles, and be animated by nobler aims than that of preventing a particular minister being ousted, or two sections of political antagonists from re-uniting. If they think that there is anything in our institutions worth a struggle or a sacrifice, they have a long conflict before them. The line which the assault will take is tolerably obvious, though of course it is impossible to speculate on the extent to which it will be successful, until we know the amount of support it will receive from the new constituencies. But the speeches of the leading radicals of the present time sufficiently indicate the points which will be the first object of attack; and we may gather from the writings of the new Oxford school of doctrinaires, the enterprises which, if the present Radicals succeed, will probably be taken up by their more extreme successors.[1]

We believe that Mr. Disraeli and Mr. Forster are right in saying, that for the present no harm is intended either to the House of Peers or to the Crown. The attempt would be a very difficult and a very profitless one. The House of Peers resists so little, and the Crown has so completely ceased to resist at all, that not only is their existence a practical grievance to nobody, but their destruction would not be felt as the removal of a serious obstacle, even by the most extreme Reformer. We do not, of course, mean that any substantial power over the political movements of the nation is likely to be left to them; but their formal position will probably be left untouched, and they may even retain some influence over patronage, and other matters of minor moment. The English, whatever their opinions, are always a practical people, and they do not waste their labour on theoretical crusades. There are plenty of undertakings elsewhere that lie nearer to the hearts of the democratic party. The Church will doubtless have the first claim upon their attention. She is threatened by two different sets of antagonists, who contrive for the present to work together, but who are really pursuing objects that are quite incompatible. There is a body powerful in numbers, but not in influence, who desire that she may cease to be an Establishment. They desire to withdraw from her all State recognition, and strip her of her endowments; but having reduced her to the temporal condition of the Roman Catholics, or the Wesleyans, they do not propose to interfere with her further. The support of all the Dissenters, that is to say, all the popular support the movement commands, will be given to this section of it. The other section is not numerous or popular, but it exercises far more influence than its mere numbers would command. It does not wish to disestablish the Church, but only to transform it. It desires that the present endowments shall continue to be applied to the teaching of something that shall be called religion. But the religion is to be 'unsectarian,' *i.e.* it is to be purged of every article of belief to

[1] Probably a reference to the proposals on Ireland, the trade unions, the land laws, etc. advanced in *Questions for a Reformed Parliament* (1867), the contributors to which, mostly Oxford men, included Frederic Harrison, Godfrey Lushington, and J. E. Thorold Rogers.

'THE CONSERVATIVE SURRENDER'

which any considerable number of persons are likely to object. The power of this party resides in the fact that it possesses an enormous hold over the class by whom public opinion is manufactured, – the journalists, the literary men, the professors, the advanced thinkers of the day. How will their prospects be affected by the newly enfranchised voters? There are a good many excellent Churchmen who believe, probably from their own parochial experience, that the poor are singularly amenable to religious influence, and that for the purposes of orthodox religion, the change from the ten-pounder to the rated householder is a change for the better. On the other side, there is an equally deep-rooted confidence that the new additions may be claimed in a body as recruits to the flag of religious Liberalism. In moving from the petty tradesman to the working man, it is believed that we have moved from an atmosphere of dissent to an atmosphere of pure scepticism. Time will show which of these anticipations is the true one. In the mean time, accident seems for the moment to favour the voluntary rather than the free-thinking wing of the attacking force. The first operations are to be against the Church of Ireland, undoubtedly a tempting, and up to certain lengths, not a formidable enterprise. If successful to the full extent of the contemplated effort, it will undoubtedly open a dangerous breach in the defences of the Established Church both of England and of Scotland. The Voluntaries are wise in their selection of the first battle-field, for if they succeed, the rest of their campaign will no longer be as hopeless as it now seems. For the time the English Church will probably be left to fight, in the main, not for her endowments but for her creed. There can be little doubt, however, that whatever principles are laid down in the treatment of Church property in Ireland will in due time be pitilessly applied to the Church of England. The question of the land will probably follow the same course. Irish discontent will be the vantage-ground from which a principle may be set up that can afterwards be used to operate against the English land-owners. There is no grievance in England that could be worked against landed property with any probability of success. But unsound principles conceded in a panic to one island are not likely for any length of time to be excluded from the other.

We do not mean to assert that either the Irish Church or the conditions of tenure in Ireland are in so perfect a state that nothing can be done to improve them; nor even in the assertion of just rights should we recommend Conservatives, in their present deplorable condition, to be rigid and exacting. The time is not yet come to enter upon these questions in detail; for it is not likely that any far-reaching schemes of change will be entertained until the new Parliament is chosen. It only concerns us now to draw, for our future guidance in reference to these two questions and to all others that may be raised, the lesson which is to be found in the events of the last two years. If the classes who are interested in these questions mean to renew the tactics which have been practised too often of late times, they have nothing but renewed disaster to expect. If they intend at the outset to draw up their forces at the extreme edge of the position they occupy, and to make a show of defending every inch of it, and then, the moment the battle becomes threatening, to abandon every post that has been attacked, the only result that can follow from their campaigning is utterly to dishearten their own troops and to inspire the forces of innovation with the most disdainful courage and the wildest hopes. If they think to save anything from the perils that surround them, they must make up their minds as to what is worth struggling for, and then not be afraid to struggle for it. Let them maturely decide, before the conflict begins, what is of essential and what is of secondary importance. Let them do their utmost to meet fair grievances half-way; and to yield, while it can be done gracefully, all that can be yielded without prejudice to any vital principle. Concessions made before the commencement of a contest are no sign of weakness, and do not, if made with judgment, compromise the defence of important points. But, if they are wise, they will endure no receding, while any further struggle is still possible, from the positions which they decide to hold. It is not safe to trust in these matters too much to the courage of others. Unless opinion forms itself as definitely on the Conservative as on the Radical side, and exacts as resolutely from those who profess to represent it a stanch [sic] allegiance to its conclusions, the scenes of the past session will assuredly be renewed in future years. It is dangerous to rely too much on the virtue or the discernment of politicians, however able or however highly placed. They live in an atmosphere of illusion, and can seldom be persuaded that any political principle is worth the sacrifice of their own careers. If momentous changes are at hand, it will be no comfort to those to whom our present institutions are dear that such changes have received their first impulse from men who will be the foremost and greatest sufferers. It is the common formula of revolutions that weakness begins what violence concludes. The time is one in which the classes who value the priceless blessings they have hitherto enjoyed under English institutions must bestir themselves, if they would see those blessings continued. To their own vigilance and their own

'THE CONSERVATIVE SURRENDER'

exertions they must trust for their security, and to nothing else. The juncture is singularly critical. The leap in the dark of the present year has thrown upon them no common burden of responsibility. If they are negligent or timid, or allow themselves to be made the sport of the ambition of politicians, complete subjection to the poorest class in the community may well be among the lightest of the evils which will reward their apathy.

'The Programme of the Radicals' (*Q.R.*, no. 270; October 1873)

INTRODUCTORY NOTE

SALISBURY'S October 1873 article was written at a period of crisis in the fortunes of the Liberal government and the Liberal party. The great Gladstone ministry which had come into power with so sweeping a majority in 1868 seemed on the verge of collapse. Its legislative achievements had largely exhausted its mandate and its energies, and had raised the feeling of powerful interests against it. Churchmen had had to swallow Irish disestablishment and the abolition of university tests (both stoutly resisted by Salisbury). The holders of landed property had seen their existing rights menaced by the principles of the Irish Land Act. The army had been disturbed by the abolition of purchase, and the publicans and their customers by the Licensing Act of 1872. On the international scene, some felt, the government had failed to uphold the country's prestige in its dealings with Russia over the Black Sea clauses of the Treaty of Paris and with the United States over the *Alabama* claims. In March 1873 the ministry had actually been defeated in the Commons over the controversial Irish University Bill, and had resigned, but Disraeli had prudently refused to take office in a minority, and Gladstone had had to go on. The end of the session had been followed by an attempt to renew the government's vitality through a number of ministerial changes. The unpopular H. A. Bruce left the home office for the presidency of the council and a peerage, and was succeeded by the former chancellor, Robert Lowe, Gladstone himself taking the exchequer; and in September John Bright rejoined the cabinet he had left in November 1870, as chancellor of the duchy of Lancaster. Another change designed to please public opinion was the removal of A. S. Ayrton from the office of works. But these moves failed to check the ministry's run of reverses in by-elections. In August and September it lost seats to the Conservatives in Dover, Greenwich, Renfrewshire, Shaftesbury, and East Staffordshire.

Not the least of the government's difficulties lay in its relationship with the Radical wing of its own party. The discontent of Radicals and militant nonconformists with what they regarded as its lack of progressive zeal was widespread and open by 1873. The education question, which Forster had made the subject of a moderate compromise in the act of 1870, was the focus of much of the criticism, and was closely linked with the general issue of the position of the established Church. There was concern, too, at the government's unwillingness to give greater satisfaction to working-class claims, especially

'THE PROGRAMME OF THE RADICALS'

over the law affecting trade unions and strike action. Now that the ministry had gone so far towards achieving the classic Liberal programme of the past, the Radicals were anxious to turn it to a fresh range of reforms, and their efforts to put pressure on it even included intervention in several by-elections. The official Liberal candidate in the Bath by-election of 1873, for example, had to endorse the educational policy of the Radical National Education League, in order to prevent a League candidate from coming in to split the Liberal vote. The divisions in the party between Radicals and moderates were plainly displayed, and that section of middle-class opinion which had had its fill of social and political change looked in alarm at proposals such as those advanced by the rising Radical star Joseph Chamberlain in the article on 'The Liberal Party and its Leaders' which he contributed to the *Fortnightly Review* for 1 September 1873.

The thirty-seven-year-old Chamberlain was not yet in Parliament, but from his Birmingham base (he was to become mayor of the city in November 1873) he had already turned himself into a leading figure of Radicalism. Much of his activity had been in the education battle, as chairman of the executive committee of the National Education League, founded at Birmingham in 1869 to campaign for a free, compulsory, and unsectarian or secular system of elementary education. But the education issue by itself was not enough to engender mass support, and Chamberlain was anxious to focus Radical energies on the broader programme which his *Fortnightly* article spelled out. After sharply criticising the government for being out of touch with the desire of the Liberal activists and the 'mass of the people' for drastic reform, he put forward the platform of 'Free Church, Free Land, Free Schools, and Free Labour', with the arrogant assertion that 'no one of ordinary foresight and intelligence will doubt that every item of it will be secured before twenty years have passed away'. 'Free Church' meant disestablishment and the secularisation of Church endowments. 'Free Land' meant the removal of the restrictions imposed by primogeniture and entail, the provision of facilities for the cheap and ready transfer of small properties, and the recognition of a tenant's right to his unexhausted improvements. The existing land system, Chamberlain argued, excessively restricted proprietorship, discouraged investment, and had depressed the condition of the 'peasantry'. 'Free Schools' signified the formal objective of the National Education League – gratuitous, secular elementary education, financed and controlled by the state. These three aims were part of the common currency of Radical politics, and Chamberlain had combined them in this slogan form in a speech at Birmingham as early as February 1872. But there was a doubt whether they possessed sufficient attraction for the working man, whose support Chamberlain was explicitly trying to harness, and, significantly, he now added to them 'Free Labour', by which he meant in practice the amendment of the law of conspiracy and of the Criminal Law Amendment Act of 1871, which severely hampered trade union activities, notably in the conduct of strikes, and the abolition of the imprisonment of employees for breach of contract under the master and servant laws, at least where no malicious injury was intended to persons or property. The whole, plus a further extension of the vote, made up a programme far in advance of what the Liberal leadership could countenance, and likely to prove unpalatable to a substantial proportion of Liberal voters.

It was this article that Salisbury took as his text when he set out to analyse the position of the Liberal party in a piece which, wrote the editor, Smith, 'seems to me to surpass almost every thing you have previously written for the Quarterly'. He saw clearly that the Liberals' difficulties were far from being the result merely of temporary and incidental factors, and the main interest of his article lies in its discussion of the fundamental trends which seemed to him to be determining the course of politics, not only in England but in western Europe as a whole. The old battle of the middle classes against the landed aristocracy and gentry, with the working classes figuring simply as auxiliaries of the former, was petering out. Since 1848 it had been increasingly submerged by a new conflict, based on the division of interest between capital and labour, which was opposing the working classes to the bourgeoisie and tending more and more to drive the latter, largely victorious in the old struggle, into a conservative posture. In this situation, the traditional lines of party in England failed to correspond with the real divisions in society. The moderate Liberals had won the religious and political 'enfranchisement' which had been their classic goal. Now, taught wisdom by the example of the Continent – most recently by the spectacle of the Paris Commune – and lacking the ingenuous idealism and faith in 'the people' of former days, they found themselves in unnatural association with Radicals whose objects they could not share, but whose support was sold dearly to their leaders as an electoral necessity. As the Radicals moved into open assault on property and the Church, the moment had come, Salisbury argued, for the moderates to break free, and to put their convictions before mere party allegiance.

The attempt to detach middle-class moderates from the Liberal party by suggesting to them that in a state of politics dominated by the challenge of the working man it was too tainted with extreme Radicalism to be a reliable agency of defence for their class interests was very much in tune with the general strategy of the Conservatives at this time. Disraeli, in March 1873, had been at pains to indicate to the middle-class public that they were entering a period in which the central issue was nothing less than the security of the great national institutions, the monarchy, the Church, and landed property, with the implication that in this situation the Conservative party would prove their natural refuge from revolutionary Radicalism. But care was taken that Conservatism should not be presented as a purely negative or obstructive force. Disraeli's 1872 references to the 'condition of the people' were not entirely forgotten: while avoiding the harassing and disruptive legislation which had characterised Gladstone's ministry, the Conservatives would not, it was intimated, neglect those necessary measures of social improvement which were a proper part of the work of government. This line, too, was echoed in Salisbury's article. It was with these themes that in less than four months' time the Conservative party was to fight the general election which gave it its first majority since 1841.

'THE PROGRAMME OF THE RADICALS'

The Liberal Party and its Leaders. By Joseph Chamberlain. 'Fortnightly Review.' London, September, 1873.

In spite of occasional vicissitudes of fortune, the elections of the autumn have left to the Government a gloomier prospect, even than that which lay before them when the Session closed. The vessel is among the breakers, and spectators scarcely are at the trouble to discuss whether she will founder: the only question is how long the inevitable moment can be put off. It is interesting to watch from the shore the desperate struggles of the gallant crew who have navigated her with so much hardihood for so long. They are ready to throw all the cargo overboard, upon either side, and even to send some of their comrades after it. In the excitement of despair, the captain even imagines he can mend his position by mastheading the first lieutenant, and putting the purser in his place.[1] But everyone believes that she cannot get off, and that the time of the famous rover, whose depredations have been so audacious, and whose terror has been so wide-spread, has come at last.

The prevalent conviction does not rest on any trivial grounds. The loss[2] of a balance of twenty seats, counting forty on a division, is serious enough, even to those who began their career with a majority of one hundred and eighteen;[3] and the importance of the numbers is much aggravated by the fact that for the last three years all the electoral conversions have been one way. No confident calculation as to the state of things next year can be hazarded: for it would be as great a mistake to count upon any settled state of politics in this country as upon any settled state of weather. English popularity, like an English summer, consists of two fine days and a thunderstorm; but thunderstorms do not last for ever. Still, with whatever qualifications, the gloom which overcasts Ministerial prospects is threatening enough. The universal conviction of impending doom is in itself a formidable danger. Friends become dull and hopeless, and blunder interminably: enemies become elated, and develop resources of which, in their depression, they had not been conscious: and the enterprising host of waiters on Providence begins to move. The great commerce of political support begins. Some prefer the export trade, and take their allegiance to a foreign market, where by selecting the precise moment of crisis a high price may be obtained. Others find that the price of their wares has risen at home,

[1] The allusions are to Gladstone, Bruce, and Lowe, respectively.
[2] In by-elections since 1868.
[3] Modern analyses put the Liberal majority after the 1868 election at about 110.

and that a profitable business is to be done without moving. One of the sorrows of a beaten Minister is that he must accept the service of swords and the patronage of causes, which in his happier hours he would have despised. And yet they bring much future embarrassment and little present help when the stress of battle comes; for then those who stand by him heartily and without conditions are apt in practice to sell their adhesion dear. Among the many trials of an unexpected reverse, undoubtedly the hardest to bear is that it opens upon the sufferer a long stream of admonitions and commentaries from his devoted friends. His misfortunes are never absent from their minds, and generally present in their discourse – serving chiefly as the shocking example of the end to which a neglect of the speaker's particular hobby will lead. The Government have not escaped this aggravated form of friendship. Their disaster has pointed innumerable morals, and served as demonstrative proof of diametrically opposite denunciations. It has been made to show that Mr. Gladstone has gone too fast, and that he has gone too slow: that he is suspected of being too fond of the Church, and of yielding too readily to the Dissenters: that he has quarrelled with the moderate Liberals when he ought to have quarrelled with the Radicals; and, on the other hand, that he has deserted the Radicals when he ought to have resisted the pressure of the moderate Liberals. It is clear that Mr. Gladstone cannot have been guilty of all the imprudences which his admiring friends lay to his charge; neither can he accept all their counsels, unless he has the faculty of walking two ways at once. But, if it is safe to judge from the failure of Mr. Baxter Langley at Greenwich,[1] and of Mr. Jaffray in East Worcestershire,[2] men whose fame has never been darkened by the faintest shade of moderation, we should doubt whether Mr. Gladstone's reign has been cut short in consequence of the undue reserve and timidity of his policy. Liberal writers are painfully inquiring into the causes that have divided the Liberal party, and the best means of restoring its shattered cohesion. The latter is a purely domestic question which we have no vocation to discuss. If its present disasters are merely due to personal blunders, or accidental misunderstandings, they are phenomena of a very transitory interest. An absurd importance has been attached to peculiarities of manner. They have an effect on the politicians of the clubs, and on the predilections of 'society.' They may

---

[1] Langley, a well-known Radical, pulled 2,379 votes in the by-election of 4 August, to the Conservative Boord's 4,525.
[2] 'East Worcestershire' is a mistake for East Staffordshire, where in the by-election of 8 August the Conservative, S. C. Allsopp, beat Jaffray by 3,630 votes to 2,893.

'THE PROGRAMME OF THE RADICALS'

not be without weight in the House of Commons; they may even turn half-a-dozen votes on a critical division. But the present difficulties of the Liberal party do not arise in either of these quarters. Society has never loved Mr. Gladstone's Ministry; and the only action taken against him by the House of Commons was caused by the sudden operation upon Irish members of a force, foreign to England, and certainly not put in motion by failures in politeness.[1] The striking phenomenon of the time is the conversion of the constituencies; and all the architects, artists, or scientific men, ever snubbed by Mr. Ayrton[2] – all the deputations that have ever smarted under the sarcasms of Mr. Lowe – would not have together made up the numbers that have deserted the Government in any single constituency; and beyond their own social circle their wrongs excite little commiseration. A change in electoral feeling which is sensible throughout the kingdom, and which is now in its third year of progress, must rest upon a wider basis than the wounded feelings of individuals. It indicates a movement of opinion that may be a change of current, or may be a mere eddy, but which at least concerns matters of wide practical range and of interest to the community at large.

No doubt it has not been due to any single cause. It has needed the coincidence of many potent forces to produce so marvellous a contrast as that between the despotism of 1869 and the impotence of 1873. We attach comparatively little importance to the administrative mistakes. They form an easy theme for party polemics, and, therefore, they have been much insisted on. But to the mass of the people they scarcely appeal more forcibly than personal defects of manner. It is only a minority of the electors who read the newspapers; and of that remnant it is a still smaller minority who read any newspapers but those of their own side. To them – if such matters have penetrated at all – the Collier appointment,[3]

[1] Salisbury is referring to the pressure of the Irish hierarchy against the Irish University Bill, which helped to cause the government's defeat by 287 votes to 284 on the night of 11–12 March 1873. The forty-three Liberals who voted against the government in this division included thirty-five Irish.

[2] A. S. Ayrton (1816–86), M.P. Tower Hamlets, and first commissioner of works from 1869 until August 1873, was notorious for giving offence by his brusque manners. Those with whom he quarrelled included the sculptor Alfred Stevens and the director of Kew Gardens, Sir J. D. Hooker.

[3] In 1871, one of four newly created paid posts on the judicial committee of the privy council was given to the attorney-general, Sir Robert Collier, who had to be raised to the bench in order to fulfil the statutory qualification. The new posts had not been supposed to provide political appointments, and the cry of jobbery was raised. Lord chief justice Cockburn protested to the government, who escaped parliamentary censure by only two votes in the Lords and twenty-seven in the Commons.

SALISBURY'S 'QUARTERLY REVIEW' ARTICLES

the indirect claims,[1] the loss of the 'Megæra,'[2] the telegraph scandal,[3] and the Zanzibar contract,[4] have only sounded like the dim echo of a distant quarrel. The legislative errors have been far more important. The interests of Englishmen are not threatened with impunity: and the danger of molesting them does not disclose itself till the threat has been uttered, and their enmity has been irrevocably incurred. They have a habit of sleeping up to the very moment of danger, which is equally embarrassing to their champions and their assailants. Politicians imagine them to be meek, and submissive, and easily despoiled, because they are insensible to the warnings which drive politicians themselves to frenzy. The sinister phantoms that haunt St. Stephen's – 'the admission of the principle,' 'the thin end of the wedge,' *proximus Ucalegon* – exert no spell upon the mind of the average Englishman. His imagination is not active, and his esteem for political logic is small. Very seldom can he be induced to see an impending danger. He watches its approach with a complacent apathy which drives his political defenders to despair.

[1] In claiming against the British government for the depredations committed on the merchant navy of the North during the Civil War by Confederate commerce raiders built in British ports (notably the *Alabama*), the United States had advanced not only claims for direct damage but also the 'indirect' claims, covering the loss incurred through the transfer of much of the American merchant marine to the British flag, the enhancement of insurance, and the prolongation of the war, together with the addition of a large sum to the cost of the war and the suppression of the rebellion. By the treaty of Washington in May 1871 it was agreed to refer the *Alabama* claims to international arbitration, but considerable ill-feeling was generated when the United States continued to press the indirect claims, which the British government thought to have been excluded from the arbitration by the terms of the treaty. Eventually, the indirect claims were ruled out by the arbitration tribunal on the initiative of the American representative, but the tribunal's award, in September 1872, still imposed damages of £3,250,000, and many people in Britain thought that the country had suffered a loss of prestige, for which Gladstone's government was held responsible.

[2] The troopship *Megæra* had to be run aground in a sinking state while conveying naval personnel to Australia in 1871. Allegations that she had been unfit for service led to the appointment of a royal commission, whose report, in March 1872, confirmed that she should not have been sent out, and made some criticisms of admiralty administration.

[3] The committee on public accounts discovered in 1873 that £800,000, partly receipts from the post office and partly deposits in the post office savings bank, which should have gone to the consolidated fund and the national debt commissioners, had been applied without parliamentary authority to the extension of the telegraphs. The postmaster-general, Monsell, had to resign, and the credit of Lowe and Ayrton, who also had some ministerial responsibility, was affected.

[4] The government was embarrassed in 1873 by a select committee investigation into an agreement concluded by the treasury for the carriage of the Zanzibar mails on what were regarded as extravagant terms. A new contract was made in accordance with the committee's report.

'THE PROGRAMME OF THE RADICALS'

He is wholly impenetrable to the argument that one change, to which he is indifferent, logically involves another which he detests. In spite of all exhortations he allows the precedent to be made, the fatal principle to be established. But the very dulness of apprehension, which has accepted the premises, fortifies him against submitting to the conclusion. Precedents are very useful as raw material for a Parliamentary argument; it might be very difficult to conduct a constitutional debate without them. But it would be wholly misconceiving their province to imagine that they encumber the political judgment of an elector about to vote. The fact that some other people elsewhere have permitted themselves to be robbed is no sort of argument to him for parting with one tittle of his rights. This contempt for inconvenient analogies, natural to unsophisticated man, is so foreign to the artificial forms of thought which the habit of debate has bred at Westminster, that it is perpetually preparing disagreeable surprises for politicians; especially for the ever-verdant innocents known as 'advanced thinkers.' They proceed in all confidence with the work of symmetrical destruction, relying upon the plea that they are 'only carrying out a principle well established by previous Acts of Parliament.' They are startled by discovering that to have established a principle in a case where the victim was weak is of very little assistance towards applying it where the victim happens to be strong; and whether the strength is derived from the lofty sympathies to which a Church can appeal, or from the less exalted associations which hang around the public-house, it is equally an obstacle to spoliation.

Into this pitfall the Government have fallen. Observing how little the interests about to be attacked sympathised with the anticipatory outcry of their Parliamentary friends, Ministers imagined that there was nothing but a party resistance to overcome. Of that illusion they have probably by this time been disabused. They are doubtless now satisfied that officers, publicans, squires, and Churchmen, have still a certain political vitality, which at least retains unimpaired the functions of feeling and of kicking. But the resentment of these classes only partially explains the phenomena of the present year. Their power, even in their utmost alarm, is limited: and a large proportion of them was hostile to the Liberals even in 1868. Moreover, the Government for the last two years have been obviously anxious to avoid further cause of offence: and under ordinary circumstances political memories in England are not so long. There are causes of yet wider range, which have removed the reproach from Conservatism, and have shorn Liberal theories of their fascination.

SALISBURY'S 'QUARTERLY REVIEW' ARTICLES

Any one who compares the present state of opinion with that which existed at the great Liberal outburst of 1830 cannot refuse to admit that a vast change has taken place. The Toryism of that year has of course no counterpart now. It applied to a state of things which, for good or evil, has passed away, and its existence would be unmeaning now. But the authority of Liberal opinions and sympathies is very different from that which they then wielded, and the ardour they inspire is far feebler. The old formulas may be recited, but the old belief in them has gone. The contrast between the tone of feeling then and now stretches over almost as wide an interval as between the illusions of youth and the disenchantment of middle age. If this generation has before it stupendous political problems which it must solve on pain of anarchy, it has at least this qualification for the task, that it has shaken free of many sweet but perilous superstitions. In the course of the last half-century the sore experience of Europe has shattered a whole Pantheon of political idols. The natural goodness of man has gone the way of the Divine right of kings. The peculiar virtues of the horny-handed sons of toil received a severe shock in 1848, and finally collapsed in 1871.[1] *Ce cher peuple*, as Robespierre used to say, is no longer the object of a very enthusiastic worship: it is a saint whose legend is discredited, and whose halo has been chipped off in many a street row. The necessity of 'faith' in politics was a favourite topic a few years ago – not the theological virtue known for eighteen centuries under that name, but a modern travestie, which consists in believing not in God but in street mobs. Since the Commune this Radical grace has been less earnestly enforced. In short, the optimist dreams which were so rife in the period of Louis-Philippe have lost their charm. Men are coming to recognise the intense difficulty which the growth of modern cities has added to the task of government – huge masses of toiling, hopeless poverty, covered in by a thin crust of gorgeous luxury. Even minds of a very Liberal cast are no longer blind to the dangers of implicitly trusting masses exposed to temptations such as these, if they be once emancipated from the restraints of habitual order and traditional submission. Mr. Bright himself seemed inclined, in a letter recently published, to accept the central doctrine of Conservatism, that it is better to endure almost any political evil than to risk a breach of the historic continuity of government.[2]

[1] I.e. as a result of the Paris Commune.
[2] The reference is possibly to the letter of 7 April 1872 (printed in *The Times*, 10 April 1872; also in Leech, *Public Letters of Bright*, pp. 152–3) in which Bright, in answer to a correspondent who had asked whether he would accept to be the first president of an English republic, remarked that the issue of monarchy or republicanism had

'THE PROGRAMME OF THE RADICALS'

This happy loss of 'faith' has increasingly coloured the political thought of this country, in proportion as the revolutionary experiment, tried out upon the Continent of Europe, has broken down; and the altered feeling has naturally gained ground with an accelerated speed during the last two years. The impression, so marked in much of the French literature of the present day, that the movement of 1789 has been a failure, has spread, though with less force, to England, and has exerted a marked influence on our internal politics. England, in truth, is enjoying at this moment one of those periods of political repose which she owes occasionally to the troubles of other countries. Insular as the nation is in genius, as much as in position, there is no people whose opinions reflect so quickly the lessons of foreign experience. Its language betrays little of this sensitiveness. The tone of our writers and speakers is rather that of oracles with whom has been deposited the one infallible secret of political construction, and to whom the vain struggles of the rest of the world to attain to a safe freedom are matters of curious observation and complacent pity. It is flattering to be portrayed as looking down with Lucretian security on the storms of political error on which the rest of the world is tossing, and it is a picture which our self-esteem would gladly cherish. But as a matter of fact such is not the mental attitude which our history, recent or distant, exhibits. It has been disturbed and chequered enough; but its vicissitudes would often present an insoluble enigma if an explanation were not to be found in the mighty working of foreign events on English feeling. As the movements of an unknown planet were calculated from disturbances in the known solar system, so an historical student, to whom no other history than that of England was accessible, might almost fix the dates of great commotions abroad from the sympathetic perturbations of public opinion here. In older times this operation was principally shown by the stimulus which the extremer forms of Protestantism received in England from the misdeeds of Roman Catholic potentates elsewhere. Protestantism had made but little way under the patronage of Henry and Edward; and even at Elizabeth's accession its fortunes were doubtful. But the contemplation of the Catholic persecutions of Alva and the Guises made England a Protestant nation. The sudden growth of the popular party during the later years of James I. and the reign of his son is, taken by itself, not easy to understand. The nation seemed to grow suddenly sensitive to assertions of royal authority, which, under Elizabeth, would

been long since decided, and suggested that any further decision might be left to posterity.

have been thought mild and scrupulous. The increase of irritability and alarm is far too rapid to be attributed to any supposed development of Liberal ideas. But the cause of it is evident enough when it is remembered that at this time the German Emperor,[1] under Jesuit guidance, was executing in Bohemia the violation of a constitution not unlike that of England, and that his success was followed by the unnumbered horrors inflicted upon Protestants by Wallenstein and Tilly. English politicians, to whom dynastic associations just then made Bohemia a familiar name, might almost be pardoned if their panic saw a new Wallenstein in Strafford.

In our own times the same law has prevailed. With increased intercourse the English have become more docile to the lessons offered in rich abundance by the vicissitudes of Continental politics. It was the French revolution of 1830 which gave the signal for the Reform agitation of that year: and favoured by apparent success of the 'three glorious days' of July in France, radical ideas enjoyed in this country a season of almost unquestioned supremacy. The exactly opposite lesson taught by the failure of the movements of 1848 and the temporary success of the *coup d'état* of 1851 was learnt with the same facility; and as the prosperity of Napoleon grew, the power of Radical ideas waned. During the first ten years of his reign no efforts and no eloquence could arouse a second Reform agitation in England. Mr. Bright devoted two years of toilsome starring in provincial towns to the task of inflaming discontent, and he is reported to have gloomily described his undertaking as that of 'flogging a dead horse.' The reactionary feeling culminated on the outbreak of the American civil war, when the belief gained ground, somewhat prematurely, that 'the republican bubble had burst.' In 1860 Lord Russell's mild offer of a 6*l.* rating franchise was ignominiously refused, and the next year a proposal to renew it was received 'with loud laughter' by the House of Commons. But as time went on it became evident that the relative force of the combatants in America had been miscalculated; and almost simultaneously the fortune of Napoleon began to fail him. The vane of English opinion veered slowly round again. Lord Russell's unlucky admonition to 'rest and be thankful,' in the autumn of 1863,[2] shortly after the battle of Gettysburgh, marks, with approximate accuracy, the moment of the change of wind. The next year, the last of the Confederate struggle, the new Reform agitation began

[1] Ferdinand II (reigned 1619–37).
[2] At Blairgowrie, on 26 September 1863, Russell opined that the feeling of the country was rather to 'Rest and be thankful' than to undertake new endeavours.

'THE PROGRAMME OF THE RADICALS'

to shape itself. Mr. Odger, in the course of it, achieved two great successes. He founded the International, and he converted Mr. Gladstone.[1] From that time forward the Reform current flowed apace. It was barely stemmed for a few months by Lord Palmerston's failing hand; and when the Northern Republicans had shown themselves finally victorious, and Lord Palmerston's opposition had been removed by death, its strength became irresistible. As early as the winter of 1865 it had roused Lord Russell from his rest and dissipated his thankfulness, and by 1867 it had gained force enough to create that general stampede of politicians of all colours which will ever make that year memorable in the history of political pledges. How far the impetus would have carried us is a matter of barren speculation. By 1870 it had abolished the Irish Establishment, and had made, upon the *corpus vile* of Ireland, the first experiment in agrarian legislation to be found on the English statute-book.[2] There was no external sign that its force was spent. Mr. Gladstone's huge majority still voted like one man, and occasional elections had so far rather tended to augment than to weaken it. To all appearance its power for subversion was unimpaired. It might have lost itself by the mere lapse of time and the growing number of its victims; it might have been embarrassed by the inability of individual convictions, however nimble, to keep pace with the rapid march of the party as a whole. As a matter of fact, however, the change came again from the outside. The progress of English legislators was arrested by the over-rapid movements of still more progressive politicians elsewhere. Early in 1871 came the Commune, and with it another sharp turn in public feeling here. The force of the Government was suddenly paralysed as by a blow from an unseen hand. Even inside Parliament the Ministry had so much lost their strength that the most important measures of that session were compulsorily postponed or withdrawn, and Mr. Cardwell's plan for disorganizing the army never passed through Parliament at all, but was imposed upon the country by a rare stretch of royal prerogative.[3]

[1] George Odger (1820-77), a shoemaker, was one of the principal working-class leaders of the sixties and seventies. As secretary of the London Trades Council, he did more than anyone to establish the First International in 1864, and became its first and only president. For his 'conversion' of Gladstone in the same year, see above, p. 176, n. 1.

[2] The Irish Land Act of 1870 was designed to help the tenants by limiting landlords' powers of arbitrary eviction and by enforcing compensation for eviction (except in the case of eviction for failure to pay rent). All evicted tenants were to have compensation for improvements, and public money was to be loaned to help tenants purchase their holdings.

[3] When the secretary for war, Edward Cardwell, set out in 1871 to abolish the purchase of commissions and promotions in the army, his bill was stopped by the Lords, and

In the constituencies the effect was prompter and more decided. The election for Durham was the first that took place under the light of the teachings of the Commune, and it was the first important check the Ministry received.[1] From that time forward their electoral history has been one of almost uninterrupted defeat.

In both England and France the designs avowed by the artisans have produced a profound modification in the political feelings of all classes of employers. The change has been brought to light somewhat suddenly by the Commune: for such startling tragedies dissipate the hesitations and perfect the half-formed resolutions of men who habitually are too busy to think out their logical position. But the process had been in operation for some time. The political antagonism of the middle class pointed formerly towards the gentry. The old contempt of the town for the country was sharpened by the jealousy which new-made wealth always feels of anything approaching to caste privilege. Difference of party, handed down from the old days of dynastic struggle, in many cases differences of religion, and more recently conflicts of interest on fiscal questions, kept the antagonism alive. In France it was infinitely more bitter, because the caste privileges had been more odious and more exclusive, and far less worthily enjoyed. During the long battle in both countries the workmen had taken at first no independent part, but had acted as a contingent of the forces of the *bourgeoisie*: and with one or two startling exceptions, in which, for a while, they were felt as an independent power, they were in the main content, up to 1848, to act in a subordinate position, and to fight that the *bourgeoisie* might win. In 1830 the mob burnt Nottingham and Bristol, in order that the middle classes, not the lower, might be admitted to power. In 1789 and 1830 it was chiefly the middle classes of the French towns who were discontented: but it was the workmen who took the Bastille and stood behind the barricades. In the elections in both countries the same close connexion subsisted. The workmen, whenever they had a chance, voted, and, when they could not vote, rioted against the common enemy. They were the rod with which the middle classes threatened, and in case of need chastised, their adversaries of the Church, and the Court, and the Manor-house. This alliance was powerful – in the end irresistible – but its fruits were unequally divided. The middle classes obtained the solid

---

the government announced the abolition of purchase by royal warrant, which obliged the Lords to let the bill through in order to secure the compensation provisions which it contained.

[1] In the Durham by-election of 28 April 1871, a Liberal majority of 52 at the general election of 1868 was turned into a Conservative majority of 38 in a straight fight.

results of favourable legislation: the workmen had the satisfaction of suffering for Liberal principles.

This arrangement lasted so long, and was so convenient, that the one class came to look upon the other as a species of political property. But in 1848 the first serious symptoms appeared of the political property thinking for itself. The workmen had by that time arrived at the conviction that they had interests of their own diametrically opposed to those of their employers; and the contest with Courts and Churches, which was the mere gratification of a sentiment, began to give place to the more deadly struggle between labour and capital. The Revolution of 1848 was commenced, like its predecessors, by the *bourgeoisie*; but they were thrust aside by the Socialists at a very early stage, and betook themselves to such refuge as first Cavaignac and then Napoleon could offer. From that time forth the divergence has been increasing. The workmen have become more independent, more obstinate, more extravagant. Their policy, a wild and bloody dream, has been expressed in action of the most practical kind – in each country according to the genius of the nation. In England and Belgium they have tried to operate through the fear of pecuniary loss: in France and Spain they have appealed to physical force. But in all these countries, whether through strikes or through revolutionary outbreaks, every opportunity has been used, during the last twenty years, with unremitting vigilance, to accomplish the wild visions of triumph over capital, upon which the workman, undiscouraged by failure, still resolutely broods.

The change produced in the political position of the middle classes by this revolt of their friends is fundamental. Their polarity has been suddenly reversed. They are attracted on the side where they were formerly repelled, and repelled on the side where they were formerly attracted. All their class relations are turned upside down. They have worked their will upon the upper classes, having gained almost everything for which they fought: but in the hour of victory they are confronted with a new enemy, once their fast and most serviceable ally. They have taken some little time to appreciate the fact; for a class does not change its course at a short notice. It can only do so as the older minds are replaced by younger, open to the perception of new circumstances, and ready to meet them by a new policy. But in both countries the conviction seems to be coming home to them at last that their old store of political maxims, ideals, antipathies, and attachments has no application to the new world that surrounds them now. How far this persuasion has operated on the recent elections we cannot accurately tell. The

Ballot[1] has evidently covered a large number of Liberal desertions: we are left to conjecture, from numerous expressions of opinion on other occasions, to which section of the party the unfaithful electors belong. But the state of middle-class feeling on the labour movement and its leaders is sufficiently notorious, and is not disputed by the opponents of Conservatism. Even Mr. Chamberlain, who takes a sanguine view of revolutionary prospects, is obliged to admit it:

There are many Liberals unfortunately belonging to the middle class who share with the Tories the alarm and disgust inspired by the growing power of trades' unions in this country.

This admission of altered feeling in the middle classes was not made without sufficient cause. That the President of a Chamber of Commerce should have formally proposed in a paper read at the British Association at Bradford to organise a league of capital against labour shows how deeply the alarm of which Mr. Chamberlain speaks has penetrated.[2] It seems difficult to exaggerate the political importance of this terror. We do not venture to predict what party or what class it will benefit, or whether it will benefit any. But it points to conditions of conflict which are absolutely new. The same process seems to be going forward on the field of politics as on the field of religion. All minor controversies, all secondary issues whose interest is chiefly traditional, are being abandoned, and men are arraying themselves for the main conflict where reconciliation seems impossible. That the aspirations and interests of the middle and lower classes should be recognised on both sides as essentially antagonistic is, at all events, a condition of internal conflict of which modern society has never had experience before.

In France the crisis has arisen in an acuter form than with us, because the continuity of their government has been broken. There are no traditions of habitual order, or local attachment, or hereditary respect to shade off the sharp division which is separating France into two camps – the employers and the employed. That the estrangement between the two can be soon healed, and good feeling grow up in spite of the collision of interests, seems beyond hope. On the one side there is the resentment of defeat and the sting of poverty, irritating into frenzy the delusions which a guilty school of shallow theorists has inculcated; on the other side there is terror that cannot be soothed, because it rests

[1] Secret voting had been introduced by the Ballot Act of 1872.
[2] The proposal made by W. Morris, chairman of the Halifax chamber of commerce, at Bradford on 19 September, bore fruit in the establishment at the end of the year of the National Federation of Associated Employers of Labour.

'THE PROGRAMME OF THE RADICALS'

on cruel and reiterated experience. The problem that lies before French statesmen would be hopeless enough even if it included no other elements of danger than the madness of the artisans and the terror they inspire. But as a crown to all other calamities, the championship of order itself is travestied by dreams as wild and pretensions as perilous as those of the International itself. The Roman Catholic clergy, not satisfied with the other difficulties which in this sceptical age they must affront, have staked the hopes of their cause upon the visionary project of replacing the Pope upon his temporal throne.[1] It involves, among other difficulties, the task of accomplishing a revolution against the feelings of the population concerned, against the desperate resistance of the Italian kingdom which is in possession, and against the wishes of the whole of Europe with the possible exception of France herself. If it is done, it can only be done against the most terrible odds, and at the risk of national extinction. But the clergy neither count the cost nor measure the obstacles. They seem to be making adhesion to this promising enterprise a condition of their support; and unless their support is freely given to the party of order, there is no doubt that M. Gambetta and his *'nouvelles couches sociales'*[2] will be the next occupants of power.

In England the tradition of order is not yet broken, and our difficulties are trivial compared to those of France. But we also are passing through a crisis on which much of our future destiny depends. We have no new institutions to discover and set up, but within their boundary our politics are scarcely less chaotic. Our political geography has to be reconstructed. The old frontiers separate those who in opinion are not divided, and classify under one name men who have now no principle in common. There is this analogy between our condition and that of France, that an exceptional responsibility lies at this juncture upon those who in that country are called the Centres, but whom for want of a less clumsy vocabulary we are compelled to designate as moderate Liberals. It is to their uncertain policy and their unnatural alliances that much of our embarrassment is due, and upon them it depends whether political conflict shall be restored to the dignity of a war of principles, or shall sink, as in America, to a reckless struggle for personal advancement. The decision of this school of politicians is at all times looked for with all the interest and all the

---

[1] The restoration of the temporal power of Pope Pius IX in Rome, which had been destroyed in 1870, was at this time a cause linked by many French Catholic legitimists with that of the restoration of the Bourbon monarchy in France.

[2] The radical republican leader Léon Gambetta had proclaimed in a speech at Grenoble, in September 1872, the entry into political life of 'une couche sociale nouvelle', composed of the urban and rural working class.

varying speculations belonging to the unknown. Like the electors who vote towards four o'clock, their vote exceeds all other and more calculable votes in value, simply because their course is doubtful. Their choice is looked for with additional anxiety, because the flow of opinion can be better judged by their movements than by any other. Steadied by no strong political belief, they yield more smoothly and promptly to the prevailing current than their better moored neighbours on the right and on the left. Their influence is specially remarkable in countries where change is made slowly, and political passions are not extravagant. In Spain no one cares what the Centres think. They are normally captives of the bow and spear; their supple fidelity is one of the easiest and least valued prizes of a successful pronunciamiento. In France they are only of importance in a strange juncture like the present, where the predominance of the army is neutralised by the exceptional loyalty of the ruling General.[1] But in England their influence has generally been commanding. It disappears during periods of strong political belief, such as that of the Restoration, or of the great revolutionary war, or of the first Reform Bill. But these epochs in England are few and far between; and during the intervals the power of the Central school of politicians, and especially of the Left Centre, resumes its importance. And in proportion as faith in all political dogmas grows dim, and enthusiasm is frozen by disappointment, the national course will be guided by those to whom this cheerless climate is familiar.

During the half-century of breathless change from which we are apparently at last to have a respite, the position of these moderate Liberals has been very remarkable. While the torrent was passing, they did not keep their feet better than other people. It has constantly happened to them to find themselves voting for that which they had denounced: accepting logical conclusions, the fear of which they had once derided as the 'hobgoblin argument;' proposing a first step as absolutely final, and then, some years later, proposing the second as a necessary corollary of the first. A forecast in 1820 of their proceedings during the following fifty years would have surprised no one so much as themselves. Like John Gilpin, 'they little thought, when they set out, of running such a rig.' But still they were marked off from the bold companions by whose side they marched, and whose ends they unwittingly served, by one strong distinction. They genuinely believed in 'finality.' The particular reform in hand was on each occasion desired by them for its own sake only – as the exceptional remedy of an exceptional

[1] Marshal MacMahon had been elected president of France in May 1873.

'THE PROGRAMME OF THE RADICALS'

abuse – as a close of controversy – as a step towards political repose. They looked forward to no vista of perpetual subversion. They did not imagine their party to exist for the purpose of eternally devising new changes, and agitating the public mind to carry them out. They would never have recognised it as a reproach that their budget of reforms was exhausted, and that they had no fresh institution to suggest for attack. It would never have occurred to them that it was the duty of a Liberal leader to collect his party, as if he were collecting moths and bats, by the exhibition of a 'blazing principle.' If they formed a party of change, it was because in their judgment great changes were required. It would not have entered into their philosophy that great changes ought to be proposed for the purpose of keeping the party of change together. The difference between the two sections is this: the moderate Liberals are Radicals *ad hoc*: the others are Radicals permanently. The one section mark trees to be cut down because they think a clearance is required; the others mark them because cutting down trees is their business; and when they have finished one job, they clamour against their leaders until they are conducted to another. It is the business of their leaders to find trees to be cut down. There lies the difficulty of the present moment. The Liberal leaders are in danger of being dethroned because they have not a fresh 'policy' – in other words, because they cannot find new and yet safe materials to gratify the destructive instincts of their followers.

To the latter section of the party it is idle to talk of political repose. They believe what they call 'progress' to be the condition of political vitality; and their definition of 'progress' is destruction. But to those Liberals who believe in finality, whose views of reform have a fixed horizon, the present is a juncture of supreme importance. The political aims of the party of movement are undergoing an entire revolution, which would have forced itself more prominently upon public attention if it had not been so far carried on with singularly little change of persons. The battle-field is changing, and the colours, and the objective point of the assailant's strategy: but a large proportion of the combatants remains the same. It is still the parson and the squire, and in the background the king and noble, who are the first objects of attack: though now there are associated with them a large class of employers of labour who used to be fighting on the other side, and who feel themselves in strange company. The assault is still conducted chiefly by poverty and philosophy; academical dreamers furnish to the movement its brains, and the Have-nots, who would gladly have without industry or thrift, supply its force. The Dissenters still contribute a large contingent; but, so far as they are not included in either of these two categories – so far as they are not hungry for endowment, or impatient of Christian belief – their alliance is traditional, depending more on habit than on present sympathy: and the same may be said of other classes of well-to-do auxiliaries, who are watching the motions of their allies with a not very friendly vigilance. But though there is in this country no very marked change in the composition of each host, the cause of battle is not the less rapidly changing.

The objects for which the moderate Liberals have contended during the last half-century may be summed up with sufficient accuracy by the word 'enfranchisement.' It is not a complete description. There was the curious struggle of Protection, when the Conservatives, under the guidance of Sir Robert Peel, were induced to take up the opinions which had been advocated by Mr. Fox; whereupon the Whigs, and after them Sir Robert Peel himself, with much discernment, and amid great public applause, appropriated to themselves the abandoned mantle of Mr. Pitt. But engrossing as this controversy was at the time, it was a mere episode in the political drama; a family quarrel between two classes who are naturally Conservative. Nor will the word enfranchisement include the violent measures with which the present Government commenced their career, and which the moderate Liberals rather acquiesced in than supported. But on the whole, enfranchisement sufficiently describes their policy. They sought to remove all political disqualification arising out of religious opinions, and – within certain limits, prescribed by the condition of popular education – all political disqualifications arising out of social rank. This was the object of their half-century's campaign. They were successful all along the line. They successively procured the admission to political equality of the Dissenters, the Roman Catholics, and the Jews, who had been professedly excluded on religious grounds, and large portions of the middle and lower classes, who had been practically, though not theoretically, excluded by the working of the Constitution. The Conservatives steadily resisted these successive relaxations; save that in the two cases of the Roman Catholics and the lower classes they came in at the end, and consented to be the instruments of passing the measures they had up to that time opposed. There was, naturally, no difference of opinion between these two opposing parties, either as to the immediate advantages of this enfranchising policy or as to the ultimate result which both desired it should produce. The Conservatives did not differ from their Liberal opponents as to the

'THE PROGRAMME OF THE RADICALS'

advantage of removing a source of discontent from the minds of powerful classes, but they feared the advantage might be bought too dearly if the Church Establishment were to be endangered by one set of measures, or the rights of property by the other. The moderate Liberals were sincere in desiring to uphold both the Church Establishment and the rights of property; but they utterly refused to believe that either would be jeopardised by their proposal of enfranchisement. The time is at hand when the value of this victorious confidence, or of these disregarded warnings, will be tested by experience. Now that the controversy is over, and the decision irrevocably taken, the only object of the Conservatives can be to prove in practice that their own alarms were baseless, and that the confidence of their Liberal opponents was wise. It surely cannot be the object of those opponents to prove exactly the opposite proposition.

Such, nevertheless, would be the result if the more violent half of the Liberal party had its way. If the views of the late Mr. Stuart Mill upon land,[1] or of Mr. Bright upon the Church,[2] or of Sir Charles Dilke upon the Monarchy,[3] or of Mr. Trevelyan upon the House of Lords,[4] were to prevail, the sinister prophecies of the Tories and Conservatives of the last fifty years would be more than justified. If it were possible to believe that the moderate Liberals, who work with these men, design and always have designed to lead the nation by insincere professions of aversion to the results they have all along repudiated, no one could deny them the praise of a very Machiavellian intelligence. But no one believes it. The Whigs and their political congeners are not the stuff out of which sincere revolutionists are made. They are not in that position in the world in which the 'nationalisation' of property, or even the confiscation of its 'unearned increment,' presents an alluring future to the mind. Their attachment to the Church is, no doubt, of a discriminating kind; but even those who are most inclined to abandon her in minor controversies shrink from the convulsion which must accompany so stupendous a confiscation as that which Disestablishment would bring with it. Yet the moderate Liberals are working heartily with the men to whom all these things are objects of intense aspiration. They, in common with

[1] Cf. p. 217, above. Mill had died in May 1873.
[2] I.e. in favour of disestablishment.
[3] Dilke, the thirty-year-old M.P. for Chelsea, an advanced Radical and republican, had caused fierce controversy by his observations at Newcastle in November 1871 on the cost of the monarchy, and by his Commons' motion of March 1872 for a full enquiry into Queen Victoria's expenditure, which received only two votes.
[4] G. O. Trevelyan (1838–1928), M.P. Border Burghs, was a leading Radical critic of the hereditary chamber.

Miall[1] and Odger, and Bradlaugh[2] and Dilke, belong to the great Liberal party. They accept the support of these men, seek to conciliate their votes, and on a pinch use their help for purposes of agitation: and they do this for the sole purpose of resisting the Conservatives, from whom, in opinion, they are separated by an almost invisible line. What is the explanation of this mysterious policy? They must clearly have some other object in view than to satisfy the political appetites of their wild auxiliaries. It is plain that the two parties to this strange alliance expect from it diametrically opposite results; and that one section or the other must consequently be deceived in the end.

It may seem a truism to assert that progress means going somewhere. Yet no one has been able to extract from the spokesmen of the 'party of progress' where in their case that somewhere is. As to some sections of the party the answer is clear enough; but by the party as a whole, these special objects are repudiated. Mr. Stuart Mill and the other philosophical Radicals knew perfectly well what the word progress meant for them; they desired to 'overthrow the principle of aristocracy;' and Mr. Mill's aims with respect to land were probably a portion of this policy. Mr. Miall and the Dissenters have a distinct object in view as their journey's end – to strip the Church of its endowments, the State of its ecclesiastical prerogatives. There are a host of smaller cliques who have peculiar views with respect to Republicanism, Intemperance, Contagious Disease,[3] and so forth; progress for them has a very distinct, though it may be a very narrow, meaning. But what does the word express to the Liberal party as a whole? It does not adopt all or any of the definitions recognised by these various subdivisions. Its authorised exponents would repudiate them with horror. Even Mr. Gladstone would think thrice before abolishing the House of Lords, and kindly bequeaths the Disestablishment of the Church to his successors. To none of the objects that we have indicated would the assent of half the Liberal party be obtained. But whither is their progress going? Progress signifies going forward; which road is forward? and what is at the end of it? Progress in the abstract, with no itinerary and no goal, is as reasonable an idea as a pilgrimage to

[1] Edward Miall (1809–81), M.P. Bradford, editor of the *Nonconformist*, and a leading supporter of disestablishment.
[2] Charles Bradlaugh (1833–91), the great atheist and republican publicist, and proprietor of the *National Reformer*.
[3] I.e. venereal disease. The Contagious Diseases Acts of 1864–9 attempted to protect the health of the armed forces by introducing a system of regulated prostitution in a number of garrison and dockyard towns. Efforts to extend their application produced a counter-movement for repeal, and the issue figured in several by-elections in the early seventies. Repeal finally came in 1886.

'THE PROGRAMME OF THE RADICALS'

nowhere in particular. To these questions no answer has even been given by the Liberal party as a whole – that is, by the moderate Liberals, who till recently have ruled it, and whom it is still essential to conciliate and reassure. As long as finality was politically tenable, progress in the abstract was little thought of. The world had heard little of 'onward marches,' or 'the increasing purpose of the age.' In the Palmerstonian era – the golden age of moderate Liberals – they knew very well that this class of phrases, though useful to writers, and conducive to a majority, were not likely to mislead the practical acuteness of their wary chief. There is no danger of a medium being taken in by his own spirits. But the state of things has changed. The Radicals have seen some of their proposals accepted, and for others they have obtained formidable encouragement from Parliament or from Liberal statesmen. What is progress? and whither is it leading? are questions which moderate Liberals, by whose aid alone the march can be continued, are bound to answer clearly to their own minds.

The Government have been in trouble during the past year: and they have accordingly been much blessed with advisers. The constant burden of the advice has been, 'Have a policy;' by which, of course, is meant a policy of change. It is of no use, they are told, to rely on past achievements; they must go forward 'to fresh fields and pastures new;' and the Government, to judge by recent appointments, are prepared to follow this advice. The moderate Liberals, who are possibly doubting in their minds as to what the progress of which they hear so much may mean, may be anxious to know which these pastures are. But on that subject they receive no information. The demand is, not that any particular pastures shall be selected, but only that the pastures shall be new. It may be worth while to inquire what pastures there are available. A map of them, for the benefit of those disciples of progress who yet retain sufficient common sense to wish to know whither they are progressing, would be a very useful Liberal publication. In default of it we will attempt such a brief survey as Radical outpourings enable us to construct. It may at least serve as an anticipatory chronology of the Liberal Ministries of the future. If it is a law of their being that in each session of Parliament they must on pain of extinction offer fresh fields for their flocks to consume and trample down, it may be interesting to know how much there is still unconsumed; and how soon we shall have reached those pleasant pastures in which the Liberals of France and Spain are happily reposing.

In surveying the Radical programme of the future, it is needless to refer to a large category of legislation on which parties do not quarrel. It is necessary to notice this class of measures because it is a favourite Radical device of the party of movement to accuse those who deprecate organic change of desiring legislative stagnation. We have been accused of hostility to all improvement, because, in pleading for repose at last from the incessant demolitions of recent years, we have made no reservation in favour of legislative changes which, unchallenged by class or party, are unquestionably needed. It would be as reasonable to blame a preacher for depreciating mathematics because he had made no allusion to Euclid in his sermon. In dealing with the contention of parties it seems irrelevant to refer to those matters on which parties do not contend. We hold them to be so far from objectionable that they, and they alone, are the proper work of Parliament, and that it is detained from its normal labours by the perpetual intrusion of revolutionary projects. To uproot institutions, to sow bitter resentments, to give to class or sect the spoliation of a rival by the brute force of a legislative majority, may possibly, in cases of extreme emergency, be a task from which governments cannot escape, but it is a field of duty to be entered with sorrow, and to be quitted with the utmost speed. In the improvement of law, of local government, of sanitary arrangements, in the alleviation, so far as statutes can procure it, of the sufferings of the poor – matters which give triumph to no class and no denomination – there is much material for the labour of Parliament, little for the manufacture of cries or the excitement of politicians. It is not for these that wire-pullers work, or party bonds are formed, or close divisions taken. They will never be more than the obligatory garnish of the programme of the Radicals.

Fiscal measures occupy an ambiguous position. They are a favourite field for passages of arms between Ministry and Opposition; but for the last twelve years they have seldom touched the great questions which are in issue between Conservatives and Radicals. They could hardly do so, unless they were prostituted to the purpose of favouring some class whose votes were valuable, at the expense of another class, or to the detriment of the exchequer. Rumour, ever unkind to falling Ministers, imputes to them a project of this kind. Recent arrangements have encouraged the belief that next April is to be an epoch in finance; that the great enchanter,[1] who has resumed the wand he had buried fathoms deep, will wave it once more over the electors, and that the popularity of 1853 and 1860 will rise again at his call. But rumour goes one step further, and even unveils the plan of his future triumph. It is to be

[1] Gladstone.

'THE PROGRAMME OF THE RADICALS'

nothing more ingenious or refined than that onslaught on indirect taxation, known as the 'free breakfast-table.' If the state of the finances shall be such as to justify a general reduction of taxation, extending to both branches, direct and indirect, the nation will accept the boon with gladness from whatever hands it comes; nor will any one grudge the benefit that will accrue to the Ministers as the messengers of such pleasant news. But if the relief is given to the indirect taxpayer alone, the proposal will cease to have a purely financial character; it will become a political transaction of the most objectionable kind. The class who only pay indirect taxation are already specially favoured in England; they bear a lighter share of the common burden than in the Republic of America or the Republic of France. To give them a special advantage in any scheme of taxation will be to aggravate an already offensive inequality. The advantages, again, of indirect taxation are already too much ignored in our actual arrangements. The fact that they are scarcely recognised by those who pay them, will outweigh to a statesman many purely economical disadvantages. It is a good thing that a tax should not be wasteful; it is better that it should not be galling. A tax may be costly in collection; it may even tend seriously to discourage the trade to which it applies: yet it will be less pernicious than one which is constructed according to the strictest rules of economical orthodoxy, but leaves a bitter resentment in the hearts of those who have to pay it. If taxes, which in policy are the least inexpedient and in equity have no special claim to remission, are taken off, a political motive for the proceeding must be assumed; and it will be readily found in the fact, that the class which is to be relieved is the most numerous at the poll. It is a pecuniary mode of appeasing discontent, to which, as we know to our cost, the Government are much attached. The method of reconciliation they pursued with the Americans[1] is the one they are said to be preparing for their own followers. Being accused of sundry unfriendly and disloyal proceedings towards their democratic supporters, they propose, instead of disproving the accusation, to settle the difficulty by paying down damages in hard cash out of the taxes. The device is so transparent, that the House of Commons could not sanction it, even if the Ministry – which we cannot believe – could stoop so low as to suggest it.

Neither is it necessary now to dwell on those questions which are occasionally discussed by speculative politicians, but which, in the present state of opinion, are either too small or too large to be regarded as a plank in any party's platform. Of the first kind the Game Laws are

[1] I.e. in the settlement of the *Alabama* claims.

a fair instance. They might, with more propriety, be called the Hare Laws: for to that important quadruped alone the serious discussion is apparently confined.[1] No one seems to quarrel with the winged game; and no one advocates the preservation of rabbits upon cultivated land. We do not anticipate that the destiny of the British Constitution will, to any great extent, turn on the destiny of the hare. This, and two or three other questions, which are referable to no general principle, excite a keen interest in particular constituencies. Pledges of a peculiarly fervid character are exacted by the electors and freely given by the candidate. But the fervour evaporates in the air of Westminster, which is fatal to sporadic enthusiasm. Hares, Hypothec,[2] and the Deceased Wife's Sister[3] may occasionally form the subject of a party division: but, whatever happens to them, their fate will not affect the political history of the country. On the other side, there are questions which are too large for partisans at present to touch. No English Radical has ventured to support the disintegration of the Empire demanded in Ireland under the name of Home Rule. A few adventurous 'fellow-labourers' of the Government, inspired no doubt by good example (it was in 1871, the year of the Commune), thought that the time was come for an assault upon the monarchy. Their eccentricities were suppressed with more vigour than politeness: and their miserable fate will probably warn off imitators for at least many sessions to come.[4] The House of Lords stands in a very peculiar position. Though not unpopular in the country, there are many theorists who would be glad to attack it, if they only knew what to do with it. Any alteration of its structure must inevitably make it more

[1] The over-preservation of hares under the game laws was a great grievance of farmers, who suffered their depredations.
[2] The hypothec, in Scottish law, is a security constituted over movable property which remains in the possession of the debtor, the best-known legal hypothec being that of a landlord over movables in leased premises. In 1871 the lord advocate introduced a bill for the abolition of hypothec, the defeat of which owed something to his own imprudence in explaining that this restriction of the rights of Scottish landlords would furnish a precedent for the abolition of the English law of distress.
[3] The bill to legalise marriage with a deceased wife's sister was a hardy annual at this period, several times approved by the Commons and rejected by the Lords.
[4] By 1871 Queen Victoria's long retirement since the death of the Prince Consort had brought her some unpopularity, and the Paris Commune helped to stimulate republican feeling, though spokesmen like Odger, Bradlaugh, and Dilke hardly rivalled their French counterparts in menace. When, in the spring, the Queen's fourth daughter, Louise, married the eldest son of the Duke of Argyle, large popular meetings at Birmingham and Nottingham passed resolutions condemning the grants voted to the couple. But the Queen's illness in the early autumn and the Prince of Wales's critical illness in December caused a swing of sentiment, and republican apologists received some rough handling.

'THE PROGRAMME OF THE RADICALS'

self-reliant, and more tenacious of its own opinions than it is now: and this is not exactly the result which Radicals desire to obtain. Its abolition would add largely to the territorial interest in the House of Commons. Moreover, the nation would shrink from surrendering its interests, without check or makeweight, to the absolute disposal of the latter body. Some substitute, therefore, for the House of Lords must be discovered: and the receipt for making a new second chamber in an old country is as hard to find as the philosopher's stone. For the present, at all events, the constitution of the House of Lords is either considered too unimportant or too perplexing to find a place in the manifestoes of the disaffected Liberals.

There are still remaining a few outlying bits which belong to the old Liberal domain, portions of political territory on which it is possible to raise the standard of enfranchisement. Efforts have been made to construct a useful cry out of the condition of the County Franchise. It does not seem a hopeful enterprise. Some day it may be practicable to inspire the agricultural labourer with so much political ambition that he will agitate earnestly for a household franchise that shall admit him to the vote. If such an agitation should arise, and if the Tories should be strongly opposed to it, it will be possible for the Liberals to enter upon the campaign with an unbroken organisation, and all the advantages of a traditional battle-cry. But there is good reason to doubt whether either of the two parties is ready to take up the position necessary for giving battle upon this question. It will be hard to inspire the Liberals with enthusiasm for an extension of the County Franchise. They have tried it already, and it has brought them no luck. Mr. Locke King's leadership has been utterly disastrous.[1] The lower we have gone into the depths of rural society, the more Conservative the strata have hitherto proved to be. Their character may change as you go deeper; but there is little ground for either asserting or denying it. It is a sheer matter of speculation, with only this one element of certainty, that the poor rural householders are and must remain the most dependent class existing among us. The Ballot in sparse districts is utterly futile, and the labourer who cultivates Radicalism, amid Tory farmers, squires, and clergy, will pass a stormy existence. On the other hand an equalisation of the Town and County Franchise must carry with it a large re-arrangement of electoral districts, and every approach to equality of electoral power will be to the advantage of the country and the detriment of the towns. We

[1] P. J. Locke King (1811–85), M.P. East Surrey, was the most persistent advocate of the reduction of the county franchise to the borough level.

are sceptical therefore of a great Liberal movement in favour of a County Reform Bill.[1] Still less is it probable that a converse enthusiasm will develop itself among their opponents. The Conservatives will never be brought into line again upon a franchise question. The recollections of the year 1867, whatever else they may have done, have at least secured this result during the lifetime of the present generation. There is no great political future for the County Franchise. Whatever legislation may ultimately take place upon it, it is not here that the 'new pastures' are to be found.

This is the last political controversy belonging to the old era. Beyond it every question on which serious controversy can arise belongs to one or other of the two great conflicts of the future, the battle of Property, or the battle of the Church. Every cry that has more than a local interest excites attention only as part of these two great controversies. The Burials Bill, and the Endowed Schools agitation,[2] would sink into questions of secondary detail if they were not part of a wide-reaching plan. Like a battlefield in actual war, they derive their significance not from the value of the ground itself, but from the importance of the country to which they open an access. After half a century of struggle, Conservatives have learned to distinguish the twofold character of grievances. There are grievances of suffering, and there are grievances of strategy. The grievance of suffering is urged in good faith by those who smart under it: and the object of their remonstrances, or their agitations, is simply to obtain redress. When redress is granted, the grievance ceases, and the agitation is heard of no more. In these days such grievances are rare: for they have been one by one detected in the course of discussion, and killed by concession. The grievance of strategy is of a very different type, and enjoys a far more tenacious life. Its characteristic is that the discontent it indicates is not cured but aggravated by concession. It is urged, not for its own sake, but for the sake of something that lies beyond. It is part of a great plan in which each move prepares the way for the move that is to follow. Success does not soothe agitation, but quickens it by giving to it an earnest of ultimate triumph. These two forms of grievance naturally call for diametrically opposite treatment. It may be worth the while of a party, or a class, to make many sacrifices for the purpose of appeasing a genuine discontent. By surrendering a portion they may save the rest: and, at all events, may cure a disaffection

[1] Nonetheless, the demand for household suffrage in counties was to be endorsed by the Liberal leadership in 1877.
[2] For the points at issue, see p. 162, n. 1, above.

'THE PROGRAMME OF THE RADICALS'

that menaces the whole community. But to make sacrifices to a grievance of strategy is to feed the evil which you seek to cure. It is to remove a difficulty from the enemy's way, to facilitate his progress to more distance objects, and to inspire him with fresh confidence in his ultimate triumph. A general who should have tried to keep the Prussians from taking Paris by surrendering to them Mont Valérien[1] would not have been more foolish than the statesman who tries to meet a grievance of strategy by concession.

It is on this ground that the Burials Bill and other similar measures have been resisted. Had they been based on genuine grievances, had they been called for by the real wants of a considerable number of persons, it would have been for the interest of the Church to make concessions in order that the discontent might be removed. But they were worked by men who did not conceal the motive of their efforts. The various measures which with more or less success have been levelled of late years against the Church have issued from one manufactory, and have borne the same well-known stamp. Such agitation as there was for them was called into existence by the Liberation Society, and has been sustained by their exertions. The Bills have been supported by their brigade, advocated in their newspapers, put forward as test questions in every borough by their agents. They and their following are the only people upon whom the grievance has pressed with sufficient weight to provoke political action. Was it ever pretended that concession on these points would satisfy them? or that it would make their hostility less enterprising or less tenacious? On the other hand, it would have removed obstacles from their path. Parliament will not take more than one step at a time. The longer any step is made to last, the longer the next project of attack must be deferred. Even if in the result it should turn out that nothing has been gained except time, yet is it no small matter to gain time: especially for the upholders of an ancient institution whose members have become sluggish from long security, and who need many and sharp shocks of alarm before they will bestir themselves in their own defence. The Conscience Clause[2] is a curious instance of the value of this policy. For many years the Dissenters devoted their utmost efforts to the establishment of the Conscience Clause in all State-aided schools. As far as education went, it was the sum and substance of their aggressive

---

[1] The fort covering the west of Paris, and a key point in the siege of 1870–1.
[2] A provision allowing parents to withhold their children from an elementary school's religious instruction if they objected to it, and designed primarily to protect children of dissenters who were obliged by lack of alternatives to attend Anglican schools. The Education Act of 1870 imposed the clause on all state-aided elementary schools.

efforts. Churchmen were pretty well aware that it would not give the Dissenters what they wanted: and, holding it to be called for by no genuine grievance, they opposed it stoutly. The battle raged for many years, during which the educational organisation of the Church was rapidly growing. At last, in 1870, it was carried. But no sooner had the Dissenters gained their object than they saw that their object was worthless. They turned round fiercely to attack the whole principle of Denominational Education. But they were too late. They had wasted many years upon the Conscience Clause, while the educational organization of the Church was growing; and now it is too strong to be disturbed.

Those smaller Church questions, which now for twenty years have occupied a large share of the Wednesdays of the House of Commons, cannot be rightly appreciated unless they are considered together with the proclaimed designs of those who moot them. They are but small fractions of the whole: but the power which succeeds in one of them will be all the stronger to carry through its avowed intention of raising all the others in succession. The smaller issues that surround the land question must be considered in the same light. The laws which in popular discussion are honoured with the names of Primogeniture and Entail are not in themselves of the first importance. Stated in more accurate but more modest language, they only concern the disposal of the estates of intestates, and power of settlors to extend their settlements over twenty-one years of unborn life. If without controversy or legislation both the proposed changes[1] were by some fairy's intervention to make their appearance on the statute-book to-morrow, we doubt if any palpable effect for either good or evil would result. Intestates are a scanty and diminishing class of people; and the existence of such a law would diminish their number further. The notion that a change in the law would make a change in public feeling on the subject, and induce men not to leave the bulk of their land to their eldest sons, is a Radical illusion, due, no doubt, to that extravagant exaltation of the State which is the peculiarity of their school. We see no reason to believe that the moral influence of the law would be greater in behalf of younger sons than it has been in behalf of widows. For centuries the law has declared that, failing other provisions, a widow shall enjoy for life one-third of her husband's lands. For centuries instruments have been uniformly executed setting the law aside, and making other, and generally much

[1] I.e. the abolition of primogeniture in cases of intestacy (with consequent division of the estate), and the restriction of settlement to living persons. Radicals saw these measures as a means to promote the subdivision of landed property.

'THE PROGRAMME OF THE RADICALS'

slenderer, provision in its place. A change in the law as to intestacy would not influence landowners more in the case of primogeniture than the ancient law of the country has done in the case of dower. The other proposed change would be equally ineffective for its intended object, the scattering of landed property. The law of Entail, as it has existed for the last forty years, is not particularly favourable to the maintenance of large estates. It works thus. A landowner executing a marriage settlement for his son settles the estate upon the son for life, and upon his unborn grandson absolutely. Of course this provision prevents the son from squandering the estate: but what about the grandson? All that the landowner has done is to tie the hands of his son whose character he knows, and who possibly may be quite trustworthy, and leave the estate utterly at the mercy of the unborn grandson, of whose character he can know nothing. In practice the danger is met, if necessary, by putting pressure, when the time comes, upon the grandson. When he grows up, or when he marries, he wants a secured allowance, and a re-settlement of the estate is the price of his allowance. But if he should for any reason prove recalcitrant, or if he should succeed to the estate early, he is free to dissipate it, and the effect of the law of entail has been to prevent his father from imposing by will any restraint upon his extravagance. The power of settling upon the unborn might be a protection if it were used exceptionally as a restraint upon sons whose extravagance had betrayed itself during their father's lifetime; but systematically employed as it is now, in marriage settlements, it tends rather to endanger than to secure the cohesion of landed estates. But the fact that these proposed changes – the distribution of land in intestacy, and the restriction of settlement to living persons – are not in themselves of great significance tells both ways. It is more fatal to the attack than to the defence. This weakness, we believe, will show itself when, if ever, they become practical propositions. They have no strength to stand alone. They will benefit no one, except perhaps the lawyers; they will remedy no grievance and relieve no suffering; they will not alter any man's social position, or ease the life of any man who is now embarrassed. All they can possibly do is to gratify the class hatreds of a clique of philosophers. If ever the cry for them becomes powerful enough to make them matter of party battle, it will be not for what they can do but for what they may prepare. They will only acquire the force necessary for political vitality when they become parts of some much larger attack upon property in land. They will then deserve to be judged by the programme of those who urge them. The only circumstance which will give them a chance of discussion will probably make their rejection certain. In the meantime their comparative insignificance must not be allowed to conceal the fact that one of them gratuitously reverses an ancient usage, and that the other is a restriction of that right of free testamentary disposition which is one of the most valued of all the incidents of property and the fair prize of industry and thrift.

There are two lines by which the free enjoyment of landed property may be assailed. It may be done by limiting the dying man's right of free bequest, or the living man's right of free contract. It may restrict either his settlements or his leases. The first method has been followed to its utmost logical extent across the Channel.[1] As an instrument for reducing society to a dead level, and exterminating the principle of aristocracy, it is unrivalled. Whether the gratification of democratic sensibilities achieved by that process is worth the loss of national cohesion which it involves, is a question which may be answered by the present experience of France. But whatever its merits in that respect, it will never be adopted in England. It would irritate to the utmost the feelings of every landowner, and it would have none but theoretic friends: for it would benefit only the rising generation of younger sons, not the generation which has a practical voice in public affairs. The proposal to abolish what are called 'primogeniture and entail' is a timid and hesitating step on the road upon which France has travelled so far. This is the utmost length to which, in view of our national prepossessions, our philosophers venture to go. We do not believe that when they come to look at it more closely, they will think this inconclusive effort worth the trouble it will cause them. They will prefer to advance in another line and seek their precedents in a different legislation. The Irish Land Act has sanctioned the principle that when two parties have made a contract as to land, the State may lawfully step in and wrest it aside in favour of one of them; presenting him with a contingent right to money payments of which, when he made the contract, he never dreamed. The only claim to this act of violence, committed on its behalf, that could be pleaded by the favoured class was that it was organised, unscrupulous, and politically strong. This is a precedent upon British soil which the assailants of the landowner are more likely to follow than any French example. It is capable of being pushed much further. The Irish Land Act reduces the landlord to the condition of a ward, forbidding him in effect to alter the occupancy of the mass of his land

---

[1] In France, the *Code Napoléon* of 1804 had abolished primogeniture and limited freedom of disposition in favour of surviving children, giving each child the right to a minimum share.

'THE PROGRAMME OF THE RADICALS'

without the permission of a barrister appointed by the Government in each county. The Irish are clamouring for a further reform which they call Fixity of Tenure. They propose to reduce the landlords further from the condition of wards to the condition of mortgagees. Whether they will ever obtain this exaction, it is hard to conjecture. If we were merely to judge of the future by the past, it would be rash to attribute any limit to the pliancy of the Imperial Parliament. We would rather hope that the lessons of experience have not been lost on us, and that the days of pulpy statesmanship are past. Parliament seems at last to have parted from the maxim that everything is to be given to those who bluster for it. But in any case they will agitate for it long and loudly: and Irish agitation is the English Radical's opportunity. The demand has been echoed at more than one meeting of Scotch farmers. The leaders of the labourers' unions[1] have done their best to use it as an instrument for combining labourers and farmers in a common campaign against the landlords. The sympathy with which they meet at present is not extensive: and their labours have hitherto made more Tories by alarm than Radicals by persuasion. But at least it is politically practical. It ensures friends by offering a bait to the acquisitiveness of a large number of persons. It satisfies the Revolutionist's standing strategy – the bribery of one class by the spoliation of another. And therefore we confidently predict that it is in this direction that the meditations of our philosophers will gravitate. Certain it is that short of this they will not find, upon the subject of land, the materials of an effective agitation or even of a good working cry. They must cross the Communist frontier before, in this direction, any 'pastures new' will reward their pilgrimage.

In the direction of the Church the same prospect lies before them. The ground around them is eaten up, and they must move: and the ground immediately in front of them is barren. There is no political nutriment to be derived from Burial Bills or Clerical Fellowships,[2] or the School Pence of little pauper boys.[3] The fair meadows of Disestablish-

[1] I.e. the new unions of agricultural workers, of which Joseph Arch's National Agricultural Labourers Union was the most important.

[2] Radicals wanted the removal of all restrictions in Oxford and Cambridge college statutes making holy orders a condition of holding a fellowship or headship. The government had refused to legislate for this in 1871, when the University Tests Act threw open lay posts to non-Anglicans.

[3] The great symbolic issue in educational politics at this moment was the 25th clause of the Education Act of 1870, empowering school boards to pay school fees for children whose parents could not afford them. Since the clause could be used to subsidise attendance at Anglican schools out of the rates, it had become the focal point of the Radical and nonconformist attack on denominational education.

ment are already upon the horizon: and thither those who mean to move any further must make up their minds to go. The active members of the Radical party are fully aware, and in no wise anxious to conceal, that this must be the next stage of 'progress.' Mr. Joseph Chamberlain, speaking apparently on behalf of the Birmingham League,[1] proposes it as the main plank in the new platform, *Free Church, Free Schools, Free Labour*, and *Free Land*. The two first objects, and the satisfaction of several minor grievances, are to be obtained by the one process of Disestablishment.

The working class, which has no sympathy with the theological side of such controversies, caring little for the issue, so long as it is presented as a question of sectarian supremacy, will speedily recognise the importance of its political aspects, and will be eager enough to claim for the nation as a whole the control and management of the vast funds which have been monopolised and misappropriated by an ecclesiastical organisation. The agitation for the secularisation of Church endowments and for dethroning the Establishment as a great political engine for repressing the freest intellectual life and thought, and for opposing the manifestation and fulfilment of the popular will and aspirations, will supersede and include all the minor subjects, such as the 25th clause, the Burials question, and the abolition of clerical fellowships. It is impossible to rouse any enthusiasm on matters of detail with such limited interest for the great mass of the electorate, and it will be easier, as well as bolder and more honest, to fight the battle on the main issue rather than to go on perpetually skirmishing with the enemy, losing heart and courage in petty contests in which defeat can hardly be avoided. After the fall of the citadel the outworks will scarcely be worth defence, and when the nation has resumed its rights over the immense property which has been so long administered by the Church, it may be anticipated that the Commissioners who now regulate the affairs of Charities and Endowed Schools will cease to be guided by sectarian considerations in the management of their trusts. – *J. Chamberlain, Fortnightly Review.*

Mr. George Potter and some of his principal associates, two years ago, pledged the trades' unions to the same course: and three of the Ministers, Mr. Bright, Mr. Stansfeld,[2] and Mr. Winterbotham,[3] have voted for it. Even Mr. Gladstone, who, in the spring, spoke out against it manfully, appears to contemplate it more favourably now. If Mr. William Gladstone's knowledge of his father's opinions is accurate, the Prime Minister neither dissuades his followers from seeking it nor doubts that they will reach it. His limbs, indeed, are too stiff to make the journey with

---

[1] I.e. the National Education League.
[2] President of the local government board since 1871.
[3] H. S. P. Winterbotham (1837–73), M.P. Stroud and under-secretary at the home office.

'THE PROGRAMME OF THE RADICALS'

them: but he sees the promised land from afar, and points their course out to them as 'the work of the new era.'[1]

There is one feature in the new programme which is remarkable, as showing the increasing community of purpose that knits together English and Continental Radicals. The agitation for a godless education – 'l'instruction *laïque*, gratuite et obligatoire' – does not on the Continent proceed from those who dissent from the dominant religion. The Protestants take little part in it. It is the distinguishing cry of those who are hostile to all religion – those who have had the lamentable courage to banish not only the ministers, but the barest mention, of religion from the grave-side of their friends, and to make this wretched bravado a point of party orthodoxy. So it is coming to be in England. The agitation against denominational education, which was commenced by the Dissenters, is gliding gradually into stronger hands. The Birmingham League began by advocating 'unsectarian education': which in its vocabulary means to say, a religious education in which the English Church shall have no share. But the compromise was soon found to be politically unworkable: and the Dissenters, in the teeth of their whole religious history, allowed themselves to be pledged to the cause of secular education. But, in changing its flag, the League is changing its spirit. It appeals to free-thinking, not to Dissenting, sympathies. Its most earnest advocates are prominent writers in the 'Fortnightly Review.' Their arguments are political and philosophical, not religious. Their antipathy to the Church is not based upon her errors in those points wherein Dissenting bodies differ from her: but on her opposition to the free-thinking and subversive tendencies of the 'party of action.' Mr. Chamberlain, in the passage we have cited, strives to inflame the working classes against the Church expressly not upon theological but upon political grounds. The argument that endowments paralyse the spiritual activity of the Church has disappeared; on the contrary, her activity is the one thing to be deprecated now. It is not the endowments of the Church, but the Church itself as a body teaching dogmatic religion, and supporting the cause of social order, that is the object of antipathy to the Liberals of the League. Mr. Morley[2] writes in the same sense:

[1] Gladstone's eldest son, W. H. Gladstone, M.P. Whitby and a lord of the treasury, had told his constituents on 4 September, discussing the question of disestablishment, that his father was not the man to take the lead in that direction, since he felt that it was 'a question for the new aera', whilst he was the leader of the old era, fast coming to a close.

[2] John Morley (1838–1923), radical journalist and author, and editor of the *Fortnightly Review*; later a leading Liberal politician and biographer of Gladstone.

SALISBURY'S 'QUARTERLY REVIEW' ARTICLES

The State Church stands for *a decaying order of ideas*, and for ideas that grow narrower and more intense in proportion as they fall more out of harmony with the intellectual life of the time. What statesmanship is that which at a time like this, and with such an outlook, invests its priests with a new function, and entrusts a fresh and holy army of misologists with the control of national instruction?[1]

This union of the Dissenters and the Infidels is one among the many unnatural alliances which are so potent an instrument for destruction in our day. It is easy to combine on a mere negative. Numbers who have no liking in common can agree upon what they hate: and they seem to think that such a bond of union is sufficient to justify political combination. In such monstrous partnerships there is always an element of treachery. There is always on each side a full intention that at the close of the operation the other side of the alliance shall not keep the chestnuts. The fruits of victory cannot be divided between parties who are diametrically opposed: they must be appropriated wholly for the benefit of one ally or the other. The only interesting question is, Which will succeed in deceiving his friend? The honest Dissenter does not wish for the success of the Infidel: the Infidel assuredly has no intention of promoting the religious doctrines of the Dissenter. But they combine to assail the Church, which for different reasons is in their way: and each party flatters itself that the other has miscalculated, and that the reward of their combined efforts will fall to it. No student of history can have any doubt which of these two calculations will prove correct. In a combined movement against established institutions it is not the Girondins who win.

But the combination of Sceptics and Dissenters is not the most conspicuous of unnatural alliances. One that is wider in range, and therefore more pernicious in its results, is now being brought forcibly before us. The language which the Radicals are at the present juncture holding to the moderate Liberals who have been acting with them so long suggests the question, What have these two parties in common now? Mr. Chamberlain is of opinion that there is nothing:

The agreement on some primary and essential points is an absolute postulate of union. At the present time, unfortunately, no such ground of union seems to exist, one section of the Liberals being content to stand still, or even, as in the case of education, to go back, and the other anxious and determined to push on with accelerated speed.

[1] The quotation is from Morley's article on 'The Struggle for National Education' (part II), *Fortnightly Review*, new series, xiv (1873), 311. 'A fresh and holy army' should read 'afresh a holy army'.

'THE PROGRAMME OF THE RADICALS'

This at least is candid. The official representatives of the party, who see many practical inconveniences in the threatened revolt, try to make things pleasant to both sides by assuring them that they can combine in a common ardour for 'progress.' They do rightly to use the word: no word has ever achieved so brilliant a success in bamboozling mankind. But surely its career of deception is nearly run. At this time of day, even the most simple-minded politician, when exhorted to agitate for progress – especially if it is to be progress at 'accelerated speed' – will ask whither this rapid progress is to take him. The Radical programme is so plainly before the world that no one can deceive himself on that head. If you translate their 'Free Church, Free School, Free Land, Free Labour' from their dialect into ordinary English, it means legislation against the employer, legislation against the landlord, legislation against the Church. By the nature of things it must be so. Progress must inevitably lead them to an assault on property, or an assault on the Church Establishment, simply because all, or nearly all, the intermediate ground has been already passed. The moderate Liberals are bound to face and answer the question whether this kind of progress is to their taste. Have they that 'agreement on primary and essential points' which Mr. Chamberlain justly declares is an absolute postulate of union? If they have not, the time must inevitably come when they and their former supporters must part. What good do they hope for their country or for themselves from the longer continuance of an alliance which both sides know to be hollow, and which neither believes can last?

But to whom, it will be asked, are they to go? Party ties are hard to snap. Personal attachments cannot be laid aside like a suit of clothes: personal distrust may be too deeply rooted to yield to the strongest political exigency. Is it to be expected that they who for the last forty years have been almost always successful, and, in their own judgment, always right, should, to avoid possible error in the future, do penance by sueing to be admitted to the fellowship of those who, in their judgment, have been always wrong? We certainly should not venture to urge upon them any such advice, if for no other reason, at all events for this, that such advice would certainly be futile. Formal transfers of allegiance on the part of large political sections have not been common in the history of English parties: and even if more frequent precedents existed, there would be much to urge against their application in the present case. The moderate Liberals, if inclined for such a course, could hardly but exact such personal arrangements as would proclaim to the world that in changing their allies they had not struck their colours or abandoned their old convictions, but were only meeting circumstances that were wholly new. They might fairly require some security that the system of undercutting had been for ever abandoned; and that they should run no risk of being put into the ridiculous position of having been frightened by the innovations of their friends into promoting the greater innovations of their opponents. Though we believe that a heavy responsibility lies upon the moderate Liberals at the present juncture, it is not necessarily by the adoption of a new party allegiance that that responsibility will be best fulfilled. The question for their consideration is whether a line of political action is not required of them now somewhat higher in its aims than the ordinary rules of party drill. The English Intransigentes[1] have no special respect for the party tie. It never hampers or retards their own action; they only use it to drag along their reluctant allies. Men who are invited for the sake of party connexions to accept a new policy which they utterly detest must ask themselves what is the value of the party tie – whether it is only the means to an end, or the supreme end for which all others must be sacrificed.

The party system, with all its anomalies, worked as it must be by contrivances and accommodations, which constantly verge on insincerity, yet has this unquestioned title to our respect – that in practice it has secured us a safe and decent Government for many generations; and in the present age of the world even this achievement is no slight distinction. But it has its peculiarities; and one of them is that it is full of pitfalls for sincere politicians. It invites to the struggle for places; it professes to honour the battle for principles; but it will not allow any set of men to be successful in both these fields of political achievement. Of course those who are not in sympathy with the prevailing opinions of the day will succeed in neither one object nor the other. They will neither attain to place nor sustain their principles. But among the sections who constitute a dominant party the two kinds of success will always be allotted in inverse proportion. It must needs be so. *Cæteris paribus*, those who give their whole strength to one object will be more likely to succeed than those who distribute it between two. A Minister has other things to think of besides his own convictions. He must get votes – especially the votes of that portion of his supporters who least agree with him – and the votes of sincere men can only be purchased by concession. When a period of ministerial distress comes round, their price rises to famine

[1] 'Intransigentes' was the name given in the early 1870s to the extremist and revolutionary wing of the Republican party in Spain, some of whose members were involved in the abortive Cantonalist revolt in the summer of 1873.

'THE PROGRAMME OF THE RADICALS'

point. A Minister in straits can only obtain the votes of his extreme supporters by throwing over, to a great extent, his own convictions, and those of his moderate supporters. Sometimes he has stood firm; on many occasions he has yielded to temptation. Whenever he does yield, the result of the bargain is that he obtains an extension of official life as the price of his indifference to principle; and they obtain some great step in their scheme of policy as the price of their indifference to office. Thus it is that the section which stamps its own convictions upon the nation's policy will seldom attain to office; and the statesmen who struggle for what is called 'power' must be content to believe in several different sets of principles in the course of their career. It would be needless as well as invidious to cite illustrations of this rule. They stand out upon the history of our time. The first class almost always have belonged to the section of advanced Radicals; the office-bearers have till recently been almost exclusively drawn from the ranks of the moderate Liberals. Accordingly the outsiders, at first despised, in the end triumphant, have been throughout consistent in their opinions; while the principles of the office-bearers have been in a condition of constant, though reluctant, change.

The office-bearers have chosen this arrangement freely; no doubt they like it; and therefore they are not fit objects for compassion. But the condition of that large number of unofficial persons, who give to the office-bearers a steady support, does seem to us somewhat forlorn. They get neither the triumph of principle nor the gratification of place. It is pleasanter, perhaps, to consider them as patterns of pure unselfishness. They work hard and pay highly for their seats; they sustain the Minister stoutly so long as he is staunch; when he eats his principles, they go through the same meal as gracefully as is compatible with the necessary speed: they are too faithful to be worth buying; their advice is not listened to, because their discontent is not feared: and their only reward is the reflection that they are procuring for their friends the subtle gratification which office apparently bestows.

This is admirable, this is beautiful, so long as the amount of principle sacrificed is small compared to the claims of friendship. But when fundamental principles and interests of the first magnitude are at stake, the position needs to be reconsidered. We have reached one of those periods of crisis in the market of political support. The adhesion of the Radicals is valuable, and they propose to sell it high. They have given the Government open notice that a fresh contract is necessary, and they have shown themselves in earnest by imposing a portion of their terms, on pain of desertion, upon the Liberal candidates at the recent elections. They do not doubt that this pressure will succeed. They calculate that the moderate Liberals will balance the surrender of principles on the one hand, and the risk of sacrificing office on the other, and, after a short interval of coy reluctance, will take the new banners in their hands and lead the Radicals to victory as before. Mr. Leatham[1] only a fortnight ago avowed the hopes of his section with great frankness, and strikingly illustrated the estimate entertained by him and them of their moderate Liberal allies:

While he was sensible, however, of the great services rendered by the Premier, his warmest admirers must feel that on ecclesiastical questions he was going in one direction and they in another, casting his lot more and more with the advocates of Church monopoly, while they were more and more resolved on a policy of justice, even at the price of party leaders or of party itself. Experience proved that if the advanced section remained firm, the Whigs would be once more prevailed upon, and that those most indignant at there being any new banners to wave would be most active in waving them...He predicted that the measures which were now the bugbears of the Whigs would be looked back on ten years hence among the respectable monuments of Whig legislation. The Whigs would crow as lustily over the disestablishment of the English Church as if it had been their pet project since 1688, describing it as the inevitable result of Whig policy ever since the repeal of the Test and Corporation Acts. A nation which prided itself on its logic and exulted in its justice could not stop short of the conclusion pointed at by that logic and reason. With their faculty of seeing things after they had happened, and of appropriating the glory of other men's labours, the Whigs would describe the disestablishment of the English Church as the crowning achievement of their policy. They must choose between movement and death, and had always shown a healthy repugnance to the latter. Far from feeling dismay at the commotion in the Liberal ranks and the consequent effects upon Toryism here and there, he hailed it as a symptom that the spirit of progress, hated by Toryism and 'funked' at by Whiggism, was coming to the front, demanding new campaigns, new watchwords, new leaders, and new victories. We were getting among real questions now – a free Church, a free school, free labour, and free land. – *Speech at Halifax*, Sept. 27.

It is for the moderate Liberals to consider whether the position thus assigned to them is honourable to them, or useful to their country; and whether the pleasure of keeping some of their friends in office sufficiently repays them for the indignity of belonging to the same party with such men as these. The moderate Liberals, and they alone, give to Radicalism

[1] E. A. Leatham (1828–1900), Liberal M.P. for Huddersfield.

'THE PROGRAMME OF THE RADICALS'

its power. In what does that power consist? Can the Radicals return a majority to the House of Commons? Can they seat their own Ministry in power? They have never been more than a slender minority in Parliament even in their most prosperous days. They have a large following in some of our great towns, and in the Lowlands of Scotland; and they have many adherents among literary men, to whom they are commended by the sharpness and symmetry of their abstract theories. But for all purposes of practical politics their power has simply lain in their dexterous manipulation of the moderate Liberals. They can threaten to secede: they can make office dependent on their good-will. And where the questions involved have seemed of secondary moment, the moderate Liberals have yielded. But now – when no secondary questions remain, and we have come, by common consent, to what Mr. Leatham calls 'real questions' – will they still continue to yield? Will they even consent to be called members of the same party with men who avowedly reckon on cajoling them, and with whom they have no longer any cause in common?

It certainly seems sufficiently grotesque that, on the one hand, earnest supporters of the Church Establishment, on the other territorial and commercial magnates profoundly interested in the rights of property, should be designated under the same political name as Mr. Chamberlain and Mr. Leatham, Mr. Bradlaugh and Mr. Odger. If it were nothing more than a case of eccentric classification, it would only be absurd. Unfortunately the name carries with it very practical results. The moderate Liberals give money, men, above all, respectability and credit to whatever cause the party, as a whole, sustains: and the Radicals now insist that they shall select the cause which this assistance is to promote. The Radicals owe a large portion of such influence as they possess to the countenance given to them by those whom they threaten. Numbers would refuse to trust them, who trust them now, if their operations were not masked by the patronage of men who are beyond the suspicion of intentionally favouring revolutionary schemes. But, it is asked, to what party are the moderate Liberals to go? And this question is thought to dispose completely of the idea that they can ever escape from the chain by which the Radicals pull them along. Shall we never escape from the Party superstition? Is absolute submission to one of two leaders the only condition under which humanity in this island may presume to express or act upon a political opinion? To sacrifice smaller objects in order that by union greater objects may be attained, is to put the party-system to its proper use, and to give to it all the authority it can claim. To lend your name and aid to revolutionary projects which you abhor, merely that you may be 'true to your party,' is to elevate the means above the end, and to degrade a reasonable usage into a pernicious superstition. A more independent bearing is required by the dangers of the time. Unless the opponents of revolutionary change will consent to wear their party trammels as lightly as their friends – unless they will learn on their side too, to bargain, and to exact, as the consideration of their support, the advancement, not of their friends, but of their principles – our institutions will always be more feebly defended and will seem to be weaker in popular support than they really are.

In truth the code of party loyalty belongs to periods in which the subjects of political conflict are well settled, and have been long defined. They have little application in face of the announcement that we are entering on an epoch of 'new watchwords and new leaders.' Let the new leaders enlist fresh troops for their new cause. Veterans cannot suffer their military allegiance to be tossed over, as a matter of course, from one standard to another – least of all at a time when the very existence of our present social order depends on the fortunes of the war. Look abroad upon the kingdoms of Europe, and see what battle it is that is raging amongst them. We may follow there, in lurid intensity, the outline of the strife which more dimly threatens us at home. It is true that the watchwords used are not precisely the same. A more delicate perception of the meaning of words would prevent a Continental audience from accepting the declamatory rubbish which is in vogue upon many English platforms. They cannot imitate our bold treatment of the fascinating adjective 'free.' They would not understand how compulsory secular education could be advocated under the name of 'free school;' they would not designate a measure for restricting the rights of landowners, as 'free land;' nor would it occur to them to preach as 'free labour' provisions for facilitating the breach of contracts, and the coercion of independent labourers into involuntary strikes. But though the words they use are less misleading and more apt, the meaning is the same. Instruction from which religion shall be banished; legislation, which, in some fashion or other shall bestow upon the artisan a share of the land and of the capital he envies, are the dream of vast multitudes abroad; and they are the chimæras towards which the new agitators would mislead our working classes here. The only difference is that portions of the Radical programme, which are only a hope to the Radicals of England, are a reality there. The Church in France has been for

'THE PROGRAMME OF THE RADICALS'

three generations disendowed; the great properties, which Mr. Chamberlain denounces, have there ceased to exist. The Church has not been stripped of her power by the process of disendowment. On the contrary, she is more powerful now than she was a century ago; but she has ceased to be national. Her Gallican sympathies are rooted out. She uses the power of the State, when she can borrow it, for her own purposes; but she is no longer its fast ally. The clergy live their life apart, using their great popular influence for no national objects, knowing no citizenship, and no interests, but those of their Church, and shaping their foreign and their internal politics solely by their regard for that one end. The comminution of landed property has not mitigated the inequalities of fortune. Nowhere do they exist more glaringly, or are felt more keenly. But it has left the supreme power of the country in the hands of a petty peasantry too ignorant to wield it, deprived of leaders to guide them, and left at the mercy of every cunning delusion contrived by the professors of political legerdemain. The doctrines hostile to capital are younger, and have not yet obtained legislative recognition; but they have been zealously propagated, and in one direction they have achieved a sinister success. They have bred a deep fanaticism of hatred in the minds of the employed against the employers, far keener than that which divides hostile creeds or races, comparable only to the bitterness of a conquered people in the first years of their subjugation towards their oppressors. Such has been the working of these articles of the Radical programme – 'free Church, free land, free labour' – in the country where they have met with the most acceptance. The effects of their operation among ourselves – if they were allowed to operate – would differ less in substance than in form. We have a right to hope that their acceptance here is an improbable contingency. As long as the Continent is content to perform, for our benefit, the dangerous experiments which are necessary to the development of political science, England may look on, and be warned in safety. Englishmen justly rely on the sound political instinct which is their natural inheritance; but if it is to save us it must be honestly followed. It must not be paltered with for any secondary end. If men of influence and position consent to stifle their true convictions in a vain attempt to cling to a political nomenclature which has lost its meaning, and to preserve a party connexion which no longer expresses any unity of sentiment or of aim, the defence of our common cause is greatly enfeebled, and in the moment of danger may be paralysed. If the new Radical Party survives, and becomes formidable, its strength will be due to the support and countenance which the Moderate Liberals have given to it by consenting to endure its political alliance. And if, during the passage of any tempest of excited feeling, the Radicals should succeed in extorting confiscatory or socialist measures, no class will suffer more than the well-to-do triflers with Revolution – the allies whose hesitating patronage they are fain to use, but whom in using they openly despise.

'Disintegration'
(Q.R., no. 312; October 1883)

INTRODUCTORY NOTE

To PASS from 'The Programme of the Radicals' to Salisbury's last *Quarterly* article is to experience only a limited sense of transition, for, as the author himself noted, there was much in 1883 to recall the circumstances of ten years or so earlier. The Disraeli ministry of 1874–80 had come and gone, destroyed by economic depression and Gladstone's thunderings against its foreign and imperial policies. The Liberals were again in power with a large majority, but again beset by multiplying difficulties, and by deepening internal dissensions resulting from the pressure of their Radical wing under Chamberlain's lead. Chamberlain was in the cabinet now, together with Dilke, and Salisbury was leader of the Conservative party, in tandem with Sir Stafford Northcote.

The government had met trouble from the start. The first session of Parliament saw the beginnng of the protracted and discreditable struggle over Bradlaugh's right to take the oath. Then imperial problems built up: fighting in Afghanistan was succeeded by the rising of the Boers in the Transvaal, ending in 1881 in the independence of the province under British suzerainty, and in 1882 came the reluctant intervention in Egypt, from which it was subsequently to prove impossible to withdraw. But above all else stood the Irish question, now assuming a central place in British politics. The agricultural depression of the late seventies had hit the Irish tenant farmers severely: thousands had got into arrears with their rents, and the level of evictions had risen sharply. The Land League, organised by Michael Davitt in 1879, took the opportunity to bring the land issue into the foreground of Irish politics, and formed an alliance with the constitutional movement for Irish independence led by Parnell, on the understanding that the latter would take up the agrarian question on the basis of peasant proprietorship. The combined force of the agrarian and parliamentary movements created drastic problems for the government, both in Ireland, where agrarian outrages proliferated, and at Westminster, where the sixty-two Home Rulers elected in 1880 sought, under Parnell, to force Parliament into recognition of Irish claims by using the procedure of the House of Commons so as to obstruct its business to an extent which they hoped would prove intolerable. Liberal policy in face of this challenge combined coercion, designed to repress agrarian crime, with conciliation, aimed at removing agrarian grievances. After the rejection by the Lords in 1880 of an emergency bill designed to protect tenants unavoidably in arrears from eviction without compensation, there was an increase in Irish unrest which led to the passage early in 1881 of a coercion bill. But with the renewal of coercion came Gladstone's second Land Act, conceding three salient aims of the agrarian agitation – fair rent, assessed by arbitration, fixity of tenure while the rent was paid, and freedom of sale. This virtually established a system of dual ownership of the land, reducing the Irish landlord to little more than a receiver of rent, but it was not enough to satisfy Parnell and the Land League, whose continued militancy quickly led to the imprisonment of the former in Kilmainham gaol and the suppression of the latter. Neither Parnell nor the government, however, wanted a fight to the finish, and negotiations between them brought about the so-called 'Kilmainham Treaty' in April 1882. Coercion was to be relaxed, the Land Act amended, and an arrears bill introduced for the many tenants who, without government help in wiping out their arrears, would be unable to take advantage of the Land Act. Parnell, meanwhile, was to try to end agrarian violence. He, Davitt, and others were released from prison, while the viceroy, Cowper, and the chief secretary, W. E. Forster, resigned. Unhappily, the Kilmainham agreement was stultified almost at once, when, in May, a small murder group calling themselves the Invincibles assassinated the new chief secretary, Lord Frederick Cavendish, and the under-secretary, Burke, in Phoenix Park, Dublin. Further coercion was inevitable, which the Parnellites were bound to oppose. Moreover, the promised Arrears Act of 1882, involving a free gift of money from the state to assist tenants unable to pay their arrears, and strongly attacked by Salisbury as an act of robbery, was so framed as to be incapable of utilisation by most of the tenants. However, the Land Act made some progress in reducing rents and thus agrarian unrest, and 1883 saw a precarious lull in the Irish struggle.

But the Liberals' difficulties were hardly lessened by this respite. The Irish problem and obstruction by the Irish nationalists in the House of Commons had helped to prevent major legislation for England, to the frustration of the Radicals. Now the latter could demand action, and Chamberlain hastened to do so. His position as president of the board of trade, with a seat in the cabinet, had little or no restraining effect on his public utterances. Using the platform rather than Parliament, he appealed to 'the democracy' with a directness and force that roused the alarm of the propertied classes and the distaste of the crown. From the first there had been tension in Gladstone's cabinet between Chamberlain and the Whig majority, and this deepened in 1883 as the Radical leader embarked upon a campaign for the franchise reform which he saw as the essential means to make the will of popular Radicalism effective upon government and Parliament, and so to introduce a new era of social change. He went beyond the simple demand for household suffrage in the counties to take up the old Chartist points of manhood suffrage, equal electoral districts, and payment of members. His Radicalism extended, too, to Ireland: he envisaged her inclusion in franchise reform (which was bound to increase nationalist strength), and pressed for local self-government, coming into sharp collision with his leading Whig colleague, Hartington. The cabinet deferred a franchise

'DISINTEGRATION'

bill to the following year, but already by the autumn, in anticipation of a new electorate, Chamberlain was beginning to formulate what was to become known as the Radical Programme.

Chamberlain's great impact depended not only on what he said but also on the pungency with which he said it, and it was in March 1883 that Salisbury, who had delivered some mordant comment in speeches at Birmingham, found himself the object of a celebrated riposte, characteristic of his opponent's style: 'Lord Salisbury constitutes himself the spokesman of a class – of the class to which he himself belongs, who toil not neither do they spin, whose fortunes, as in his case, have originated by grants made in times gone by for the services which courtiers rendered kings, and have since grown and increased, while they have slept, by levying an increased share on all that other men have done by toil and labour to add to the general wealth and prosperity of the country.'

It was Salisbury's concern in his October article to rally the 'constitutional' forces against the challenge of Radicalism, and to claim for the Conservative party the function of representing the cause of national unity in opposition to 'disintegration'. The elements of 'disintegration' he saw in the waning of patriotic spirit and in the growth of class antagonism, leading towards an attack on property. The latter especially alarmed him in that he had little confidence in the House of Commons as an instrument of arbitration. Impressed by the leverage that the almost unfettered constitutional supremacy of the Commons under 'democracy' allowed sections of its membership to exert upon ministers, he was driven to cast envious glances at the safeguards with which American democracy sought to limit the power of the legislature and to protect the executive from enslavement to it. The Commons, he argued, did not represent the deliberate judgement of the nation in its dealings between classes. Too often, the fate of great issues and interests was dependent on the tactics dictated to ministers by the necessities of survival in a division. In particular, people's rights and property were sacrificed in the bargaining necessary to compose the internal troubles of the Liberal party. Here, of course, the main villains were the Radicals, who extorted violent measures as the price of their allegiance. Salisbury gave a highly coloured and exaggerated sketch of Radical aims, which, he alleged, extended to equality of status and possessions and the extirpation of religious dogma. But also worthy of blame were the Whigs, who vainly attempted to contain the advance of Radicalism by the demoralising policy of step-by-step concession. Salisbury was as anxious as ever to make the Whigs feel the full humiliation and falseness of their position, and to insinuate that the time to break with Radicalism had come. In a speech in June he had asserted that the modern Liberal party had far less in common than the Conservatives with the Liberal party of fifty years ago, and that it was now the Conservatives who were defending, and Liberals who were attacking, the old Liberal values. The futility of the Whig practice of continual yielding to pressure was demonstrated, he argued, by the example of Ireland, unreconciled to English rule despite a century of concessions. Salisbury had no illusions about the state of Irish feeling, but he had no thought of surrender to it. To Home Rule as to Radicalism his negative was absolute.

The article was immediately recognised as Salisbury's, and caused some stir. Its pessimistic tone was deprecated even by the Conservative *Standard*, while its scepticism about the viability of parliamentary institutions under democratic rule seriously perturbed *The Times*, which spoke of 'a sweeping attack on Parliamentary government as it exists at present in England', and remarked that, though Salisbury posed as the champion of the constitution, 'his principles, logically developed, would be quite as fatal to the Constitution as any that he attributes to the Radical party'. The public discussion of the article as his production annoyed Salisbury, who would not acknowledge authorship, and said in private that since anonymity could not be secured he would not write again for the *Quarterly*. He kept his word.

Speeches of the Right Hon. W. E. Forster, M.P., at Devonport and Stonehouse. London, 1883.

The most marked characteristic of Mr. Gladstone's governments is the regularity of the law which appears to govern their birth and their decay. So far as we can at present see, the present Administration is likely to run a course closely parallel to that of 1868. It was called into existence by the same stupendous effort of oratorical exaggeration.[1] Its earlier years have been devoted to the same blind policy of buying off Irish discontent by a partial surrender of long-established rights. While legislating with the force of Irish insurrection at its back, it has in both cases shown great activity, a sinister originality in legislative innovations, and a dictatorial haughtiness in forcing them on its opponents. In both cases, as soon as the threat or scarecrow of Irish insurrection was no longer available in its support, its legislative faculty has become half-paralyzed; its vast majority has begun to melt away, and has become a precarious reliance for ordinary work; and its proud spirit has sunk into a submission to any rebuffs that an undutiful House of Commons might have a fancy to inflict. The parallel is striking: whether its later features will correspond to this beginning it would be rash to conjecture. Measuring the progress of decay simply by the lapse of time, Ministers are in their present career at a point corresponding to that which they occupied in April 1872. They were just then under the cloud of the great discredit attaching to the Washington Arbitration;[2] a miscarriage

[1] The reference is to Gladstone's Midlothian speeches of 1879-80 against the Beaconsfield ministry, paralleling in intensity the campaign he had conducted on the Irish Church issue in 1868.
[2] I.e. of the *Alabama* claims.

'DISINTEGRATION'

which had much analogy with their recent blundering over M. Lesseps' claims,[1] and was due to the same type of statesmanship. In some respects their condition is worse than it was then, for they had then received no great Parliamentary blow like the division on the Affirmation Bill;[2] nor had they begun to experience the irritating recurrence of small defeats in the House of Commons.[3] On the other hand, the dissatisfaction of the country in 1872 had shown itself more evidently in the bye-elections, than it has hitherto done during the present Administration. The general tenor of the polls, so far as their numbers have shown any change, has been in the Conservative direction; but there has been no election so significant or so important as that of East Surrey in September 1871.[4] Vacancies of important Liberal seats have been curiously rare; and there is therefore nothing in our experience, as far as it has gone, to discourage Conservative expectations. But the slowly-developing effects of the Ballot have been too vast to admit of any confident forecast. The Ballot is the régime of surprises. A large number of the electors, without fixed opinions, are swayed from day to day by the feelings any chance cause may raise, and it is a matter of mere accident which of these random impulses is dominant at the critical moment when the vote is given. In a system of open voting these capricious changes are checked by a respect for the opinion of the voter's friends, and for the pledges

[1] Dissatisfied with the management of the Suez Canal by the Frenchman de Lesseps's company, British shipping and business interests proposed in 1883 to construct an alternative canal across the Suez isthmus. De Lesseps resisted this on the ground that his 1854 concession gave him exclusive rights over the isthmus, and, after negotiation, the British government reached an agreement with him whereby his company was itself to make a second canal, reduce its dues and tolls, and increase English representation in its management, while Britain would help to secure the necessary concessions for the new canal and would lend up to £8m towards its construction. This arrangement, which effectively endorsed de Lesseps's claim to exclusive rights, was heavily criticised as too favourable to him, and the government had eventually to abandon it.
[2] On 3 May 1883 the government had been defeated in the Commons by 292 votes to 289, on the second reading of the bill which it had introduced to legalise affirmation of allegiance, in order to provide for the case of the atheist Charles Bradlaugh, who, three times elected M.P. for Northampton, had been unable to take his seat because a majority of the Commons would allow him neither to take the parliamentary oath nor to affirm his allegiance. Seventeen Liberals and thirty-six Parnellites voted against the government in this division.
[3] In addition to the defeat on the Affirmation Bill, the government had been beaten in the Commons on the Bradlaugh case in February 1882 (286 votes to 228) and on an amendment to the Crimes Bill for Ireland in July 1882 (207 to 194).
[4] The East Surrey by-election of 24 *August* 1871 provided one of the then government's first serious losses, the Conservative Watney having a majority of 1,163 where the Liberals had had a majority of 384 in 1868.

already given; but these influences lose their power in the obscurity of the Ballot. Elections sufficient to turn the scale are decided by comparatively few votes, and any passing wave of feeling may catch a sufficient number at the last moment to reverse the majority in the House of Commons. General Elections, therefore, will probably be always as unexpected in their results as those of 1874 and 1880.

But whether the present current of affairs is or is not to lead, after the precedent of ten years back, to the fall of the Liberals from office, it seems already to have greatly diminished their substantial power of doing harm. The discipline of their party is broken: the enthusiasm which lifted them into office and bore them through the first two years of administration has cooled down into a very critical preference: and they can no longer command the unity of purpose, within or without the Cabinet, which is necessary to devise or carry measures of far-reaching change. To many Conservatives this is a very satisfactory stage to have reached in the advance of their own party; so satisfactory, that they may be willing to halt there for an indefinite period of repose. A Liberal Government in office, too weak for violent legislation, is, perhaps, the condition of things most favourable to the maintenance of the Constitution – for the professional advocates of change find themselves by the force of circumstances retained to defend inaction; but when the brief is taken from them, when they have no longer the responsibility of putting their sentiments into practice, the clamour for subversive change revives. This view of the political situation is naturally attractive to those Conservatives who have little interest in politics except the maintenance of the institutions of their country. So far as it merely affects the occupancy of office, we have no desire to controvert it. But if it is used as a basis for the inference that there is less cause than there was for Conservative vigilance and activity, it may lead to a disastrous error. Though the present Government may have lost the power of action, it has not for that reason lost the liability to be pushed. The present position of political forces is not one that bodes rest or peace for any length of time. The torpor, bred probably of disunion, into which the Ministry are sinking, may prevent them from undertaking for the present any new enterprises against Church or property. But it is not from the initiative of a Ministry that the greatest disturbances spring. We are inclined to agree with Mr. Chamberlain, that great changes are probably approaching, though we doubt whether they will precisely correspond to his expectations, or will be of the kind which is likely to appear on any party programme. But if this view is justified

'DISINTEGRATION'

by the facts, we are entering on an epoch of sharp contention, in which the country will need all the strength that can be given to it by the union and energy of the Conservative party.

There are prophets who would persuade us that the political barometer stands at 'set fair,' and that any such fears or hopes are the offspring of partisan imaginations. We could wish that we saw on the political horizon any signs to justify this complacent optimism. To our minds there are many indications of an unstable equilibrium in our present political condition. We do not refer merely to the more ephemeral topics on which a political writer might naturally dwell. The blunders, the shortcomings, the misadventures of the present Ministry, the contradiction between the promises which landed them in office and the tenor of their actual practice since those promises have achieved their purpose – out of these things a formidable indictment can be constructed. Such topics have been and will be submitted to the verdict of the constituencies by many trenchant pens and tongues. But it is not only from these that the misgivings spring, with which we look upon the future. It is a necessary result of political discussion as carried on in this country, that the individual has too large a portion of our thoughts and the principle too little; and controversy is apt to be made up, not so much of political argument, as of a series of political biographies of an adverse character. But the evils against which we have to struggle will last longer than any living men. There is abundant call for the vigilance and energy of those who love their country and its institutions, not merely because the policy of the statesmen of the hour is mischievous, but because of the dangerous temper of men's minds which the acceptance of that policy reveals. Some of our evil symptoms have outlasted in a form more or less acute several shifts of Ministry, and require not only a change of persons, which in its nature must be an experiment, but a change in our political methods and ideas. We need to restore, not laws or arrangements that have passed away, but the earlier spirit of our institutions which modern theory and crotchet have driven out. There is a general disposition among those who in the constituencies are opposing the party now in power, to substitute the word Constitutional for the word Conservative in their political language. It is the fruit of a true instinct. The object of our party is not, and ought not to be, simply to keep things as they are. In the first place, the enterprise is impossible. In the next place, there is much in our present mode of thought and action which it is highly undesirable to conserve. What we require is the administration of public affairs, whether in the executive or the legislative department, in that spirit of the old constitution which held the nation together as a whole, and levelled its united force at objects of national import, instead of splitting it into a bundle of unfriendly and distrustful fragments.

The dangers we have to fear may roughly be summed up in the single word – disintegration. It is the end to which we are being driven, alike by the defective working of our political machinery, and by the public temper of the time. It menaces us in the most subtle and in the most glaring forms – in the loss of large branches and limbs of our Empire, and in the slow estrangement of the classes which make up the nation to whom that Empire belongs. The spirit which threatens to bring it upon us is of course most marked in the home administration: but it has left broad and discouraging traces on our external policy as well. Half a century ago, the first feeling of all Englishmen was for England. Now, the sympathies of a powerful party are instinctively given to whatever is against England. It may be Boers or Baboos,[1] or Russians or Affghans, or only French speculators – the treatment these all receive in their controversies with England is the same: whatever else may fail them, they can always count on the sympathies of the political party from whom during the last half century the rulers of England have been mainly chosen. What a marvellous illustration of this spirit is being enacted before our eyes in India! The very maintenance of that empire – the stupendous achievement of thousands ruling over millions to whom they are strange in colour and creed and race – depends on the respect in which the superiority of the English race is held. To gratify some theorists at home who have weight in Parliament, we are deliberately humiliating the English race in the eyes of the natives; and we are announcing the policy, which we cannot fulfil without suicide, that race-distinctions in the bestowal of administrative offices shall cease.[2] It is a striking, though by no means a solitary indication of how low, in the present temper of English politics, our sympathy with our own countrymen has fallen. Of course, we shall be told that a conscience of exalted sensibility, which is the special attribute of the Liberal party, has enabled them to discover, what English statesmen had never discovered before,

---

[1] In Anglo-Indian usage, a disparaging term for Hindus or, more especially, Bengalis with a superficial English education.

[2] A particular subject of contention both in India and in England in 1883 was the so-called 'Ilbert Bill', designed to enable the Indian government to appoint natives as justices of the peace, with jurisdiction over European British subjects outside the presidency towns (native magistrates already had such jurisdiction in the presidency towns).

'DISINTEGRATION'

that the cause to which our countrymen are opposed is generally the just one. Undoubtedly, their conduct may conceivably be accounted for by this lofty theory. Many actions in life are susceptible of a double explanation. When a commander surrenders a fortress which he might have held, he generally attributes his capitulation to the tenderness of his humanity, which shrank from the shedding of blood. When a man allows himself to be kicked without resisting it, he will very likely assure you that it is due to the Christian meekness of his character. The credence which in either case is given to this sort of explanation, will depend very much on its consistency with other portions of the explainer's habitual conduct. Those who have observed in other parts of the Liberal record – say in their Irish policy – a perfect detachment from the lower impulses of party interest, may possibly conclude that their colonial and foreign policy arises from an excess of Christian abnegation. For ourselves, we are rather disposed to think that patriotism has become in some breasts so very reasonable an emotion, because it is ceasing to be an emotion at all; and that these superior scruples, to which our fathers were insensible, and which always make the balance of justice lean to the side of abandoning either our territory or our countrymen, indicate that the national impulses which used to make Englishmen cling together in face of every external trouble are beginning to disappear.

But it is in home affairs that the ominous tendency of which we have spoken is most conspicuous, and it is in these that the danger threatens us the most closely. Of course, when the word disintegration, as a possible peril of the present time, is mentioned, the mind naturally reverts to Ireland: and Ireland is, no doubt, the worst symptom of our malady. But we are not free from it here; it is beginning to infect us in this country also, though the stage is less advanced and the form is less acute. While scorn is thrown upon the old instincts of patriotism which animated all ranks and divisions of men with common aspirations, the temper that severs class from class is constantly gaining strength. Those who lead the poorer classes of this country are industriously impressing upon them, with more or less plainness of speech, that the function of legislation is to transfer to them something – an indefinite and unlimited something – from the pockets of their more fortunate fellow-countrymen; and it is too much to hope that a doctrine, which teaches that a disregard of the Tenth Commandment is the highest duty of citizenship, should not gradually impress itself on the minds to which it is addressed. On the other hand, by a necessary consequence, the members of the classes who are in any sense or degree holders of property are becoming uneasy at the prospect which lies before them. The uneasiness is greatest among those whose property consists in land, because they have been the most attacked; but the feeling is not confined to them. No one will say that this anxiety is without foundation. Things that have been secure for centuries are secure no longer. Not only is every existing principle and institution challenged, but it has been made evident by practical experience that most of them can be altered with great ease. The mechanism by which small changes are made, – by which the humble daily work of legislation ought to be done – is rusty and inefficient to the last degree. But the mechanism by which large and revolutionary changes are carried out is singularly rapid and effective in its action, and requires a very small preponderance of force to set it in motion. It is needless to dwell on the feelings of the Irish landowners, who think that their property, often their whole property, has been taken from them under a mockery of judicial forms, to satisfy the clamour of the secular enemies of their class and of England, whose loyal pioneers and foremost champions they have been. Twice despoiled by the power whose support they were, they are preparing, with heavy forebodings, to combat the third attack, which seems imminent in no distant future. Their hard fate – which if any one had prophesied twenty years ago, he would have been derided as a Tory alarmist and a calumniator of Liberal virtue – has not left the corresponding classes in England indifferent or unaffected. The shadow of the same danger has passed near the English landowner, and his fate is still uncertain. Some people think the peril has gone by, and that for the time he is safe; others look upon the handling he has recently undergone as a mere warning of what is to come – the premonitory tremor of the earthquake wave which has been fatal to his Irish brother, and is travelling slowly towards him. Perhaps, however, such desponding minds may derive comfort from the reflection that here their class is not, as in Ireland, the only, or even the most prominent, embodiment of wealth. It is fairly probable that, under the peculiar circumstances of English society, if anybody is to be eaten, it will be the fundholder and the capitalist who are destined to be eaten first. The fate of the English landowner depends very much upon the vigour and resolution with which he defends himself; and the same may be said of any other body of men threatened by legislation which is inspired by electioneering motives. In the present day those interests are in the least jeopardy, which will give the greatest trouble if molested. But the important feature of these attacks and apprehensions, in a wider view, is not so much the possible destiny of particular sections of the community which

'DISINTEGRATION'

they may foreshadow, as the general distrust which they inspire. Every action of the House of Commons is now watched with keen anxiety by classes in this country whose numbers are not small, and whose influence is very far from insignificant. Churchmen, landowners, publicans, manufacturers, house-owners, railway shareholders, fundholders, are painfully aware that they have all been threatened: that their most vital interests are at the mercy of some move in the game of politics, and they are watching with pardonable interest to see whose turn will come next. The collapse of principles formerly looked on as immovable has been so complete, the changes of front executed by parties and individuals have been so astounding, that no one can foresee into what unexpected region of political doctrine the Legislature will make its next excursion.

It is an unfortunate circumstance that, just at the time when the House of Commons is attaining to a supremacy in the State more decided than it ever possessed before, it should appear to be entirely losing one of the most necessary attributes of a ruler. The broad distinction between a civilized and an uncivilized community is this – that in a civilized community individuals or bodies of men who quarrel submit their difference to an arbitrator, while in a savage state they fight it out. The arbitrament of a ruler is substituted for the arbitrament of intestine war. It is of the essence of the civilized system that the arbitrator should be in the main impartial; and the kings or chiefs, to whom in ruder times the power of arbitration was confided, satisfied, or were believed to satisfy, this requirement. The first deadly blow against kingly power was struck when the differences of religion arose; for then, for the first time, the king ceased to be impartial on a matter which concerned all his subjects, and on which they were bitterly divided. He became perforce a partisan, and in that capacity he forfeited the trust of his subjects. Other and more potent causes have subsequently worked in the same direction; but it was with the differences of religion that the change of feeling towards monarchy in modern times began. Assemblies have inherited the function of political arbitration where it has dropped from the hands of kings; and while their power was undeveloped, or while they were drawn from a limited portion of the community, their impartiality, though not quite unimpeachable, has sufficed for the preservation of their moral authority, and of the confidence reposed in them. With us, as in other Anglo-Saxon societies, the Representative Assembly is no longer taken from a limited section of the community, and it has succeeded with us, far more than any assembly in America, in shaking itself free of all restrictions upon its power. But with this development of its character and strength, the loss of its fitness to arbitrate has become apparent. The movement of society is reversed; we are going back to the ancient method of deciding quarrels. Our ruler is no longer an impartial judge between classes who bring their differences before him for adjustment; our ruler is an Assembly which is itself the very field of battle on which the contending classes fight out their feuds. The settlement by arbitration has given place again to the settlement by civil war; only it is civil war with gloves on. Of course the decisions thus given vary in their character without limit; and all confidence in fixed principles or a determinate policy is gone.

Undoubtedly, in a modern state, the only arbitration possible between classes is the judgment – the cool and deliberate judgment – of the generality of the nation. At the best it may not be an ideal form of arbitration; in ordinary circumstances its genuine decisions are hard to obtain: but it is the only one available under modern conditions of political life. The reproach to which the House of Commons acting for the nation is liable, is that it does not in its dealing between classes, even approximately, represent this deliberate judgment. If its policy is unstable, and its action is watched from year to year with uncertainty and dread, it is because its mode of procedure is ill-fitted to ascertain or faithfully to transmit the decisions of the nation in the issues submitted to it – because it suffers them to be dictated by impulse or falsified by sectional bias. If it ever forfeits completely – as it perhaps some day may forfeit – the confidence of large classes of the community over which its authority extends, the cause must be sought partly in the unexampled extent of its powers, which permits hastiness of decision, partly in the peculiar play of parties within its walls, which vitiates the fidelity of its action as an exponent of national opinion.

Hack phrases are a dangerous snare to an age too hurried and too busy to think. We live under a Parliamentary Government: we have lived two centuries under a Parliamentary Government: all other Anglo-Saxon communities live under a Parliamentary Government. Whether in the three cases the same word means the same thing, no one is careful to enquire. The phrase blinds us to the peculiar position, a position wholly without any precedent or parallel, occupied at the present day by the House of Commons. Our Government was called a Parliamentary Government a century ago, as it is now. But the control of the machine was largely shared by the Crown and the aristocracy. Now it is entirely in the hands of the democracy. It is impossible to express in words a wider difference. We have passed from one pole of political ideas to its exact opposite. The consequence is, that arrangements which worked perfectly well under one system are wholly unsuited to the other. We have carried over from one condition of political existence to the other the doctrine that the Ministry, the depositary of all the powers of the State, holds office as tenant at will of the House of Commons. A single motion carried any one night in that House – the sudden result of panic or mere impulse, or of clever canvassing, or of an intrigue among various groups, will displace a Ministry, and reverse a policy. When a majority, or a large proportion of the members who had the power of giving this vote, were the nominees of royal or aristocratic patrons, this system presented no great inconvenience in practice. Whatever other evil results such a system of government may have involved, it was not likely to sin on the side of instability. The limited class who nominated a majority of the members had their attention constantly fixed on politics, and their opinions varied little, or only at long intervals: and the members who represented them moved in a predetermined course, to which they were vigilantly restricted. But a democracy, consisting of men who must be ordinarily engrossed by the daily necessities of self-support, only attends to public affairs partially and fitfully. During the long intervals which elapse between the periods when they do give their minds to politics and pronounce an intelligent decision, they pay no attention to the subject at all. Their voice is mimicked by some one else, who speaks in their name, and affects to act under their authority. It may be some one whom in some informal manner the majority of them have chosen; or it may be one whose mandate is altogether technical, indirect, and unreal. It matters little for those whose vital interests are practically left unprotected at his mercy. It is no longer the voice of their countrymen at large, which arbitrates between them and their opponents and decides their fate. It is the will of one man, or one set of men, – themselves holding on to power by a capricious and precarious tenure; compelled to fight for it night after night, amid the conflicting passions and ambitions of the various groups in the House of Commons; but omnipotent so long as these groups can be manipulated with success. It is a transparent mockery to tell the classes whose great litigation it is the supreme function of legislation to determine, that the verdict of their countrymen is expressed in the decisions which in any parliamentary crisis may be dictated to a Ministry by the exigency of tactics in the House of Commons. This is not the Parliamentary Government under which the nation lived a century ago, when the position of a strong Minister was secure from the sudden revulsions of feeling in the House of Commons; but, on the other hand, when his action was effectively controlled by the still vigorous power of the aristocracy and of the Crown.

Again, it is a popular impression that our existing system has the sanction of the experience of the Great Western Republic; and that American institutions are practically the same as ours, differing only in that they are a little more democratic. The resemblance is entirely superficial. The elements of instability and insecurity, which are so rife in our institutions as they at present practically stand, have been wisely excluded from the American system. Our House of Commons has come into its position, as it were, by accident. It is like the junior member of a great mercantile firm, who has suddenly become all-powerful, not in pursuance of any articles of the partnership, but simply because the senior partners have fallen into poor health, and have retired. No provision was made in the articles to meet such a contingency; and his power is absolutely unrestricted. The House of Representatives at Washington is in a very different position.[1] The constitution of the United States was framed by men, deeply mistaken, as we think, in that they were hostile to monarchy, but yet fully sensible of the dangers that attended the democracy they chose; and it was with these dangers fully in their view that they limited the functions and counterpoised the power of the supreme assemblies they set up. Both in America and England the popular vote indirectly chooses the party from which the Ministers are to be drawn, in the one case by the election of a President, in the other by the election of a House of Commons; but the tenure of the Ministers is very different. In America they practically hold during the four years' Presidential term; they do not sit in Congress, and cannot be displaced by any action of Congress short of an impeachment. The difference between a secure and a precarious tenure affects the mind of the politician as much as that of the agriculturist; and accordingly American Ministers do not find it necessary to recommend legislative measures with an eye chiefly to the party interests of the moment and to the composition of their majority from day to day. One of the results of this condition of things is the comparative absence of a class of legislation with which in England we are too familiar. No group of members has the power of intimating to a Minister, 'Unless this or that measure on which we have set our hearts is supported by the Government, they must not count on our support in the next critical division.' Personal

---

[1] The remarks on the American constitution which follow had the benefit of being scrutinised by Sir Henry Maine, who advised some changes in Salisbury's original version.

'DISINTEGRATION'

purity is unhappily low in American politics; and, unless they are maligned, the lesser bribery, the bribery of individuals, frequently takes place. But the greater bribery, the bribery by legislation, the bribery of classes strong in political power at the cost of those who are weak – this kind of corruption is comparatively unknown.

But the most remarkable feature in the institutions of democratic America is the strength of the safeguards which have been erected to prevent hasty or violent legislation. The co-ordinate authority of the Senate is exercised with as much freedom and with as little hesitation as that of the House of Representatives. The veto of the President is not rusted with disuse; but is an effective constitutional check, not unfrequently applied. But the most remarkable of the restrictions which have been set up to prevent the Legislatures in America from misusing their power, is the provision which removes a most important class of subjects entirely out of their reach. The foundations of the Constitution are placed upon a firmer basis than the caprice of any Assembly. It cannot be altered by the ordinary authorities to whom the general work of Legislation is confided: but only by the assent of three-fourths of the whole nation, specially consulted for the purpose.* And this inviolable Constitution includes the assertion of principles which we, too, once believed to be inviolable in England, but which are now freely sold in the market-place of politics. Take the question of the sanctity of contracts, a principle for which our present Parliament takes every opportunity of evincing its contempt. The question belongs in America to the jurisdiction, not of the Central, but of the Local Legislatures; and the provision of the Constitution (Art. i. sect. 10) is, 'No State shall pass any *ex post facto* Law, or Law impairing the Obligation of Contracts.' This golden law cannot be set aside by the pressure of any malcontent section of partizans, or the Parliamentary strategy of any Minister. If any American Legislature had passed a measure similar to the Irish Land Act, the Supreme Court would have annulled it as unconstitutional.

We are well aware that such precautions could not be engrafted on the institutions which have grown up in England. Our hope, such as it is, must be in the possibility of the House of Commons returning to the better spirit of its earlier traditions. We cite the American safeguards, not

---

* The Congress of the United States may propose amendments in the Constitution by a two-thirds vote of both Houses, *or*, upon the application of two-thirds of the State Legislatures, it may call a convention to consider and propose amendments; but in either case the proposed amendments must be ratified by three-fourths of the State Legislatures, or by conventions called in three-fourths of the several States.

as the suggestion of a possible remedy, but as an illustration of the singular danger in which we stand. By a process of political evolution, which affects not us only, but the whole western world, ultimate power is passing into the hands of much larger multitudes than ever exercised it before. It is as useless to repine at this process, as to repine because we are growing older. It is patent on the face of history that the aggregates of men who form communities, like the aggregates of atoms that form living bodies, are subject to laws of progressive change – be it towards growth or towards decay. And it is evident from the example of the communities in which men have come unfettered by the past to the choice of their own political arrangements, the United States, and our own Colonies, that the numerical majority, when it chooses to assert itself, is in effect the living power of our particular time. There is no experience at present to show that this fact is incompatible with the government of England on the sober principles, respectful of the rights of all, with which our Constitution is instinct; and therefore there is nothing in it which, as Constitutionalists, we need deplore. But what is to be deplored, is that the change is not recognized: and that no inclination is shown to provide against its inevitable difficulties and drawbacks. Our arrangements are just what they were when the machine was worked by an aristocracy and checked by a very active Royal Power. We show in our political movements the same immobility of habit as that which distinguishes the emigrating Englishman. Just as he is prone to carry to a burning climate the dress, the diet, the hours, the manner of building, suitable to the temperature of his own country, and can hardly be prevailed upon to change them, so we have migrated from the old system of politics to the new, and imagine that the appliances of political life which suited the calmer and more equable climate which we have left, are maintainable in the full glare of Democracy. It is melancholy to note that American Institutions, which we shrink from as an extravagant embodiment of the Democratic idea, have yet known how to guard effectively against some of the worst dangers of Democracy to which we still remain exposed.

This entire absence of protection for the varied interests of the country, in the conduct of what is an entirely novel experiment in Government, is calculated to create anxiety and distrust among those who have anything to lose, – a category which, we are glad with Mr. Forster[1] to believe, includes a large proportion of the working class. These apprehensions

[1] W. E. Forster, having resigned the Irish secretaryship in April 1882, was now outside the government.

may not be shared by the mere optimist, who solves every difficulty by an effusive profession of trust in the people. That is an admirable sentiment, which has formed the text for many political declamations – especially of the kind which abound in the early stages of a revolution. No one was fonder of the sentiment than Lafayette. The worst feature of it is that, excellent as it is, it is wholly irrelevant to sublunary concerns. The 'people,' as an acting, deciding, accessible authority, are a myth. Except on rare emergencies, when they are excited by some tempest of passion, or some exceptional emergency, the 'people' do not speak at all. You have to put an utterance into their mouths by certain conventional arrangements, under which assumptions are made which, though convenient, are purely fictitious: as for instance, that those present at the process of voting represent the absent; that a majority, however small, represents the whole; that a man's mind is a perfect reflex of the minds of fifty thousand of his fellow-citizens on all subjects, because he was chosen, as the best of two or three candidates, in respect to a particular crisis and a particular set of subjects, by a bare majority of those who took the trouble to vote on a particular day. These fictions may be convenient, they may be inevitable; but they do not alter the facts. You do not get the voice of the people; but something which, for good and sufficient reasons, you choose to dignify by that name. But when confidence in the people is invoked as a sublime emotion which should calm all doubts and fears, it is necessary to remember that we are asked to repose our trust, not upon a voice which really proceeds from the people, but upon the utterances of men whose right to speak on their behalf is purely conventional.

But at all events the apprehension that under present arrangements the action of the Legislature does not represent the calm judgment of the people, is not confined to Conservatives. Here is a testimony to its soundness which comes from no Tory mouth:

The first danger which accompanies political progress in this age is over-hasty legislation: and the next is the danger from wire-pullers. Why do I say the danger from over-hasty legislation? For this reason – that there never was a country in which the same wave of excitement would go from end to end, as it naturally does in England. At this moment we are closer together, we are more like one another, we have communication by railway and by telegraph, we have our cheap press, so that when any event happens which excites the country, there is a response from John o' Groat's to the Land's End almost instantly. There never was a country so likely to be moved by any special feeling as is Great Britain at the present time...That, I think, forms the danger that under any sudden excitement legislation might be passed which we should afterwards feel had been too hastily passed...I confess I think that we ought to look out for safeguards against over-hasty legislation...I should like those who care about politics to study American politics; and you may be surprised to find that real Conservative safeguards are much more powerful there than they are here. – Mr. FORSTER *at Stonehouse*, August 16.

While we entirely agree with Mr. Forster in lamenting the want of adequate safeguards, we question whether overhasty legislation is the only, or even the greatest danger. No doubt we do suffer from waves of feeling which sometimes hurry Parliament into rash proceedings. They are usually raised by some sentimental cry – as in the case of the Contagious Diseases Acts, or the Plimsoll agitation, which was produced by the existence of genuine evils, but which issued in demands that were entirely extravagant.[1] In cases of this kind, Englishmen often have cause to regret the checks of the American constitution, which with us are ill replaced by the delays arising from obstruction and loquacity. But these hasty and ill-informed cries, though sometimes, as in the case of the Bulgarian atrocities,[2] rising to the level of a national mania, usually affect matters of secondary importance, and are only felt within a narrow area. The evil which we have to dread, and which makes us long for some, at least, of the constitutional safeguards possessed by our kinsmen – especially when we think of Ireland – is the system of political bargains to which great Legislative changes are frequently due. The bargains are not, it need hardly be said, compromises between the two parties in the State. They are the upshot of the internal negociations by which the dominant party, the party of action, from time to time maintains or re-establishes discipline in its ranks. Peculiar facilities are afforded for this traffic by the unchecked, or almost unchecked, prerogatives of the House of Commons; indeed, if its powers were not so enormous, such a traffic could hardly live. If the change demanded by a group as the price of its obedience could not be effected without securing the assent of other bodies of equal power and, perhaps, the sanction of a popular vote, the prospect of obtaining it would always be precarious, and the value of the offer as a means of obtaining support in Parliament would

[1] The campaign on behalf of the merchant seaman mounted from 1870 by Samuel Plimsoll, Liberal M.P. for Derby, was aimed primarily at stopping the sending of men to sea in overloaded, over-insured, and unseaworthy vessels by securing the compulsory survey of merchant ships and the observance of a maximum load line, and was largely responsible for the passage of the Merchant Shipping Act of 1876.

[2] I.e. the atrocities committed by Turkish irregular troops in response to guerilla risings in Bulgaria in 1876, which provided the occasion for the opening of Gladstone's crusade against Turkish misrule and against the foreign policy of the Beaconsfield government.

be indefinitely diminished. Instead of value paid over the counter, the Minister would only be able to give a bill drawn at long date on a questionable security. But on his side he would not have the same motive for making the offer. It is the possession by the House of Commons of the power of dismissal at a moment's notice, that gives all its force to a well-timed threat of desertion. Without it no malcontent group of supporters could extort promises from the Minister on the eve of a critical division, for critical divisions would not exist.

Undoubtedly the evil has only become serious in very recent times. The facilities for bargaining, offered by the position which the House of Commons occupies in the State, have only become of grave importance since the composite character of the Liberal party has become more strongly marked. We constantly see, in Liberal writings and speeches, exhortations to the various sections of the party to practise mutual forbearance. They are entreated to 'give and take;' in other words, they are exhorted to barter. If they were agreed, 'giving and taking,' or bartering, would be unnecessary; but, precisely because they are not agreed, it is necessary to ascertain by 'the higgling of the market' on what terms of mutual surrender they can be kept together.

If the votes that are bought and sold in this curious traffic were paid for merely in the political counters of honours and places, though the transaction would be morally much more corrupt, the concern of the public in them would be mainly speculative. But the rights of classes, the property and living of numbers of non-political men and women, are the currency in which this commerce is conducted. The owners of land in Ireland have bitterly felt, how hard a destiny it is to live in a land where votes are the aliment on which rulers live from day to day, and where those votes must be paid for by sacrificing the ancient and unquestioned rights of a defeated class. They are the most conspicuous victims of this necessity; but they have not been the first, and they will not be the last.

Only those who carefully watch the progress of legislative measures, and the principles on which they are constructed, can realize how much the destinies of many innocent classes are affected by the busy bargaining which goes on in the heart of the Liberal party. For the Liberal party has not only its full share of the individual disagreements which beset all bodies of men acting together for common ends, but, in addition, it lies under the constant peril of disruption caused by profound divergencies of opinion between its principal sections. The difference may be expressed briefly, though perhaps roughly, by saying that the Radical desires equality, and the Whig does not. Those Radicals who have taken the trouble to think out their opinions, and are not restrained by any prudential motives from avowing them, wish for equality right through, without qualification or limit. They wish for equality among religions: and the tendency of their school is to attain it, not only by stripping all religious bodies of endowments, but also by the extirpation of all dogmas which make a distinction between one religious body and another. They wish for equality among individuals: and therefore they are opposed to all honour or privileges which are transmitted by inheritance. From the same desire they are opposed to all inequalities of property: and by the action of taxation, of succession laws, and of sundry other devices borrowed from the Socialist armoury, they hope to attain an absolute level, first in the ownership of land, and afterwards in all other kinds of ownership. We do not say that the desire for equality, in the fulness with which we have expressed it, is avowed by all those who are usually known as Radicals. Many do not think out the necessary result of the formulas they use. Others, again, who have fully thought the subject out, do not express publicly the full extent of the changes they really desire. Reticence is the quality which above all others is cultivated by the habits of parliamentary life. It may seem a paradox to say so, but free institutions tend rather to restrain than to promote freedom of speech among those who work them. The essence of the method of government prevailing in free countries is that men should act together in considerable masses for the attainment of public ends. In doing so, they do not desire to invite more adverse criticism than is absolutely inseparable from the particular proposal which at that particular moment they are advocating. Therefore it is their interest as a body to repress any avowals of opinion pointing to other and further proposals by which hostile feeling may be roused. The advocacy which suits them best is that which confines itself strictly to the project in agitation, and gives no ground for the suggestion that it is meant to smooth the way for some ulterior and more formidable design. The men, therefore, who will rise in a party of change, who will be trusted as its agents and leaders, are those who can argue for the change that it [sic] is in issue, without revealing that any of those who promote it mean, with its help, to ask for larger changes further on. More eccentric and outspoken persons, who not only think out their principles, but have the indiscretion to think aloud, sin against the general prospects and welfare of the party, and do not, unless they are gifted with extraordinary eloquence, gain influence in it. Reticence, beyond the limits of the questions popular at the moment with the

'DISINTEGRATION'

party, is an obligation of prudence which is felt by all Radical politicians, and which the greater mass of them are too politic to resist. It would, therefore, be wholly unsound to conclude from the reticence habitual to the Radicals that the party generally does not sympathize with the doctrines, which at present only a few of the freer pens express.

But in truth there is nothing insisted on more strongly by the Radical party than that their ultimate aspirations are not to be measured by the demands which they make now. In their own phrase, they are, above all things, a party of progress. They always rejected with vigour the famous recommendation to 'rest and be thankful.' They heap unmeasured contempt upon the weaker spirits who at any point wish to be satisfied with what has been achieved, or to bind the party of to-day by reservations, or disclaimers, or protests, which were found necessary to facilitate the advance of yesterday. They always love to compare themselves to an army on the march; it has its regiments who lead the van, and its regiments who bring up the rear. But, at whatever pace or in whatever order its individual members may advance, the characteristic of the whole body is that it is always on the move from something old to something new. They profess that their unresting advance is always in a straight line, and that it is along the road to which they complacently give the name of 'progress.'

But if it be progress, it must be progress somewhere. Whither are they 'progressing'? The question has often been asked, and has never been definitely answered. Yet there must be an answer. There must be some objective point towards which this long march is directed. There must be some ideal land of promise in which their long wanderings are to end. The Radicals can hardly conceive themselves as filling in politics the part of the 'Wandering Jew.' He was undoubtedly the most remarkable and most consistent devotee of progress that the mind can contemplate – progress in which the traveller looks forward to no resting-place, but moves for moving sake. The language used by Radical advocates is often only consistent with the supposition that this is the kind of progress to which they are devoted; but it is more reasonable to assume that their unceasing labour is not aimless, and that at least the more active spirits among them have a definite object, which they perfectly understand, and which they do not find it convenient to communicate. The obvious mode of determining the end towards which a traveller is going, is simply to produce the line on which he has hitherto moved; and, ascertained in this manner, the object must necessarily be the equality not only of conditions but of possessions, and the extermination of religious dogma.

Radicalism, acting with these objects, and pursuing them by the method of political disintegration, is not a very unusual or surprising phenomenon. History has not yet furnished us with materials wide enough or minute enough for constructing anything like a science of the diseases and decay of States. But it may at least be said that in popular governments a particular cycle of phenomena has frequently reappeared. Freedom greatly tends to the increase of industry and commerce; and, as they increase, wealth is accumulated, and inequalities of fortune necessarily become more and more marked. For some not very evident reason, they are borne more impatiently than the inequalities of an aristocratic type, which have almost always originated in conquest. Perhaps it is because these latter tend, though very slowly, to wear away by lapse of time, and cannot be renewed; while the inequalities of mere fortune, far from wearing away, grow with the increasing growth of material prosperity. After a time the contrast becomes very intense. Vast multitudes have not had the chance of accumulating, or have neglected it; and whenever the stream of prosperity slackens for a time, privation overtakes the huge crowds who have no reserve, and produces widespread suffering. At such times the contrasted comfort or luxury of a comparatively small number becomes irritating and even maddening to look upon; and its sting is sharpened by the modern discoveries which have brought home to the knowledge of every class the doings of its neighbours. That organizer of decay, the Radical agitator, soon makes his appearance under these conditions. He easily persuades those who are too wretched, and have thought too carelessly to see through his sophistry, that political arrangements are the cause of the differences of wealth, and that by trusting him with political power they will be redressed. He does not tell his dupes how it is possible they should live if industry languishes, or how industry and enterprise can flourish if men once conceive the fear, that the harvest of wealth which they or theirs have sown, and reaped, and stored, may perchance be wrested from them by the politician. It is not the interest of the Radical that they should look further than the momentary satisfaction of their jealousy or their need; and by those who have the knack of preaching in politics, spoliation is easily painted the colour of philanthropy. Then arises that long conflict between possession and non-possession, which was the fatal disease of free communities in ancient times, and which threatens so many nations at the present day. Our grounds of induction are narrow, and are drawn chiefly from States of small extent and power. But, so far as they go, there is no reason to believe that this malady, when it once fastens on a free State, can have any other than a fatal issue. The length of time during which it runs must depend, as in all other battles between disease and health, upon the robustness of the constitution with which it has to contend. But it slowly kills by disintegration. It eats out the common sentiments and mutual sympathies which combine classes into a patriotic State. The internal dissension becomes constantly more rancorous; the common action and common aspirations become feebler. The organized body loses its defensive force against an external shock, and falls under the power of the first assailant, foreign or domestic, by whom it may chance to be attacked after the final stage of political debility has set in.

Are we yet stricken by this malady? It is hard to say; for the real living political forces of our people lie habitually so much in repose, than [sic] an observer is always in danger of mistaking the professional polemic of politicians for conflicts really involving the great classes of which the nation is composed. But the existence of disquieting symptoms can hardly be doubted. If classes are not in actual conflict, they are at least watching each other with vigilant distrust. The feebleness of Parliament is not an accidental disorder. It means something more than a mere defect in machinery, or an excess of senatorial loquacity. The failure of the mechanism to move, means that there is nothing like a general desire that it should move. A certain number of advanced Radicals are keenly anxious that its activity should be restored, as is evident from the speeches of Mr. Bright and Mr. Chamberlain; and a similar anxiety may prevail among the considerable contingent of crotcheteers who, with an optimism which is not at the mercy of events, are counting the moments until their nostrum is adopted, which is to save the nation. But there are a great number of people who look at the tendencies of Parliament with misgiving and mistrust; who feel wholly unable to predict what particular upas-tree[1] it will next address itself to cut down; and who much prefer a legislative stagnation, however inconvenient in some particulars it may be, to the unknown hazards of Parliamentary activity.

The other chief section of the Liberal party, the Whigs, with whom the Radicals have to negociate, and whom it is their principal function to squeeze, are in many respects a more interesting study. The Radicals attract attention principally on account of their energy, and of the future which is supposed to be in store for them. The lineaments of the great

---

[1] Gladstone, in October 1868, had likened the Protestant ascendancy in Ireland to a upas-tree, 'darkening and poisoning the land so far as its shadow can extend'.

enemy with whom we have to struggle, and by whom our destruction may be brought about, must always be interesting; but they are in no sense singular. Our Radicals scarcely differ in their objects or their methods from the Radical parties of other countries, except in the necessary variations impressed on them by the diversity of their 'environment.' But the other important section of the party, the Whigs, are an absolutely special product of this half-century; and there is nothing in past or present history that resembles them. They bear the name of a great party which has played a splendid part in English history; but they inherit little from it but its name. They are not even an independent body; they are only a section of the great political federation in which they are merged. The doctrines which won the fame of their eminent predecessors do not belong to this age and country. The great work at which they laboured in their time, the curbing of priestly and royal power, is now as obsolete as the Crusades. The present Whig party is a mere survival, kept alive by tradition after its true functions and significance have passed away. It is not so numerous as it once was, for the contradiction between its present policy and the doctrine of its most accredited teachers in the past is too transparent; and, moreover, the enlarged constituencies, who dislike fine distinctions, understand a Tory and understand a Radical, but have great difficulty in making out a Whig. Nevertheless there still survives a considerable section, who occupy an intellectual position that is absolutely unique among present or past politicians. A Whig who is a faithful member of the present Liberal party has to submit to this peculiar fate, not only that he inherits the political opinions he professes – a lot which befalls many Englishmen – but that he also inherits a liability to be compelled to change them at the bidding of the leader whom the Radical party may have chosen for him. Lord Somers and Charles Fox have bequeathed to him a collection of political doctrines, among which the advantages of individual freedom, and the sacredness of property, occupy a prominent place; and these, as a Whig, he is bound to uphold. But as a Whig he is also bound to remain a member of the great Liberal party, which has recently equipped itself with a brand-new set of opinions, in which individual freedom and the sacredness of property are treated as matters of very light account. As a Whig he has prejudices in favour of the Established Church, and the House of Lords, and our 'mixed form of government'; but it requires no prophet to see what the great Liberal party is likely to do with these institutions. It is not possible for human ingenuity to fulfil, without occasional backslidings, these conflicting claims of duty: to be at the

'DISINTEGRATION'

same time an historical Whig, faithful to the legend of Lord Somers, and an obedient disciple of the progressive doctrines which from time to time are revealed to the great Liberal party by Mr. Chamberlain or Mr. Parnell. This strain upon their political consciences is telling sensibly upon the happiness and tranquillity of this ancient party. For their many sins in past generations, they are condemned in the present to the political torment of constantly voting against their principles for measures they detest, in order to support a Ministry they distrust. It may seem to many, who are not born within the circle, to be a grievous fate; and their submission to it may be a matter, not only of admiration, but of surprise. But what is to be done? They are born Whigs; and they must remain Whigs, and vote with their party, – whoever leads it, and wherever it may be going. Descent and ancestry have their obligations; the tyranny of caste is not unknown even in the West. There are many strange and unattractive functions which, under the laws of caste, a Hindoo cheerfully accepts as the inherited burden of his life; but probably few of them suffer more than an educated Englishman, who thinks that it does not consist with the honour of his family to profess in public the opinions he really holds, or to oppose the political changes on which in his heart he looks with horror. Such a stress upon conviction is too severe to be permanent, and the ranks of the party are sensibly thinning under its pressure. Many have come to the conclusion, that genealogical consistency in the choice of political associates is of less importance than the maintenance of sound principles in legislation: and therefore have either openly joined the Constitutional party, or co-operate with it upon all the great questions of the day. Others have taken the plunge into advanced Radicalism, and are the foremost to scoff at the old-fashioned pretensions of the friends they have left behind. But the majority have neither the courage to abandon their Whig professions, nor to part from their Radical allies. They may often be met helplessly lamenting their sad fate; for the only solution of their difficulties that has yet presented itself to them is a combination of public loyalty with private imprecation. During Mr. Gladstone's reign their sufferings in public life have been undoubtedly severe. They do not feel Mr. Chamberlain's enthusiasm for manhood suffrage, or the payment of members; they hardly echo his disinterested condemnation of all who do not make their living by toiling and spinning. They do not share the contempt with which freedom of contract is now usually mentioned by Liberal writers and statesmen; and the sight of a quarter of the Irish landlords' property being presented to the tenantry in order to persuade them to vote right and abstain from murder, was not to the Whig magnates a consoling or re-assuring spectacle. Their feelings must have weighed heavily upon them when public utterances were required of them. Nevertheless, they have performed their part without flinching: and have always been ready to applaud everything – to enlarge in glowing periods upon the beauties of the Land Act, and the uniform success of Her Majesty's Government. Their fate always reminds us of an unpleasant story of the French revolution at Arras, quoted by M. Taine from a journal of the time:

L'histoire que voici arriva à quelques-uns de nos amis. Avec beaucoup d'autres on les avait amenés d'un ville éloignée, sur des charrettes découvertes, et, accablés de fatigue ils avançaient vers la prison où on devait les déposer. Au moment de leur arrivée plusieurs personnes allaient être guillotinées. Lebon, qui, selon son ordinaire présidait à ce spectacle, fit arrêter le convoi, afin que les prisonniers fussent eux-mêmes témoins de l'exécution. Mes amis et leurs compagnons, terrifiés, furent obligés non seulement de paraître attentifs à la tragédie, mais à chaque tête coupée de prendre part aux cris de *Vive la République*. – Taine, *Un séjour en France de 1792 à 1795*.

The question naturally suggests itself, what motive can men have to play so disagreeable a part, to whom no motives of ordinary self-interest can speak with much effect. Party passion, the corporate patriotism of the Whig connection, no doubt counts for a good deal. 'The cause for which Hampden died in the field, and Sidney on the scaffold, the government of England by the Whigs,' as Lord Beaconsfield puts it, is still capable of exciting some enthusiasm. Every one likes his own side to win. But they probably justify it to themselves on grounds of a wider patriotism. They start with the fatalist belief, which has been so common since the French Revolution, that ultimately the Radicals must win; and they contemplate the institutions of the country, the endowments of Established Churches, the rights of property, and so forth, much as Valentinian or Honorius might have looked upon the wide territories of the Roman Empire. The barbarians would certainly break in at last: nothing could prevent them from overrunning it. But if it were yielded to them in fragments from time to time, a frontier here, and a province there, the final onset might be indefinitely delayed. Every position that is conceded, they well know, can never be recalled, and makes the next demand less easy to resist. But still the evil day is put off. The Whigs have constituted themselves the superintendents and distributors of this political Danegeld. They know that the material for the concessions with which the enemy is bought off is not inexhaustible, and therefore they conduct their bargains with all possible thrift. They never give more than is just

'DISINTEGRATION'

sufficient to induce the Radicals to keep the Whigs in office. Thus 'the cause for which Hampden died,' &c., is asserted, and at the same time the utmost prudence is shown in husbanding the resources of the Constitution. We do not doubt that the Whigs on each occasion make what they believe to be the best bargain of which their necessities allow. But we doubt still less that the insincere system of political thought and action, which they have done so much to encourage, has tended powerfully to undermine the respect in which Parliamentary Government was formerly held. Whatever temporary advantages their method may have presented – and we do not dispute that they were attractive – it has laboured under the fatal vice which always attaches to the plan, in any department of policy, of 'buying off the barbarians.' It takes the heart out of defence; it dissolves cohesion; it splits up an organized society into a mob of struggling interests. The idea that the convictions of politicians are never stable, that under adequate pressure every resistance will give way, every political profession will be obsequiously re-cast, is fatal to the existence of either confidence or respect. Neither trust nor fear will, in the long run, be inspired by a school of statesmen who, whatever else they sacrifice, never sacrifice themselves. In order to know the end to which this system will bring us, we do not need to exercise any gift of forecast. In Ireland the experiment has been tried. Our policy, in that island, has been made up of steps, each of which was the recantation, under pressure, of principles once loudly and ostentatiously proclaimed as sacred. How has it fared with the English Government in that country? Is it too much to say that, as the issue of a long series of measures framed under these conditions, we are approaching a crisis more formidable than we have ever passed through before?

Unfortunately, no possibility of doubt is left to us as to the character of the feelings with which we are regarded by a large mass of the Irish people. In a recent speech, Mr. Healy[1] has described it in language, which puts clearly enough the view of the situation taken by the extreme adversaries of English rule:

Nine-tenths of the people hate you, and the other tenth despise you, for they know that you are only an engine for the extraction of rent and extraction of taxes.

We may fairly hope that matters are not quite so bad as this. But in face of the recent electoral experience of Ireland, we cannot flatter

[1] T. M. Healy (1855–1931), M.P. Monaghan, and one of Parnell's most prominent associates in the Home Rule movement; later first governor-general of the Irish Free State, 1922–8.

ourselves that it errs, except in somewhat exaggerating the dimensions of the evil. The origin of this unhappy animosity has been made the subject of many passionate disquisitions; but it seems to us that the course of events has tended to refute the explanations which have usually been given. It used to be attributed to the difference of religion, and the persecutions Catholicism has undergone. But it existed before the division between Catholics and Protestants had arisen; and at this moment, when it seems to have reached its culminating point, Catholic influences are weaker with the Irish than they have ever been before. Moreover, persecution was not directed against the Irish Catholics alone; but it has left no corresponding bitterness in the minds of the English Catholics, who, being nearer to the seat of power, often suffered more severely. It seems to us that a truer philosophy was expressed by the late Mr. Vincent Scully,[1] when he told the House of Commons, that only one contingency would seduce the Irish from the Roman Catholic creed; and that was the possibility of its becoming the creed of the English. Another solution of the problem, which of late has been frequently advanced, is that we are suffering under an outburst of the slowly pent-up wrath which was excited by the commercial restrictions imposed upon Irish industry during the last century. The weak point of this argument is the undoubted fact, that never was Ireland so easy to govern, so submissive under the hand of England, as during the time when the severest of those restrictions were in force. The truth is that, barbarous and indefensible as they were, they were consciously felt as a burden by only a very limited portion of the population; and even upon them the enormous facilities for smuggling caused the burdens to press with no intolerable severity. The last theory which has been advanced to account for the state of Irish feeling is the theory of the Upas Tree. It was the State Church; it was the condition of landed tenure, and the misdeeds of the landlords. But the teachings of experience, so far as they have gone, do not give more support to this theory than to previous explanations. A docile electorate gave full powers to Mr. Gladstone; he swept away an ancient Church; he plunged his hands deeply into the coffers of the landlords, and scattered largess among the Irish tenantry, in the hope to win their affections, or at least their adhesion. No one can question the efficiency of his legislation as regards the landlords; they have felt the full force of the blow, and many of them have been driven from their homes, ruined and broken men. But no road has been found to the hearts of

---

[1] 1810–71; M.P. Cork County 1852–7 and 1859–65; a zealous Roman Catholic and advanced Liberal.

'DISINTEGRATION'

the peasantry; their appetites have only been whetted for more loot; their conviction that it can be gained by outrage has been signally confirmed. They will not even pay for the booty that has already been secured the poor guerdon of electoral support. The Government that has stripped the landlord to buy the peasant, does not seem to enjoy the preference even of a minority at the ballot-box. At the two last county elections there was a Conservative party, which was in the minority; and there was a Separatist party, which was in the majority; but for the Liberal Government there were no partisans at all.[1] The feeling towards England is worse, not better than it was; and the party of Mr. Parnell, already on the verge of being a majority, grows with every vacancy. There is no appearance at present that Irish disaffection will be charmed away by the sacrifice of Churches or landlords. Of course the authors of these nostrums tell us we must patiently wait, and our faith shall be rewarded in due time. This is the consolation to which political alchemists are apt to have recourse, whenever the great projection fails. All that can be said with confidence is, that half a generation has passed away since the Upas Tree speech was made, and that no symptom of relenting on the part of the Irish peasantry has yet been shown.

Why is an Ireland the special lot of this country, so philanthropic, so popular and liberal in its sentiments of government, so anxious to divest its policy of even the suspicion of egotism? Other countries have conquered dependencies in their time; it is not an exceptional atrocity peculiar to the history of England. In other places the process has not been accomplished with rose-water; but nevertheless the issue has been complete assimilation of the conquerors and the conquered, and the creation of a united people. There is much in the past history of Ireland that would be horrible if it took place at the present day; but there is nothing in it monstrous or singular – nothing worse than has been done elsewhere by invaders in a conquered province – nothing that was out of harmony with the morality of the age in which it took place. And yet the possession of an Ireland is our peculiar punishment, our unique affliction, among the family of nations. What crime have we committed, with what peculiar vice is our national character chargeable, that this chastisement should have befallen us?

We seem to have the power of conquest, but not to have the faculty of assimilation. The inhabitants of the Flemish Pas de Calais, or of the

[1] Salisbury is referring to the by-elections in Monaghan and Sligo in June and August 1883, respectively. The Home Ruler beat the Conservative by 2,376 to 2,011 in the first, and 1,545 to 983 in the second. There was, however, a Liberal candidate in Monaghan, who got 274 votes.

Celtic Brittany, are not in national sentiment and affection distinguishable from other Frenchmen; and the same, fifteen years ago, could have been said of the German Alsace. Poland has not been a hundred years in the hands of Russia, and has been the theatre of cruelties which have passed into a proverb. Finland has been under the sceptre of the Tsars for a still shorter period. Yet the mass of the population in both Poland and Finland are far more friendly to the domination of Russia than the Irish peasantry are to the rule of England. Conquest followed by incorporation is the process of national formation by which a congeries of petty tribes becomes a great and united nation; and the cruelties which often mark its progress are no bar to the cordiality of the union when it is complete. Ireland had been long under the lordship of England when the conquest of Granada was achieved: does Granada now remember that it is a conquered province? Why is it that in Ireland alone this law does not act, and that no process of assimilation sets in to cover over and heal the rancour of the past?

It may be said that the early conquest of Ireland was merely nominal, that it was never a reality until the reign of Elizabeth; and that for a century after her death the power of England over Ireland was paralyzed by intermittent civil war. There is some truth in this explanation, though it is hardly adequate to account for the entire failure of England to naturalize her rule even in the counties where for many centuries her power was not disputed. But the phenomenon has been still more marked in later times, when the superior strength of this island was not open to challenge in any part of Ireland. The pacification effected by William III. was complete. Willingly or unwillingly, all armed resistance was thenceforth abandoned. So absolute was the submission, that when England was threatened with civil war in 1715, and again in 1745, there was no sympathetic movement of any importance in Ireland, though a diversion on that side would have been profoundly embarrassing to the English Government. If there were a '15 or a '45 at the present day, should we have to deal with no sympathizing action in the sister island?

There is no more curious, and no more instructive contrast than that which is offered by the two periods – the ninety years which preceded 1780 – and the century which has followed it. The first period is one of absolute repose. After the first few years Parliament hardly heard the name of Ireland. England had abundance of enemies at home and abroad; but they did not find in Ireland either help or countenance. Dean Swift's attack on Sir Robert Walpole's Government was a mere war of pamphlets; and the agrarian disorders which began to show

'DISINTEGRATION'

themselves towards the end of the period were as yet very partial, and attracted little attention. On the whole, Ireland at this time was governed with less expenditure of force, and caused less anxiety, than Scotland; and occupied little place among the cares of the Government, or the political history of the time. Yet this was not a period of good government. The laws against the Roman Catholics passed at the beginning of it are a byword for blind ferocity; and the commercial restrictions, adopted at the bidding of the mercantile interests in England, exaggerated the same selfish policy as that which had inspired the Navigation Laws. As the century wore on, the worst penal laws against Roman Catholics fell into disuse, and the commercial laws were largely evaded; nevertheless, if we may trust Dean Swift's invective, the condition of the peasantry was far more wretched than it is now, even in the poorest districts.

The second period – the century which has elapsed since the year 1780 – presents a marked contrast in every respect. With scanty intervals, Ireland has been the principal occupation of the Parliament and the Government at Westminster. The internal history of Ireland has been a continuous tempest of agitation, broken by occasional flashes of insurrection. The legislation of the period has been a continuous stream of concession. And by these words we do not mean merely that the views of the Legislature changed; and that having previously pursued one particular policy they afterwards pursued its opposite. Concession implies two processes: it means refusal changed into consent by pressure. The poet's description of Julia, who 'vowing she would ne'er consent, consented,' would serve for a description of Britannia's attitude to Ireland ever since the appearance of Lord Charlemont and the volunteers.[1] The consequence has been that condition of feeling, which enables Mr. Healy, without obvious absurdity, to assert that nine-tenths of the Irish people hate us, and the other tenth despises us.

But what is there in this epoch of 1780 to make it a turning-point in Irish history – a letting in of the waters of strife which rage higher every day. It was a momentous juncture in many ways. It was the era of Ireland's escape from direct subjection to England; which was brought

[1] The development of the volunteer movement in Ireland from 1778, in response to the threat of French invasion, provided the organisational means for the expression of the rising political self-consciousness of the Protestant nation, and made inevitable the readjustment of the relationship between Ireland and England. Freedom of trade for Ireland was won in 1780, and in February 1782 the Ulster volunteer companies adopted resolutions drawn up by the patriot leader Lord Charlemont which asserted Irish legislative independence, and were followed by the British government's recognition of the independence of the Irish parliament and judicial system later in the year.

about, it must be owned, mainly by our kinsmen and representatives in Ireland. The majority of the people, the Roman Catholic descendants of the old race, had little or no share in that revolution. It was a *coup de main* cleverly timed at the moment of England's supreme embarrassment, but executed in the main by the Irishmen of English and Scotch extraction – by those whom the Nationalist newspapers of to-day now revile as 'West Britons.' It was the worst day's work for themselves they ever did in their history. They little dreamt for whose use they were establishing the maxim, that England's necessity is Ireland's opportunity.

But this same date of 1780 marks another era in our constitutional history, which is still more closely connected with the present state of the Irish difficulty. It was the time when the transformation of Whig policy commenced. It was then that for the first time the Whigs sought political strength by allying themselves with revolutionary movements. They did not seek such extraneous sources of strength earlier, because they did not want it. Till the accession of George III. they were all-powerful in the State, for the Tory party had been entirely effaced ever since 1714; and for some years after his accession their power was little diminished. But when all constitutional propriety was outraged by the Tories taking office, a new chapter in their policy was opened. They cast about for aid; and they called in extreme politicians, rebels or Radicals, to help them. The bargain has been an unfortunate one for them, as well as for their country. In England it ultimately broke up the old Whig party, and has placed the residue which retained the party name at the mercy of the Radicals. In Ireland their political action has been more immediately disastrous. It would not be possible abstractedly either to condemn or praise, in the lump, the measures of concession which, thus reinforced, the Irish have extorted from the English Parliament; but for our present purpose they cannot be judged apart from the conditions under which they were passed. Neither Grattan, nor O'Connell, nor Parnell would have succeeded, but for the assistance of the Whigs. The measures they advocated would either have not passed at all, or would have passed in another shape. But the important thing is, that but for that assistance they would not have passed as the result, in the eyes of all the world, of the pressure which successful disorder could exercise on the deliberations of the House of Commons. Putting aside the matter of the measures involved, which in this case was less important than the manner – the capitulations of 1782, 1829, and 1881,[1] have been

[1] Respectively, the grant of Irish parliamentary and judicial independence, Catholic emancipation, and Gladstone's second Land Act.

disgraceful to the English Parliament. But the attack which extorted them would not have been so powerful or so furious, but for help within the fortress – but for the encouragement and aid which the Whigs gave to agitators whose ultimate designs, as they well knew, were fatal to the integrity of the Empire.

It was an unhappy circumstance, that the Irish race came gradually to the full exercise of political power as electors to the United Parliament, at a time when its credit was deeply shaken by the successive victories it had yielded to revolt; and to a great extent by means of those very victories. It hardly seems credible that statesmen should have expected that the power so obtained would be used to promote the supremacy of England, which had just been partially shaken off. But political forecasts were of a far more roseate hue in those days than now. Up to the time of the Roman Catholic Emancipation, the Roman Catholics of Ireland, which is roughly the same thing as saying the ancient Irish race, had not exercised practically any political power. It had either been in the hands of England, or of Irishmen of English and Scotch extraction. With the Roman Catholic Emancipation a new era began; and to the majority of statesmen it seemed an era full of hope. The abolition of such a religious disability was in accordance with sound ideas of justice and toleration; and it seemed likely to place a spiritual influence that was all-powerful on the side of England. But the event has not justified the sanguine expectations of those times. Lord Melbourne is reported to have said before he died, 'Everybody but the fools was in favour of Roman Catholic Emancipation; but it has turned out that the fools were right.' The Irish hatred has been stronger than Catholic reconciliation: and the universal conviction that the measure was extorted has quenched all gratitude for the boon. The result, as far as after half a century of experience we may judge it, has been to add another illustration of the difficulty of keeping people as subjects against their will by the instrumentality of highly popular institutions; and the more real the popular institutions are, the more arduous does the undertaking become. Undoubtedly the subjection is not severe in its character; and it exists as much for the benefit of the smaller as of the more numerous race. For many years this nation has flattered itself that the dislike to English rule was a pretence of the agitators, and was not the real feeling of the people; or at all events that it was confined to a small minority. But as one restraint after another upon the expression of their true opinions has been removed, the fact is becoming plainer and plainer, that a large mass of the inhabitants of Ireland, specially composed of those who are not of English or Scotch descent, are disaffected to English rule, and only submit to it because they have no opportunity of throwing it off.

Englishmen have failed to foresee the course which events would take in Ireland after Roman Catholic Emancipation, because they are blinded by the metaphors which are habitual in political discussion. It is given to few phrases to cover so much untruth as to the word 'Self-government.' There is something so attractive in it, that even foreign nations have borrowed it of us, and speak of people who are governed by a majority among themselves as having obtained 'self-government.' The structure of the word suggests that it means very much the same thing as 'self-control' – the noblest and freest condition to which the individual can aspire. Yet it is a hollow metaphor and nothing more. The 'self' which governs and is governed does not exist: it is a mere abstraction or convenient mode of speech. It is a collective word for a multitude of real 'selves,' of whom a large portion are very far indeed from being 'self-governed.' Whenever the majority of such a community really have the same political wish, they can give effect to it; and in that case they – the majority only – can be said with truth to be self-governed. The minority are no more self-governed than if they lived in Morocco. They have to do what they do not like, because the majority like it: which is the very reverse of being self-governed. In regard to that particular question they are not free. No doubt, in a homogeneous community this condition of subjection is, or may be, only transitory. The minority of to-day may be in the majority of to-morrow: a man who is in the minority on one question may be in a majority on the next. He has nothing to complain of: for, while on some questions he is free, and dictates to his neighbour, on others, when he has to submit to dictation, he is probably governed with tolerable fairness. As regards such communities, no better way has been discovered of managing human affairs. Self-government is therefore, in their case, a very desirable state of things; though the word is far from meaning exactly what it says. But this accident happens to so many political phrases, that it would not be worth noticing, if only homogeneous communities were in question.

But the matter assumes an entirely different aspect, when we come to apply the word to a community which is not homogeneous. If it consists of different elements that have not been fused together; if large masses of citizens are separated into jealous or hostile sections, by deep divisions of creed or race, or even of interest, the word 'self-government' is not only a bad metaphor, but becomes flagrantly deceptive. In such cases one section of the community is in a permanent minority on a whole

'DISINTEGRATION'

department of questions, which are probably precisely those that it has most at heart. In regard to them, it has to accept, not its own solution, but the solution of the hostile majority, which is perhaps diametrically the reverse of its own. By no license of language can such a permanent minority be spoken of as self-governed or free. Are the Catholics of France self-governed, or free? It may well be that they would be more free under the rule of a despot who was indifferent, and therefore impartial, upon the class of questions which interest them most, than under a popular government in which there is a majority pledged by the strongest motives always to vote against them. It is in a great degree on this account that a despotic government is more successful than a democracy in securing the peaceable government and the ultimate fusion of an empire made up of hostile races. It may certainly account for the fact, that admission to the English Parliament has not operated in any degree to reconcile to English rule those to whom it was previously an object of aversion. The change has been in the other direction. The more the party, that in an Irish Parliament would be dominant, have recognized their isolated condition as a permanent minority in the assembly at Westminster, the stronger has their wish to escape from Westminster become. Certainly the English majority cannot blame itself for having made any undue use of its prerogatives. It has been generous of its concessions; in the eyes of Conservatives generous often at the cost of justice and of the rights of other men. But such concessions have conveyed to the minds of the minority a conviction rather of our softness than of our liberality, and has [sic] stimulated the resolution to exact the supreme concession from those who have already been brought to concede so much.

Unhappily they do not lack efficient weapons. It has been given to them to illustrate in the most forcible colours the inefficiency of the party system for governing a disaffected population. A permanent minority does not readily acquiesce in a position of helplessness. Being unable to use its vote for its own objects with any effect, it takes measures to sell it to those who can. In a homogeneous assembly, on the Parliamentary system, the conspicuous men as a rule either hold office, or hope to do so. But the leaders of a permanent minority can have no such aspirations, if their constituents are in earnest. As long as their opinions are in hopeless disaccord with those of the majority, it is evident they never can be members of a government resting on the concurrence of the majority. Ceasing, thus, to be themselves candidates for power, they are free to practise on the weaknesses of those who are. Their votes in a division can be made the price of legislative concessions. Party leaders in the heat of conflict will give much to win a division; and they can, not unfrequently, be brought to offer more than is consistent with the interests of their country or the pledges of their party. The principle of this strategy is by no means new in politics. It is the simple device practised by those far-seeing electors, who are, or were, accustomed to defer the final decision of their hesitating convictions till within a few minutes of four o'clock.[1] It is the ordinary plan by which a Radical group induces a Whig Government to win it back to the fold on the eve of a confidence division. We have seen it at work in the German Parliament, where, in Herr Windhorst's dexterous hands, it has conducted the great Chancellor himself several stages upon the dreaded road to Canossa.[2] But upon no political field has it been practised with so much tenacity and resource as by the Irish party in the English Parliament since the Emancipation Act of 1829.

For some time they met with no great success, and experienced one or two severe reverses. The Lichfield House compact[3] procured nothing for the Irish party, except a certain influence over the distribution of patronage; but it wrecked the Whig Government in the affection of the constituencies. The 'Pope's Brass-band' of 1852 was prophetically named; for little else except noise apparently resulted from its existence. It landed a few of its members in subordinate Government offices, and then broke up with an evil savour among the scandals of the Tipperary Bank.[4] But though the Irish party achieved little of positive gain in the way

[1] It had been a common practice of electors in corrupt constituencies to withhold their votes until late in the day, in order to command a better price for them.

[2] Ludwig Windthorst (not 'Windhorst'), the leader of the Catholic Centre party in the Reichstag, was a skilful parliamentary tactician and a bitter opponent of Bismarck, whose desire for Centre party co-operation after the liquidation of the Kulturkampf and the falling away of National Liberal support he was able to exploit. One of his devices was to avoid committing his party on a measure until a late stage.

[3] The name given to O'Connell's agreement with the Whigs in March 1835, as a result of which his followers combined with them and the Radicals to force Peel out of office in the following month.

[4] Salisbury is not quite accurate here. The independent group of Irish M.P.s which was nicknamed 'the Pope's Brass Band' came into being in 1851, not 1852, due to resentment among Irish Liberals of Russell's Ecclesiastical Titles Bill. It formed an alliance with the Irish Tenant League, and after the general election of 1852 mustered forty-eight members. But it was weakened when two of its leaders, Keogh and Sadleir, accepted minor posts under Aberdeen, and it never achieved anything solid, finally disintegrating in 1859. Its end hardly owed much to the collapse in 1856 of the Tipperary Joint-Stock Bank, following the suicide of Sadleir, the bank's founder, who had been engaging in financial malpractice. If anything, this event helped the independent group by substantiating the charges it had made against Sadleir's character since his desertion.

'DISINTEGRATION'

of legislation, they succeeded in introducing a new element into the calculations of Parliamentary strategists. The question how the Irish vote was to be secured was the absorbing problem which weighed on the minds of the whips on the eve of every critical division. Still the practical results were of a secondary kind. Until 1868 their efforts were principally devoted to foiling Stanley's and Peel's schemes for mixed education. But a new epoch opened with Mr. Gladstone's accession to power. In his Lancashire speeches of that year he offered the largest bribe that has ever been given for Parliamentary support. He saw with the eye of genius the opening for business, presented not only by the Irish representation, properly so called, but also by the large Irish populations which the Reform Bill of 1867 had added to the register in many of our great towns; and he made them a splendid offer which he sagaciously judged was sufficient to sweep the market – the complete destruction of the Irish Church, a deep dip into the landlords' pockets, with the early prospect of renewing the process, and the entire overthrow of the system of education, for which England had been contending for half a century. Another boon he was about to give them, though much was not said of it at the time – perhaps a more momentous gift than any other. The Ballot, to which the Prime Minister about the same time became a convert, was destined finally to transfer supremacy at the Irish polls to the anti-English party.

The results of these transactions were, for the moment, brilliant to both sides. The Irish gained measures for which they had long wished, but for which five years before they would not have dared to hope; and Mr. Gladstone gained for three years a submissive and unquestioning majority. If, however, he imagined that by sacrificing the landlords and the Church he had permanently gained the Irish vote, events speedily disabused him of his mistake. The Irish party are shrewd bargainers, and they took an early opportunity, on the University Bill, of acquainting him that their adhesion was a matter of business, and not a question of gratitude.[1] They indicated the policy from which they have never swerved, that an English party cannot purchase their co-operation by any single service, however splendid, but must earn it by a continuous tribute of concessions, until the great end is reached. That the Land Act of 1870 should develop into the Land Act of 1881 was to be expected. Lord Beaconsfield at the time pointed out that compensation for disturbance must lead to an attack on rents; not only as a logical conclusion, but as

[1] Cf. p. 297, n. 1, above.

a necessary consequence of the altered balance of power. The forces whose conflict had ended in the Act of 1870 were arrayed against each other again; but their relative strength was fatally altered. Legislation had made the landlord powerless, and a former defeat had made him hopeless; while the Irish party were strong in the confidence bestowed by past success and present resources, for they knew by experience how much could be extorted from the political necessities of Mr. Gladstone, and how powerful were the means of pressure in their hands. The most noteworthy circumstance about the struggle, of which the Arrears Act has been the momentary close, is the novelty in tactics due to the ingenuity of Mr. Parnell. For the purpose of obtaining particular concessions, he still pursues the plan which was pursued by O'Connell and by Butt,[1] of purchasing them by offering the votes of his detachment in exchange. But in order to attain gradually to the main end which the Irish party have at heart – escape from the rule of England – he has hit upon another device. It is of no use to attempt to purchase Home Rule of English party leaders, by any offer of Parliamentary support, however captivating; for even if they wished to do so, they could not enforce such a policy upon their followers in the House, or in the nation. But it has occurred to him that Parliament and the country may concede as a matter of mere weakness what they would never consent to on its merits. Bad as they think it, it is possible they might accept it as the alternative to something more intolerable still. He thinks that perhaps we may in the end prefer that Ireland shall be ruled by the Irish, rather than that England should not be ruled at all. We might be willing to grant an Irish Parliament if there was no other way of maintaining our own Parliament in a condition of vitality. Accordingly he has set himself to the task of hampering and paralyzing the legislative machine, so that little or no useful work can be got out of it, even by the expenditure of the most excessive labour.

The plan is not wanting in ingenuity, and, so far as it has gone, has met with an encouraging amount of success. Of course it implies the lowest possible estimate of the resolution and courage of those with whom he has to deal; but it will not on that account necessarily fail. It is pursued, according as opportunity offers, but not always with uniform effort; for it is not the only path by which the Irish party hope to attain their end. At present they follow two distinct but converging lines of advance towards the great objective point – separation. Mr. Parnell tries to operate on Parliament itself; and, for that purpose, to extort all the

[1] Isaac Butt (1813–79), lawyer and M.P., leader of the Home Rule movement 1870–8.

'DISINTEGRATION'

changes in the electoral law which are likely to increase the strength of his Parliamentary contingent. He sees that at the head of forty votes he can make Parliament almost unworkable; he naturally infers that, at the head of eighty votes, he can make the presence of the Irish Members quite unbearable to the rest of the House of Commons; and he doubts not that in their agony Englishmen will reflect on the fact, that it was the Union with Ireland which bestowed this blessing on Parliament. Mr. Davitt,[1] being outside Parliament, hopes to reach the same end by another path. He holds the common belief, that it is the Irish landlords who induce Parliament to retain its hold of Ireland, and consequently argues that, if they were extirpated, Parliament would be lukewarm on the question of the Irish Union. Accordingly, he proposes the extirpation of the landlords, by the simple process of taking their land from them. This strategy throws him more completely upon the ordinary resources of the 'party of action' in every country. He has little share in the special advantages which Mr. Parnell derives from the working of our party system; but, on the other hand, he sails before the wind of popular greed and passion. He is engaged in the task of persuading the most lawless and land-loving peasantry in the world to despise the law and to seize the land; and he is not likely to be deterred by a temporary Crimes Act from pursuing so hopeful an enterprise. It may possibly prove more arduous than he expects. He probably proceeds on the assumption that there is no limit to the compressibility of a Liberal Government. It must be admitted that, up to this time, the existence of such a limit is a matter of faith rather than of experience. But whether the English people will be equally compressible, when once they understand the question, remains to be seen.

Both agitators appear, for the moment at least, to be advancing prosperously upon their respective paths: and the peril which they are creating for England will tax to the uttermost the manhood of her sons. For it is one out of which no immediate issue is yet disclosed to view; except a courageous maintenance of the rights of the Empire, and a patient struggle with the resistance, however stubborn it may be, however

[1] Michael Davitt (1846–1906), Fenian organiser, was active in the foundation of the Land League in October 1879, and in bringing together the agrarian and Home Rule agitations. After the Land League's suppression in October 1881, he helped to form the National League. He had served nearly eight years' penal servitude in 1870–7 for treason-felony, and was imprisoned again from February 1881 to May 1882 (when he was released as a result of the Kilmainham agreement), and from January to May 1883. Influenced by Henry George, he was an advocate of land nationalisation, which brought him into conflict with Parnell.

long it may last, against which those rights must be vindicated. Experience must surely have satisfied us, by this time, that there is no other safe path to pursue. Ever since the Union, the course of English policy has been to remove one by one the various restraints which prevented the will of the numerical majority from being supreme in Ireland. So far as this policy has gone, it has been marked at each step by an increase in the proportion of the constituencies which have expressed their dislike of English rule. To re-impose such restraints when they have been once removed is notoriously difficult, and no one suggests that it would be practicable in the present case. On the other hand, there is nothing to encourage the belief that a greater success is likely to attend the efforts which the Government are making to move further along the same line. Registration Bills[1] and Reform Bills will only elicit in a more emphatic and authoritative form the very aspirations which embarrass us, and which, when they are expressed, it will be the inevitable function of the English majority to quench. To persist in such homœopathic remedies is to neglect the teaching of a century of experience. Such measures can have no other recommendation, except that, for the moment, they will lead Mr. Parnell's contingent through the Ministerial lobby in a certain number of divisions.

One issue there is which, in the judgment not only of the Conservative party, but in that of the great majority of Englishmen, is absolutely closed. The highest interests of the Empire, as well as the most sacred obligations of honour, forbid us to solve this question by conceding any species of independence to Ireland; or in other words, any licence to the majority in that country to govern the rest of Irishmen as they please. To the minority, to those who have trusted us, and on the faith of our protection have done our work, it would be a sentence of exile or of ruin. All that is Protestant – nay, all that is loyal – all who have land or money to lose, all by whose enterprise and capital industry and commerce are still sustained, would be at the mercy of the adventurers who have led the Land League, if not of the darker counsellors by whom the Invincibles have been inspired. If we have failed after centuries of effort to make Ireland peaceable and civilized, we have no moral right to abandon our post and leave all the penalty of our failure to those whom we have persuaded to trust in our power. It would be an act of political bankruptcy, an avowal that we were unable to satisfy even the most sacred obligations, and that all claims to protect or govern any one beyond our own narrow island were at an end.

[1] I.e. to facilitate the registration of voters.

'DISINTEGRATION'

In the presence of such considerations, we hardly care to speak of the strategical objections. But these are formidable enough. If Ireland is not with us, she is against us. If her Government does not obey the orders given from Westminster, it will speedily become subordinate to the greater Ireland that is growing up beyond the ocean. Napoleon was wont to say that Antwerp was a loaded pistol held to the mouth of the Thames. The coast of Ireland, in unfriendly hands, would be something more than a pistol held to the mouths of the Clyde and the Mersey and the Severn. And we must not dismiss such extreme conditions from our minds as possibilities which cannot be realized. We shall have speedily enough to choose between them and the reconquest of Ireland, if once Home Rule be granted. Any political power conceded to an Irish assembly will be made the fulcrum by which more will be exacted, until complete practical independence is secured.

The impossibility of England's acceding to Home Rule is too plain to need enforcing. The proposal is not as yet advocated, even by the most advanced of the leaders of progress. If the country had simply to choose between accepting and resisting separation, the decision would be given promptly and without hesitation. But a more difficult task is before this country. It must guard itself from being led, under the guise of legitimate indulgences or of carrying out accepted principles, into concessions which will make Home Rule inevitable. Have we strength left to do this? or has the disintegration gone so far that these concessions too will be won by the process which has proved effective for all that have gone before? We may have the resolution to refuse Home Rule as a whole. Have we the resolution to refuse it in instalments? Or will our bargaining politicians, when votes grow scarce, open their market once more for a final clearance sale of all that remains of English rule in Ireland?

The air is filled with rumours of new negociations and successful bargains. Another 'deed without a name' – another fortuitous concurrence of mutually benevolent intentions, like that which took place at Kilmainham – is likely to place the Irish vote at the disposal of the Government for the purposes of a Reform Bill. Such complaisance at such a crisis will deserve warm recognition; and it will be duly given in the form of a Bill for the establishment of local government in Ireland, which is to be conducted by elective Councils.[1] What limit is to be assigned to the

---

[1] The Queen's speech of 1881 had promised a measure for the establishment of county government in Ireland on a representative basis, and an Irish member had introduced a bill for elective county councils earlier in 1883.

powers of these Councils, we cannot say: but we can predict with absolute confidence that, whatever it is, the whole energy of the Councils will be devoted to procuring its abolition. And no doubt the day will come, when votes will again be in request for a critical occasion: and the entire emancipation, and possibly the consolidation, of these Councils will be the price. Will the Whigs be parties to this arrangement also? A quarter of a century ago our system of government was described by Prosper Mérimée, a perfectly impartial witness, in these terms:

Ce qui me frappe surtout dans la politique anglaise de notre temps, c'est sa petitesse...Tout se fait en Angleterre en vue de conserver les portefeuilles. On fait toutes les fautes possibles pour conserver une trentaine de voix douteuses. On ne s'inquiète que du present, et on ne songe pas à l'avenir.

Is this always to be so, even to the end? And if so, how long can the final disintegration of the Empire be postponed?

Index

Aberdeen coalition (1853), 148-9
Acton, Lord, 4
Adullamites, 79, 80, 83, 194, 226-7
Affirmation Bill (1883), 339
Afghans, 342
agricultural labourers:
  and politics, 317
  union leaders of, 323
  wages of, 51n
Alabama claims, 292, 315, 338-9
Alexandra of Denmark, Princess of Wales, 159-60
Allsopp, Sir H. (1st Baron Hindlip), 96n
Althorp, Viscount, 243
Alva, Duke of, 301
America, United States of, 30, 72-4, 165, 174, 189, 275, 292, 307, 315, 345, 350, 352
  constitution of, 31, 101, 174, 337, 348-9, 375
  democracy in, 31, 32, 72-3, 101, 105, 126, 136, 158, 189-91, 208, 337, 348-9, 350
  'indirect' claims of, 298
American Civil War, 5, 8-9, 34, 72-4, 159, 162, 173, 189-90, 193, 197, 302, 303
  impact of on Salisbury, 11
American Revolution, 105
Andover, 138
Annual Register, 159
Antwerp, 133, 375
Argyll, 8th Duke of, 111, 267
aristocracy, 59, 187
army reform, 286, 292, 303
Arnold, Matthew, 4
Arrears Act (1882), 336, 372
Arundel, 142
Australia, 41
Austria, 111, 128, 159-60, 190
Ayrton, A. S., 292, 297

Bailly, J.-S., 126
Baines, Edward, franchise bill of, (1864) 160, 176, 177; (1865) 262
Balfour, A. J., 101
ballot, 305-6, 317, 339-40, 371
Baring, Sir F. T., 115
Bath, 293
Bath, 4th Marquis of, 86

Baxter, Dudley, 195
Beaconsfield, 1st Earl of, *see* Disraeli, Benjamin
Beales, Edmond, 283
Beaumaris, 204
Beesly, E. S., 89
Belgium, 133, 218, 305
Bentinck, G. W. P., 150
Bentley's Quarterly Review, 4
Berwick, 143
Beverley, 204
Birkenhead, 113, 139, 204
Birmingham, 113, 138, 141, 203, 204, 293
Bismarck, Prince Otto von, 105, 370
Blackburn, 141
Bodmin, 138
Boers, 56, 335, 342
Bohemia, 302
Bolton, 141, 204
Bradford, 141
Bradlaugh, Charles, 90, 312, 331, 335
Brand, Henry, 238
Brazil, 55, 56n
Brecon, 140
Bridgwater, 204
Bright, John, 31, 58, 72, 90, 112, 132, 133, 194, 221, 234, 239, 283, 292, 300, 311, 324, 357
  and America, 72-3, 197, 224
  fiscal policy of, 66, 123, 125-6, 135, 144, 155, 215
  and France, 112, 129, 133
  and the land, 58, 68, 113, 125, 150, 215, 216-17, 224
  and Reform, 62, 68, 71, 76, 113, 125-6, 135, 144, 150, 155, 193, 196, 197-8, 200, 205-6, 212, 213, 220, 224-5, 232, 242, 244, 263, 302
Brighton, 201
Bristol, 204, 304
Bruce, H. A., 292, 295
budget of 1860, 66, 112, 115-24, 134-5, 136
building societies, 217
Bulgarian atrocities, 352
Burials Bill, 66, 162, 318, 319, 323, 324
Burke, Edmund, 231
Burke, T. H., 336
Burnley, 113, 139, 201

377

INDEX

Bury, 141, 204
Butt, Isaac, 372
Buxton, Charles, 76

cabinet responsibility, theory of, 269–71
Cairns, Sir Hugh (1st Baron and 1st Earl Cairns), 262
Cambridge, 204
  women's colleges at, 18
Canterbury, 204
Cardiff, 204
Cardigan, 140
Cardwell, Edward, 111, 119, 303
Carmarthen, (borough) 204; (county) 140
Carnarvon, 140
Carnarvon, 4th Earl of, 81, 93, 254, 255, 264
Castlereagh, Viscount, 5, 37, 55
Catholics:
  emancipation of, 310, 366–7
  English, 362
  French, 369
  Irish, 146, 147, 362, 365, 366
Cavaignac, General, 305
Cave, Stephen, 177
Cavendish, Lord Frederick, 336
Chamberlain, Joseph, 52, 90, 101, 108, 293–4, 306, 324, 325, 326, 331, 333, 335, 336, 340, 357, 359
  on Salisbury, 337
change, 24, 36, 38–9, 106, 283
Charlemont, 1st Earl of, 365
Charles II, king of England, 195
Charles X, king of France, 244
Chartism, 243
Chatham, 141, 204
Chelsea, 113, 138, 201
Cheltenham, 204
Cheshire, 237
  South, 140
Chester, 204
China, British relations with, 55, 56n, 122
Chippenham, 138
Church of England, 66–7, 78, 157, 162, 231, 292, 296, 311, 318, 340, 358
  and the Conservative party, 67, 84, 274, 287
  and education, 51, 66, 319–20, 323, 324, 325–6
  threats to, 66–7, 159, 257, 285, 288–9, 293, 294, 311, 312, 319–20, 323–6, 327, 330

Church of Scotland, 289
church rates, 66, 159, 161
Churchill, Lord Randolph, 1, 94
Cirencester, 138
cities, difficulty posed by growth of to government, 300
civil service, competitive examination for, 97
Clanricarde, 1st Marquis of, 227
Clarendon, 4th Earl of, 207n, 227
class conflict, 26–7, 35, 58, 79, 87–90, 102, 104, 107–8, 124–6, 144, 182–3, 219, 242, 294, 304–7, 337, 342, 343–4, 346, 356–7
class differences, 27–9
clerical fellowships, 323, 324
Cleveland, 4th Duke of, 207n
Cobden, Richard, 73, 112, 123
Cobden Treaty (1860), 112, 117, 118, 127–8
Code Napoléon, 217, 218
Colchester, 204
Collier case, 297
Comte, Auguste, 199
concession, 290
  perils of, 37–8, 318–19
conscience clause, 319–20
Conservatism, 27, 39, 72, 96, 106, 109, 300
conservative classes:
  dangers of complacency among, 34, 71–2, 283–4
  duty of, 34–5
  in 1867, 85, 278–9, 281–4, 287; tactics for, 290–1
Conservative party, 310–11
  basis of, 27
  in 1832, 59
  in 1832–46, 310
  in 1846–66, 60–6, 74, 77–9, 111, 113, 114, 138–9, 145–6, 148, 149–58, 159, 160, 168, 193, 243, 260
  in Reform crisis of 1866–7, 79–85, 91, 194–5, 219, 223, 226–7, 229, 237, 246, 247, 248–9, 250, 251, 253–7, 260, 261–4, 265–6, 267, 273, 274, 277, 280, 281, 284–7, 289
  after 1867, 86–7, 90–7, 107–8, 294, 306, 312, 314, 317, 318, 330, 337, 339, 340, 341, 359, 363, 374
  Salisbury and, 1–2, 62, 86–7, 93–7, 102, 107–9, 256
conservative tactics, 36–9, 290
Contagious Diseases Acts, 312, 352

378

INDEX

corn laws, 147
Cornwall, 246
  West, 138
county constituencies:
  political conditions in, 317
  under-representation of, 75, 201, 202
  urban element in, 62, 113, 140, 195, 200-2
  see also: franchise; Reform, parliamentary; Reform acts; Reform bills
Coventry, 204
Cowper, 7th Earl, 336
Cranworth, Lord, 265
Crown, 288, 294, 311, 316
  power of, 269, 346, 348

Darlington, 201
Davitt, Michael, 335, 336, 373
deceased wife's sister, marriage with, 316
defence, national, 111, 112, 126-7, 133-4
democracy, 1, 29-34, 68-70, 72-3, 85, 93-4, 97-8, 100-3, 104, 105, 125-6, 144, 157, 158, 186-7, 190-1, 194, 195, 207-8, 220, 347, 350, 369
  in America, 31, 32, 72-3, 101, 105, 126, 136, 158, 189-91, 208, 337, 348-9, 350
  in British colonies, 208
  in France, 31, 72, 98-9, 126, 136, 158, 190, 333
Denmark, 159-60, 162, 168n, 173, 189-91
Derby, 141, 204
Derby, 14th Earl of, 86, 371
  as leader of the Conservative party, 61-6, 79-85, 108, 113, 114, 149, 151, 154, 159, 193, 194, 195, 226, 227, 249, 251, 253-7, 260-1, 262, 263-4, 266-7, 272-4, 275, 276, 277, 281, 282, 287
Derby, 15th Earl of (known as Lord Stanley, 1851-69), 226, 227, 262, 270
  on Conservatives, 2
Derbyshire, North, 140
despotism, 369
Devizes, 138
Devon, South, 138
Devonport, 204
Dilke, Sir Charles, 90, 311, 312, 335
Disraeli, Benjamin (1st Earl of Beaconsfield), 1, 2, 8, 87, 94, 96n, 107, 139, 193, 280, 288, 360, 371
  as Conservative leader, 61-6, 80-6, 92-3, 108, 113, 114, 148, 149, 150, 151-4, 156-7, 159, 194, 195, 226-7, 253-7, 261, 262-4, 265, 266, 272, 285, 286, 287, 292, 294
  relations with Salisbury, 63, 93, 114
  on Salisbury, 9
dissenters, 67, 159, 288, 292, 296, 310, 312, 319-20, 325, 326
Dorchester, 138
Dorset, 140
Dover, 204, 292
Du Cane, C., 119
Dudley, 141, 204
Dunkellin, Lord, 227, 230, 247, 263
Durham (city), 204, 304
Durham (county), 237
  North, 140

education:
  elementary, 51, 285, 286, 292, 293, 319-20, 323, 324, 325-6, 330, 332
  Irish, 371
  women's, 17-18
Edward, Prince of Wales (later Edward VII), 160
Elcho, Lord, 193, 196, 226
elections, 42, 213, 339-40
  corruption and intimidation in, 46, 164, 189, 216
  cost of, 247
  general: 1865, 77, 193, 236; 1868, 91; 1874, 92-3, 294, 340; 1880, 88, 340; 1885, 96; 1886-1900, 96
  voting papers in, 247
electoral registration, 247
Elementary Education Act (1870), 292, 323, 324
Elgin, 8th Earl of, 111
Empire, 56-7, 102, 342
endowed schools, 66, 159, 318, 324
Endowed Schools Bill, 162
Englishmen:
  influence of foreign events on, 301-4, 333
  political characteristics of, 125, 180, 298-9, 301, 333, 350, 351, 352, 376
entail, law of, 320-2
equality, 28
  Radical desire for, 353-4, 355
Essays by the late Marquess of Salisbury K.G.: Biographical (1905), 5
Essays by the late Marquess of Salisbury K.G.: Foreign Politics (1905), 5-6
Essex
  North, 138
  South, 138, 140, 201

INDEX

ethics, 22–3, 258
Evesham, 138
Exeter, 2nd Marquis of, 3, 62n, 81, 114

Fawcett, Henry, 210
Fenians, 277
Ferdinand II, Holy Roman Emperor, 302
Ferdinand II, king of Naples, 209
Finland, 364
Finsbury, 142
foreign policy, 26, 53–6, 130–3, 160, 162–3, 182, 286, 292, 342–3
  ethics of, 53
Forster, W. E., 167, 193, 261, 263, 279–80, 285–7, 288, 292, 336, 338, 350, 351–2
Fortnightly Review, 325
Fox, Charles James, 265, 310, 358
Fox, Henry, 265
France, 105, 215, 218, 270, 301, 302, 307, 308, 313, 315, 342, 363–4
  Catholics in, 369
  church and clergy in, 307, 332–3
  class conflict in, 304–5, 306–7, 333
  commercial treaty with, 112, 117, 118, 127–8
  democracy in, 31, 72, 98–9, 126, 136, 158, 190, 333
  foreign relations of, 111–12, 127–30, 133, 160, 307
  land law in, 322, 333
  legislative assembly of, 165–6
  see also: Franco-Prussian War; French revolutions
franchise:
  of 1832, 42, 44, 46, 75–6, 164, 174, 188, 193, 194n, 195–6, 201
  reform of, *see* Reform, parliamentary; Reform acts; Reform bills
  right to, 44–7, 160–1, 175–6, 178–9, 180–8
  for women, 18n
Franco-Prussian War, 25, 98
free trade, 50
freedom:
  conditions of, 49
  and democracy, 32–3
  and political society, 180–2
  and working classes, 218
French revolutions, 245–6
  1789, 34, 37, 105, 126, 175, 304, 360
  1830, 302, 304
  1848, 305
Frome, 142

Frost, John, 243
Froude, J. A., 4

Gambetta, Léon, 307
game laws, 315–16
Garibaldi, Giuseppe, 163
Gateshead, 142, 204
Gibbs, E. J., 195, 201, 203
Gibson, T. Milner, 153, 168
Gladstone, W. E., 4, 54, 77–8, 79, 80, 84, 98, 106, 155, 160, 166, 168, 170, 239, 240, 250, 256, 270, 273, 335, 338, 359, 371
  as chancellor of the exchequer, 66, 111–12, 115–24, 126–7, 132, 133, 134–5, 144–5, 161, 229, 234–5
  on the franchise (1864), 44–5, 159, 160, 175–80, 188–9, 191, 193, 221, 235
  hostility of to the landed interest, 66, 134–5, 150, 236–7
  as prime minister (1868–74), 292, 295, 296, 312, 314, 324–5, 330, 362; (1880–3), 372
  and the Radicals, 66, 78, 176–7, 193, 194, 197, 232–5, 250–2, 296, 303
  and the Reform Bill of 1866, 193, 196, 197, 198, 199, 200, 202, 206–7, 209, 221, 223, 226–30, 232–9, 261, 263
  self-deceit of, 234–5, 236
Gladstone, W. H., 324
Glasgow, 125, 143n
Globe, 286
Glorious Revolution (1688), 265
Gloucester, 150
Gloucestershire:
  East, 140
  West, 140
Goschen, G. J., 237
government, 37, 38, 39, 40–53, 58–9, 77, 129, 259–60
  by party, 269–76, 369–70
  and public opinion, 41, 100–1, 173–4
  purpose of, 41, 45, 48, 52–3, 182–3
  representative, 180–7, 351, 354; in Britain, 39, 40, 42–6, 59–60, 75–7, 98–103, 105, 174–5, 187–9, 260, 338, 344, 345–8, 349, 350–3 (*see also:* House of Commons; House of Lords)
  self-, 57n, 368–9
  social and economic role of, 48–53
Grattan, Henry, 366
Greece, 162
Greenwich, 204, 292, 296
Grey, 3rd Earl, 76, 207n, 249

380

INDEX

Grey, Sir George, 235
Grosvenor, Earl, 226, 230, 238
Guildford, 138, 204
Guise family, 301

Halifax, 1st Viscount, 207n
Hall, Carl, 190
Hamilton, Lord George, 86
Hardy, Gathorne, 262
Harrison, Frederic, 90
Hartington, Marquis of, 336
Harwich, 138
Hastings, 204
Haverfordwest, 204
Healy, T. M., 361, 365
Heathcote, Sir William, 194
Helper, H. R., 189
Henley, J. W., 154, 281
Herbert, Sidney, 48n, 111
Hertford, 138, 204
Hertfordshire, 140
history, 20, 24-5, 104
Hodgkinson, G., 256
Honiton, 138
Hope, A. J. B. Beresford, 3-4
Horsman, Edward, 124, 226
House of Commons, 42-3, 59, 102, 116, 174-5, 188, 216, 229, 230, 269, 274, 296-7, 317, 337, 345-8, 349, 351, 352-3, *and minor refs. passim*
  of 1859-64, 161-73
  Irish obstruction in, 335, 336, 372-3
  power of over executive, 43, 99-100, 173, 174, 275-6, 337, 347, 353
  Salisbury and, 14
  working of, 94-5, 163-74, 189; in 1867, 277-8
House of Lords, 39, 101n, 172, 223, 224, 311, 312, 316-17, 358
  in 1832, 245
  in 1867, 280, 288
  reform of, 40, 59
House of Representatives (American), 165, 348
housing of the working classes, 52, 286
Huddersfield, 174
Hudson, George, 121-2
Hull, 204
Hume, Joseph, 243
Hungary, nobility of, 215
Huntingdon, 138
Hyde Park:

meetings in, 277
riots in, 253, 281, 282
hypothec, law of, 316
Hythe, 204

immaculate conception, doctrine of, 261-2
imperialism, 57, 108
income tax, 69, 118, 121, 122, 123, 124, 126-7, 135, 144, 161, 281
India, 56-7, 342
international law, 53
international relations, 53-4
International Working Men's Association (First International), 88, 303, 307
'Invincibles', 336, 374
Ipswich, 141
Ireland, 37, 38, 56-7, 108, 146, 257, 274, 286, 287, 335-6, 337-8, 343, 352, 353, 361, 370-6
  course of English rule in, 361-8, 369, 374
  land question in, 285, 287, 289, 323, 335-6, 344, 359-60, 362, 371-2, 373
  (*see also:* Irish land acts)
Irish Church, 77, 146, 150, 287, 289
  disestablishment of, 292, 303, 362, 371
Irish Home Rule, 57n, 95, 316, 335, 338, 372-6
Irish Home Rulers, 335, 336, 363, 372-3, 374
Irish land acts:
  1870, 292, 303, 322-3, 371
  1881, 336, 349, 360, 366-7, 371
Irish University Bill, 292, 297, 371
Irishmen in House of Commons, 171
Italy, 111-12, 130, 132-3, 162, 173, 307

Jaffray, J., 296
James, Edwin, 30
Japan, 56n
Jewish disabilities, removal of, 62n, 154, 310
joint-stock companies, as analogues of the state, 183-6
Jones, Ernest, 125

Kaffirs, 56
Kensington, 113, 138, 201
Kent, West, 138, 140, 201
Kidderminster, 142
'Kilmainham Treaty', 336, 375
King, P. J. Locke, 317
Knaresborough, 138, 174

INDEX

Knightley, Sir Rainald, 266

Lafayette, Marquis de, 351
Lambert, John, 199
Lancashire, 159, 237
  North, 138, 140
  South, 138
Lancaster, 204
Land League, 335, 336, 374
land questions, 66, 69, 125, 185, 195, 215, 216–18, 236, 285, 287, 289, 292, 293, 294, 303, 311, 312, 320–3, 330, 332, 333, 344, 354
  see also: Ireland, land question in
landed interest, 22, 134–5, 154, 195, 236, 344, 345
  and the Conservative party, 64–5, 95
  Salisbury and, 21–2, 51, 66
  taxation of, 66, 121, 134–5, 145, 202, 236
  under-representation of, 75, 201–2, 237
Langley, Baxter, 296
Lansdowne, 4th Marquis of, 207n, 227
lawyers in House of Commons, 170
Layard, A. H., 168
Leatham, E. A., 330, 331
Leeds, 113, 138, 140, 141
legislation, 94–5
  private bill, 167
Leicester, 141, 204
Leicestershire:
  North, 140
  South, 140
Leominster, 138
Lesseps, Ferdinand de, 339
Lewis, Sir G. C., 116, 118
Liberal party, 93, 308–9, 310–11, 329
  basis of, 27
  in 1846–66, 50, 60–1, 62, 66–7, 74, 77, 78, 138–9, 145–6, 148, 150–1, 154–6, 160, 168, 176, 193, 197–8, 229, 234–5, 236
  in Reform crisis of 1866–7, 79, 80, 194, 196–7, 198–200, 219, 222–3, 226–34, 237, 238, 247, 253–4, 255, 259, 265, 272, 286–7
  after 1867, 86, 87, 88, 89–92, 94, 108, 292–9, 303–4, 306, 307–15, 317–18, 326–8, 329–32, 333–4, 335, 336–7, 338–9, 340, 341, 342–3, 352, 353–61, 363, 373, 374
  Whigs in, 60–1, 66–7, 74, 77, 79, 80, 89, 194, 195, 206, 207, 216–17, 220–5, 226–7, 231–2, 234, 249–50, 251–2, 311, 330, 336, 337, 354, 357, 358–61, 366–7, 376
  see also: Radicals
Liberalism, 248, 289
  decline of, 300–1
Liberation Society, 162, 319
licensing, 48
Licensing Act (1872), 292
Lichfield, 2nd Earl of, 207n
Lichfield House Compact, 370
Lincoln, 204
Lincoln, Abraham, 73
Lincolnshire, North, 138
Liverpool, 113, 127, 138, 141, 204
London, 96, 142, 201, 245–6
  City of, 117, 142
  Treaty of (1852), 159, 168
  University of, 113, 139
Louis XVI, king of France, 37
Lowe, Robert, 77, 226, 228, 263, 292, 295, 297
Lucraft, Benjamin, 250, 251
Ludlow, 138
Lymington, 138
Lytton, 1st Earl of, 56

Macaulay, Lord, 132
Macclesfield, 141, 204
MacMahon, Marshal, 308
Maidstone, 204
Maine, Sir Henry, 4
Maine Liquor Law, 218
majority, tyranny of, 32–3
Maldon, 138, 204
malt tax, 65, 121, 122
Manchester, 113, 138, 141, 143n, 204
'Manchester school', 111, 112, 123, 126, 131, 132, 133
Maoris, 56n
Marlborough, 138, 204
Marlborough, 7th Duke of, 270
Marlow, 138, 204
Marx, Karl, 26n, 89
Marylebone, 30–1, 142
master and servant, law of, 185, 293–4
Megæra, 298
Melbourne, 208
Melbourne, 2nd Viscount, 244, 367
members of Parliament, property qualification for, 154
Mérimée, Prosper, 376
Merioneth, 140
Merthyr Tydvil, 142

382

INDEX

Miall, Edward, 312
middle classes:
 character of, 59
 in politics, 59–60, 85–6, 89–91, 92, 95–7, 135, 231, 245, 280, 293, 294, 304–6, 309, 310
Middlesex, 138, 140, 201
Mill, John Stuart, 30, 32, 217, 236, 311, 312
Milnes, Richard Monckton (1st Baron Houghton), 128
monarchy, 129
 British, *see* Crown
 decline of, 345
Moncreiff, J., 233
Monmouth, 204
Monmouthshire, 140
Montesquieu, C. L. de S. de, 276
Montgomery, 140
Morley, John, 325–6
Morning Chronicle, 3
Morning Star, 133
Morny, Duc de, 165–6
Morris, W., 306

Napoleon I, emperor of France, 117, 130, 375
Napoleon III, emperor of France, 72, 111, 127–30, 133, 302, 305
National Education League, 293, 324, 325
National Review, 5, 52
National Union of Conservative and Constitutional Associations, 96–7
nationalism, 55, 115
'natural leaders', 28–9
natural rights, 180–1, 183, 187
negroes, 56
New Social Movement, 52
New Zealand, 56n
Newark, 204
Newcastle, 5th Duke of, 111
Newcastle-on-Tyne, 204
Newcastle-under-Lyme, 204
Newman, Professor Francis, 139
Newport, 204
Nice, annexation of (1860), 111, 130
Norfolk, West, 138
North Carolina, 190
Northampton, 204
Northamptonshire, South, 140
Northcote, Sir Stafford (1st Earl of Iddesleigh), 1, 5, 93, 119n, 194, 262, 280, 335

Northumberland, South, 140
Norwich, 143
Nottingham, 204, 304

O'Connell, Daniel, 243, 366, 372
Odger, George, 69, 78, 90, 303, 312, 331
old-age pensions, 52
Oldham, 204
Osborne, R. Bernal, 168n
Overend, Gurney & Co., failure of, 4n, 264–5
Oxford, 204
 women's colleges at, 18
Oxford Essays, 4
Oxford Union, 10, 49
Oxford University election (1865), 78

Palmer, Sir Roundell, 233, 280
Palmerston, 3rd Viscount, 61, 63, 77–8, 111–14, 147, 149, 159, 160, 161, 162, 168, 193, 197, 223, 228, 229, 231–2, 234, 236, 270, 272, 303, 313
paper duty, repeal of, 112, 124, 197, 229, 234–5
Paris, 245, 319
 Commune of, 88, 89, 294, 300, 303, 304, 316
 mob in, 105
Parnell, C. S., 335, 336, 359, 363, 366, 372–3
party, 43–4, 60, 85, 103, 108, 157, 222, 230–1, 257, 267, 327, 328–9, 331–2
 government by, 269–76, 369–70
patriotism, deficiency of, 342–3
Paul I, emperor of Russia, 209
paupers, treatment of, 52
Peace Society, 127
Peel, A. W., 210
Peel, General Jonathan, 81, 254, 255, 264, 266
Peel, Sir Robert, 1, 82n, 108, 123, 146–7, 150, 151, 152, 268, 371
 his finance, 118–21
 and repeal of the corn laws, 272, 280, 310
Peelites, 63, 64, 111, 149–50
Pembroke, 204
Peterborough, 142, 204
Pinto-Duschinsky, M., 2
Pitt, William (the younger), 5, 37, 310
Plimsoll agitation, 352
Poland, 162, 172, 210, 364

INDEX

political conflict, 284, 341
  economic and social basis of, 26–7, 242
  encouraged by party system, 43–4
  morality of, 37, 268
  pendulum movement of, 35–6, 283
  permanence of, 35
  psychological basis of, 27
  sporting element in, 248
political equilibrium, 36, 283
political ideas, 26, 180
political institutions, 259–60
  functions of, 41
  nature of, 39
  reform of, 39–40
politicians, 44, 190–2, 269, 274–5, 284–5, 290
politics, 34–5, 187, 190, 191, 283
  dynamics of, 25–7
  English, drawbacks of, 98, 191–2, 284–5
  and ethics, 22–3, 37, 82, 180, 187
  principle in, 43, 328–9
  see also: party; *entries beginning with* 'political'
Poole, 142
poor law board, its electoral statistics (1866), 193, 196, 198–200, 202–3, 206–7
'Pope's Brass Band', 370
Portsmouth, 141, 204
Potter, George, 209, 250, 251, 324
Preston, 141, 204
primogeniture, 320–2
principle, in politics, 43, 328–9
progress, 25, 309, 312–13, 327
  political, 40
property as basis of political conflict, 26, 182–3
protection, 50, 61, 149, 260, 310
Protestantism, growth of in England, 301–2
Proudhon, Pierre-Joseph, 125
Prussia, 99n, 159–60, 190, 270
  government of, 98–9
public opinion, 41–2, 100–1, 134–5, 173–4, 246, 259–60, 289

Quarterly Review, 4–6
Quintus Curtius, 156

Radicalism, 38, 68, 302
Radicals, 44, 96, 366
  in 1846–66, 58, 72–4, 76, 77, 85, 112, 113, 151–3, 154, 156, 157, 176–7, 193, 195, 197, 234–5, 279

  in 1866–7, 201, 217, 223, 232–4, 244, 250, 261, 286–7, 288
  after 1867, 87, 89–90, 102, 292–4, 296, 309–10, 311–12, 313–14, 316–17, 320, 323–7, 328, 329–31, 332, 333–4, 335, 336–7, 353–6, 357–8, 359, 360, 361, 370
Reform, parliamentary, 1, 5, 23, 35, 39, 40, 62, 68, 71–2, 75–85, 93, 96, 108n, 111, 112–14, 124–6, 135–51, 154–6, 159, 160, 161, 175–80, 184–5, 193–268, 277, 279–82, 294, 302–3, 310, 317–18, 336–7, 359, 374, 375
  see also: franchise
Reform acts:
  1832, 36–7, 46, 59, 79, 85, 194, 242–4, 245, 268; context of, 136, 244–5, 308
  1867, 40, 85, 87, 256, 257–8, 279, 282, 371
Reform bills:
  1852, 147, 155
  1859, 62, 113, 137, 154; (Bright's) 205–6
  1860, 113, 135–44, 154–6, 238, 302
  1866, 79, 193–5, 197–207, 219–20, 222–5, 226–30, 232–9, 245, 246, 253, 255, 261, 263
  1867, 81–5, 253, 254–6, 259, 260, 261, 264, 265–6, 277, 280–2
  1884, 93, 108n
Reform League, 257
reformers, 39
Reigate, 204
religious questions, 24, 157, 182, 325–6, 345, 354, 355
  see also: Burials Bill; Church of England; Church of Scotland; church rates; clerical fellowships; endowed schools; Endowed Schools Bill; Irish Church
Renfrewshire, 292
republicanism, 129, 312, 316
revolution, 74–5, 290
  and Reform crisis (1866), 244–6
revolutions of 1848, 305
  influence of in England, 302
Richmond, 138
Ripon, 138, 174
Robespierre, Maximilien, 209, 300
Rochdale, 141
Rochester, 204
Roebuck, J. A., 152
Rolt, J., 144

384

INDEX

Roman question, 307
Rome, ancient, 190, 207-8
Royal Society, 195
Russell, Lord John (1st Earl Russell), 114, 133, 162, 193, 197, 198n, 227
  political record of, 146-8
  and Reform, 42, 79, 112-13, 136, 137, 142, 145, 147-8, 150-1, 155, 160, 164, 188, 226, 243, 249, 302, 303
Russia, 292, 342, 364
Rye, 204

St Albans, 150
St Ives, 204
Salford, 141, 204
Salisbury, Marchioness of, 15
Salisbury, 2nd Marquis of, 4, 9, 10, 114
Salisbury, 3rd Marquis of (known as Lord Robert Cecil to 1865 and as Viscount Cranborne, 1865-8), *minor refs. in introduction and introductory notes, passim; for his views on and refs. to particular subjects, see those subjects*
  life: childhood, 9-10; at Oxford, 3, 10, 11, 12, 49; elected for Stamford, 3; marriage, 4, 15; becomes Indian secretary (1866), 79, 227; resigns (1867), 81, 255; goes to Lords (1868), 86; enters Disraeli's cabinet (1874), 93; becomes leader of Conservative party, 93
  mental and personal characteristics, 9-20; difficulty in social intercourse, 10, 13; diffidence, 12, 83; dislike of fighting, 10n; emotional involvement in politics, 10-11, 15, 105; empiricism, 18-20; grasp of reality, 13-15; health, 3, 9-10; heterodoxy, 19; intellectual isolation, 14; lack of racial prejudice, 56; neuroticism, 10-11; partisanship, 43, 108n; pessimism, 11-12; taste for executive power, 98
  social and political thought, 2-3, 21-57, 104-5, 106, 108-9; affected by temperament and social position, 21-2; materialism of, 25-6; organic view in, 25, 39; 'principles' in, 22; relation of to ethics, 22-3; scientific pretensions of, 25; utilitarianism of, 23-4
  interests: history, 20; photography, 19-20; science, 20
  capacity for democratic appeal, 97
  character of his Conservatism, 1-3, 104-5, 106, 108-9
  and Conservative party, 1-2, 62, 86-7, 93-7, 102, 107-9, 256
  controversial characteristics, 8-9, 11, 15, 104
  economic views, 50-1
  at foreign office, 14
  at India office, 56
  journalism, 3-9, 71-2, 93, 103-4, 106-7, 114, 338; as source for his thought, 6-7; style, 8-9
  as a landed aristocrat, 21-2
  nepotism, 97
  religion, 15-17, 47
  strength and weakness as a politician, 82-4, 106-8
  Chamberlain on, 337
  Disraeli on, 9
Saturday Review, 3-4, 6
Savoy, annexation of (1860), 111, 128n, 130, 136
Scarborough, 204
Schelling, Friedrich, 200
Schleswig-Holstein question, 56, 159-60, 168n, 173, 190, 229
Scully, Vincent, 362
Seeley, J. R., 54n
Seward, W. H., 189
Shaftesbury, 292
Sheffield, 140, 141, 143n, 204, 211, 213
Sherman, J., 189
Shrewsbury, 204
Shropshire, North, 140
Sieyes, Abbé, 39
Smith, William, 5, 294
social evolution, 28
social reform, 47-53, 286, 294, 314
Socialism, 88, 95
Somers, Lord, 224, 358
Somerset, East, 138
Somerset, 12th Duke of, 207n, 227
South Africa, 56
South Shields, 141, 205
Southampton, 204
Southwark, 205
Spain, 305, 308, 313
Spencer, 5th Earl, 207n
Stafford, 205
Staffordshire:
  East, 292, 296n
  South, 138
Stalybridge, 113, 139, 201

INDEX

Stamford, 3, 42, 49
Standard, 3, 338
Stanley, Lord, *see* Derby, 15th Earl of
Stansfeld, James, 163, 324
state, character of, 181, 184-5
state intervention, 48-53
Stockport, 141
Stoke, 141, 205
Strafford, Earl of, 40, 302
Stratford, 201
Sunderland, 205
Sunderland, 2nd Earl of, 265
Surrey, 201
  East, 140, 339
  West, 140
Sutherland, 3rd Duke of, 207n
Swansea, 205
Swift, Dean, 364, 365
Switzerland, 133

Taine, Hippolyte, 360
Tamworth, 205
taxation, 26, 66, 69, 112, 118-27, 131, 134-5, 144-5, 155, 182, 184-5, 186, 195, 215-16, 219, 220, 231, 281, 314-15, 354
  of the agricultural interest, 66, 121, 134-5, 145, 202, 236
Tewkesbury, 138
Thetford, 138
Tilly, Count Johann, 302
timber duty, 121
Times, The, 114, 338
Tipperary Whiteboys, 146
Tocqueville, Alexis de, 30
Tory party, in eighteenth century, 366
Toryism of 1830, 300
Totnes, 138
Tower Hamlets, 137, 142
trade unions, 69, 70-1, 143, 155, 175, 176, 195, 210-14, 251, 281, 286, 293, 306
Trevelyan, G. O., 311

university tests, abolition of, 292

Victoria, Queen, 108n, 127, 160, 227
Victoria (state of), 47, 76
Vienna, Congress of, 128
Virginia, 190

Wakefield, 174
Wallenstein, Albrecht von, 302
Wallop, Lord John, 18
Walpole, Sir Robert, 265
Walpole, Spencer, 154, 194, 200
Walsall, 141, 205
Walsh, Sir John, bt., 115
Wandsworth, 201
war, 98
Warrington, 142, 205
Warwickshire, South, 140
Washington, 208
Wells, 138
Westbury, 205
Whigs, *see* Liberal party, Whigs in
Whitehaven, 142
Wigan, 141, 205
Wilhelm I, king of Prussia and German emperor, 99
William III, king of England, 364
William IV, king of England, 244, 245
Wiltshire:
  North, 140
  South, 140
Winchester, 205
Windthorst, Ludwig, 370
Winterbotham, H. S. P., 324
Wolff, Sir Henry Drummond, 86-7
Wolverhampton, 141, 205
women, capacities of, 17-18
women's colleges at Oxford and Cambridge, 18
women's suffrage, 18n
Woolwich, 201
Worcester, 205
Worcestershire, East, 296
working classes:
  in politics, 33, 58, 68-71, 74-5, 77, 79-80, 87-90, 124-6, 135, 144, 174, 177, 179, 183, 184-5, 186-7, 193, 195-6, 198, 202-6, 208-18, 220, 221, 223, 237, 240n, 241, 242, 244-6, 253, 254, 258-9, 261, 262, 279, 292-4, 300, 304-5, 306-7, 310, 324, 325, 332, 343, 350
  and religion, 289
  right of to the suffrage, 46-7, 76, 79, 80, 187
  social welfare of, 49-53, 294, 314

Yarmouth, 141, 205
Yorkshire, 237
  North Riding, 138
  West Riding, 113, 138, 140
'Young England', 63

Zanzibar contract, 298

Cambridge Studies in the History and Theory of Politics

TEXTS

LIBERTY, EQUALITY, FRATERNITY, by *James Fitzjames Stephen*. Edited, with an introduction and notes, by *R. J. White*

VLADIMIR AKIMOV ON THE DILEMMAS OF RUSSIAN MARXISM, *1895–1903*. An English edition of 'A Short History of the Social Democratic Movement in Russia' and 'The Second Congress of the Russian Social Democratic Labour Party', with an introduction and notes by *Jonathan Frankel*

TWO ENGLISH REPUBLICAN TRACTS, PLATO REDIVIVUS or, A DIALOGUE CONCERNING GOVERNMENT (*c.* 1681), by *Henry Neville* and AN ESSAY UPON THE CONSTITUTION OF THE ROMAN GOVERNMENT (*c.* 1699), by *Walter Moyle*. Edited by *Caroline Robbins*

J. G. HERDER ON SOCIAL AND POLITICAL CULTURE, translated, edited and with an introduction by *F. M. Barnard*

THE LIMITS OF STATE ACTION, by *Wilhelm von Humboldt*. Edited, with an introduction and notes, by *J. W. Burrow*

KANT'S POLITICAL WRITINGS, edited with an introduction and notes by *Hans Reiss*; translated by *H. B. Nisbet*

MARX'S CRITIQUE OF HEGEL'S 'PHILOSOPHY OF RIGHT', edited, with an introduction and notes, by *Joseph O'Malley*; translated by *Annette Jolin* and *Joseph O'Malley*

STUDIES

1867: DISRAELI, GLADSTONE AND REVOLUTION. THE PASSING OF THE SECOND REFORM BILL, by *Maurice Cowling*

THE CONSCIENCE OF THE STATE IN NORTH AMERICA, by *E. R. Norman*

THE SOCIAL AND POLITICAL THOUGHT OF KARL MARX, by *Shlomo Avineri*

MEN AND CITIZENS: ROUSSEAU'S SOCIAL THOUGHT, by *Judith Shklar*

IDEALISM, POLITICS AND HISTORY: SOURCES OF HEGELIAN THOUGHT, by *George Armstrong Kelly*

THE IMPACT OF LABOUR, 1920–1924. THE BEGINNING OF MODERN BRITISH POLITICS, by *Maurice Cowling*

ALIENATION: MARX'S CONCEPTION OF MAN IN CAPITALIST SOCIETY, by *Bertell Ollman*

Printed in Great Britain
by Amazon